JUSTICE IN BLUE AND GRAY

JUSTICE IN BLUE AND GRAY

A Legal History of the Civil War

Stephen C. Neff

HARVARD UNIVERSITY PRESS

Cambridge, Massachusetts

London, England

2010

Library of Congress Cataloging-in-Publication Data
Neff, Stephen C.
Justice in blue and gray : a legal history of the Civil War / Stephen C. Neff
p.   cm.
Includes bibliographical references and index.
ISBN 978-0-674-03602-4 (alk. paper)
1. War and emergency powers—United States—History.   2. Secession—United States—
History.   3. Military law—United States—History.   4. Slavery—Law and legislation—
United States—History.   5. Amnesty—United States—History.   6. United
States—History—Civil War, 1861–1865—Claims.   7. War (International law)—History.
8. United States—History—Civil War, 1861–1865.   I. Title.
KF5060.N44 2010
973.7′1—dc22   2009029638

To Nancy, with love

Contents

Acknowledgments

My thanks and praise go to many persons and institutions, only some of whom (and which) can be mentioned here. For invaluable time of research leave, I am jointly, and immensely, grateful to the Arts and Humanities Research Board of the United Kingdom, and to my home institution, the University of Edinburgh School of Law. For hospitality in the United States during that period of leave, my great thanks go to the George Washington University School of Law in Washington, D.C., where the intellectual stimulation was as notable as the hospitality. In the way of hospitality during that sojourn, special thanks are also due to John and Georgene Chastain and family, as well as to Michael and Linda Cosgrove.

For editorial assistance, sprinkled with occasional (and much merited) stern criticism, my special thanks go to Ashley Theunissen, as well as to William Hutchison and my wife, Nancy. For general intellectual stimulation, assistance, encouragement, and related acts of kindness, my praises go (alphabetically) to William Gilmore, Christine Gray, Susan Karamanian, Hector MacQueen, Alexander McCall Smith, Geoffrey Marston (posthumously), Peter Raven-Hansen, Frederick Shiels, Ralph Steinhardt, Simonetta Stirling, Stephen Tierney, Arthur Wilmarth, and Robert Windmill. This book, alas, is all too paltry a reward.

Introduction

Americans are, notoriously, the most legalistic of peoples. Whether this is a matter of pride or of shame may be the subject of vigorous debate. What is beyond debate, however, is that this native genius (if that is the right word for it) was in fullest evidence throughout the greatest crisis in the country's history, the Civil War of 1861–1865. This book is a history of that crisis, as seen through a legal lens.

Of all wars in recorded history, none equals—or even comes close to equaling—the Civil War in the role played by law. To be sure, many other conflicts have thrown up legal issues high in both volume and importance. The First World War is probably the most striking case. But the American Civil War was unique in that a remarkably large proportion of the legal issues and disputes that arose were actually litigated and decided in the courts.[1] The result was a veritable ocean of judicial pronouncements about all aspects of the war—including the secession process, battlefield tactics, and confiscation of property, as well as regulation of trade, enforcement of the blockade, and the ending of slavery, and encompassing the protection (or as the case may be, infringement) of civil liberties, questions of separation of powers and the limits of governmental prerogatives under the Constitution, the ruling of occupied lands, and much more besides. Our task is to explore this ocean, from its deepest currents to its most striking landfalls.

Only secondarily, therefore, is this book a treatment of the Civil War as such. It is primarily a case study of the myriad ways in which law plays an important role in a crisis of giant political and military dimensions. It is a means for affording nonlawyers the opportunity of a close inspection of the science of law in action. It is a study of how the pronouncements of the men of books interacted with the brute (and often brutal) facts of life created on the ground by the men of action. The American Civil War has the distinction of providing the best, and grandest, example of that process at work. The intention is to give a detailed picture of how legal issues arose in that extraordinary crisis, what impact they had on the human beings who were caught up in the myriad aspects of the struggle, and how those issues were dealt with by courts of law. In a number of areas, resolution of important issues is still awaited at the present day; and these will be pointed out in the course of the narrative.

The readers of this book should be assured that they are assumed to possess no prior knowledge whatever of legal studies. Legal concepts will be carefully explained as they arise. For the convenience of those who require a reminder of the meaning of legal terms, a glossary is provided at the end, containing capsule definitions of all such terms that are used in the course of the discussion.

Although this is a book of history, it is not *only* about history. Law is a constantly living, evolving subject, with the past gliding its way into the present (and the future) with a silence that is as deceptive as it is inexorable. Many— in fact virtually all—of the issues that faced the policy-makers of the 1860s are still with us today, in a more or less recognizable form. Indeed, some are all too vividly present, such as debates over executive powers, infringements of civil liberties, and the fate of unlawful belligerents. Only the issues relating to the abolition of slavery have a clearly "historical" flavor, in the everyday sense of that term. And even they, as will be seen, were of lasting importance in the way that they shaped the legal contours of race relations long after the war ended. An effort is therefore made, throughout the book, to indicate later developments in the areas of law covered.

Since this is not a book for professional lawyers (though it is humbly suggested that they too can learn much from it), a rigorous effort has been made to exclude matters in which the weight of technicality would overbear the historical significance of the topic. Readers will therefore be relieved to know that procedural issues have been, as nearly as possible, wholly dispensed with. There has also been a fairly merciless simplification of questions of property law (which, as many a first-year law student can attest, is the most maddeningly arcane of legal subjects). Consequently, issues such as "corruption of blood" or the obsessive search for the "location" of a fee simple will be—much in the manner of the gruesome tale of Sherlock Holmes's "giant rat of Sumatra"— kept safely outside of our purview.

Mundane considerations of length also dictate—with all the sternness that an ironclad word limit can impose—that many portions of the story must be more lightly treated than they merit, and some must even be left out altogether. In general, the policy is that subjects which are largely administrative in nature are left aside, in favor of topics involving issues of legal principle. On this basis, the subject of trading-with-the-enemy regulation in general, including the details of the notorious cotton trade in particular, is largely omitted. (This is an aspect of the conflict which still awaits a comprehensive treatment.) The working of the military-conscription policy also falls largely outside the scope of the book for this reason, as does the large subject of prisoners of war, including the arrangements for prisoner exchanges and for the extensive granting of paroles by both sides. The subject of Union policy in the occupied territories is covered only at the level of general principles, on the thesis that it is really more closely connected thematically (if not quite chronologically) to Reconstruction than to the war itself. Finally, it must be confessed that the focus is strongly on the Union side of the conflict. The reason is simply that it is the law from that side, rather than from the Confederate one, which has gone on to become part of our present legal heritage.[2]

This account will be organized chiefly according to subject matter, although it will also be at least broadly chronological. The first chapter will summarize the debates over the legal nature of the federal Union and, more specifically, the arguments presented on the lawfulness of secession. It will also deal with the debates and uncertainty as to the legal character of the conflict. The second chapter will concern the exercise of governmental powers, both executive and legislative, in the emergency. In these first two chapters, constitutional law will therefore be the principal lodestar.

The third chapter will take us outdoors, to the fields of battle, where the concern will be with the law governing the conduct of war. It will also take us into a new legal realm, that of *international* law—and specifically that part of it known, for obvious reasons, as the laws of war. Here, the concentration will be on several areas of law that remain at least as controversial today as they were in the 1860s: guerrilla warfare, questions of combatant status, and the carrying of the horrors of war to civilian populations. The fourth chapter will concern property questions, of two rather different kinds: the occupation of enemy territory, and issues relating to the confiscation of property belonging to disloyal persons. Chapter 5 will concern the process of emancipation, tracing the legal difficulties that arose in the extinguishing of the very concept of private property in human beings. The sixth chapter will deal with civil liberties, particularly executive detentions and trials of civilians before military commissions.

The next two chapters will return to international law. Chapter 7 will address the various neutrality issues that arose in the wake of the recognition of belligerency by Britain, France, and other countries, culminating with an account of the international arbitration between Britain and the United States over the sundry questions associated with the fitting-out of warships in neutral territory. The eighth chapter will relate the various legal devices that the Union navy and prize courts contrived, in the course of litigation over ship captures, to increase the effectiveness of the blockade policy. In all of these areas, the Civil War broke important new ground.

The termination of the war, along with its many legal aftereffects, is dealt with in the ninth and tenth chapters. Chapter 9 covers the legal questions posed by the disappearance of the Confederate federal government and the questions of the legal effects of acts by the Southern states during the secession period, along with criminal prosecutions and civil actions directed against individuals great and humble. The final chapter concerns the Johnson administration's clemency policy and its legal limitations, together with an analysis of the various legal paths by which at least some persons obtained at least some compensation for losses that they had sustained in the conflict.

It only remains to note that one major theme runs, like a thread, through a very large portion of this history. That is the manner in which the war, from beginning to end, was—at least in the eyes of the Union authorities—a dualistic, Janus-faced affair: involving sometimes a resort to *sovereign* rights and at other times a resort to *belligerent* rights as the legal basis for actions taken. In very brief terms, sovereign rights are peacetime rights, arising from the Constitution and ordinary laws of the land. Belligerent rights are peculiar to a state of war. Their source is international law, and they spring automatically into action when a state of war takes effect. Sovereign rights and powers are applied to citizens of the law-making power in question, whereas belligerent rights and powers are invoked against enemy nationals.

In concrete terms, this meant that the Union authorities sometimes treated the Confederates as enemies in an "ordinary" armed conflict—that is, virtually as foreign nationals—while at other times treating them as rebellious citizens of the Union itself. In other words, the Confederates were treated sometimes as enemies and sometimes as criminals, with the Union government correspondingly functioning sometimes as a belligerent and sometimes as a sovereign. When acting in a belligerent capacity, the Union was guided by the international rules on the conduct of war. When operating in its sovereign capacity, it was constrained by the statutory law of the land and, ultimately, by the strictures of the Constitution. The story of the constant interweaving of these two categories of rights is, in a nutshell, the grand theme of the legal history of the American Civil War. It is systematically told for the first time here.

I

Breaking a Nation

That a State, as a party to the constitutional compact, has the right to secede . . . cannot . . . be denied by any one who regards the constitution as a compact—if . . . the [federal system] should fail to fulfil the ends for which it was established. This results, necessarily, from the nature of a compact—where the parties to it are sovereign; and, of course, have no appeal.

—John C. Calhoun

Unless the Confederate States may be regarded as having constituted a de facto government for the time or as the supreme controlling power within the limits of their exclusive military sway, then the officers and seamen of their privateers and the officers and soldiers of their army were mere pirates and insurgents, and every officer, seaman, or soldier who killed a Federal officer or soldier in battle, whether on land or the high seas, is liable to indictment, conviction, and sentence for the crime of murder. . . . Wisdom suggests caution, and the counsels of caution forbid any such rash experiment.

—Justice Nathan Clifford

In the years leading up to 1860–1861, Americans disagreed with one another about a great many things. But two issues may be singled out, from the legal standpoint, as being particularly fundamental. The first one concerned the nature of the federal Union which had been formed in 1787–1789. The essence of the debate may be stated very simply. One view, held predominantly in the North, was that the federal system of government had been created by the *people* of the United States as the ultimate holders of sovereign power—with the people making a once-and-for-all conveyance (or surrender) of their powers, but carefully granting some of those sovereign powers to the federal government and the remainder to the states. The opposing view, held predominantly in the South, was that the people had *previously* granted the *whole* of their sovereign powers to the states, prior to the drafting of the Constitution—

with the Constitution then being the creation not of the people directly but rather of the states. On this view, the Constitution was properly seen as an ongoing contractual arrangement between the states, that is, as an arrangement in which the states, by agreement with one another, delegated some (but only some) of their sovereign powers to the newly created federal government. On this seemingly abstruse issue hung the momentous question of the right of states lawfully to secede from the federal Union.

The second fundamental legal question concerned the nature of the armed conflict that broke out in the spring and summer of 1861. Was it a law-enforcement exercise, albeit on a gargantuan scale? Or was it better seen as a war in the true legal sense of that term? To supporters of the Confederacy, the answer was starkly clear: it was a war in the fullest legal sense, conducted between two entirely independent countries. Therefore, every element of the struggle was governed by the laws of war (i.e., by the *international* law regulating the conduct of war). In the North, there was naturally a powerful reluctance to concede that the conflict was a war in that fullest possible sense. The furthest that the federal executive was willing to go was to conduct the land hostilities *as if* the conflict was a true war. In other respects, the crisis would be regarded as an internal *rebellion,* to which the ordinary criminal laws of the country could (at least in principle) be applied. This too may seem an abstruse issue. But a host of harshly practical consequences flowed from it.

A Union Less Than Perfect

The supporters of the Confederacy adamantly maintained that the secession of the Southern states in 1860–1861 was a lawful act.[1] This insistence was rooted in a particular view of the legal nature of the federal Union—specifically, on the position that the Union was, in essence, an ongoing contractual arrangement between the states. Flowing logically from this core belief was the conclusion that each state (i.e., each party to that contract) possessed a legal right to dissolve the contract if it was breached by other states parties. This contract, or Constitutional compact, was held to have been concluded under the general law of nature between the states as sovereign and independent nations in their own right, with the federal government being the *product* of that arrangement.

To appreciate fully the character of this argument, it is well to contrast it with two other potential justifications of secession the Southerners *might* have employed in 1860–1861 but (for the most part) did not. One is what might be called a revolutionary justification. The other might be termed (for lack of a better expression) an "inherent-power" justification. A very brief glance at each of these should suffice for present purposes.

A revolutionary justification, by its nature, is concerned with *unlawful* action by subjects against a sovereign. Revolutionary force might, of course, be justified by resort to a "higher law" than that of the sovereign in question, as had been the case in the great example of revolution that was always high in the minds of Americans—their own independence struggle against Great Britain in 1775–1783. The colonists' struggle may have been justifiable. But that justification came not from the law of the nation-state which held sovereign power over the insurgents, but rather from some "higher law," such as the law of "Nature and Nature's God" (in the famous words of the Declaration of Independence).

Revolutionary action, in other words, always involves a violation of the law in force *at the time at which the revolt takes place.* It becomes lawful only in retrospect—that is, *if* it succeeds, *de facto,* in its aims, as had happened in the case of the American colonists. At that point, the defeated sovereign concedes the lawfulness of the revolutionary deeds, which are thereby retroactively validated. Legality follows (with due meekness) in the footsteps of power. But power comes first, and legality second.[2] The secessionist argument of 1860–1861 was not of this character, for it posited that secession was lawful not in retrospect in the event of success, but rather at the very time at which it occurred.[3]

An "inherent-power" argument is similar to a revolutionary one in that it concedes (at least implicitly) that secession might be unlawful at the time that it occurred. This second line of thought, however, deals with that difficulty in a rather different way: by making a careful distinction between a *right* to secede and a *power* to secede. On this view, independence was seen as an inalienable attribute of sovereign states, something that sovereign states could not give or bargain away. The Constitutional contract, on this thesis, must therefore be understood to be not a surrender of this key sovereign power, but instead something very much more modest: an agreement to refrain from *exercising* that omnipresent prerogative.

The key point here is that the power to secede remains in existence even in the face of a contractual arrangement to refrain from wielding it. Secession might be unlawful, in the technical sense of being a breach of the Constitutional contract. It would, however, be *effective* because the full panoply of powers associated with sovereignty had never actually been surrendered or extinguished. This may appear to some to be an overly sophistical argument. But it should be noted that it is alive and well in present-day international law, where it is generally held that sovereign states possess an inherent power to withdraw from international organizations such as the United Nations, even if (as in the case of the UN) there is no express provision in the relevant treaty or charter providing for withdrawal.[4] This argument was not, however, advanced by the Southerners at the time of the secession crisis of 1860–1861, although it is interesting to note that it was endorsed during the war by one of the Confederate attorney generals.[5]

Compacts and Their Breach

The principal legal justification of secession differed from both of these. It is curious that it has never been baptized with a widely accepted label. For present purposes, it may be referred to as a "breach-of-compact" argument. This was, in essence, a contention that secession was a lawful remedy for breach of the Constitutional compact by the Northern *states* (as opposed to the federal government). This justification was rooted in what may be referred to as the "compact-of-states" theory of the nature of the federal Union, or just the "compact" theory for short. Its core notion may be stated very simply: that the federal Union consisted of an aggregation of sovereign *states,* bound together by a contract concluded between one another. The states, on this view, were, in their inception, sovereign entities living in a state of nature *vis-à-vis* one another (i.e., possessing no common sovereign ruling *over* them). The federal Union was therefore not, on this view, formed by individuals acting in their personal capacities.

Support for this position was provided by no less an oracle than James Madison, who, in the *Federalist,* expressly pointed out that the ratification of the Constitution was to be "given by the people, not as individuals composing one entire nation, but as composing the distinct and independent States to which they respectively belong." The result was that the United States consisted, in Madison's words, of "so many independent States," as opposed to constituting "one aggregate nation."[6] In the early nineteenth century, the doughtiest champion of this compact theory of the nature of the federal Union was the South Carolina politician and political theorist John C. Calhoun.[7] In the period of the Civil War itself, its most stalwart champion was

Alexander Stephens, vice president of the Confederacy and a considerable legal and political thinker.[8]

For present purposes, the principal feature of this compact theory was its insistence on the Constitution as a contract between the states as sovereign entities—with the federal Union then being a creation of the states. On this thesis, the *whole* of the sovereign powers of the country resided in the states. The federal government consequently possessed no sovereignty in its own right, but simply exercised a number of specific powers delegated to it by the states. The Constitution was the instrument of that delegation. It therefore had a sort of double role: first, as an agreement, or compact, between the states in which each state agreed with each other one as to precisely *which* sovereign powers would be entrusted to the federal government; and second, as the actual charter creating that federal government and endowing it with those agreed powers. The first of these roles—as a compact between the states—was the fundamental one, from which the second followed naturally.

This compact theory had a number of important logical implications. One was that the interstate compact was necessarily governed by the general *natural-law* rules on contracts, since the states were not part of any larger polity at the time the contract was concluded. That is to say, the states were, in the common expression of the time, in a state of nature *vis-à-vis* one another at the time of contracting. That general *natural* law of contracts, it was widely agreed, gave to each contracting party a remedy in the event that the contract was violated: a right to terminate the agreement. This was, in effect, a right—i.e., a true *legal right*—to secede from the federal Union formed by the contract. Moreover, this legal right of secession did not depend on or require any explicit provision in the text of the Constitution because the right existed as a general, universal principle of law—in Stephens's words, "by the same laws of Nations which govern in all matters of treaties or conventions between Sovereigns."[9]

The specific complaint of secession advocates was that the Northern states—*not* the federal government itself—were in breach of the Constitutional compact by virtue of their flagrant and deliberate flouting of the federal Fugitive Slave Act of 1850.[10] That law established a federal mechanism for the efficient retrieval of runaway slaves. Some of the free states, however, attempted to interfere with the process, chiefly by means of habeas corpus writs issued by state judges, which purported to liberate slaves from the custody of fugitive-slave commissioners charged with returning them to their owners. It is true that the federal Supreme Court held these state actions to be unlawful in a notable case in 1859.[11] But that decision, at least in the view of prominent Southerners, had little practical effect. The Constitution, lamented the Georgia politician Howell Cobb, had been "basely broken" and "wantonly violated" by Northern states, ten of which (he maintained) had the plain design of annulling the Constitutional provision on fugitive slaves.[12] He bluntly referred to them as "the ten nullifying States."[13] Stephens was of a similarly outspoken view. Thirteen of the Northern states, he contended, had "openly and avowedly disregarded their obligations" under the fugitive slave and extradition clauses of the Constitution. A compact thus broken, he concluded, was no longer binding on the other parties.[14]

On the fugitive-slave question, there was some considerable sympathy in the North for the Southern position. President Buchanan, for example, in his final annual message to Congress, conceded that, if the Northern states did not repeal their various laws interfering with the Fugitive Slave Act, then the Southern states would be justified in mounting a "revolutionary resistance to the Government of the Union."[15] In a similar vein, a federal judge in New York, in January 1861, when instructing a grand jury, admitted that "the slaveholding states have just cause of complaint against some of their sister states," which had adopted legislation "in direct conflict with one of the plainest provisions of the constitution of the United States."[16]

In keeping with this compact theory, several of the Southern state secession ordinances contained detailed lists of allegations of violations of the federal Constitution by the Northern states. South Carolina, for example, followed up its ordinance of secession with a declaration setting out the reasons for its drastic action. The fourteen free states, it averred, "have deliberately refused, for years past, to fulfill their constitutional obligations." It went on to identify two specific passages of the Constitution that had been trampled on: the fugitive-slave provision, and the duty of extradition of criminals. (Regarding extradition, it was alleged that persons wanted in the slave states for the offense of inciting a servile insurrection were not surrendered by Northern state governments.)[17] The result, South Carolina proclaimed, was that "these ends for which this [federal] Government was instituted have been defeated, and the Government itself has been made destructive of them by the action of the non-slaveholding States." The final straw was the election of Lincoln, which meant that "all hope of remedy is rendered vain."[18] These complaints were echoed by Georgia's ordinance. The Fugitive Slave Act of 1850, it pronounced, "stands today a dead letter for all practicable purposes in every non-slave-holding State in the Union."[19]

Opposing Views

The compact theory of the federal Union did not, to put it mildly, go unchallenged. In the early nineteenth century, its most redoubtable foe was that ardent champion of the Union cause and renowned practicing lawyer Senator (and two-time secretary of state) Daniel Webster of Massachusetts. He devoted much effort, in his portion of the Webster-Hayne debate of 1830, to refuting the compact theory, which he condemned as "a total misapprehension . . . of the origin of this government, and of the foundation on which it stands."[20] The federal government, he insisted, "is the independent offspring of the popular will. It is not the creature of State legislatures." The correct view of the American system of government, Webster insisted, was that the people of the United States, in adopting the Constitution, had created a system of divided or shared sovereignty, parceling out certain designated sovereign powers directly to the federal government and conferring the remainder onto the states. As a result, the federal government and the states were *both* sovereign—each in its own area of authority.[21]

The federal Supreme Court gave what appeared to be strong support to the Webster thesis—ironically, in the very case in 1859 which had barred the states from interfering with federal enforcement of the Fugitive Slave Act. In this case, *Ableman v. Booth,* the Court stated that sovereignty did not lie exclusively with either the states or with the federal government. Instead, it was parceled out between the two, with the result that each of these authorities was supreme over the other in its *own* allotted area. As Chief Justice Roger B. Taney put it on behalf of the Court:

> The powers of the General Government, and of the State, although both exist and are exercised within the same territorial limits, are yet separate and distinct sovereignties, acting separately and independently of each other, within their respective spheres. And the sphere of action appropriate to the United States is as far beyond the reach of the judicial process issued by a State judge or a State court, as if the line of division was traced by landmarks and monuments visible to the eye.[22]

The implications of this dual-sovereignty thesis (as it might be termed) were important. On this view, the federal government possessed a measure of sovereignty in its own right, and *not* merely as the fruit of a contract concluded between *other* entities (the states). If the federal government was merely the product of a contract, as the compact theory had it, then it effectively ceased to exist when that contract was dissolved. More specifically, if any state withdrew from the compact with just cause, then the federal government must automatically cease to have *any* lawful authority over it. If, however, the federal government was sovereign in its own right, as the Webster thesis held, then the federal Union had a permanent existence, independently of the states—with, crucially, the right to defend and enforce its sovereign rights (limited though they might be) against *anyone* who attempted to subvert them. In the eyes of many—including the Lincoln administration—that was essentially what the federal government did in 1861–1865: it enforced its laws against those who sought to violate them. The Civil War, on that view, was a law-enforcement or police exercise by the federal government, albeit on the grandest of scales.[23]

The Birth of a (Purported) Nation

The details of the secession process and formation of the Confederate States of America in 1860–1861 have been fully recounted elsewhere.[24] It is therefore only necessary here to note some of the salient legal points that have not always been fully appreciated. In every Confederate state except one (Tennessee), separation was brought about by a specially organized state convention. (In Tennessee, the state legislature adopted a declaration of independence from the Union.) The purpose of this process was to reverse the ratifications of the 1787–1789 period, which had been undertaken by special state conventions rather than by legislatures (as required by the Constitution itself).[25]

More specifically, though, the compact theory of the Union held that the actual parties to the constitutional compact were the *people* of the states acting in a sovereign capacity, that is, deciding directly, on their own, to enter into a contract with the peoples of the other states similarly organized. Logically, therefore, the dissolution of that same contract must be undertaken by the very parties which had originally formed it. As the Georgia Supreme Court explained, in a judgment during the war, the secession conventions were a means by which the people of the state could exercise, in a direct manner, their inherent sovereign right of self-government. In such a convention, the Court stated, the people act "in a capacity, higher than, and superior to any government, State or Federal, theretofore created, or adopted by them."[26]

In general, the states underwent no *internal* legal change by virtue of the secession, although they now purported to be fully independent nation-states. It
was not long, however, before the associationist urge took hold. In February
1861, representatives of the seven seceded states convened in Montgomery, Alabama, for the formation of a new, and improved, federal union, designated
the Confederate States of America. This convention, unlike its Philadelphia
predecessor of 1787, was not content simply to draft a constitution. It went
on to constitute itself—without any explicit mandate to do so—as the provisional government of a new federal nation. A provisional constitution was
quickly adopted, with a permanent one following only a month later, in
March 1861.[27] The departures from the United States Constitution were not
great. In the later words of Confederate Attorney general Thomas H. Watts,
the new Constitution was "almost a transcript" of its 1787 predecessor, with
most of the changes made being mere alterations of phraseology "to exclude
doubtful and dangerous constructions."[28]

One of these alterations was in the preamble, which was reworded so as to
contain a clear endorsement of the compact theory of the new union, which was
explicitly stated to have been formed by "each State acting in its sovereign and
independent character." There was no express statement in the text of the Confederate Constitution as to whether the Confederate federal government was
sovereign, but a later opinion by Attorney General Watts pronounced it not to
be (i.e., that sovereignty lay exclusively in the hands of the states, with the federal government acting, in effect, only as an agent).[29] Slavery, not surprisingly,
received rather more explicit protection in the Confederate Constitution than in
the Union one. There was, for example, an express ban on the adoption of any
law "denying or impairing the right of property in Negro slaves." The slave *trade,*
however, in the form of importing slaves from abroad, was prohibited. This provision was inserted in the interest of earning recognition of the new nation from
foreign states. The only exception was that the Confederate Congress could au-
thorize importing slaves from the Union slave states.[30]

Some contentious questions received very little attention in the Confederate Constitution. Most notably, no express right of secession was included in
the text. Indeed, the union was explicitly stated to be "permanent." Perma-
nence must be understood to mean, in this context, *indefinite* duration, because, according to the compact theory, a contract between sovereign entities
was inherently dissoluble in the face of a persistent breach by any of the parties. It was apparently agreed that this natural-law right to of termination con-

stituted an effective (if tacit) right of secession, so that there was no need to re-iterate it in the text of the document.[31]

Insurrection and War

A fundamental legal issue that brooded incessantly over the entire 1861–1865 struggle was the question of the legal nature of the conflict—whether it was a case of mere rebellion by disgruntled individuals against the lawful authorities or a war in the true sense of the term.[32] Specific issues beyond number hinged on this most basic question. For the present, the significance of the distinction need only be stated in broad terms. If the conflict was regarded as a law-enforcement operation, then the implication was that *all* supporters of the Confederate cause, from the highest to the lowest, were criminals or rebels and subject to prosecution and punishment as such. If, on the other hand, the con-flict was regarded as a true war, then supporters of the Confederacy were not criminals but instead were *enemies*. The difference was enormous, for in the law governing war, it was no crime to be an enemy. In other words, it is no crime to be a national of an enemy state or even a serving soldier in an enemy army. An enemy is liable to be defeated on the field of battle, and as a conse-quence to be compelled to agree to more or less onerous peace terms. But an enemy is not, as such, liable to prosecution and punishment in the *national* courts of the opposing state.[33]

An alternative, and succinct, way of stating this contrast is to say that, in a case of rebellion by its own citizens, a government acts in a *sovereign* capacity, as the enforcer of its own national laws. Against enemies, in contrast, a gov-ernment operates in a *belligerent* capacity. The bodies of law applicable to these different forms of activity are quite distinct. When acting in a sovereign mode, a government wields whatever coercive weapons are given to it by its own constitution or domestic law. When acting in a belligerent capacity, the government's powers are determined by *international* law—specifically by the portion of it known (for obvious reasons) as the laws of war. This funda-mental question of whether the Confederates were rebels (i.e., criminals) or enemies—and, by the same token, whether the Union government was oper-ating in a sovereign or a belligerent mode—would pervade the entire legal his-tory of the struggle.

This dilemma existed only on the Union side. To the Confederates, there was no doubt that the conflict was a war in the true sense of the term because

the two sides were wholly independent states. The principal concern of the
Confederacy was not, therefore, over the nature of the conflict as such, but
rather over the question of where the responsibility lay for starting it. For various reasons, including its quest for the recognition of its independence by foreign governments, the Confederates had an interest in not appearing to be the
aggressors.

Unsheathing the Sword

As a purportedly independent country, the Confederacy possessed an inherent, natural-law right to full control over its own territory. This right began
to be asserted with vigor on the very morrow of secession, with seizures of federal property situated in the Southern states—customhouses, military installations, naval facilities, post offices, courthouses, and the like. There was little
actual resistance to these takeovers, as the federal custodians were usually
vastly outnumbered by local forces (and sometimes sympathetic to secession
or even actively supportive of it). President Buchanan forthrightly denounced
the seizures as "purely aggressive, and not in resistance to any attempt to coerce a State or States to remain in the Union."[34] The Confederates, however,
regarded these measures as assertions of right, in the interest of gaining full
control over their own territory by expelling trespassers.[35]

On the Union side, there was also a certain wariness about resorting to
force but for a rather different reason: because of doubts over whether the federal government possessed the constitutional right to employ armed force to
coerce a seceded state back into the Union. Calhoun had insisted, in the nul-
lification crisis, that neither the federal government nor the states could lawfully employ armed force against the other.[36] Chief Justice Taney agreed,
although he never had occasion to place this view into a legal judgment.[37] So
did Jeremiah S. Black, Buchanan's last attorney general, who gave extended
consideration to the point shortly after Lincoln's election.[38] The President was
entitled, he concluded, forcibly to defend federal property (such as forts, customhouses, and post offices) from attack and to recapture it if taken. The recapture of the Harper's Ferry Arsenal after the John Brown raid of 1859 was an
example. The regular enforcement of federal law, however, was a different
matter. That was to be effected through the ordinary mechanisms of courts
and magistrates rather than by military action.

Black conceded that, in certain special circumstances, federal armed forces
could be dispatched to ensure that the normal judicial processes operated ef-

fectively. But the secession crisis was quite different, in his view, since there were no federal courts or magistrates in the Southern states, hence no one for the troops to aid. Federal armed forces, he contended, could not be sent into a state on a mission of conquest. "[T]o send a military force into any State, with orders to act against the people," he maintained, "would be simply making war upon them."[39] Neither the President nor Congress possessed such a power to wage war against a state. Congress's constitutional power to declare war referred, in Black's view, only to the power to declare war against a *foreign* state, not against a member state of the Union itself. The militia could be summoned and placed in federal service, but only in three specified situations that were expressly stated in the Constitution: executing federal laws (in aid of judges and marshals), suppressing insurrection, and repelling foreign invasions.[40] On the thesis that "insurrection" meant rebellious activity by individuals rather than by states as such, none of these cases authorized a use of armed force to compel a seceded state back into the Union.

The practical problem concerned the two forts in Southern territory that were strongly garrisoned by Union forces—Fort Sumter in Charleston Harbor and Fort Pinckney in Pensacola. It was difficult for the Confederates to attack them without seeming, at least to the naked eye, to be aggressors. At Fort Sumter in particular, a wary and nervous waiting game was played. In January 1861, South Carolina state forces fired on a Union ship called the *Star of the West* when it attempted to deliver supplies to the Fort Sumter garrison. On being hit, the ship turned back. Since the Union garrison in the fort refrained from firing at the South Carolina forces, the incident was a minor one. But it was a very near thing.[41] In April 1861, however, the Confederates finally chose to mount a full-scale attack on Fort Sumter. President Lincoln reacted by mobilizing the armed forces of the United States for the military subduing of the entire Confederacy. There was, however, considerable room for debate as to whether the ensuing struggle qualified as a *war* in the true sense of the term. In order to shed light on this question, it is necessary to say a few words about what was meant by the expression "civil war" in mid-nineteenth-century legal usage.[42]

Legal Conceptions of War and Civil War

The principal cornerstone of legal thought about war in the nineteenth century was the conception of a *state of war*. In the proper legal sense, that concept, as it was envisaged in the nineteenth century, may be briefly defined as a

legal situation in which it is lawful for the contending sides to commit a range
of violent acts against one another—acts which would be unlawful in a state
of peace, such as killing and capturing, taking prisoners, and occupying enemy territory. On that much, there was universal agreement among nineteenth-
century lawyers. Since practically time immemorial, civil strife had been
considered distinct from war in the true sense, since war in the true sense was
generally seen to be possible only against a *foreign* foe. This had been the case
in Roman law, as well as throughout the European Middle Ages.[43] Disturbers
of the peace at home—i.e., criminals—were dealt with by entirely different
means from the waging of war. They were combated not by armed forces but
rather by police, magistrates, and criminal courts. Moreover, criminals were
dealt with on a strictly individual basis, with actual proof required of wrongdoing in each specific case in which punishment was to be applied.

In the course of time, it was realized that the two types of crisis do not, in
practice, separate quite so cleanly into the two categories just described. For
one thing, there could be situations in which the degree of turmoil or resistance to laws was so great that the armed forces were required to ensure obedience, instead of the regular police and magistrates. In addition, sometimes
the insurgent forces possessed a high degree of organization—even to the
point of running a *de facto* government in a portion of the nation's territory. In
such cases, the line between criminality and war could become seriously
blurred.

The most prominent authority on this subject for the Americans of the
1860s was the notable Swiss international-law writer of the eighteenth century,
Emmerich de Vattel. In his famous book *The Law of Nations* (1758), he set out
what became the basis of modern international legal doctrine on civil wars. He
held that, under certain rather special conditions, a condition of internal conflict would become, from the standpoint of international law, fully equivalent
to an interstate war. This was a situation in which rebellious subjects wholly
rejected their ruler's right to govern them—that is, where the insurgents' goal
was either to overthrow their government and take it over themselves or to secede and form a separate state. Vattel labeled this a "civil war" in the true legal
sense of the term. A civil war, in this strict sense, was fully equivalent to an interstate war, on the ground that the insurgents and the government constituted, in fact if not strictly in law, two distinct nations.[44] Whether an internal
conflict actually fell into this category of civil war in the international legal
sense was to be determined by the overall facts of the situation. This was nec-

essarily so, since the government side, in the usual course of things, would not be expected to recognize insurgents as being on a par with a foreign armed force. It will be seen that the British and French (and other) governments effectively adopted this position when they recognized the Confederacy as a belligerent power—though not, significantly, as a fully independent *state*.[45]

In May 1861, the subject was treated somewhat more cautiously by Henry W. Halleck—shortly to become a high-ranking Union general—in his treatise *International Law*. He echoed Vattel in holding a true civil war to be fully equivalent to an interstate war—with the laws of war and neutrality fully applicable. Unlike Vattel, however, he held that cases of attempted secession were not true civil wars, but instead fell into the lesser category of "mere rebellions." In such cases, the ruling government applied *only* its own national laws and not the international law relating to war.[46]

It is necessary to stress that these seemingly hair-splitting distinctions had concrete implications of the highest order, which should be carefully noted. If the crisis was regarded purely as a rebellion—i.e., as a law-enforcement operation—then the federal government would be acting in a *sovereign* capacity. It would possess those powers—and *only* those powers—expressly given to it by the Constitution. The single most outstanding consequence is that Confederate supporters would be regarded as ordinary criminals, subject to prosecution for whatever federal crimes they might have committed (such as treason). Convictions would have to be obtained, however, in the normal manner—on a person-by-person basis, with proof in each case beyond a reasonable doubt, and with all due process of law accorded to the accused persons. That meant that accused persons would have to be accorded such rights as a presumption of innocence, a right to counsel, trial by jury, and so forth.

If the crisis were to be regarded as a war, then the legal position becomes radically different. In this case, the federal government would be operating not as a sovereign but instead as a belligerent. It would proceed against the Confederates not on a person-by-person basis but rather collectively, wielding the powers granted by international law to warring nations. These consisted, most outstandingly, of the right to kill and capture members of the enemy armed force and forcibly to occupy enemy territory. They also encompassed the right to capture enemy private property on the high seas and to mount and enforce blockades around enemy seaports. In a situation of belligerency, however, there could be no criminal prosecution of enemy soldiers for carrying out lawful orders of their sovereign. Enemies, in short, were to be *defeated* but not *punished*.

The American Conflict of 1861–1865

The federal executive did its best, throughout the 1861–1865 crisis, to insist that, ultimately, the crisis in which it was embroiled was a rebellion and not a war in the strict sense. It was a law-enforcement action—on a large scale, to be sure—to enforce the *ordinary* law of the land against recalcitrant *individuals* in the Southern states. In support of this position was the fact that Congress never issued a declaration of war—or at least it never issued a declaration explicitly so labeled. It is true that troops were summoned (both state militia forces and the federal army), but there is no constitutional stricture that the armed forces can *only* be employed in war. On the contrary, the Constitution expressly provides for the use of state militia forces in federal service in order to "execute the Laws of the Union" and to "suppress Insurrections."[47]

It may also be noted that, when Congress convened to deal with the crisis on July 4, 1861, it proceeded to enact new criminal legislation to meet the emergency. One of these laws made it a crime to conspire to levy war against the United States (i.e., to commit treason).[48] Another new law made it an offense to recruit persons for the purpose of committing "armed hostility" against the United States.[49] A new piracy statute was also enacted, allowing action to be taken against ships (and their crews) which were *intending* to commit acts of piracy, as well as against those who had actually committed such acts in the past.[50] All of these initiatives bore the clear mark of a government acting in a sovereign, rather than a belligerent, mode.

At the same time, however, several initiatives taken by the federal government appeared, at least to the naked eye, to be marks of belligerent action. Three were of particular importance. One was the proclamation of a blockade of the Southern ports by President Lincoln in April 1861.[51] A blockade was widely regarded as quintessentially a belligerent operation. A second belligerent (or apparently belligerent) measure was a trade interdiction against the Southern states authorized by Congress in July 1861 and then implemented by President Lincoln the following month.[52] Prohibitions against trading with enemies, like blockades, were widely regarded as a hallmark of a state of war, since they (like blockades) targeted a whole population without regard to the guilt or innocence of particular individuals. Finally—and most important of all—there was the Union government policy of conducting its operations against the Confederate forces wholly in accordance with the international law of war. This included, crucially, granting prisoner-of-war treatment to captured Confederates, from the very outset of the struggle.

The Union government offered explanations for each of these three policies just identified, in an earnest effort to refute the view that they were belligerent actions. The trade interdiction policy—or "nonintercourse" policy as it was commonly known—was explicable as an exercise by Congress of one of its ordinary powers under the Constitution: the power to "regulate Commerce . . . among the several States."[53] Judicial support for this interpretation was provided by federal courts during the struggle.[54]

The blockade was explained in different terms: as a concession by the federal government to foreign countries, in the interest of avoiding distracting disputes that might otherwise arise. The federal government, it was contended, might have closed the Southern ports by legislation, as an exercise by Congress of its normal constitutional power to "regulate Commerce with foreign Nations."[55] The problem with such an action was that many countries (including, as it happened, the United States itself) contested the right of countries to close a port by fiat *unless* the government of the country was actually in effective control it. If the government was *not* in actual control of the port, then, as a matter of *international* law, it was only allowed to effect the closure by blockading it. The federal government position, therefore, was that, simply to avoid disputes with foreign countries, it would, as a matter of its own free choice, effect the closure of the ports by the belligerent power of blockade rather than by the *sovereign* power of legislation.

Regarding the application of the laws of war to the conflict, the Union government took a similar position—that its resort to belligerent methods was a matter of free choice and not of legal obligation. Simply in practical terms, it was unfeasible to mount hundreds of thousands, if not millions, of individual prosecutions for treason. In addition, if the Union refused to accord prisoner-of-war treatment to captured Confederates, then it was virtually certain that the Confederacy would retaliate by treating Union prisoners as criminals. The result would be increased bitterness on both sides that would impede the reconciliation process that would be necessary at the conclusion of the conflict. The Union therefore never wavered in its policy of treating soldiers in the Confederate armies as enemy belligerents rather than as traitors. But the Union also never wavered in its position that this was a unilateral humanitarian gesture, a matter of grace and free will on its own part, and not of true legal entitlement on the part of the Confederates themselves.[56]

In several important respects, the Union policy of treating the Confederates *as if* they were enemy belligerents rather than domestic criminals was subject to some sharp limitations. For one thing, the policy applied *only* to the conducting of military operations on land. Confederate forces on the high seas were treated not as lawful belligerents (i.e., as enemy naval forces or privateers) but rather as pirates. The Union also refused to accord any degree of legitimacy to Confederate governmental measures.[57] Nor did the federal government regard residents of the Confederate states as being excused from obedience to federal laws, such as the payment of taxes. In addition, the Union government reserved the right to rule over Confederate territory as a full sovereign and not merely as a belligerent occupier, as would be the case in a true war.[58] Even the concession of belligerent status to Confederate land forces applied only *during* the actual hostilities. The Union government gave no guarantee that Confederates might not be prosecuted for treason *after* the armed conflict had ceased.[59]

The federal executive's dualistic approach (as it might be termed) to the legal nature of the conflict was vividly illustrated early in the war by its policy of treating seagoing Confederates significantly differently from their land-based brethren. Seagoing Confederates were to be treated as pirates rather than as privateers. The legal distinction between these two types of entrepreneurial activity may be explained briefly. A privateer was a ship specially fitted out by private parties in time of war for the augmentation of their nation's war fleet, as a sort of volunteer naval vessel, although privateers typically engaged in the capture of enemy merchant ships (which were typically unarmed) and did not participate in battles against enemy warships or battle fleets. Privateering was expected to be a profitable investment activity, since the privateers were typically entitled to a share of the proceeds of any captures they made. A person seeking to engage in this adventurous form of business required a commission from a government, in the form of a license known generally as a *letter of marque*. Captures made pursuant to such a commission would qualify as legitimate acts of war. In the absence of the legal authority provided by a letter of marque, captures would be mere acts of piracy (i.e., robbery on the high seas for personal ends). A letter of marque was therefore a legal shield against prosecution for piracy, entitling a captured privateer to be treated instead as a *bona fide* prisoner of war.

The power to issue letters of marque was expressly granted to Congress in the original United States Constitution, and faithfully reproduced in the Confederate one.[60] By 1861, however, the issuing of letters of marque and employing of privateers had passed out of fashion, at least among the major European powers. Indeed, in 1856, the major European maritime states adopted what was known as the Declaration of Paris, which contained some notable rules of maritime war—including a sweeping statement that "[p]rivateering is, and re-

mains, abolished."[61] The United States did not support the abolition of privateering and, for that reason, declined to become a party to the Declaration,
thereby retaining the legal right to employ privateers. The Union did not,
however, envisage making use of this prerogative in the Civil War. Instead, it
chose an altogether different maritime strategy: relying on the regular navy to
mount a comprehensive blockade of the Southern ports.[62] (Midway through
the struggle, in March 1863, Congress authorized the President to grant letters
of marque; but Lincoln never availed himself of the power.)[63]

The Confederacy, in sharp contrast, decided to employ privateers, since it
entirely lacked a regular navy at the outset of the conflict. The importance of
privateering for the Confederacy was vividly indicated by its Congress's declaration of war against the United States. Only one section of the law actually
announced the state of war. The other fifteen or so provisions were given over
to detailed arrangements for issuing letters of marque.[64] Some forty-eight of
these were eventually issued by the Confederate government, although fewer
than half of the holders actually managed to put to sea.[65] They mostly sailed
out of Charleston, New Orleans, or Hatteras Inlet.[66]

At the very outset of the hostilities, the Union government made it clear that
it would not recognize any lawful authority on the part of the Confederacy to
issue valid letters of marque. In the blockade proclamation issued at the start of
the war, it was flatly stated that persons who molested American shipping "under the pretended authority" of the Confederacy would be treated as pirates.[67]
This refusal on the Union's part to recognize the legal validity of Confederate
letters of marque set the stage for one of the earliest legal confrontations of the
War.[68] This began with the capture in June 1861 by the Union navy of a Confederate ship, the *Savannah,* off the coast of Charleston. The vessel held a letter
of marque from President Jefferson Davis. The federal authorities, however, instituted criminal charges for piracy against the twelve crew members of the *Savannah* and proceeded to trial in a civilian court in New York.[69]

In their defense, the seamen naturally contended that their endeavors had
been lawful acts of war, by virtue of the privateering commission they held
from the Confederate government. In his charge to the jury, Justice Samuel
Nelson of the federal Supreme Court (sitting as a circuit judge) rejected this
defense. He stated that the court had no power, on its own initiative, to recognize the validity of the Confederate government as either an independent state
or as a lawful belligerent. That power, Nelson held, belonged exclusively to the
political branches of the government; and the courts had no choice but to fol-

low their lead. In modern terminology, it would be said that these recognition issues were political questions, hence outside the scope of judicial scrutiny. Since the Union government clearly had not recognized the Confederacy as a separate country, the court had no choice but to decline to recognize the holding of a Confederate letter of marque as a defense to a piracy charge. In the event, however, a jury deadlock prevented conviction (although the prisoners were kept in detention and not set free).[70]

A second trial of Confederate would-be privateers, held at virtually the same time in Philadelphia in the autumn of 1861, had a different outcome. This concerned an ex–slave ship which was issued with a letter of marque and, like the *Savannah,* was captured by the Union navy. The jury instructions of Justice Robert C. Grier of the federal Supreme Court (sitting as a circuit judge), like those of Nelson, stated that it was for the legislative and executive branches of the government, not the courts, to determine whether a purportedly independent nation was actually to be treated as such. Since the federal government clearly did not recognize the Confederacy as an independent state, no validity could be accorded to the letters of marque held by the defendants.[71] On this occasion, the master of the ship was convicted of piracy, along with three members of his crew.[72] In practice, however, the United States refrained from following through with this criminal-law policy, in part because of the threat of retaliation by the Confederates against Union prisoners.[73] On the motion of the district attorney, the privateers were remanded into military custody and effectively treated as prisoners of war.[74] They were never even sentenced, and eventually were exchanged for Union prisoners of war.[75]

These two privateers' cases should be understood to signify that, in eyes of the Union courts, the Confederacy could not be regarded as an *independent nation-state* (in the absence, that is, of recognition by the executive or legislature). Rather different, though, was the question of whether the Confederacy might be entitled to exercise the lawful rights of war on some *other* ground. This issue came before the full bench of the federal Supreme Court in March 1863, in the very heat of the conflict, in the famous Prize Cases.[76] These cases concerned captures not of Confederate privateers but rather of merchant ships from neutral states which were attempting to trade with the Southern states. Captures of neutral ships on the high seas could lawfully be made only in two principal circumstances: violations of a lawful blockade, and the carriage of contraband of war (i.e., arms, ammunition, and the like) to an enemy. It was absolutely crucial to both of these that a state of war, in the strict legal sense, be in existence at the time. Absent a state of war, the United States could have no legal ground for interfering with neutral-state trading vessels.

The issue in the Prize Cases, therefore, was whether a state of war actually existed at the time that President Lincoln proclaimed the blockade of the Southern states (April 1861). If it did not, then the blockade policy would amount to nothing more (or less) than a policy of systematically violating the rights of neutral traders, contrary to international law. In such an event, the President could lawfully enforce the blockade against the United States' *own* nationals; but could not enforce it against ships from neutral states without violating international law. In the words of Justice Nelson, who dissented from the majority's ruling, the conflict would be a mere "private war" of President Lincoln's, rather than a war in the true meaning of international law.

In effect, then, the federal Supreme Court was being called on to determine the legal character of the ongoing conflict—whether it amounted to a war, or instead had some lesser status, such as a purely civil commotion. The Court held (with Justice Grier writing for the majority) that, on this vital question, the political branches of the government did *not* have the exclusive say, as they did over the issue of the independence of the Confederacy. Instead, the legal status of the conflict was an objective question—*not* a purely political judgment—to be determined by the courts, on the basis of the overall facts (or "accidents") of the situation. In making their determination, the courts should look to such factors as "the number, power, and organization of the persons who originate [the rebellion] and carry it on."

> When the party in rebellion [the Court pronounced] occupy and hold in a hostile manner a certain portion of territory; have declared their independence; have cast off their allegiance; have organized armies; have commenced hostilities against their former sovereign, the world acknowledges them as belligerents, and the contest as a *war*.[77]

More specifically, the Court held that the crucial test for the existence of a civil war (in the strict legal sense) was whether "the regular course of justice is interrupted by revolt, rebellion or insurrection, so that the courts of justice cannot be kept open." In such a circumstance, "civil war exists and hostilities may be prosecuted on the same footing as if those opposing the government were foreign enemies invading the land."[78] Applying these criteria, the Court went on to conclude that the conflict was a true state of war—and that, consequently, the blockade policy was a lawful act of war which, as such, could be applied against neutral ships on the high seas.

Also considered by the Court was the question of whether a war, such as the present one, could be initiated without a declaration by Congress, as the Constitution requires—or at least seems to require. The conclusion on this point was that the congressional power to declare war only refers to situations in which the United States is the party initiating the contest. It is possible, the Court held, for a state of war to be thrust upon the United States by another party. The Mexican War was advanced as an example. Armed conflict—and a state of war—was already in progress when Congress acted, so that the congressional action was merely recognition of an *existing* state of war, rather than the initiating of a war. This was proclaimed on the very face of the legislation, which was entitled "Act for Prosecution of the *Existing* War against Mexico."[79] The substantive text expressly averred that a state of war had been created by the action of Mexico. The present situation, the Court concluded, was much the same. A war had been forced on the United States by an organized power with a well-defined territorial base.[80]

The Court did not shrink from the clear implication of its ruling: that, since a state of war existed, the Confederacy must be allowed to exercise the rights of war, as those were set out in international law, even if it was not a wholly independent state.[81] In modern parlance, the Confederacy would be said to be a *belligerent community* or *belligerent power,* even if it fell short of being a state. This ruling, it should be noted, was incompatible with the view of the federal government in one important respect: that it held the recognition of belligerent status of the Confederacy to be a question of *law,* to be decided by courts, rather than a question of *policy,* to be decided by the political branches of the government. Recognition—or, as the case may be, nonrecognition—of the Confederacy as an independent state remained in the hands of the executive; but the recognition of the Confederacy as a belligerent power was now held to be a justiciable issue, to be determined by courts on the basis of fixed, objective criteria.

It may also be noted that the Supreme Court's judgment in the Prize Cases was incompatible, certainly in spirit if not in letter, with the jury instructions given in the earlier privateers' cases. The matter is not altogether free from doubt, admittedly, because the jury instructions in those cases had concerned the question of the outright independence of the Confederacy rather than of its status as a belligerent power. The prevailing view in international law, though, was that the issuing of letters of marque to privateers was a legitimate act of war—hence a prerogative of the Confederacy, even in the absence of full independence. A federal court in California so held in 1864, citing the Prize Cases in support of its conclusion.[82]

The judgment in the Prize Cases came from a sharply divided Court, with five judges in the majority and four dissenting. Justice Nelson, speaking vigorously for the dissenters, contended that the various objective factors cited by the majority only determined the existence of a war in what he called a *material* sense, as distinct from a war in the true *legal* sense. For a war to exist in the true legal sense, he insisted, it must be duly declared by Congress, as expressly provided for in the Constitution—and this stricture applies, he maintained, to civil wars as well as to wars against foreign powers. The President, he conceded, has substantial powers to bring the armed forces of the United States, together with the militias of the states, into action against insurgents—but such action only amounts, in law, to "a personal war against those in rebellion," that is, against those who are *actually* disloyal to the Union government. A true war, in contrast, converts the *entire* population of the enemy state into enemies, merely on the basis of their nationality, without regard to any actual commission of hostile acts on the part of particular individuals. And only Congress, not the President, can institute such a true state of war.

On this thesis, Nelson concluded that a legal state of war only commenced on July 13, 1861, when Congress enacted the legislation conferring two key powers onto the President: the power to close ports in rebellious areas; and the power to declare the inhabitants of designated areas to be generally in a state of insurrection.[83] Only at that point, Nelson contended, did the actions of the federal government cease to be directed against rebellious persons exclusively, and come to be directed instead against whole regions and populations. Consequently, any captures of neutral vessels prior to that date were violations of international law.[84]

It may be said that, from the standpoint of *international* law, the majority in the Prize Cases had the better of the argument. They had, after all, the authority of the venerable Vattel on their side. It was also the general position of international-law writers in the nineteenth century that the existence of a state of war did not depend on the issuing of a formal declaration, but instead was to be inferred from the facts.[85] From the standpoint of American constitutional law, however, the matter is considerably more uncertain, in large part because formal declaratins of war are, at least in practice, no longer promulgated. In practical terms, therefore, disputes now tend to turn on the general question of presidential prerogatives in the area of foreign affairs, including the employment of American troops for limited purposes which fall short of a state of war, in the traditional sense.[86] Fortunately for the United States, no occasion has arisen for a reconsideration of the issues presented in the Prize Cases.

One final word is in order regarding this momentous ruling. It carefully distinguished between the two great categories of public right and power: *belligerent* and *sovereign*. Sovereign rights and powers belong only to independent nation-states. Belligerent rights and powers, in contrast, can be wielded by lesser entities, such as rebellious regions within established states. Belligerent communities of this lesser sort are therefore allowed to take and hold prisoners of war, to invade and occupy the territory of their enemies, to mount blockades, and so forth. But they are not allowed—or at least not *automatically*—to have legislation recognized by foreign powers or to send and receive diplomats, because these are rights reserved to sovereigns. An important consequence of this state of affairs is that civil conflicts are, in an important sense, asymmetrical (in modern terminology), in that the government side is permitted to employ *both* sovereign *and* belligerent powers in the suppression of the rebellion. The rebels, in contrast, possess only belligerent rights.[87]

The Union government did not hesitate to take advantage of what it saw as its legally privileged position. In practice, it employed a complex and somewhat untidy mix of sovereign-right and belligerent-right measures to bring the rebellious Southerners to book. On the field of battle, it acted as a belligerent. Off that field, however, it acted as a sovereign. From the very outset, the Union government insisted that it was fully entitled to operate in this dual capacity (as it might be termed), and courts generally supported this stance. A prize case in 1862 in Massachusetts, for example, held that Confederates "are at the same time belligerents and traitors, and subject to the liabilities of both." By the same token, it was stated, the United States has "the double character of a belligerent and sovereign, and has the rights of both. These rights co-exist, and may be exercised at pleasure."[88] This dualistic character of the Union war effort would reverberate throughout the Civil War—and indeed well beyond it.

The Confederacy Declares War

From the Southern standpoint, the issue of the legal nature of the conflict was far simpler. It was regarded unproblematically as a fully *international* war,

since the Confederate States of America was (in the Confederates' own eyes) a
fully independent country.[89] From the Confederate vantage point, it was even
contended that the United States *did* declare war against it, even if not in the
form of a declaration explicitly so labeled. According to Confederate president
Davis, a message that Lincoln had sent to the governor of South Carolina on
April 8 amounted to a "declaration of hostile purposes"—a declaration Lincoln then repeated "in more specific terms and on a much more extensive
scale" in his call for troops on 15 April.[90]

For the removal of any doubt on the subject, the provisional Confederate
Congress proceeded to enact a formal declaration of war against the United
States on May 6, 1861.[91] This declaration, though, basically asserted that a
state of war *already* existed, by virtue of Union aggression. The preamble of
the act noted that "earnest efforts . . . to establish friendly relations" had been
spurned by the United States and, furthermore, that that country had raised
military and naval forces against the Confederacy with an intention "to over-
awe, oppress and finally subjugate the people of the Confederate States." To
meet this dire emergency, the President was authorized to employ the country's armed forces "to meet the war thus commenced." In all events, the important point is that, according to the Confederates, the crisis was fully a war, by
virtue of *either* a Union declaration creating a state of war *or* a *de facto* invasion
of Confederate territory by United States armed forces.

It is therefore interesting, and ironic, that neither side in the great struggle
of 1861–1865 regarded the contest as a *civil war.* The North regarded it was a
law-enforcement enterprise, as the subduing of a rebellion (albeit on a large
material scale), rather than as a war. The South regarded it as a war, but not as
a *civil* war, since it saw itself as an independent nation. That we now refer to
the crisis, without hesitation, as the "Civil War" is an indication of a happily
diplomatic resolution of this delicate and potentially emotive point.[92] Even
lawyers, who are famously long of memory, have largely reconciled themselves
to this terminological compromise.

2

Desperate Measures

No doctrine, involving more pernicious consequences, was ever invented by the wit of man than that any of [the] provisions [of the Constitution] can be suspended during any of the great exigencies of government. Such a doctrine leads directly to anarchy or despotism. . . . [T]he theory of necessity on which it is based is false; for the government, within the Constitution, has all the powers granted to it, which are necessary to preserve its existence.

—United States Supreme Court

In time of war, without any special legislation, not the commander-in-chief only, but every commander of an expedition, or of a military post, is lawfully empowered by the constitution and laws of the United States to do whatever is necessary, and is sanctioned by the *laws of war,* to accomplish the lawful objects of his command.

—Supreme Court of Ohio

The American Constitution contains only two provisions on emergency situations. The first confers on Congress the power to summon the state militia for any of three stated purposes: to "execute the Laws of the Union"; to "suppress Insurrections"; and to "repel Invasions."[1] The second provision—which unfortunately is very opaquely worded—is known as the suspension clause. It provides that the writ of habeas corpus can be suspended if (but only if) "the public Safety" requires it, in "Cases of Rebellion or Invasion."[2] The opacity of the wording lies chiefly in the failure of the text to state explicitly who possesses the power to invoke the suspension. There is no provision in the Constitution for suspending any of the normal operations of political life by, say, postponing elections, or for suspending basic liberties such as the right to a fair trial or a presumption of innocence. Nor are extraordinary powers of substantive law-making provided for, such as the enactment of *ex post facto* criminal laws or legislation by executive decree. However dire the emergency facing it, the federal government possesses only the powers that the Constitution grants to it, either expressly or by fair implication. As Justice Stephen J. Field later insisted (though in a dissenting opinion) in a Supreme Court case in 1884, "[t]he wants of the government could never be the measure of its powers."[3]

It seemed outrageous to many observers at the time that the Constitution could have been written—or that it should now be interpreted—in such a way as to prevent the federal government from taking drastic action in the face of well-nigh the direst emergency that could be imagined. It is not, therefore, surprising that a school of thought would arise that would press for a broad interpretation of the express powers of the Constitution, so as to allow considerably greater latitude to the federal government than had hitherto been thought possible. The label given to this line of thought was the "adequacy of the Constitution" school of thought.[4] Among the key supporters of this school of thought was William Whiting, the solicitor of the War Department, whose book *War Powers under the Constitution,* first published in 1862, was said to have gone through no fewer than forty-three editions by 1870.

In the 1861–1865 crisis, both the President and Congress made more expanded uses of their powers than they had previously done—thereby raising some serious doubts as to whether their constitutionally granted powers might have been exceeded in the process. From the President came two initiatives that were particularly controversial in this matter: the assumption of the power of suspension of habeas corpus; and the imposition of martial measures, which entailed executive law-making and the subjection of civilians to military trials. From Congress came various measures, of which three will particularly occupy our attention: the enactment of an income tax; the creation of an inconvertible legal-tender paper currency; and the establishment of a system of military conscription.

The President Takes Command

The express constitutional powers of the President fall into three broad, and ill-defined, categories.[5] First is simply "[t]he executive Power," which is stated to be "vested in a President of the United States."[6] No definition is provided of the actual contents of this executive power. The second category of presidential powers comprises various specific powers which are historical descendants of the legal powers of the British Crown, such as the power to pardon persons convicted of crimes and to veto legislation. The third category consists of the powers incident to the President's role as the commander-in-chief of the armed forces. These powers, like the general executive ones, are not explicitly spelled out in the text of the Constitution.

President Lincoln was not slow to make maximum use of his constitutional powers. At the outset of the armed struggle, he took several decisive steps which may be briefly noted. First was the summoning of 75,000 militia troops from the states, in the proclamation of April 15, 1861.[7] This was legally unproblematic, as statutory authority existed, in the form of the Militia Act of 1795.[8] A second measure was the issuing of a call for volunteers to augment the size of the regular army. For this step, there was no specific legal authority. Most problematically, the President had no money to pay these troops with—at least not legally—since the Constitution expressly prescribes that "[n]o money shall be drawn from the Treasury, but in consequence of appropriations made by Law."[9] Notwithstanding this stricture, Lincoln paid some $2 million of Treasury funds for the assembling of these forces. When the Congress eventually met, on July 4, 1861, it dealt with this matter by means of a ratification law of August 6, 1861, which stated that all proclamations and orders regarding the army and navy, and the calling out of the militia, were "hereby approved and in all respects legalized and made valid, to the same intent and with the same effect as if they had been issued and done under the previous express authority and direction of the Congress of the United States."[10]

In addition to these measures, the President took several others that were considerably more controversial legally, of which four will call for detailed attention. First was the proclamation of the blockade, in April 1861. Second was the suspension of the right of habeas corpus. Third was the resort to martial law. Fourth, and most momentous of all, was the freeing of slaves in the rebellious states by way of proclamation. The emancipation of slaves will be considered in due course.[11] The first three will be considered here.

Proclaiming a Blockade

Among the earliest of President Lincoln's measures after the attack on Fort Sumter was the instituting of a blockade against the entire Confederate coastline, on April 19, 1861.[12] Questions soon arose as to whether the President had the authority to do this in the absence of a declaration of war by Congress.

The problem arose because a blockade was regarded as a belligerent measure—that is, as a feature of a state of war. And the President, some contended, had no power to create a state of war on his own initiative, since the Constitution clearly conferred that power on Congress.[13] The nearest that there was to a congressional declaration of war, it was argued, was the Non-intercourse Act of July 13, 1861, in which Congress authorized the President to impose a comprehensive prohibition against trading with the rebel areas.[14] Lincoln proceeded to impose the prohibition on August 16, declaring at the same time that the inhabitants of the eleven Southern states were "in a state of insurrection against the United States."[15] The thesis was that trade prohibitions were so closely connected with states of war as to amount to the equivalent of a declaration of war. If this contention was accepted—and it won support from federal attorney general Henry Stanbery after the war—then the inevitable conclusion was that any captures made for blockade violation in the period between April 19 and August 16 (or July 13 at the earliest) must have been unlawful.[16] In that event, prize courts must order the release of all such vessels.

This question—the legality of captures for blockade violation during the three- or four-month gap period—was the specific issue that was at stake in the Prize Cases which reached the Supreme Court in 1863—with the decisive question being whether the President, *without* the authorization of Congress, could lawfully impose a blockade on his own initiative.[17] The Court held that he could. This was on the ground that a civil war, as distinct from an international war, would never be expected to commence by way of a formal declaration of war. As observed previously, the existence of a state of civil war is identified instead by various objective indicators such as the degree of organization of the insurgent forces and so forth.[18] The real question, then, in the Court's view, was to decide who had the authority to determine whether those various indicators of civil war were present or not. In the Court's ruling, it was the President who had that power; and his determination must bind the courts.[19]

The result, then, was that, in effect, the congressional power to declare war applies *only* to wars against foreign countries, not to civil wars. It should be carefully noted that, strictly speaking, the President cannot "declare" a civil war in the sense of *creating* a state of war by act of will. The state of civil war is created by the facts of the situation, not by fiat or act of will. The President's prerogative, therefore, is better seen as *acknowledging* or confirming the state of war, rather than actually *creating* it. In the particular case at hand, the Supreme Court held that the President had confirmed the existence of a civil war by the very act of instituting the blockade. Consequently, the war commenced in April 1861 and not in July or August.[20]

There was a vigorous dissent on the Court from this conclusion, with Justice Samuel Nelson writing for the minority.[21] He insisted that there was a distinction between, on the one hand, the use of the militia to deal with an emergency and, on the other hand, a true war. The militia, Nelson maintained, was deployed, in the manner of a police force, only against *individual* miscreants for alleged violations of the municipal law of the United States. Its summoning by the President in April 1861 was therefore an exercise of "a power under the municipal law of the country and not under the law of nations." At that stage, the conflict was only what Justice Nelson called a "personal war"—specifically, an enforcement action aimed against *individual* wrongdoers. Only with Congress's adoption of the Non-intercourse Act of July 13, 1861, was the conflict transformed, by Congress, into what Justice Nelson called a "territorial war," in which the entire population of another state were enemies, regardless of any personal wrongdoing. The President, in the view of the dissenters, possessed no power to "convert a loyal citizen into a belligerent enemy" by fiat.[22] This argument did not carry the day with the majority of the Court. It did, however, persuade a postwar British-American arbitral panel, which considered precisely the same question. It, like Justice Nelson and the minority in the Prize Cases, regarded the war as having commenced only with the Non-intercourse Act of July 13, 1861—meaning that all captures made prior to that date were unlawful.[23]

Suspending Habeas Corpus

The second of Lincoln's controversial actions was the suspension of habeas corpus. The text of the Constitution's Suspension Clause makes express provision for this, albeit in an obliquely negative manner. "The Privilege of the Writ of Habeas Corpus," it states, "shall not be suspended" *except* "in cases of Rebellion or Invasion."[24] The principal problem, though, is that this clause, being phrased in the passive voice, signally fails to state which organ or organs of government are allowed to suspend in those exceptional circumstances. Moreover, as of 1861, there had never before been a suspension, so that there was no precedent available for guidance. There was, however, scholarly authority, in the form of Supreme Court justice Joseph Story's famous commentary on the Constitution, to the effect that Congress, rather than the President, possessed the suspension power.[25]

At the commencement of the crisis, Congress was not in session. (Nor was Lincoln in any great hurry to convene it.) The President therefore began taking action on his own. The early suspensions were on rather a piecemeal basis, without public proclamation, in the form of confidential orders or authorizations to military commanders. An early concern was to safeguard the railroad lines from the loyal states of the Northeast to Washington. For this purpose, Lincoln privately authorized his chief army commander, General Winfield Scott (of Mexican War fame) to suspend habeas corpus privileges to persons who were arrested "in the vicinity of [any] military line" between Philadelphia and Washington.[26] The first suspension of habeas corpus by public proclamation soon followed, on May 10, 1861, covering areas in southern Florida (Key West, the Tortugas, and Santa Rosa).[27] Local commanders were authorized, like Scott, to institute suspensions of habeas corpus.[28] Subsequent suspensions in the Northeast followed, extending the measure to military lines as far away as Bangor, Maine.[29] One of the suspensions was very narrowly targeted, affecting only a single named individual.[30]

Challenges to the President's authority on this front soon emerged. An early one occurred when a federal district judge in the District of Columbia sought to withdraw a person from the Union forces on the ground that he was a minor who had enlisted without the consent of his parents. (For the purpose of habeas corpus law, military service is treated as a form of detention, in that a person, once enrolled in the colors, is not free to leave the service at will.)[31] The judge issued a habeas corpus writ, addressed to the commander of Fort McHenry in Baltimore, where the soldier was stationed. Not only did the commander refuse to surrender the soldier; he also arrested the attorney who served the writ. To complete the humiliation, Secretary of State Seward stopped payment of the judge's salary. The other judges in the relevant federal circuit reacted very sourly to this turn of events, characterizing the executive action as "without a parallel in the judicial history of the United States." But the judges also candidly confessed their impotence in the face of "the vast military force of the executive." The court, they lamented, had "no physical power to enforce the lawful process of this court on . . . military subordinates against the president's prohibition."[32]

A much more famous case was soon to follow. This concerned a certain John Merryman, a Confederate sympathizer of some prominence in Maryland. He was allegedly the officer of a prosecessionist company involved in the destruction of railroad bridges. In the course of federal crackdown on disloyal elements in Maryland, he was arrested by the armed forces and incarcerated in

Fort McHenry.[33] In April 1861, he sought, and obtained, a habeas corpus writ from Chief Justice Taney, whose judicial duties included service as a federal circuit judge in the circuit that included Maryland. (At that time, all Supreme Court justices did, so to speak, double duty as Supreme Court justices and also as trial and appellate judges in the various federal circuits.) Taney, in his capacity as circuit judge, issued the writ, addressed to General George Cadwalader, the commander at Fort McHenry.[34]

Cadwalader declined to comply with the writ, on the ground that he himself was empowered to suspend habeas corpus. He informed Taney of this view and politely requested him to postpone further action in the matter.[35] In response, Taney issued an opinion on the questions of law raised by the incident, concluding that the prerogative of suspending habeas corpus belonged solely to Congress. In so holding, he invoked the authority of Story. He also relied on the fact that the suspension clause was placed in Article I of the Constitution, which concerned the powers and constraints on Congress. The opinion concluded in a diplomatic (if not quite a conciliatory) vein, with an invitation to the President to defuse the crisis. Perhaps, Taney speculated, General Cadwalader had exceeded his instructions, thereby relieving the President of any personal blame. In that event, however, the President should rectify matters by determining "what measures he will take to cause the civil process of the United States to be respected and enforced."[36]

Lincoln, however, was in no mood for compromise. He refused to take steps to enforce the circuit court's actions.[37] The administration also tenaciously disputed Taney's legal reasoning. In his opening address to the newly assembled Congress on July 4, 1861, Lincoln dealt forthrightly with the matter, delivering a riposte to Taney's ruling of some six weeks earlier. He stressed the gravity of the crisis and asserted that the writ of habeas corpus "practically . . . relieves more of the guilty, than of the innocent." It was therefore essential that this traditional right must "to a very limited extent, be violated." The alternative, Lincoln insisted, was that all *other* laws of the United States would be violated. "[A]re all the laws, but one [i.e., that of habeas corpus], to go unexecuted," he asked, in a famous rhetorical flourish, "and the government itself go to pieces, lest that one be violated?" His answer was unambiguous: that "the single law" of habeas corpus must be sacrificed in the interest of preserving the whole structure of federal power and right. He conceded that some contended that only Congress, and not the President, had the power to impose such a sacrifice. But "it cannot be believed," Lincoln maintained, that "the framers of the [Constitution] intended, that in every case, the danger should run its course, until Congress could be called together; the very assembling of which might be prevented, as was intended in this case, by the rebellion." He then promised that a detailed argument for habeas corpus suspension as an executive prerogative would be put forward in due course by the attorney general. The question of whether there should, at some future point, be legislation on the subject was left by Lincoln, rather vaguely, to "the better judgment of Congress."[38]

The country had not long to wait for the promised opinion of the attorney general. Edward Bates, on the very next day, submitted a lengthy exposition on the subject—and very interesting it proved to be.[39] Bates's opinion was, on the one hand, considerably more nuanced than Lincoln's congressional message of the previous day but was, at the same time, even more assertive of the prerogatives of the executive. The approach of Bates differed from that of the President in emphasizing not so much the President's power to *suspend* habeas corpus as his power to *override* or counteract it. Bates asserted, in effect, an inherent power on the part of the President to arrest and imprison "insurgents in open arms against the Government," notwithstanding any habeas corpus orders to the contrary. This approach enabled him to concede that, strictly speaking, only Congress could suspend the *privilege* of the writ of habeas corpus. But suspension, in this strict and narrow sense, only referred, in Bates's view, to depriving litigants of the right to *seek* the remedy, or to stripping courts of the power to *issue* the writ. Separate from these was the question of the duty of the executive to *obey* a writ once it was issued. On this vital point, Bates maintained that the President possessed a distinct power, as part of his *general* powers as chief executive, to decline to obey orders for the release of particular prisoners.

Such a policy of deliberate disobedience of court orders by the executive, to be sure, must be (in Bates's words) "temporary and exceptional and . . . only intended to meet a pressing emergency." But he went on to maintain that the President was "the sole judge" of whether or not such an emergency was in existence at a given time. Moreover, the President's judgment on this point was not reviewable by courts. "[T]he whole subject-matter," he asserted, "is political and not judicial. The insurrection itself is purely political." It would be difficult, in the whole of American history, to discover a broader assertion of presidential prerogatives.

Judicial opinion on the question of the suspension power was divided during the war, though with the weight of opinion on the side of Taney. In the federal system, a district court in New York and a circuit court in California held, like Taney, that the suspension clause power belonged to Congress rather than to the President.[40] The state supreme courts of Wisconsin and Indiana were of like opinion.[41] A federal circuit court in Vermont, however, supported the view that the President possessed the suspension power under the suspension clause (while also holding that the President could not delegate the exercise of that power to subordinate officials such as the secretary of war).[42] Although there has, even now, been no definitive pronouncement on the question by the federal Supreme Court, the prevailing opinion is that of Taney: that the suspension power belongs to Congress.[43]

It is interesting that, during the Civil War, it was the judiciary which pressed the case for the suspension right as a congressional, rather than a presidential, prerogative, and not Congress itself, which remained largely quiescent on the matter. Be that as it may, the possibility of a clash between the executive and legislative branches of the government on the subject was definitively averted when, midway through the conflict, Congress provided a statutory basis for suspensions of habeas corpus. The Habeas Corpus Act of March 1863 expressly granted the suspension authority to the President.[44] But the legislation was ambivalently drafted, in that it actually granted to the President the right (along the lines argued by Bates) to override habeas corpus orders, and did not actually strip the courts of the right to issue such orders in the first instance. In cases in which a prisoner was being held "by the authority of the President," the person holding the prisoner would so inform the court. On such certification being given, "further proceedings under the writ of habeas corpus" would be "suspended" for so long as the presidential "suspension" policy was in force. In all events, though, even if the meaning of "suspension" of habeas corpus remained tantalizingly vague, the practical effect was clear: the executive could imprison persons suspected of disloyalty without the effective constraint of habeas corpus proceedings.

The 1863 law did not, at least in any explicit way, state that the prior suspensions had been unlawful (although one federal court, after the war, held that the statute implicitly amounted to a rejection of the President's claim to possession of the suspension power).[45] In the Wisconsin state courts, a constitutional challenge was mounted against the act on the thesis that it constituted an improper delegation to the President of Congress's own suspension prerogative. The Wisconsin Supreme Court, however, held the delegation to be lawful, though only with very palpable misgivings.[46] Since that time, the federal

Supreme Court has clarified the position on this matter. Congress is permitted to delegate tasks to the executive which fall into its constitutional sphere, provided that, in so doing, it lays down "an intelligible principle" for the executive to follow. This suffices to ensure that the role of the executive is merely to implement the policy set by Congress, and not to substitute the executive's own will for that of the legislature.[47]

Lincoln made use of the authority conferred by the 1863 act in later habeas corpus suspensions. This occurred most notably in September 1863, in the face of a crisis brought about by a rash of habeas corpus writs which threatened seriously to undermine the Union's conscription process (which will be considered presently). The chief problem was posed by judges who issued habeas corpus writs for the release of conscripts *after* their induction. Some lawyers even developed something of a specialization in this area—most famously (or notoriously) a New York lawyer named William F. Howe, who became popularly known as "Habeas Corpus Howe" for his ability to obtain releases of persons from military service. Navy Secretary Gideon Welles grumbled that sailings of warships were sometimes delayed by judges issuing habeas corpus writs on behalf of seamen.[48] These habeas corpus actions were especially numerous, and disruptive to the conscription process, in Pennsylvania.[49]

Lincoln reacted by invoking the Habeas Corpus Act, to deny the benefit of the writ to persons enrolled in the armed forces, as well as to persons who had committed any offenses against the armed forces.[50] The following year, he invoked the act again, to suspend habeas corpus in Kentucky, in the context of a proclamation of martial law in the state, in the face of an impending Confederate invasion.[51]

By means of this combination of executive and legislation action, the Union government succeeded in closing off habeas corpus actions in the federal courts as an effective avenue of opposition to the war policies of the Lincoln administration. Other legal pathways, however, remained to be explored by intrepid dissenters, including habeas corpus relief from *state* courts, which were not covered by the federal suspensions. These other activities will be explored in due course.[52] For the present, it is only necessary to note that the constitutional provision for suspension of federal habeas corpus action was successfully—if somewhat untidily—put into effect for the first time in American history, first by presidential action alone and subsequently by a combination of congressional and executive initiative.[53]

Martial Law

The nearest thing that the President possesses to a *general* emergency power in American Constitutional law is the power to impose martial law. The Constitution, however, nowhere makes explicit reference to the subject, which is therefore left shrouded in a certain degree of juridical mystery. The root of the concept lies in something called the "law of war" or *jus belli* in English law, which came into play in the face of either insurrection or invasion. It was, naturally, contrasted with the law of peace, or *tempus pacis* (meaning literally "time of peace"). The famous British jurist Edward Coke explained the difference in the seventeenth century:

> When the Courts of justice be open and judges and ministers of the same may by law protect men from wrong and violence [he explained] and distribute justice to all, it is said to be time of peace. So, when by invasion, insurrection, rebellions, or such like, the peaceable course of justice is disturbed and stopped, so as the courts of justice be as it were shut up, *et silent leges Inter arma,* then it is said to be time of war.[54]

In early American history, courts took a stricter view of martial law than Coke did. The Louisiana Supreme Court, in particular, did so when it considered the lawfulness of certain actions taken by General Andrew Jackson in the face of the British invasion of the New Orleans area in 1814–1815, during the War of 1812. The court treated martial law as, in essence, a sort of emergency conscription measure.[55] A declaration of martial law extended, the court held, only over the *very* ground actually controlled by the armed force in question, with the effect of transforming that tightly circumscribed area into a military encampment—with the result that all persons of military age and capacity located within it were now subject to the orders of the commander. The court also held, however, that a commander's martial-law powers extended no further than the area that was *actually* under his immediate control. In the case in question, the court held that the declaration of martial law could not encompass the whole city of New Orleans, given that the commander's actual encampment was all of four miles distant from the city.

A few words are in order regarding the relationship between martial law and the suspension of habeas corpus. There can be a close association between the two, because the imposition of martial law might entail a suspension of habeas corpus. In such a case, it is arguable—though judicial authority on the point is lacking—that martial law is an alternate mechanism, independent of the suspension clause, for restricting habeas corpus. That is to say, it is possible that habeas corpus is actually suspendable in two distinct ways: by Congress, pursuant to the suspension clause; and by the President (or subordinate military commanders), pursuant to the President's commander-in-chief power.

It should also be noted that martial law and habeas corpus suspension differ in two very important respects. The first is that martial law is the more powerful instrument of the two, by a large margin, because it entails, at least potentially, a *total* replacement of the ordinary civil law by military rule. Martial law, in other words, is, to put it bluntly, a form of military dictatorship. Suspension of habeas corpus is far more limited in nature, being "merely" the suppression of one particular remedial pathway for the contesting of one particular wrong (unlawful detention).

The second key difference between martial law and habeas corpus suspension is in their geographical coverage. Martial law, as noted above, is rigorously local in character, extending no further than the area *actually* threatened by the rebellion or invasion, and perhaps even (on the Louisiana Supreme Court's view) no further than the area actually occupied physically by the armed forces of the martial-law commander. This geographical straitjacket confining martial law was confirmed by the Supreme Court of Wisconsin in a case in 1863, which held that martial law could only be exercised in the actual "theatre of war."

> Within those [geographical] limits [the Court proclaimed] let the war power rage, controlled by nothing but the laws of war. But outside of them let the constitution, with all its safeguards, remain undisturbed. Let it stand like the cities of refuge or the temples of the gods, a shield against illegal violence, even to the guiltiest traitor that ever raised his sacrilegious hand against it.[56]

The Indiana Supreme Court, in a similar (if less florid) vein, held firmly that the President was only allowed to impose martial law "locally and temporarily, where actual or immediate impending force renders it a military necessity."[57] The Pennsylvania Supreme Court was of a like view.[58] Shortly after the war, the federal Supreme Court added its voice, holding martial law to be "confined to the locality of actual war."[59] Martial law may therefore be said to amount to a *total* displacement of the ordinary law within a *limited* area. Suspension of habeas corpus, conversely, may be described as a *limited* suspension of the rule of law on, potentially at least, a *nationwide* geographical basis.

With this background in mind, we may consider some of the more legally adventurous uses made of martial law by the Lincoln administration and the
Union armed forces under his auspices. It became apparent early in the war that
very elastic views could be taken of the local-character aspect of martial law. In
August 1861, General John C. Fremont declared the entire state of Missouri to
be under martial law.[60] The question of the nature and extent of the powers held
by a martial-law commander received detailed consideration in a case in the
Court of Claims after the war. The case concerned various contracts that Fremont had entered into, purportedly on behalf of the federal government, which
failed to conform with existing federal rules.[61] It was held that a martial-law administrator's powers, being rooted in the principle of necessity which operated
during an emergency, justified departures from "normal" law (with the consequence that the contracts were binding on the federal government).

Fremont's successor, Halleck, was less zealous about abolishing slavery and
also more restrained in his view of martial law. He doubted the validity of Fremont's martial-law declaration, apparently because of the lack of a prior presidential authorization.[62] His doubts on this score were eventually assuaged by
Lincoln, who in December 1861 expressly allowed him to exercise martial law
"in your discretion to secure the public safety and the authority of the United
States."[63] Armed with this reassuring authority, Halleck proceeded to declare
martial law, not over the whole state of Missouri as Fremont had done, but only
over the city of St. Louis, plus areas "in and about" all railroads in the state.[64]

There were a number of additional declarations of martial law by Union
commanders. In February 1862, for example, martial law was declared over the
whole of the state of Kansas, coupled with an express pronouncement that the
civil authorities of the state were "manifestly unable to preserve the peace and
give due security to life and property." The purpose of the declaration was to
deal with guerrilla bands, which were to be put down "with a strong hand and
by summary process." Trials of persons participating in such bands were to be
by military commissions.[65] In 1864, in the face of a northward countersurge by
Confederate armed forces, martial law was declared over the whole state of
Kentucky.[66] This action was noteworthy because the declaration contained
both a suspension of habeas corpus and the establishment of martial law—
indicating (rightly) that the two were distinct from one another, although
sometimes imposed simultaneously.

The most audacious martial-law initiative of the entire war was taken by
the Lincoln administration itself in August and September 1862, when it prom-

ulgated a series of legislative measures by executive decree, with nationwide reach. On August 8, 1862, Secretary of War Stanton issued two proclamations, one dealing specifically with draft evasion and the other with "the suppression of disloyal practices."[67] To deal with draft evasion, two rules were laid down: first, that no one eligible for the draft into the militia was allowed to leave the United States; and second, that any draft-eligible person who left his county or state before the draft was made would be liable to arrest. The second order, concerning disloyal practices, provided that persons accused of such activities—which were not defined even in the most general terms—would be tried by military commissions rather than by the civil courts. The substance of this second proclamation was then embodied in a set of general orders to the armed forces.[68]

The Stanton orders of August 8, 1862 were of only temporary duration. The following month, they were superseded—with their substance retained—by a presidential proclamation of September 24, 1862.[69] This candidly stated that "disloyal persons are not adequately restrained by the ordinary processes of law." Persons who discouraged enlistments of volunteers, as well as persons guilty of "any disloyal practice," were now liable to arrest by the armed forces, without access to habeas corpus relief. These persons were expressly stated to be "subject to martial law." If placed on trial at all, they would be tried by military commissions and not by civilian courts.

There were immediate and loud objections to these measures by persons who were worried about the concentration of excessive powers in the hands of the federal executive. Prominent among the objectors was Benjamin R. Curtis, a former associate justice of the federal Supreme Court (in 1851–1857) and staunch opponent of the spread of slavery. In his pamphlet *Executive Power*, issued in the wake of these measures of August and September 1862, he protested that the administration was, in effect, placing the entire country under martial law and making law by presidential fiat.[70]

Judicial reaction to these bold executive initiatives was mixed. A federal circuit court in Vermont approved them as a valid exercise of the power of martial law.[71] So did a federal circuit court in Ohio.[72] Not all courts were so deferential to the executive. In 1864, the Indiana Supreme Court held that the President could exercise law-making powers *only* in a strict martial-law context, specifically, in the immediate theater of actual hostilities. Outside that strict limit, the President could not create new criminal offenses by executive proclamation. To subject persons to trial by executive fiat for acts that were not criminal according to either state or federal law was denounced by the court, in language bordering on the intemperate, as "but a mode of applying lynch law."[73] The Indiana court's righteous indignation exceeded its practical effectiveness. During the war, no effective judicial constraint on vigorous executive action materialized.[74]

Legislating in New Realms

The crisis of 1861–1865 posed challenges to the powers of Congress as well as to those of the President. The nub of the difficulty here may be stated with the utmost simplicity. The Constitution does not grant to Congress an open-ended power to legislate. Instead, it grants the power to legislate on some seventeen specified subjects. The result is that each and every enactment of Congress must find its justification in one of the seventeen areas expressly set out. In two areas particularly, Congress broke new ground during the Civil War: the raising of money, and the raising of manpower for the armies. On the money-raising front, there were two innovations: an income tax and the issuing of a nonconvertible paper currency that was declared by law to be legal tender. Regarding manpower, the innovative step was military conscription. All of these gave rise to interesting legal disputes.

Taxing Incomes

In principle, the revenue-raising powers of Congress are sweeping. The Constitution confers onto Congress a broad power to "lay and collect Taxes, Duties, Imposts, and Excises."[75] Only one kind of tax is expressly prohibited outright by the Constitution: on exports.[76] There are, however, constraints on the *manner* in which taxes may be laid, depending on whether the tax in question is *direct* or *indirect*. Indirect taxes are required to be "uniform throughout the United States."[77] Illustrated in the simplest way, this uniformity requirement means that Congress cannot, for example, impose one tariff rate on imports into New York and another rate on the same goods imported into Baltimore. Direct taxes are subject to a quite different constraint: they are required to be "apportioned among the several States" according to their populations.[78]

During the Civil War, Congress enacted four additional types of tax, to supplement the federal government's two normal revenue sources, which were customs duties and land-sale proceeds. Two of these new taxes—excise taxes and inheritance taxes—posed little in the way of legal problems. A third one was a direct tax—basically a land tax—enacted in 1861, duly apportioned among the states as required by the Constitution.[79] In the event, this only lasted for one year, bringing in little (if any) revenue that would not have been raised by other means. Its principal significance was the role that it later played as a vehicle for the confiscation of land in the Southern states, an aspect that will be considered in due course.[80] The fourth tax—on incomes—posed slightly more difficulty. It was enacted early in the conflict, at the same time (and in the same legislation) as the direct tax.[81]

The details of the income tax, while interesting, are not germane here, where the only question is as to the constitutional basis of it.[82] In principle, there was no doubt as to Congress's power to tax incomes. There was consequently never any question of the income tax being regarded as an emergency measure. (It continued in force well after the war, until 1873.)[83] The only legal question was whether it was direct or indirect within the meaning of the Constitution. If the tax was classified as direct, then it would have to be apportioned among the states, on the basis of the states' populations. This means that the aggregate amount of a direct tax generated from each state must be the same proportion of the total proceeds of the tax as that state's population bears to that of the whole Union. In other words, a state that contains 10 percent of the population of the country must generate 10 percent of any direct tax the federal government levies. (In calculating population for this vital purpose, five slaves are held equivalent to three free persons, according to the famous "three-fifths rule.")

The reason for this apportionment requirement was a fear, especially on the part of Southerners, during the drafting of the Constitution, that Congress might levy a direct tax on some item—such as slaves—that was considerably more prevalent in one section of the country than another. Such a tax would then, of course, weigh particularly heavily on that one section. To guard against such an eventuality, the drafters of the Constitution took care to ensure that the burdens of direct taxes would fall equally on all states—at least in terms of the proportion of populations. So this was, in effect, a sort of uniformity requirement, but with the uniformity in question being between *states* as collectivities, rather than between individual taxpayers, as in the case of indirect taxes.

The apportionment requirement has the practical effect—which was quite deliberate—of making it exceedingly difficult for the federal government to impose a direct tax in good conscience, that is, without leading to manifest

unfairness. Consider, for example, a quintessential illustration of a direct tax,
a tax on land. Suppose further that there are two states with equal populations
and land areas but unequal economic circumstances. One state has very fertile
soil, and consequently a population that is wealthy per capita; the other has
very unproductive soil, and consequently a population that is much poorer
per capita. The two states must produce the same aggregate sum of money
from the land tax, simply because they have equal populations. But the actual
burden of the tax will be much greater on the residents of the poorer state,
since they have to generate the tax revenue from an inferior economic base. (It
should be appreciated, in this context, that the Constitution only requires apportionment of the aggregate proceeds of the tax between the states; with the
actual duty to *pay* falling onto the individuals within the states.) Largely for
this reason, there was opposition to the land tax of 1861 in the western states,
which were poorer and more agricultural than the eastern ones and consequently more severely affected by it. As a result, the tax was suspended after
one year of operation and later terminated entirely.[84]

In the case of an income tax—*if* it were to be classed as a direct tax—the in-
equity caused by the apportionment requirement would be particularly glaring,
for the same reason as that just given for a land tax. The inevitable effect would
be to compel residents of states with low per-capita incomes to pay a higher rate
of tax than residents of wealthier states. In short, such a tax would inevitably be
regressive. If, in contrast, the income tax was regarded as an indirect tax, then
it could be levied at uniform rates (to the individual taxpayers) nationwide, so
that persons with the same income would pay the same tax nationwide.

The principal legal question about the income tax was therefore whether it
should be classified as direct or indirect. Unfortunately, the Constitution provided no definition of these terms. But Alexander Hamilton had briefly expounded on the matter in the *Federalist* of the 1780s. Direct taxes, he stated,
"principally relate to land and buildings;" while indirect taxes comprise, "in
general, all duties upon articles of consumption."[85] Perhaps a better approach
would be to consider taxes on acts or transactions to be indirect, and taxes on
objects as such to be direct. On this reasoning, a sales tax can readily be seen
to be indirect, in that it is a tax on the *act* of buying and selling, rather than a
tax on the actual goods that are bought and sold. Similarly, customs duties
would be indirect, on the thesis that they are imposed on the act of importation. In all events, there was hoary authority from the earliest days of the
Supreme Court, in 1796, to the effect that *only* two kinds of tax are direct

within the meaning of the Constitution: a poll tax (i.e., a head tax on persons) and a land tax.[86]

Common sense—admittedly no infallible guide on matters legal—would seem to dictate that an income tax be classed as indirect, on the ground that it is in essence a transaction tax. It may be regarded as, so to speak, a sort of sales tax on the buying and selling of the service of employment. Indeed, there seems to have been very little inclination, during the period of the Civil War income tax (1861–1873), to view the matter in any other light. On several occasions between 1869 and 1881, the federal Supreme Court firmly rebuffed contentions that the income tax was a direct tax.[87]

It only remains to mention that the issue resurfaced in 1894, when Congress again sought to enact an income tax—but this time in a significantly different political context.[88] This measure was vigorously attacked on the political ground that it was a socialistic tool, a device of class warfare or of radical wealth redistribution thinly disguised as a "mere" revenue-raising device. The legal issue, however, remained as before: whether an income tax was direct or indirect. In what can only be described as an inspired legal tactic, the opponents of the measure carefully focused their attack exclusively on the taxation of income derived from land (such as rental income). It was contended that, since a tax on land *itself* was universally conceded to be direct, it was logical to hold that any tax on income *derived* from land must likewise be direct. No objection was raised to the taxation of income consisting of salaries, interest, or profits from ordinary manufacture and trade. In 1895, the Supreme Court accepted this argument—and then went on to hold that the *entire* income-tax scheme must be struck down, on the basis that the taxation of income from land was so integral a part of it.[89] There the matter stood until 1913, when the Sixteenth Amendment to the Constitution took effect, expressly empowering the Congress to tax income "from whatever source derived, without apportionment among the several States."

Greenback Dollars

Another major legislative innovation of the Civil War period was the legal-tender legislation, the effect of which was, purportedly, to confer significant economic value onto intrinsically worthless pieces of paper. Paper currency as such was, of course, nothing new. Private banks had been issuing notes for many years, which passed from hand to hand and therefore constituted a sort of *de facto* paper currency. Legally, though, these notes were simply promises by the issuing bank to pay a designated amount of specie to the holder of the note, from the bank's *own* resources. If the bank had sufficient specie on hand when the note was presented for payment, then all was well. If it did not, then the holder of the note simply received no payment. That was the risk that he or she knowingly incurred when accepting the note as currency.

The important point, for present purposes, is that these private bank notes were not *legal tender*. That means that there was no legal *requirement* that a creditor accept the bank notes in payment of a debt, in lieu of specie. The creditor could refuse the notes and insist on payment in coin. If, on the other hand, the notes were legal tender, then the debt was discharged when the notes were presented, even if the creditor refused to accept them. In other words, it would be, for all practical purposes, mandatory for the creditor to accept the notes as the equivalent of specie.

In the early stages of the Civil War, the Treasury Department issued notes which were, for all practical purposes, equivalent to private bank notes in *not* having legal-tender status. But that mattered little to the holders of them because, in practice, holders could present the Treasury notes at any time to private banks, which would pay the face value in specie. The banks would then, of course, hold the notes and present them to the Treasury Department in due course for payment, again in specie. In the face of dramatic growth in the aggregate value of the note issues, the holders began increasingly to doubt whether the banks actually held sufficient specie for payment. The result, naturally, was a rush to cash in the notes. Then, in December 1861, the banks, alarmed at the rate of specie withdrawals, announced a suspension of specie payments.[90]

This action by the banks caused consternation in the Treasury Department and led the Union government to adopt a drastic double expedient for future issues of Treasury notes.[91] The first was that future Treasury notes would *not* be stated to be convertible into specie, as the previous note issues had been. There was comparatively little controversy about this step, since it was generally believed that, at some point in the not-too-distant future following the war, the government would provide for the redemption of these "greenbacks" in coin, as it eventually did in 1875.[92] (The colloquial label for the notes referred to the color of the paper on which they were printed.) Far more controversial was the second aspect of the new policy: conferring legal-tender status onto the greenbacks, with the effect that it was now mandatory for creditors to treat "note money" as fully equivalent to "coin money" of the stated value (to employ terminology common at the time). This legislation was enacted in February 1862, with some considerable misgivings (not least by Treasury Secretary Salmon Chase himself).[93]

The specific legal issues concerning the greenbacks were many, but they may be said to fall conveniently into two categories. First was the impact of legal-tender status of greenbacks on private parties, including (crucially) the extent to which private parties could avoid some of the unwelcome consequences of holding greenbacks. Second was the question of whether Congress possessed the Constitutional power to confer the status of legal tender onto pieces of paper that were intrinsically valueless.

Regarding the impact of legal-tender status of greenbacks on the activities of private parties, a variety of issues arose. One was the question of retroactivity— whether payments pursuant to contracts concluded *before* the adoption of the Legal Tender Act were affected by the legislation. During the war, various courts went both ways on this question.[94] Only in 1869 did the federal Supreme Court finally resolve the question. Chief Justice Salmon P. Chase (appointed by Lincoln to the post in 1864), who had previously been secretary of the treasury, wrote for the majority of the Court, ruling against retroactivity, on the ground that the intention of the parties to the contract must be the paramount consideration.[95] And parties to contracts made prior to the legal-tender legislation must necessarily have contemplated that payment would be in specie.[96]

A related question was whether private parties, when making contracts *after* the adoption of the Legal Tender Act, could "contract out" of the law, by agreeing between themselves that their particular transaction must be discharged in specie and not in paper. There was never a definitive decision by the courts on this point.[97] Two states—California and Nevada—enacted legislation expressly allowing contracting-out. When these were challenged in the respective state courts, the California law was upheld, but the Nevada one struck down.[98] The point seems never to have been definitively resolved by the federal Supreme Court.

The largest question about the greenbacks was whether Congress possessed the power to confer legal-tender status onto notes. Attorney General Bates gave an informal opinion that it did.[99] Several state supreme courts also considered the matter in the course of the conflict. All of them upheld it, with varying degrees of enthusiasm.[100] Not until 1870, however, did the federal Supreme Court have the opportunity to pass directly on the question, in a pair

of cases which, between them, provided what some might regard as an embarrassingly clear revelation of how large a subjective element there is to the art of
adjudication. In short, the two cases reached diametrically opposite conclusions on the very same point.

In the first case, the greenback issue was struck down as unconstitutional
by a five-to-three majority.[101] The power to confer legal-tender status onto
notes, the majority pronounced, was not encompassed within the power to
"coin Money."[102] (In fact, the Court had already held "coin money" and "note
money" to be "essentially unalike in nature.")[103] Nor was the legal-tender
power incidental to the constitutional power of Congress to "regulate the value"
of money, or to borrow money.[104]

A year later, in a reconsideration of the issue, things were different—or at
least the composition of the Supreme Court bench was. The retirement of one
justice (Robert C. Grier), combined with the creation of a new Court seat,
opened up two simultaneous vacancies. To these two seats, President Ulysses S.
Grant appointed William Strong of Pennsylvania and Joseph P. Bradley of New
Jersey (who went on to become one of the most eminent judges in the Court's
history). Both adhered to the minority view from the previous decision, so that
there was now a five-to-four majority for upholding the constitutionality of the
legal-tender acts.[105] Never before or since in the history of the Supreme Court
has there been so rapid a reversal of position on so major an issue.[106]

This second Legal Tender Case gave the question a far more thorough airing
than the earlier judgment had. (It consumes some 120 pages in the Supreme
Court Reports.) More important, this second judgment broke new and important ground on the subject of federal legislative powers in general, chiefly in
holding that it was not necessary to identify any *single* provision in support of
the legal-tender legislation. Instead, it was allowable to group "any number" of
individual grants of power together and to "infer from them all that the power
has been conferred."[107] The Court went on to take a broad view of the coinage
power in particular, expressly holding that "a strict literal construction" of it was
inappropriate. That power, instead, should be liberally construed as conferring
onto the federal government "a general power over the currency."[108]

Another major innovation of this new legal-tender decision was its articulation of an implicit power of Congress to take steps during an emergency
which might not be justified in normal times. "It is not to be denied," the new
majority pronounced, "that acts may be adapted to the exercise of lawful

power, and appropriate to it, in seasons of exigency, which would be inappropriate at other times."[109] It went on to hold, with great firmness, that the legal-tender policy had been urgently necessary as a means of financing the government in the life-and-death crisis that the country had recently faced. It was true, the Court cautioned, that there had to be "some relation between the means and the end"—specifically, that an emergency measure must be tailored to the needs posed by the actual situation at hand. But the Court also expressly stated that this relation need not be "direct and immediate."[110] Moreover, the Court made it clear that this was the real basis of its ruling.[111]

This second legal-tender decision was not the Supreme Court's final word on the subject. The question arose again in 1884, in the context of a challenge to the constitutionality of a law of 1878 that provided for the reissuing of greenbacks after they had been turned in to the government and exchanged for specie.[112] The key question now was whether Congress possessed a *general* power to impress paper with legal-tender status, even in the complete absence of a grave national emergency. The Court now held, for the first time, that it did.[113] The specific basis of the power was now identified as the borrowing clause—broadly interpreted, of course, and also "fortified" by the coining clause, the commerce clause, and the power to regulate the value of money. These various powers, in combination, bestowed on Congress a general power to "establish a national currency," without any requirement that a national emergency be present.

More broadly yet, however, the Court now emphasized the legal-tender power as an inherent attribute of sovereignty. The power to confer legal-tender status onto government notes, it stated, was stated to be "one of the powers belonging to sovereignty in the civilized nations, and not expressly withheld from the Congress by the Constitution." It would be difficult to overstate the potential significance of this line of reasoning. It amounts to a contention that there is, in effect, a *second* source of federal-government powers, deriving not from the Constitution, but instead from the status of the United States as a sovereign entity. A similar argument of an independent source of federal power (this time in the field of foreign affairs) was put forward by the Supreme Court in 1936.[114] To the present day, there has been little exploration of this potentially fertile—or alarming—means of expanding federal power. But some fear—while others hope—that a potential legal revolution may yet be lurking in this interesting doctrine.

Military Conscription

From the present perspective, it is not easy to appreciate the constitutional issues that were at stake on the question of conscription. The idea that citizens have a legal duty to perform military service was hardly a novel one. More specifically, the principle of mandatory service was intrinsic to the system of state militia forces, which consisted, by definition, of the entire male population of each state that was capable of bearing arms. Militia forces, in other words, were a kind of permanent—though generally dormant—pool or reserve of military manpower, capable (at least in theory) of being summoned into action as and when needed, by government proclamation. This was, of course, the fabled "minuteman" tradition. What was new in the Civil War, then, was neither the idea nor the practice of compulsory service as such, but rather its *federalization.*

The Constitution clearly provided for a dual system of armed forces, directly reflecting the federal character of the government. The states continued to possess their own separate armed forces in the form of the militia bodies. In addition, though, Congress was given an express power to "raise and support Armies" for the service of the federal government.[115] Compulsion always played an important part in this dual system—but in different ways at the state and federal levels. At the state level, there was a duty of *individuals* to perform militia service as required. At the federal level, there was a power of, so to speak, collective conscription—in the form of a power enabling Congress to arrange for "calling forth the Militia to execute the Laws of the Union, suppress Insurrections and repel Invasions."[116] This meant that the federal government could conscript the state militia forces, as ready-made bodies, into federal service.

In the Militia Act of 1795, Congress made use of this power, entrusting to the President the right to call out the state militia "whenever the laws of the United States shall be opposed or the execution thereof obstructed . . . by combinations too powerful to be suppressed by the ordinary course of judicial proceedings."[117] President Lincoln took this step on April 15, 1861, in the immediate aftermath of the attack on Fort Sumter.[118] Some two weeks later, on May 3, 1861, he took the separate and additional step of increasing the *federal* armed forces by the only means then available to him: calling for individual volunteers.[119] The President had no authority to place individuals compulsorily into the federal government's *own* forces.

The implementation of conscription in 1862–1863 came about, fittingly, in two stages. First came the Militia Act of July 1862.[120] This created a kind of hybrid arrangement whereby the federal government assumed the right to enroll individuals by compulsion into the various *state* militia forces. In any state which did not possess adequate machinery for raising the militia forces that were summoned (or if existing machinery was not being adequately employed), then the President could step in fill the ranks himself, by making "all necessary rules and regulations" for enrollment and enlistment. (The ominous word "conscription" was carefully eschewed in setting out this policy.) It must be appreciated that the troops which were raised were enrolled not into the federal armed forces but rather into the militia units of the state in question—with those militia units, then, in turn being brought, as existing collectivities, into federal service. The constitutional foundation of this policy was clearly the power of Congress to "provide for calling forth the Militia."[121] When the policy was judicially challenged, the Wisconsin Supreme Court had no trouble holding it to be constitutional on that basis.[122]

The second, and decisive, stage was the conscription of individuals *directly* into the *federal* armed forces, with the state militias now playing no role. This occurred on March 3, 1863, when Congress enacted what was delicately called the Enrollment Act (still avoiding the frightening word "conscription").[123] By this law, all males from the ages of eighteen to forty-five were stated "to constitute the national forces" of the United States. Two separate processes were provided for: enrollment (i.e., registration) and *actual* conscription. Once enrolled, a person was liable, for a two-year period, to be selected for service. Persons so chosen were to serve for the duration of the conflict or for three years, whichever was shorter. A nationwide system of commissioners was established to run the system. For this fully federal arrangement, which broke important new ground, the constitutional authority was the power of Congress to "raise and support Armies."[124]

The administrative details of the system, and its political and social consequences, are a fascinating story (which have received surprisingly little attention from historians); but the present concern is with the legal issues it raised.[125] The most serious doubts as to the constitutionality of the conscription policy concerned not civil liberties, but rather the less emotive (to some) issue of the balance of power within the federal system between the federal government and the states. Concerns on this score were strongly held by no less a

figure than Chief Justice Taney, who, as a personal exercise, drafted a detailed
argument against the constitutionality of the conscription policy. This document reads much like a draft judgment, awaiting delivery in the event that a
conscription case were to come before him (which, in the event, it never did).[126]
The essence of Taney's position was that a power of individual conscription in
the hands of the federal government was incompatible with the federalism
arrangement enshrined by the Constitution. The federal government, Taney
maintained, was authorized to *employ* state militia forces in situations of emergency. But it was not authorized to *undermine* the state militias by, in effect,
poaching their members and putting them directly into federal service instead.
The fact was, in Taney's view, that every single individual whom the federal
government conscripted into its service was one person withdrawn from his
state militia duty—with that militia correspondingly weakened. Continuing
on this line of reasoning, what (Taney wondered rhetorically) would prevent
the federal government from utterly destroying state militias by conscripting
every single one of their members into federal service?

That the Taney view commanded at least some support in judicial circles became dramatically apparent in 1863, when the Pennsylvania Supreme Court
held the federal conscription policy to be unconstitutional on the reasoning set
out by Taney, in a case arising out of a suit for an injunction against the federal
officials who were operating the conscription machinery in the state.[127] (Counsel for the federal government, incidentally, declined to appear in the case.) In
material terms, the judgment had little effect, since the judges, despite their
finding of unconstitutionality, declined to issue the injunction. Moreover, the
decision was soon reversed, in the manner of the later Legal Tender Cases, after
the replacement of one of the judges who had voted for unconstitutionality.
The new judge was Daniel Agnew, an articulate and forceful supporter of broad
federal powers, and one of the stalwarts of the adequacy-of-the-Constitution
school of thought. His accession to the bench tipped the balance in favor of upholding the federal law, in a rehearing of the case.[128]

Federal courts, as matters developed, had very little occasion to consider
conscription issues.[129] The federal Supreme Court did not rule on the constitutionality of it, either during the war or in its aftermath. Taney's paper on the
subject therefore lay unused, awaiting discovery early in the twentieth century.
Not until 1918, when the federal government again resorted to direct conscription in the First World War, did the federal Supreme Court finally rule on the
matter. By that time, the Taney position had been rendered obsolete by major

changes made in the structure of the state militia forces, most notably by the replacement of old-style militias by the modern National Guard in 1903.[130]

These new state forces were not, like the militia, based on the traditional thesis of a whole population in arms. Instead, they were carefully designed to function as a kind of reserve for, or adjunct to, the federal armed forces.[131] As a result, the idea that there was some kind of opposition or incompatibility between federal and state forces, on which Taney's constitutional objections had been premised, was no longer applicable. This was reflected in the Supreme Court's dismissal of that argument with little more than a passing mention. Nor had the Court much more patience with other legal objections. The contention that conscription was an impermissible infringement of basic personal liberty was scornfully held to be "so devoid of foundation that it leaves not even a shadow of ground upon which to base the conclusion."[132] Conscription was held, straightforwardly, to be authorized by the congressional power to raise and support armies.

The raising of armies was naturally one of the most important essential operations of the Civil War (or of any war), for both sides. Of even greater importance was what those armies did once they were formed and of how they went about the grim business of overcoming their enemies. To this fearsome enterprise, too, the rule of law was brought to bear. This was found not in the United States Constitution, but rather in the body of international legal rules known, appropriately enough, as the laws of war.

3

Fighting by the Rules

What is the law which governs an army invading an enemy's country? It is not the civil law of the invaded country; it is not the civil law of the conquering country: it is military law,—the law of war.

—U.S. Supreme Court

Burning private houses, or uselessly destroying private property . . . is barbarous; but I approve of taking or destroying whatever may serve as supplies to us or to the enemy's armies.

—Henry W. Halleck

The laws which regulate the conducting of hostilities—the *laws of war,* as they are known for obvious reasons—come wholly from the international law of war, as it evolved primarily in European state practice over the many centuries since the Middle Ages.[1] Under the American Constitution, Congress is given the power to "make Rules for the Government and Regulation of the land and naval Forces" of the country.[2] It duly exercised this power in 1806, when it enacted the Articles of War, which were still in force at the time of the Civil War.[3] It is also empowered to "make Rules concerning Captures on Land and Water."[4] The question of whether Congress can, by way of these provisions, grant to the American forces powers *beyond* those allowed by the international laws of war is one that has, happily, not (or not yet) arisen.[5]

The principal feat of codification of the laws of war during the Civil War era was achieved, however, not by Congress but rather by the executive. This was in the form of the Lieber Code, written by, and named after, the eminent lawyer and political theorist Francis Lieber. Lieber was Prussian by birth, but his liberal outlook, coupled with a modest degree of political activism, had led to his exile, first to other parts of Germany, then to other countries in Europe (including Italy and Germany) and eventually, in the 1830s, to the United

States. He taught history and political economy at South Carolina College for over twenty years, where his strongly nationalist views of the nature of the American Union made him unpopular. In 1856, he moved to New York and began teaching at Columbia University. From the start, he was an ardent supporter of the Union cause. The first year of the war saw him lecturing on the highly topical subject of the laws and usages of war.[6]

Lieber became a close associate of Union general Henry W. Halleck, who was himself a legal writer of some renown. Halleck had served as secretary of state of California in the 1850s, a task which involved him in a number of legal issues relating to the integration of the English- and Spanish-based legal systems in the newly acquired territory. From this work grew a general treatise on international law, published at the outset of the war in May 1861, which was largely an updated version of Vattel's classic treatise, written in 1758.[7] Halleck and his treatise, as events proved, both had great futures ahead of them. Halleck himself soon became the highest ranking Union general, as a result of his command of Union forces in the West in the first year of the conflict—the only instance in American history of a leading writer on international law holding such a position. His treatise, in the meantime, endured into the twentieth century as a leading American work in the field of international law.[8]

Halleck, of all people, was therefore disposed to be sensitive to the many legal issues that were bound to come his way in the course of his work as the commanding Union general. More specifically, Halleck recognized the need for a convenient and usable summary of the laws of war—succinct but comprehensive, readable but detailed—for use by serving soldiers. For the compilation of such a summary, Halleck turned to Lieber for assistance. In April 1863, the Lieber Code, as the work has been appropriately known ever since, was completed and duly promulgated by President Lincoln as a set of general orders for the whole of the Union armies.[9] Since the code was a restatement, or summary of the *existing* laws of war, rather than actual new legislation, it did not require congressional approval.

The Lieber Code may be said, without undue exaggeration, to be something of a legal masterpiece—a sort of pocket version of Blackstone's famous *Commentaries on the Laws of England,* though confined to the particular subject of the laws of land warfare. It was not simply a list of rules, as might be implied by the label "code." It was, in addition, a miniature commentary on those rules, explaining, if only in the briefest terms, the basic principles underlying the specific commands and prohibitions. As such, it made a lasting contribution to the development of the subject. Shortly after the Civil War, the prominent Swiss international lawyer Kaspar Bluntschli drew heavily on the Lieber Code in his highly influential textbook on international law, even including the code in full in the appendix of the book.[10] The Lieber Code was also drawn on in 1874 by a conference of international legal experts in Brussels, which compiled a draft code (or *projet,* as it was termed) of laws of war.[11] This Brussels *projet,* in turn, became the basis for a codification of the laws of war by the First Hague Peace Conference of 1899, this time in the form of a legally binding treaty.[12] The "Hague Rules," as they are called, remain to this day, in their slightly modified form of 1907, as the basic statement of the international laws of war.[13]

The legal talent found within the Union's Department of War was also very impressive, starting at the very top with Edwin Stanton, who was secretary of war for most of the conflict. An experienced lawyer, Stanton had been, in his early career in Ohio, an associate and protégé of Samuel Chase. He later served, though only briefly, as attorney general in the closing months of the Buchanan administration. When Chief Justice Taney died in 1864, Lincoln considered Stanton as his replacement, although in the event that honor went to Stanton's old associate Chase, who had recently left his post as secretary of the treasury.[14] (After the war, Stanton was appointed to the Court by President Grant—only to die four days after his approval by the Senate, before taking his place on the bench.)[15] The War Department's solicitor was a former Harvard Law School professor named William Whiting, who would be one of the most energetic defenders of the various legal measures taken by the Lincoln administration. Also in the War Department was Joseph Holt of Kentucky, a former federal attorney general, who became judge advocate general (or head lawyer) of the armed forces. Holt was a brilliant legal mind, in whom rigor was considerably more apparent than mercy. He would play a memorable role as the aggressive chief prosecutor of the Lincoln assassins. Of this collection of War Department lawyers, it has been said that "no university law faculty or private firm in the nation" was its equal.[16]

These distinguished legal minds had much to occupy them. Controversies and accusations about violations of the laws of war during the Civil War were legion; and they have yet to be submitted to systematic study. The present focus will be not on isolated incidents of violations, such as disputes over misuse of flags of truce or acts of individual marauding by soldiers, but rather over controversies concerning deliberate policy measures—all too many of which will be chillingly familiar to present-day observers. Three subjects in particular will command our attention: challenges posed by new technology; questions of entitlement to combatant (or belligerent) status; and issues relating to injuries to and the protection of civilians. Before looking at these particular areas, it will be necessary to make some remarks about the general character of the law of war, as that subject has a number of aspects that are unfamiliar to laypersons (as well as to civilian lawyers).

The Rule of Law and the Heat of Battle

The military life is a different world from the civilian one. This is true in many respects, not least from the standpoint of law. In their belligerent operations—that is, in their actual assaults on the enemy armed force—serving soldiers are exempt from the ordinary civilian law of the land in which they operate, whether that be their home country or that of the enemy. "All municipal law of the ground on which the armies stand, or of the countries to which they belong," the Lieber Code tersely stated, "is silent and of no effect between armies in the field."[17] The fact that a soldier is exempt from the civil law of the territory in which his belligerent operations are carried on does not, of course, mean that he operates outside the law. It means that he is subject instead to a different body of law from civilians (i.e., to the laws of war). Violations of the laws of war are known, naturally enough, as *war crimes.*

It is well, at the outset, to take note of certain very general features of the laws of war which may be unfamiliar to nonlawyers. One of the most fundamental points is that this body of law is a peculiar combination of privilege and constraint. On the side of constraint, the laws of war contain various prohibitions, much along the line of criminal offenses in civilian life. Certain acts are forbidden on the ground that they are intrinsically wrongful, meaning that they are prohibited in *all* circumstances, without regard to the specific context at hand. A ready example is *pillage,* which is the taking of private property for mere personal gain. There are absolute prohibitions too against certain kinds of weapons, such as poisons (at the time of the Civil War) or chemical and biological weapons (at the present time). In addition, certain tactics are prohibited, such as policies of no quarter (i.e., killing enemy soldiers who have surrendered or been captured).[18]

The other aspect of the laws of war, concerning the granting of legal privileges, or *belligerents' rights*—sometimes alternatively known as the *rights of war*—will be less familiar or intuitive to laypersons. It concerns things that soldiers are *permitted* to do, which would be unlawful in ordinary civilian life. Most important, soldiers are permitted to kill and capture members of the enemy armed force and to occupy territory belonging to a foreign sovereign. In legal parlance, these are known as *acts of war.*

Acts of war are not criminal offenses, as they would be if committed by civilians in peacetime, since the soldier is not acting on his own account. Instead, he functions, in a manner of speaking, as a minister of his government, performing a public service for his country. As the Lieber Code put it: "So soon as a man is armed by a sovereign government and takes the soldier's oath of fidelity, he is a belligerent," with the legal result that "his killing, wounding, or other warlike acts are not individual crimes or offenses."[19] Precisely because acts of war are not criminal offenses, a soldier who is captured is not subject to criminal proceedings for committing them. Instead, he becomes a *prisoner of war,* meaning (broadly) that he is subject to a special, nonpunitive form of detention. This entitlement to prisoner-of-war status is regarded, rightly, as one of the most valuable legal privileges that lawful belligerents possess.

To these general statements about the legal privileges of belligerents, a major caveat must be entered. That is, that soldiers are immune from criminal prosecution only if their actions fall into the category of acts of war in the legal sense—that is, only if their acts are lawful according to the laws of war. Any acts not so authorized are, by definition, war crimes; and for these, a soldier can be prosecuted, either by his own superior officers or by the enemy armed force into whose hands he might fall. With these very general considerations in mind, we may turn to two specific aspects of the laws of war which are apt to be particularly unfamiliar to laypersons, and therefore subject to very great misunderstanding: military necessity; and enforcement measures such as reprisals.

Military Necessity

Military necessity is a concept that is much misunderstood (and not only by laypersons). It is a somewhat unfortunate expression because it risks being taken, erroneously, to refer to an emergency situation in which transgressions of the laws of war are justified. Such a notion is deeply mistaken. Military necessity, in its true legal sense, refers to situations in which acts which are *permitted* by the laws of war in principle become exercisable in practice. In the words of the

Lieber Code, military necessity comprises "measures which are indispensable for securing the ends of the war, *and* which are lawful according to the . . . law and usages of war."[20] The Code went on to specify that military necessity *never* permits such evil practices as "the infliction of suffering for the sake of suffering or for revenge," or the infliction of torture to extort confessions, or the use of poison.[21]

The effect, then, is that, when military necessity is present, the rights of belligerents may lawfully be exercised to their fullest extent. When military necessity is *not* present—when the acts contemplated are not (in the words of the Lieber Code) "indispensable for securing the ends of war"—then the rights of belligerents are correspondingly *not* exercisable to their fullest extent.[22] The effect is to prohibit the infliction of merely malicious injury. In the terse formulation of the Lieber Code, "Unnecessary or revengeful destruction of life is not lawful."[23] The later Hague Rules, in the same spirit, put the same point in terminology that is still extant in the laws of war: that the causing of "unnecessary suffering" is prohibited.[24] Whether military necessity is present or not in a given case depends crucially on the prevailing military situation at the particular time and place in question. In this highly important sense, military necessity operates to *restrict* the liberties of belligerents, not to expand them.

Military necessity also operates, however, in a somewhat different manner: as a kind of balancing or cost-benefit exercise (in modern parlance) between harm done and advantage gained. This aspect of military necessity is clearest when considerations of "collateral damage" to civilians are in question (again resorting to modern terminology). The Lieber Code acknowledged this point by expressly stating that damage to civilians which was "incidentally unavoidable" was not unlawful. As will be seen presently, the American Civil War offered some striking examples of ways in which the "incidental" damage to civilians could be, under certain circumstances, quite substantial. In this sense, military necessity can, admittedly, have a flavor of license rather than of restriction.

A particularly instructive illustration of military necessity in action arose out of General William Tecumseh Sherman's order, after the capture of Atlanta in September 1864, for the complete evacuation by Union troops of the entire civilian population from the city.[25] The opposing Confederate general, John T. Hood, promptly denounced the action as an "unprecedented measure," transcending "in studied and ingenious cruelty, all acts ever before brought to my attention in the dark history of war."[26] The mayor of the city, along with two councilmen, also protested the move.[27] Sherman, however, provided a careful justification of his action to Halleck, emphasizing that the removal had been carried out with "liberality and fairness" and without the employment of force. The houses of the town, he explained, were required for "military storage and occupation." In addition, it was necessary to concentrate the Union forces as tightly as possible, so as to minimize the length of defensive perimeter lines.[28] Halleck responded that he "fully approved" of Sherman's action and even opined that Sherman had a positive duty to act as he did.[29] So long as there was no absolute prohibition against the involuntary evacuating of civilians (as there was not), and so long as a genuine military purpose was being served, the action was lawful.

Enforcement Methods—Reprisals

The chief method of enforcing the laws of war has always been for each country to discipline its own soldiers for the commission of war crimes, by subjecting them to courts-martial.[30] Various other methods exist as well. One is for war criminals who are captured by the opposing side to be tried by their captors. On a number of occasions during and after the Civil War (with exact figures not presently available), the Union forces court-martialed captured Confederates for war crimes.[31]

Some laypersons (and lawyers too) will have misgivings about one side in a war putting its enemies on trial. There is no denying that such a situation is far from ideal, and that risks of injustice will often be present. It should be pointed out, though, that, since the same laws of war are applicable to both sides, and provided that the trial is fairly conducted, there will be no injustice to the accused person. The single most conspicuous example from history of one side subjecting prisoners to trial for war crimes occurred in the Nuremberg Trials after World War II, when eighteen of the twenty-two defendants were accused of war crimes of various kinds, sixteen of whom were convicted.[32] In analogous proceedings in Tokyo, twenty-four Japanese government and military officials were accused of war crimes; and ten were convicted.[33] Since 2002, the International Criminal Court, situated in The Hague, has had jurisdiction to try accusations with thirteen persons under indictment for various acts as of mid-2009. The first trial commenced in January 2009.

Laypersons are likely to be considerably more uneasy still with regard to various other, more robust methods of enforcement of the laws of war: reprisals, hostage-taking, and forfeiture of belligerent status. Each was resorted to during the Civil War, so a few words on them are necessary.

The very word "reprisal" is apt to fill some laypersons with dread. The legal meaning of reprisal, however, is importantly different from its everyday usage, with its connotation of vindictiveness.[34] Reprisals in the legal sense are intended to be a law-enforcement mechanism, for deployment in response to some *prior* violation of the laws of war. Their function is not to satisfy some primitive lust for revenge on the part of victims of the prior violation, but rather to induce the law-breaking side to alter its behavior in the future. In the words of the Lieber Code, reprisals are "a means of protective retribution," as distinct from "a measure of mere revenge."[35] In practice, this fine distinction could sometimes be lost in the heat of conflict.

Three aspects of reprisals call for special attention. The first is that a reprisal is an action which is *intrinsically* unlawful. The act is excused, however, as a matter of regrettable necessity, if it is the only means feasible for inducing a prior wrongdoer to halt his wrongdoing—that is, if the reprisal act fulfills, in the specific circumstances, a genuinely remedial function as a law-enforcement measure.

The second key feature of reprisals is that they are nonpunitive, in the strict and technical sense that they are measures taken against someone *other than* the original wrongdoer himself. Such a policy is likely to strike laypersons as being flagrantly unjust. And there can be no doubt that, ideally, the *very* person or persons who committed the original infraction of the law should be the ones to suffer the punishment (by way of court-martial). In many cases, however, the problem was that the actual miscreants could not be identified or located. This aspect of reprisal was demonstrated most clearly in the Union response to guerrilla-style action, which will be considered presently.

The third crucial point about reprisals in the legal sense is that they must be proportionate in severity to the original wrong to which they are a response. In the case of *belligerent reprisals*—reprisals intended to deal specifically with violations of the laws of war—this requirement tends to take the extreme form of *retaliation.* This is a situation in which the reprisal taker commits *precisely* the same violation of the laws of war as the original wrongdoer did. This is, of course, the classic situation of "an eye for an eye, and a tooth for a tooth." Given the hierarchical nature of armed forces, it also means "a rank for a rank." That is to say, that, if a major on one side is unlawfully put to death, the other side will respond by selecting a major in its custody and putting *him* to death. The original wrongdoer was repaid in his own coin, as it were, right down to the penny.

Military lawyers have never been under any illusions as to the dangers involved in the resort to reprisals. The Lieber Code candidly described them as "the sternest feature of war," to be employed only when more moderate methods are not available. And it readily admitted that too ready a resort to reprisals carries the risk that a conflict will descend into "the internecine wars of savages."[36] For that reason, a reprisal should only be taken as a last resort, and only after "careful inquiry" into the alleged wrongdoing it is intended to address.

An early example of a reprisal policy in action occurred in 1861 in the wake of the Union piracy trials of the Confederates captured at sea.[37] As noted, the prisoners held letters of marque from the Confederate government (i.e., official permission from that government to engage in captures of Union ships and cargoes on behalf of the Confederacy); but the Union authorities refused to accord these letters any legal validity. There was widespread outrage in the Confederacy about this policy. Jefferson Davis even wrote personally to Lincoln on the subject, expressly threatening to engage in man-for-man retaliation if the convicted prisoners were put to death.[38] The Confederate Congress explicitly gave its approval to Davis's policy.[39]

This was no idle threat. A lottery was duly held, in solemn circumstances, in one of the Confederate prisons for the selection of the very Union prisoners who would be marked out for death. As it happened, the Union did not carry out the death penalty on the convicted prisoners and eventually exchanged them for Union captives in Confederate hands.[40] Perhaps the most notable instance, on the Union side, of a reprisal measure approved at the highest levels of government was in response to Confederate provision of inadequate rations to Union prisoners. The reaction of Secretary of War Stanton was to order an across-the-board reduction of 20 percent in rations for Confederate prisoners of war in Union custody.[41]

The subject of reprisals has continued to be a part of the laws of war, although in a somewhat shadowy fashion, with little explicit acknowledgment in the written law. This is due, in large part, to a palpable unease on the part of lawyers on the question. The Brussels Conference of 1874, for example, declined even to discuss the topic. The matter was raised at the Hague Peace Conferences of 1899 and 1907 but did not find its way into the Hague Rules.[42] The Institute of International Law was slightly bolder on the subject. Its *Manual on the Laws of Land Warfare,* compiled in 1880, stated reprisals to be necessary in the event that the actual persons who committed war crimes could not be located and punished individually.[43]

The principal judicial consideration of reprisals in the modern era occurred in the various war-crimes trials after the Second World War. The leading case condemned reprisal killing as a "barbarous practice"—but pointedly stopped short of holding it to be, *per se,* a war crime. Instead, the ruling hedged it about with conditions. For example, it is necessary that the policy be announced in advance. Reprisal killing cannot be undertaken in connection with distant events, in circumstances in which there would be no actual deterrent effect on the conduct of the original wrongdoers. In addition, innocent civilians cannot be made the victims—unless, that is, "the population as a whole is a party to the [original] offence, either actively or passively." Finally, the ruling insisted that there be "a judicial finding that the necessary conditions exist." But even these strictures could be dispensed with in cases of especially urgent need.[44]

If reprisals have never been altogether prohibited in war, there has nonetheless been a steady rise in specific restrictions on them—on the forms that they can take, and on the persons against whom they can be directed. The Lieber Code contained only one important restriction: that enslavement could never be a permissible form of reprisal.[45] A principal concern over the years was over the taking of reprisals against prisoners of war. The Lieber Code explicitly held that this *was* permissible.[46] Later developments, however, have reversed that position. Most notably, the Geneva Convention of 1929, on prisoners of war, expressly prohibited the practice.[47] Since World War II, prohibitions against various forms of reprisal directed at civilians have been agreed. In particular, Protocol I of 1977 to the Geneva Conventions prohibits *attacks* on civilian populations by way of reprisal (but is silent on lesser actions such as economic measures).[48] The Protocol also bars reprisals against a host of more specific potential targets, such as places of worship and potentially dangerous installations such as dams and power plants.[49]

Enforcement Methods—Hostage-Taking

Similar in spirit to reprisals was the taking of hostages. But there were several differences between the two processes. Reprisals were typically in response to some past and completed act of wrongdoing. Hostage-taking was usually designed to deal with some ongoing wrong—with the hostages then to be released when satisfaction was obtained. Hostages were therefore in the nature of involuntary sureties. In addition, belligerent reprisals were usually on a me-

chanical tit-for-tat basis, with the reprisal closely matching the prior wrongful
act. Hostage-taking, in contrast, which was essentially an act of kidnapping
and false imprisonment, could be in response to *any* kind of conduct on the
part of the opposing side. Nevertheless, the similarities between the two activities were so close as to make them sometimes difficult to distinguish from one
another.

An instructive instance of hostage-taking occurred in Fredericksburg, Virginia, in 1864 after the Battle of the Wilderness, when a group of energetic
townspeople managed to capture sixty Union soldiers, whom they then dispatched to a military prison in Richmond. In response, Stanton ordered the
capture of sixty-four citizens of the town, to be held as hostages until the soldiers were released. Over the next two months, both the soldiers and the civilian hostages were released as part of a negotiated exchange.[50]

Hostage-taking, in this new sense, has received relatively little attention
from either historians or lawyers.[51] The subject was not covered in the Lieber
Code (unless it may be thought that, by interpretation, the provisions on
reprisals extended to hostage-taking as well). Since hostages were typically
civilians, the later codifications of the laws of war—with their emphasis on the
relations between the enemy armed forces—did not deal with the matter. At
the Nuremberg Trials in 1946, mounted against German leaders of the Third
Reich in the wake of the Second World War, the war-crimes charges were
stated to include the *killing* of hostages, though not the *taking* of hostages.[52]
In a war-crimes trial that was conducted at about the same time, the tribunal
(comprising American service personnel) was rather more permissive, holding
that even the killing of hostages could be lawful as a very last resort.[53]

The Fourth Geneva Convention of 1949 finally laid down an express prohibition against the taking of hostages, although it appears that this only applies to the taking of *civilian* hostages.[54] The 1977 Protocol reinforced this
prohibition (whatever its precise scope) by making it clear that the it applies
to hostage-taking by both civilian and military authorities.[55]

A final word on hostage-taking is in order. As a device (if a rude one) for
enforcing the laws of war, it bears no significant resemblance to what is often
referred to as "hostage-taking" in the context of terrorism and similar activities, such as the incident of the American "hostages" held in Tehran in
1979–1981. Hostage-taking (so-called) of that kind is in the nature of simple
kidnapping and blackmail—straightforward criminal acts unconnected to the
conduct or laws of war.

Enforcement Methods—Forfeiture of Belligerent Status

The third of the drastic measures for enforcement of the laws of war was forfeiture of belligerent status on the part of either named individuals or categories of persons. It must be emphasized that this refers to forfeiture of status as a punishment for wrongdoing, and *not* to the failure to qualify as a lawful belligerent in the first place (a matter to be considered presently). Such a person has no entitlement to treatment as a lawful belligerent, but that is not the result of any crime or misconduct on his part but simply is, so to speak, a mechanical consequence of his failure to meet the criteria for classification as a combatant in the first place.

Quite different from this is the practice of stripping a person of a combatant status to which he was duly entitled, as a punishment for some kind of crime. Union General John Pope was singled out for this dubious honor in August 1862, for his adoption of a policy of harsh treatment of civilians within occupied areas under his command in Virginia (a matter to be discussed presently).[56] In November of that year, two other named Union officers were also marked out for denial of prisoner-of-war treatment, for "a series of wanton cruelties and depredations" allegedly committed in Tennessee.[57]

The most extreme form of forfeiture of belligerent status is the condition known as *outlawry*, which is a wholesale forfeiture of the *whole* of one's legal rights. It is a sort of juridical excommunication, with the person in question being placed entirely outside the framework of the law. No contracts made by such a person would be regarded as valid. No debts owed to him need be paid. He would have no standing in any court of law to enforce any rights, so that trespassers and thieves could interfere with his property with impunity. He could not make a valid will or contract a lawful marriage. More drastically, he had no legally protected security of person, so that he could be assaulted at will—and even killed like a wild beast—without having any recourse. (The use of the word "outlaw" simply to mean a lawbreaker or villain is, of course, an inexact popular appropriation of the term.)

There were two noteworthy proclamations of outlawry during the Civil War, both by the Confederate side. The first was in August 1862, directed against Union general David Hunter. His offense was the enrollment of ex-slaves in occupied areas of coastal South Carolina into the Union forces—which (as will be seen presently) amounted in Confederate eyes to the fomenting of slave revolt. For this misconduct, he was not to be treated as a public enemy (i.e., as a lawful belligerent). If captured, he was to be placed "in close confinement for execution as a felon."[58]

The other prominent proclamation of outlawry was directed against General Benjamin Butler. He earned this signal distinction for his activities as the commander of Union forces in New Orleans after its fall to Union forces in April 1862—and in particular for his notorious order that any woman acting disrespectfully toward his troops would be treated as "a woman of the town plying her avocation."[59] The decree of outlawry was issued by President Davis in December 1862, formally pronouncing its unchivalrous subject "a felon deserving of capital punishment" and declaring him "an outlaw and common enemy of mankind."[60] If captured, Butler was simply to be hanged on the spot, without even the pretense of a trial. In addition, any commissioned officers who served under Butler, although not suffering the severe penalty of outlawry, were nonetheless not to be accorded prisoner-of-war status, but instead were to be "reserved for execution."

The Lieber Code expressly held that declarations of outlawry, of the kind pronounced against Butler, were violations of the laws of war. "The sternest retaliation," it stated, "should follow the murder committed in consequence of such proclamation."[61] The modern law of war follows the Lieber Code in this regard, strictly forbidding forfeiture of belligerent status for any prior action, however heinous. A belligerent may be punished—after a fair trial—for any *specific* crimes he may have committed. But in no event is he stripped of his combatant (or belligerent) status.[62]

With these general remarks about the laws of war in mind, we may proceed to look at three particular sets of legal issues that arose in the Civil War in this area. These are: the challenge of technological developments (in this case, land mines); disputes about combatant (or belligerent) status; and the fate of civilians and civilian infrastructure in war.

Challenges of the New Technology

It is an intrinsic feature of the science of law that rules are commonly phrased in rather general terms, so that their application to particular situations can involve exercises of fine judgment. In addition, legal rules are commonly (and virtually unavoidably) crafted with the experiences of the past in mind. As a result, rapid changes in technology can pose particularly knotty challenges to regulators, as many examples in the modern world illustrate. As a result, military lawyers, like generals, are virtually condemned to fight today's wars on the basis of yesterday's rules.

In the Civil War, the principal technological innovation which gave rise to legal debate was the invention and first use of land mines. These "torpedoes" or "sub-terra explosive shells" (as they were called in a pre–Madison Avenue age) were the brainchild chiefly of Confederate General Gabriel J. Rains. He first employed them in the Peninsular Campaign of 1862, by placing small shells in roads to delay the advances of Union forces.[63] He conceded that their effect was largely a "moral" one, as they were too small to do serious damage.[64] These new devices did, however, succeed in causing pandemonium among the astonished Union cavalry forces—a success that stimulated the Confederates to plant some thirteen hundred of these novel devices around Richmond to fend off General George McClellan's Army of the Potomac.

There were objections on both sides to the deployment of this marvelous innovation. On the Union side, McClellan denounced the use of mines as "murderous and barbarous conduct."[65] He reported that the Confederates were employing them near wells and springs, as well as in carpetbags and flour barrels—employing them, in other words, as what would now be called booby traps. There were misgivings on the Confederate side too about making use of these devices. General James Longstreet—whose own forces had benefited from their use—disliked the laying of mines in roads and issued orders against the practice, on the ground that it was not "a proper or effective method of war."[66] Rains objected to any policy of "rigid philanthropy for the enemy" (as he sourly put it), pointing out that land mines were simply an alternative form of ambush, which was clearly a lawful means of war. Land mines were also, he contended, justifiable as a means of countering the Union's great superiority in supplies of gunpowder.[67]

The matter was brought immediately to the attention of Confederate secretary of war George W. Randolph. His solution was to apply the general principle of military necessity to the matter. So long as a genuine military function was being served, he concluded, mines were permissible. For example, it was allowable to plant shells in parapets to defeat an assault, or on roads to hinder an ongoing pursuit. But it was not admissible, he pronounced, "to plant shells merely to destroy life and without other design than that of depriving the enemy of a few men."[68]

In the course of time, it became apparent that many commanders were less skittish than Longstreet about using mines. They were employed again in 1863 to protect fortified posts at Charleston, which was under siege by Union forces. They were also planted around Fort Fisher in North Carolina, helping to prevent the fall of that fortress to Northern forces until January 1865. In November 1864, President Davis personally ordered them to be used in southern Georgia, to slow Sherman's advances.[69] Their use for the defense of Fort McAllister near Savannah, Georgia, in December of that year accounted for the major share of casualties in the capture of that installation.[70] Sherman countered by putting Confederate prisoners of war to work clearing the mines.[71]

There was never any judicial consideration of the lawfulness of this new technique of war; and land mines passed smoothly into the growing armory of new weapons in a period of ever quickening technological advancement. Only in the late twentieth century were rules to cover these matters devised. A treaty concluded in 1980 placed various restrictions on the use of mines in civilian areas.[72] Then, in 1997, a convention was drafted which completely prohibited the use of antipersonnel land mines by states parties (which do not, incidentally, include the United States).[73]

Unlawful Combatants

The laws of war obviously determine *what* may lawfully be done in war—i.e., what acts qualify legally as acts of war, which are thereby shielded from criminal prosecution. Somewhat less obviously, the laws of war also determine *who* is authorized to commit those acts—i.e., what persons possess what is called *combatant status* or *belligerent status*. The basic rule on this point is—or appears to be—simple enough. Belligerents are persons who are officially enrolled in the armed forces of the opposing sides.

It has not always been so. In the Middle Ages, it was held that, in time of war, the two societies were, as such, comprehensively enemies to one another—with the result that *any* national of either state was permitted, on his own initiative, to inflict damage on the other side. This older position found verbal reflection in the texts of declarations of war as late as the seventeenth century. In 1672, for example, King Louis XIV of France, in declaring war against the Netherlands, commanded "all his Subjects . . . to fall upon the Hollanders."[74]

Even by that time, however, this conception of war as a state of universal hostility between populations was going out of fashion, at least in European warfare. The newer practice was that the business of waging war (which could and did become something very like a business in seventeenth- and eighteenth-

century Europe) was to be discharged exclusively by designated specialists—
specifically, by uniformed professional soldiers trained, equipped, and organized specifically for the task. By the middle of the eighteenth century, Vattel
was able to state with confidence that the only persons who were allowed to
engage in belligerent acts were those who were commissioned or instructed to
do so by their sovereign.[75]

Persons who lack the requisite governmental authorization do not possess
"the peculiar rights of belligerents" (in General Sherman's quaintly candid expression).[76] Consequently, any killing or capturing which they do is, simply,
homicide and kidnapping, criminally punishable as such. These persons have
no entitlement to treatment as prisoners of war. They are commonly known,
in modern parlance at least, by such labels as "illegal combatants" or "unlawful belligerents" or "unprivileged belligerents."

During the American Civil War, there were rancorous debates, in a variety
of areas, about entitlement to the coveted privilege of belligerent status, with
each side strenuously objecting that the other was employing persons in its
service who did not qualify, on various grounds, as lawful belligerents. The
Confederates contended that ex-slaves were not lawful combatants, while the
Union sought to deny that status to guerrilla warriors of various descriptions.
In each case, the persons concerned, being regarded as beyond the protection
of the laws of war, were exposed to some very rough treatment.

Servants in Arms

The Confederate government took the position that ex-slaves could not be
lawful belligerents. The laws of war were somewhat ambiguous on this point.
There was authority, dating at least from the seventeenth century, to the effect
that it was unlawful to suborn a national on the enemy side to assassinate his
ruler or one of his army's generals.[77] But matters were not so clear on the question of fomenting discontent generally among the enemy population. Vattel
held that to "seduce the enemy's subjects" into disloyalty was *not*, strictly
speaking, unlawful, although, in the spirit of chivalry, he regarded the practice
as seriously dishonorable.[78] The Lieber Code had no provision one way or the
other on the matter. Nor has the question figured in later codifications of the
laws of war.

In all events, the Confederate thesis was that it was not permissible for the
Union to wage war against the Southern way of life, or against the South's internal social arrangements—and that the Union's policy of employing black

troops, which began officially in July 1862, blatantly infringed this fundamental principle.[79] Confederate secretary of war James Seddon maintained that such a policy could have only one purpose: "to subvert by violence the social system and domestic relations of the negro slaves in the Confederacy," thereby adding the element of "servile insurrection" to the normal calamities of war.[80] For this reason, the Confederate government regarded the enrollment of slaves in the Union army as "a departure from the usages of nations and an abandonment of the rules of civilized warfare."[81] It will be observed that this line of reasoning logically entailed that it would be lawful for the Union to enroll *free* blacks in its forces. Howell Cobb, the Confederate general and statesman (and also noted lawyer), readily conceded the point.[82] Seddon, however, surmised that, in practice, Confederates would fail to appreciate this fine distinction.[83]

The Confederate response to the Union's policy of enrolling blacks into its forces took the form, most notably, of a refusal to accord belligerent status either to the black troops themselves or to white officers who commanded them. On May 1, 1863, the Confederate Congress adopted a Joint Resolution, in response to Lincoln's Emancipation Proclamation, stating that such white officers, if captured, should be tried for the offense of inciting servile insurrection, with a possible death penalty awaiting them if convicted.[84]

A similar fate awaited the black Union soldiers themselves. This policy of nonrecognition of belligerent status manifested itself in several concrete ways. For one thing, Confederates commonly would not treat with black Union soldiers (or their white officers) under a flag of truce.[85] More seriously by far, the Confederates held that black soldiers were not entitled to prisoner-of-war status when captured. Nathan Bedford Forrest, for example, was very explicit that, in his view, black soldiers were captured *property* (with legal title passing to the captors) rather than captured *persons*.[86] With remorseless logic, the Confederate authorities did not permit black soldiers to benefit from prisoner-exchange arrangements which were concluded by the Union and Confederate armed forces in July 1862.[87] The refusal of the Confederacy to yield on this issue was a major factor in leading the Union to discontinue the prisoner-exchange policy the following year.[88]

The breakdown of the prisoner-exchange arrangement, in turn, had serious consequences for many soldiers (mostly white) who were held captive in the South. With the halting of prisoner exchanges, the Southern prison camps became more and more crowded; and conditions in them deteriorated markedly. Andersonville Prison Camp in Georgia was the most notorious case—leading (as will be seen) to two war-crimes prosecutions after the war.[89] For the present, it is only necessary to note that behind this tragic episode lay the stubborn Confederate refusal to accord prisoner-of-war status to captured black troops.

For the black soldiers themselves, the Confederate nonrecognition of belligerent status could have consequences that were more direct, and more shocking yet. By November 1862, Seddon approved a drastic policy of summarily executing armed slaves found in the Union forces.[90] It would appear, however, that this practice was never incorporated into general orders applicable to the Confederate military at large. In addition, it should be appreciated that glimmers of humanitarianism were not altogether lacking. Seddon did express a concern over "the possible abuse of this grave power" stemming from "over-zeal on the part of subordinate officers." Therefore, executions should be ordered only by commanding officers and not by subordinates.[91]

Policies of summary execution of black Union soldiers certainly found a receptive audience in some quarters. In June 1863, General Edmund Kirby Smith, commanding the Trans-Mississippi Department, wrote to his subordinate, General Richard Taylor, expressing the hope that Confederate troops "may have recognized the propriety of giving no quarter to armed negroes and their officers."[92] In cases where this policy was not carried out, the black soldiers should be turned over to state authorities for disposition according to ordinary peacetime legal processes. The state of South Carolina, in particular, expressed itself anxious to prosecute black Union troops (both slave and free) for violation of the state's criminal law on the fomenting of servile insurrection.[93]

In the second half of the war, allegations began to spread that the Confederates were adopting a policy of giving no quarter to black troops (i.e., a policy of killing defeated or surrendered soldiers instead of taking them prisoner). In June 1863, in the wake of the Battle of Milliken's Bend, in Louisiana, accusations surfaced of the shooting of black prisoners by their Confederate captors. General Grant asked the Confederates for assurances that the individuals responsible for this act would be punished and that the Confederate command expressly disavow the act. At the same time, he assured Confederate general Taylor that the black troops had been regularly mustered into the Union forces and were therefore entitled to equality of treatment with white forces.[94]

It has been contended that, in Arkansas and Louisiana in late 1863 and early 1864, Confederate forces engaged in "an ongoing program of racial intimidation" involving the murder of black troops.[95] There were accusations, for example, that, near Lake Providence, Louisiana, in June 1863 a Confederate

colonel, when attacking a Union fort, urged his troops to take no black prisoners. At Marks' Mills, Arkansas, in April 1864, over a hundred black troops
were reported massacred. In April 1864, the Battle of Poison Spring, Arkansas,
which occurred during General Nathaniel Banks's Red River Campaign, gave
rise to another incident. Union forces admittedly had been engaging in loot-
ing, although there is no evidence that black troops played any major role in
that activity (or perhaps any role at all). It was noted, though, that black
troops formed a remarkably high proportion of the Union dead, sparking accusations that captured black troops had simply been murdered on the spot
instead of being made prisoners of war.[96]

The single most notorious of all the Confederate atrocity incidents against
black soldiers—and the most famous battlefield atrocity of the entire conflict—
was the "Fort Pillow Massacre," as it has come to be commonly known. It occurred in April 1864, when the famous Confederate general Nathan Bedford
Forrest attacked, and took, Fort Pillow near Memphis. Prior to his assault on
the installation, he made a demand for its unconditional surrender—backed by
an express, if imprecise, threat of no quarter. This was refused, and the fort was
duly stormed and taken, with about half of the defenders being killed. Here, as
at Poison Springs (which occurred only about a week later), black troops comprised a suspiciously high proportion of the Union casualties.

Immediately, gruesome rumors began to circulate as to the systematic murdering of black prisoners. The matter was taken up by the Joint Committee on
the Conduct of the War of the Union Congress, which dispatched two of its
members to Fort Pillow on a fact-finding mission. They interviewed over seventy persons, including many who had been wounded during the battle, and
concluded that over three hundred blacks (including many women and children) had been killed.[97] The Committee's investigation was hardly an exercise in
courtroom-style objectivity. It seems likely, though, that Forrest did not *expressly*
order the commission of murder or commit any killings himself. But there is no
serious doubt that a massacre of black soldiers did occur on that occasion.[98]

One other incident of the murder of black troops should be noted, as it
would become the most important of all of them from the legal standpoint. This
was the little-known Battle of Saltville, Virginia, in October 1864. Although it
never acquired anything like the high public notoriety of the Fort Pillow incident, it did lead to a war-crimes trial after the conclusion of the hostilities.[99]
Here, too, the basic allegation was that black troops, when captured, were murdered rather than being taken as prisoners.[100] Initial reports had it that some 150

black soldiers were summarily dispatched, although more careful investigation later made it more likely that the true figure was in the range of fifty.[101]

The Union consistently took the position that black troops in its ranks were entitled to the privileges of lawful belligerents on an equal basis with whites. The Lieber Code forthrightly insisted on this point. "The law of nations," the code flatly pronounced, "knows no distinction of color." More specifically, it declared that it was not open to a belligerent to declare that persons of "a certain class, color or condition" should not enjoy the full range of belligerents' rights.[102] The practical problem, however, was how to bring the enemy side around to this enlightened view.

The obvious means of countering the various Confederate practices was by way of reprisal. At least one Union commander showed himself willing to go down this path. General Hunter, in South Carolina, wrote directly to President Davis in Richmond on the subject, threatening to execute the highest ranking Confederate officer in his hands, in response to each instance of reenslavement of captured black soldiers. He also demanded the revocation of the order of August 1862, on the treatment of white officers of black troops as felons, threatening to execute *all* Confederate officers and slaveholders in his jurisdiction if it was not withdrawn.[103] President Lincoln made it clear that he was of a like mind on the matter. In July 1863, he issued an order from the White House expressly setting out a man-for-man reprisal policy. It had two components: first, that, for every Union soldier who was killed in violation of the laws of war, a Confederate soldier would be executed; and second, that, for every Union soldier who was enslaved, a Confederate soldier would be put to work at hard labor on public works.[104]

In practice, reprisals were risky in this highly sensitive area. It was rumored that black troops, with "Remember Fort Pillow" as a rallying cry, set about killing Confederate soldiers instead of taking them captive. Forrest alleged that black soldiers had taken a solemn oath on their knees in Memphis to murder any Confederate soldiers whom they captured.[105] An intense debate among the Lincoln cabinet over how to respond to the Fort Pillow incident revealed a deep division of opinion over the question of reprisals (with attorney general Bates being particularly outspoken in opposition).[106] As it happened, there were no prosecutions, either during the war or afterward, for the Fort Pillow affair.

The occurrence of racial atrocities is perhaps the darkest stain on America in its Civil War. But it is appropriate to note that the picture in this area was not unrelievedly bleak. The Confederate authorities themselves were shocked by the reports of the killings at Saltville. Robert E. Lee expressed his "unqualified reprobation" of them and ordered the arrest and trial of the general who was in overall command, Felix Robertson.[107] General Robertson eluded capture, though, and lived until 1928 (when, at his death, he was hailed as the last surviving Confederate general). The individual most directly responsible for the killings, a ruthless and homicidal guerrilla leader named Champ Ferguson, was not so fortunate. As will be observed in due course, he was captured, tried, and put to death after the war.[108]

Partisans

From the Union standpoint, the principal problem with regard to issues of combatant status concerned the employment by the Confederates of irregular forces of various descriptions as auxiliaries to their principal armies.[109] The principal issue concerned the extent to which self-appointed persons operating on an independent basis, outside of the military command structure of the country on whose behalf they are fighting, were entitled to the privileges of belligerents.

The problem arose in the very early days of the war, most notably in Missouri but also elsewhere. To sort out the law on this matter, the aid of Francis Lieber was naturally enlisted. Prior to the compilation of his famous code, he was asked by Halleck to expound and clarify the state of the law on the particular subject of guerrilla warfare. Lieber duly obliged, producing his pamphlet on the subject, *Guerrilla Parties Considered with Reference to the Laws and Usages of War,* in 1862.[110] Halleck had five thousand copies printed and distributed to the Union Armies. The following year, Lieber incorporated the main conclusions into his code. There, he made an elaborate series of distinctions between different categories of persons according to how tightly or loosely they were integrated with the official armed forces of the enemy—ranging from partisans to spies, saboteurs, "armed prowlers," and guerrillas in the true legal sense. These different categories of persons were entitled, Lieber explained, to various different forms of treatment.

One of Lieber's concerns was over *partisans.* These were defined in the code as "soldiers armed and wearing the uniform of their army, but belonging to a corps which acts detached from the main body for the purpose of making inroads into the territory occupied by the enemy."[111] Similar to partisans—and similarly entitled to the privileges of belligerents—were members of *free corps*. These were stated to be "troops not belonging to the regular army, consisting of volunteers, generally raised by individuals authorized to do so by the government, used for petty war," though not incorporated into the regular armed forces.[112]

Lieber carefully pointed out the dangers involved in making use of partisans and free corps, particularly their proneness to indiscipline. There was, however, no blanket rule against employing them, as there was, in Lieber's opinion, "nothing inherently lawless or brigand-like in their character."[113] Partisans in particular, he explained in his pamphlet, were "part and parcel of the army."[114] As such, they were entitled to the rights and privileges of belligerents, including (crucially) the right to be treated as prisoners of war when captured. Any individual misdeeds that might have been committed by these persons could be dealt with on a case-by-case basis, "on the principle of retaliation."[115]

The Confederate Congress made statutory arrangements for the employment of partisan forces in April 1862. It specified that the bands of "partisan rangers" (as they were labeled) must be "regularly received into service" and that they must receive the same pay and rations as regular soldiers, as well as being subject to the same regulations (i.e., they were to obey the laws of war in their operations). Any arms that they captured were to be delivered to the Army quartermaster, for which the captors would be paid the full value.[116]

One of the most famous, or notorious, of the Confederate partisan forces was that of Colonel John S. Mosby (the "grey ghost"), who operated in the Virginia theater. His force did not maintain a continued existence, but instead assembled at a signal, on an *ad hoc* basis. The targets of this group were generally not the Union armed forces, but Union infrastructure. One of the group's more spectacular feats was the derailing and robbery of a train on the Baltimore and Ohio Railroad line in October 1864. There were no injuries, but the band made off with $173,000. (When the money was divided among the members, in their customary fashion, each received $2,100 for his labors. Mosby himself, also true to custom, gallantly declined to take any share.)[117]

Mosby's counterparts in the Western theater were Nathan Bedford Forrest and John Hunt Morgan. Both of them raised and equipped their own forces and then operated them as adjuncts to the regular Confederate armies. Both also engaged in a number of spectacular raids. Morgan's great raid of December 1862, for example, led to the capturing of some eighteen hundred prisoners, plus the seizure of about $2 million of federal property. In July of the following year, he even carried the struggle into the Union states, crossing the

Ohio River and raiding Indiana and Ohio. On that occasion, he was captured
and imprisoned, civilian-style, in the Ohio State Penitentiary; he managed to
escape from it and resume his raiding. By 1864, however, his force had become
little more than a band of "riotous looters" (in the words of one historian).[118]

Robert E. Lee regarded Mosby as "strict in discipline" and as performing
"excellent service" for the Southern cause.[119] The Confederates insisted that
Mosby's forces, when captured, should be accorded treatment as prisoners of
war, on the thesis that his forces were "regularly enlisted soldiers in the Confederate service—as much so as any in the field."[120] The Union authorities accepted this, at least in principle.[121] But not always in practice. In 1864, General
Philip Sheridan reported that he had one of Mosby's men hanged and six others shot when he apprehended them.[122]

Not all of the partisan forces were as disciplined as those of Mosby. Within
the Confederate government and armed forces, there came to be considerable
misgivings over the employment of partisans. The most prominent objector
was Robert E. Lee, who complained that the partisan policy "gives license to
many deserters and marauders" who "commit depredations on friend and foe
alike." He also pointed out that the policy had the effect of discouraging enlistment in the regular forces, as would-be soldiers were lured from the regular
life by the prospect of adventure, independence, and booty.[123] Secretary of
War Seddon was of a like view.[124] So, eventually, was the Confederate Congress. In February 1864, it repealed the earlier authorization of partisan operations and required all existing bands to become part of the regular cavalry.[125]

Spies

Spies constitute a category of persons whose legal status is of a very peculiar
character. It must be understood from the outset that the legal definition of
spy differs considerably from the general lay stereotype. Basically, a spy is a soldier during time of war who acts clandestinely (i.e., not in uniform), within
enemy or enemy-held territory, for the purpose of gathering information and
relaying it to his own forces.[126] The fictional James Bond, along with his real-
life counterparts in the CIA and similar organizations, is therefore not a spy in
this strict legal sense because they are not soldiers operating during time of
war. Spying should also not be confused with treasonous conduct. A disloyal
person living within the Union lines who conveyed information to the Confederates might well be guilty of treason. But he or she would not be a spy—

again by virtue of the fact of not being an enemy soldier operating out of uniform. Finally, spying should be distinguished from sabotage (which will be treated presently), even though, in practice, there has long been a tendency, even among lawyers and judges, to conflate them. Spying in the strict sense refers to the gathering of information, *not* to such matters as the destruction of property or the killing of persons.[127]

The oddest aspect of spying from the legal standpoint is its seemingly contradictory treatment by the laws of war. On the one hand, spying is *not* forbidden by the laws of war. At the same time, however, it *does* entail a forfeiture of combatant status—meaning that a person who is caught in the act of spying (i.e., out of uniform) has no entitlement to treatment as a prisoner of war. He is therefore subject to prosecution and punishment under the ordinary criminal laws of the country in which he is captured. The result, very oddly, is that spying is an activity that is simultaneously lawful *and* punishable—lawful, that is, according to the *international* law of war, but simultaneously punishable by the state being spied on, under its own *national* law. Another way of putting this point is to say that, while spying is not a *war* crime, it *is* an *ordinary* crime.[128]

As if this position were not peculiar enough (from the standpoint of laypersons), it should be added that the United States has a long-standing practice of not adhering to the international-law rules on this subject. Instead of treating captured spies as *ordinary* criminals, the American practice has been to regard them instead as war criminals (i.e., as violators of the laws of war). The chief manifestation of this policy is the fact that spies captured by the United States have been tried before military rather than civilian tribunals, and accused of violations of the laws of war. The leading precedent in this regard was the treatment meted out to Major John André during the American War of Independence. When found with incriminating documents, in connection with the treason of Benedict Arnold, he was tried by a military commission and hanged. The Articles of War of 1806 provided for the continuation of this policy and prescribed the death penalty.[129] Supplementary legislation, enacted during the Civil War, in February 1862, extended the coverage of this law to time of rebellion as well as in time of war.[130]

It is interesting to note that the Confederacy adhered to the international-law position, at least in principle. Its position was that military tribunals had no jurisdiction to try accused spies.[131] It remains to be seen how, or whether, American practice will be brought into line with the international legal rule.

Prowlers, Saboteurs, and Terrorists

Another group of persons identified in the Lieber Code were *armed prowlers,* defined as persons "who steal within the lines of the hostile army for the purpose of robbing, killing, or destroying bridges, roads, or canals, or of robbing or destroying the mail, or of cutting telegraph wires."[132] In the more popular parlance, they were known as "bushwhackers." A more modern term would be "saboteurs." An important point to note about these persons is that, by definition, they entered Union areas from outside. Consequently, persons who actually lived within the area controlled by the forces that they were attacking were *not* saboteurs. They were either ordinary criminals, if living in Union or Confederate home territory, or else "war rebels" or "war traitors," if they lived in occupied territory (a matter to be treated in due course).[133] Saboteurs (or armed prowlers) in the true sense, Lieber insisted, were *not* legitimate belligerents. Even if they wore a uniform when engaging in their activities, they were not entitled to prisoner-of-war status if captured. In Lieber's view, they were on a par with simple assassins; and it was legitimate to shoot them when found.[134]

The robust approach of the Lieber Code in this regard was not consistently followed. At least in the early part of the war (prior to the promulgation of the code), bridge-burning and similar acts that were done by soldiers under military auspices were treated as ordinary warfare. For example, Confederate general Sterling Price, in the early part of the war, authorized his forces to engage in the destruction of bridges behind Union lines in Missouri. Halleck responded by stating that, provided the activity was undertaken by persons "wearing the garb of soldiers and duly organized and enrolled as legitimate belligerents," then it would be regarded as a lawful act of war—and the perpetrators, if captured, would be duly treated as prisoners of war. He made it clear, though, that persons sent "in the garb of peaceful citizens and under false pretenses" would not be accorded that treatment.[135]

In practice, saboteurs who were sent from the opposing side, disguised as civilians, were treated on a par with spies. A striking example of this policy action was provided in 1862 by the fate of the participants in the famous Andrews Raid, which was carried out in Georgia by a band of Union soldiers in civilian garb (and led by a civilian, James J. Andrews). They hijacked a train, with the intention of burning bridges and cutting telegraph lines behind them as they drove north. The project did not succeed (although it provided the occasion for a thrilling Great Locomotive Chase), and the members of the band were captured. Initially, they were held as hostages; but seven of them were then prosecuted as spies before a Confederate military court. In their defense, they contended that they were regular soldiers engaged in a *bona fide* military mission (notwithstanding their civilian disguises), with no element of clandestine information-gathering—and that consequently they could not be treated as spies. They were nonetheless convicted of spying and hanged.[136]

Later in the war, some rather more elaborate plans were hatched by the Confederates for clandestine activity behind enemy lines, under government auspices. In January 1864, for example, a certain Professor R. S. McCulloh was authorized by Confederate secretary of war Seddon to organize bodies of men for the destruction of property in Union-held areas. The diligent professor's reward was to be 50 percent of the value of any property destroyed. Some would condemn this policy as amounting to nothing less than state-sponsored terrorism. Secretary Seddon, however, made it very clear that these nonacademic activities were to be "governed by the law of nations" and that civilians were not be harmed. Destruction was to be confined to "army and navy supplies and such other property as may be directly serviceable to the enemy in waging war." The plan did not, in the event, bear fruit.[137] The following month, on the very day that partisan activity was abolished by statute, the Confederate Congress placed this state-sponsored sabotage policy, secretly, onto a statutory footing by giving the War Department formal authorization to make such arrangements.[138]

In practice, if not in strict theory, sabotage has tended to be treated in much the same manner as spying. In the United States, that means that persons accused of sabotage will be tried in military courts as war criminals. A notable example during the Civil War was one Robert C. Kennedy, who was tried before a military tribunal, charged with spying and with "irregular and unlawful warfare." His program could properly be termed terroristic, since the plan (apparently) was to burn down the city of New York. The execution proved, however, to be unworthy of the ambition, since nothing more threatening actually occurred than a minor fire in a hotel, in December 1864. Kennedy, nonetheless, was convicted and sentenced to hang.[139]

Not until the Second World War did the federal Supreme Court have occasion to consider the treatment of sabotage. This occurred when a group of German saboteurs were landed in American territory by a German submarine, with the intention of committing various acts of destruction against the American war-production sites. Significantly, the group included one American national. They were tried before a military commission and convicted of violations of the laws of war—with the approval of the Supreme Court in a well-known case in 1943.[140]

The international law of war continues to be in a state of grave uncertainty in this important area. It is suggested that perpetrators of terrorist attacks—i.e., of attacks on civilian groups (by such means as the planting of bombs in restaurants)—should not have combatant status or entitlement to prisoner-of-war treatment. There is some authority to this effect in British courts, although it is not free from ambiguity.[141] More problematic is the case, such as the Andrews Raid, in which the perpetrators are military personnel acting clandestinely, but carrying out *bona fide* military operations. On the one hand, the general policy of the law of war is to be liberal in the according of combatant status, in the interest of humanitarianism. On the other hand, clandestine activity does constitute a deliberate blurring of the line between military and civilian spheres, which is incompatible with the spirit (if not strictly the letter) of the laws of war. There continues to be a very urgent need for clarification of international law on this vital point.

Guerrillas

Guerrillas, in the legal sense, are persons who wage war on their own account, entirely independently of the official military apparatus of the side that they support, and on a part-time rather than a full-time basis. The Lieber Code did not actually use the term "guerrilla," but it explicitly denied the status of lawful belligerents to

> men, or squads of men, who commit hostilities, whether by fighting, or [by] destruction or plunder, or by raids of any kind, without commission, without being part and portion of the organized hostile army, and without sharing continuously in the war, but who do so with intermitting returns to their homes and avocations, or with the occasional assumption of the semblance of peaceful pursuits, divesting themselves of the character or appearance of soldiers.[142]

Such persons, the code stated, "are not public enemies, and, therefore, if captured, are not entitled to the privileges of prisoners of war, but shall be treated summarily as highway robbers or pirates."[143]

Out in the field, General Sherman expressed much the same view when he described guerrillas as "wild beasts unknown to the usages of war." In order to qualify as lawful belligerents, he insisted, persons must be "enlisted, enrolled, officered, uniformed, armed, and equipped by some recognized belligerent power, and must, if detached from a main army, be of sufficient strength, with written orders from some army commander, to do some military things."[144]

Some Confederates begged to disagree with Sherman, maintaining that their side was fully entitled to resort to this unconventional form of warfare. Brigadier General Daniel Ruggles was one of these. When writing to Benjamin Butler in 1862, he invoked not the laws of war as such, but instead the fundamental natural-law right of self-preservation.

> It is to be observed [Ruggles insisted] that the first great law of nature, the right of self-defense, is inherent in communities as well as individuals. No law condemns the individual who slays the robber or the assassin, and no just law can condemn a community for using all its power to resist the invader and drive him from their soil.[145]

Invoking the precedent of practices during the American War of Independence, Ruggles went on to assert that "one belligerent has [no] right to complain of the name or form which the other may choose to give to its military organizations. The right to adapt these to the peculiar service required has been universally conceded."[146] In a similar vein, Confederate general Theophilus H. Holmes wrote from Little Rock, Arkansas, to his Union counterpart, General Samuel R. Curtis, that the Confederacy "cannot be expected to allow our enemies to decide for us whether we shall fight them in masses or individually, in uniform, without uniform, openly or from ambush."[147]

A common form of guerrilla activity during the Civil War was interference with communication and transport, a scourge that afflicted both armies. Bridge-burning and the cutting of telegraph wires were the most conspicuous activities, and both sides were prepared to take drastic action against it, along the lines advocated by Lieber. The major Confederate concern was with eastern Tennessee, where a pro-Union insurgency raged. Judah Benjamin, during his brief tenure as Confederate secretary of war, ordered that, if bridge-burners were caught in the act, they should be summarily tried by military commission and, if found guilty, executed on the spot.[148]

The Union side suffered in much the same way in Missouri, where Halleck, in his tenure as Union commander there, largely echoed Benjamin. In December 1861, he issued a set of general orders, warning bridge-burners that, if caught in the act, they would be "immediately shot." In areas where such acts occurred, the local pro-Confederate population would be compelled to provide their labor for repairs. Local towns and counties would be compelled to contribute to the cost of repairs, unless it was established that the acts could not have been prevented. "[P]retended" Union supporters were required to disclose any information that they possessed about sabotage activity, on pain of being treated as accomplices of the perpetrators.[149]

The following year, Halleck's successor in Missouri, General John M. Schofield, urged the adoption of a policy of "extreme and speedy punishment" of guerrillas.[150] In central Missouri, the announced policy—stated in rather general terms—was that guerrillas should be "pursued and exterminated without mercy."[151] In the Kansas Department, things were spelled out in slightly more detail. Guerrillas—described as "unnatural enemies of the human race"—were to be "summarily tried by drum-head court-martial" and, if found guilty, to be executed on the spot.[152] In southwestern Missouri, another afflicted area, it was similarly ordered that any guerrillas who were caught in action were to be shot. Anyone suspected of harboring them was to be arrested and tried by military commission.[153] In Virginia, General Pope ordered that persons caught in the act of destroying railroads, telegraphs, and the like were to be shot on the spot.[154]

It soon became apparent that some care needed to be taken in the meting out of such drastic, and irreversible, punishments. In July 1862, General Schofield indicated a concern that antiguerrilla policies not get out of hand. Spies, he stated, were *not* covered by the antiguerrilla policy and therefore were not to be subject to summary execution. Nor were persons who merely incited insurrection. Indeed, even the actual guerrillas were to be subject to summary proceedings *only* if "the formal process of law has failed to arrest the evil." And even then, they could only be summarily executed if they were "actually taken in arms engaged in their unlawful warfare."[155] On some occasions, a more positive approach was taken to guerrilla war. In northeastern Missouri, in October 1862, an offer was made to treat guerrillas as prisoners of war, and even to release them on parole, *if* they halted their guerrilla activities.[156] The following year, in the Missouri-Kansas border area, guerrillas who surrendered were promised exemption from "military punishment" (i.e., summary trial and execution), although not from prosecution for treason in the civil courts.[157]

If the response to guerrilla warfare on the Union side was sometimes robust, there were also grave misgivings within the Confederate leadership about resorting to this kind of warfare. Confederate secretary of war Randolph, for example, commenting on the situation in Missouri in mid-1862, expressed the hope that guerrilla war could be rendered unnecessary by the instituting of "a system of regular warfare" in its place.[158] Even the dashing General Nathan Bedford Forrest professed to dislike guerrillas, to the point of (supposedly) approving of the Union policy of hanging them when caught.[159]

It would be pleasing to report that the many legal issues which surfaced in the Civil War concerning irregular forms of warfare have been satisfactorily resolved since then. That is, however, far from the case. The question of entitlement to combatant (or belligerent) status was a divisive one among international lawyers throughout the remainder of the nineteenth century, and indeed remains so to the present day. The Hague Rules of 1907 lay down the basic rule: that persons who are *not* members of the armed forces of their country are only entitled to the "rights . . . of war" if four specific conditions are all met. First, the persons must be "commanded by a person responsible for his subordinates." Second, they must have "a fixed distinctive emblem recognizable at a distance." (Notice that this is not explicitly a requirement of a full uniform.) Third, they must "carry arms openly." Finally, they must "conduct their operations in accordance with the laws and customs of war."[160]

Any irregular would-be belligerent who fails to meet *all four* of these criteria is not entitled to the "rights . . . of war." That is to say, such a person has no legal right to kill and capture persons on the opposing side in the conflict, and no entitlement to treatment as a prisoner of war if captured. This position was reaffirmed in the wake of the Second World War by an American war-crimes tribunal.[161] Hostile activity on a purely self-appointed basis, without the support of an organized government, the tribunal held, is "criminal and deprives the participants of belligerent status." As a result, "a civilian who aids, abets or participates in the fighting is liable to punishment as a war criminal under the laws of war. Fighting is legitimate only for the combatant personnel of a country." The Tribunal candidly assessed the status of irregular warriors in language that could easily have come straight from the 1860s:

> Just as the spy may act lawfully for his country and at the same time be a war criminal to the enemy, so guerrillas may render great service to their country, and, in the event of success, become heroes even, still they remain war criminals in the eyes of the enemy and may be treated as such. In no other way can an army guard and protect itself from the gadfly tactics of such armed resistance.[162]

There is one caveat—and potentially a very large one—to this seemingly simple and clear set of rules: that an irregular who fails to meet one or more of

the four criteria, although not entitled (as noted) to the "rights . . . of war," is
nevertheless, in general principle, "under the protection and the rule of the
principles of the law of nations."[163] Although this caveat (known to international lawyers as the "Martens Clause," after the German lawyer who formu-
lated it) has existed since the First Hague Peace Conference of 1899, there is
considerable uncertainty over its real meaning and effect. It seems likely that
this proviso would preclude policies of drumhead "trials" and summary executions which were meted out during the Civil War. But there is no definite authority on the matter as yet. It may be noted, in addition, that the preamble
to the Hague Convention on Land Warfare also states that "unforeseen cases"
in war should not "be left to the arbitrary judgment of military commanders."
This provision too lacks authoritative interpretation.

The position on irregular forces was rendered substantially less clear by
Protocol I of 1977 the Geneva Conventions. Simplifying very drastically, it
may be said that combatant status will not be forfeited by a soldier who operates out of uniform and who carries concealed weapons in the period leading
up to the actual mounting of an attack.[164] The Protocol does not actually say
that such conduct is lawful. It merely states that engaging in it will not result
in the forfeiting of combatant status. This provision has been condemned as a
guerrilla's or terrorist's charter, and there are grounds for concern on that
point. At the same time, it may be noted that the provision would (probably)
also protect special-forces units which operate clandestinely behind enemy
lines and who might otherwise be exposed to being treated as spies. To this extent, the regular armed forces of developed countries would benefit from the
provision, as well as "asymmetrical" warriors (in modern terminology). For
present purposes, all that can be said here is that this area of the law continues
to be in urgent need of clarification—perhaps now more than ever before.

Warring on Civilians

At the very heart of the laws of war is the idea that the sharpest possible separation between the civilian and the military spheres of life must be maintained
at all times. This principle has a dual aspect, restricting the role of civilians in
war in two opposite ways. On the one hand (as observed above), it meant that
civilians should not be *participants* in war. On the other hand, it also meant
that civilians should not be *victims* of war.

This idea that civilians should be as little troubled by war as possible grew very gradually over the centuries. During the Middle Ages, a number of categories of persons were marked out as being protected from acts of war—including ecclesiastics, women and children, traveling merchants and pilgrims, peasants, and students.[165] By the eighteenth century, there was a consensus, at least among western European countries, that civilians in general should be as little troubled by the waging of war as possible—a practice that Vattel rightly regarded as "highly commendable and well worthy of Nations which boast of their civilization."[166]

In 1868, soon after the American Civil War, the principle received its most formal confirmation as a cornerstone of the laws of war, in the Declaration of St. Petersburg, adopted by a conference of some sixteen major powers. "[T]he only legitimate object which States should endeavour to accomplish during war," the Declaration pronounced, "is to weaken the military forces of the enemy."[167] Five years before that, the Lieber Code had taken essentially the same position. "In modern regular wars of the Europeans, and their descendants in other portions of the globe," it stated, "protection of the inoffensive citizen of the hostile country is the rule; privation and disturbance of private relations are the exceptions."[168] The unarmed citizen was "to be spared in person, property, and honor as much as the exigencies of the war will admit."[169]

Unfortunately, the "exigencies of war" tend to be omnipresent, and sometimes in a very large and tragic fashion. During the Civil War, four types of military action affecting civilians were particularly in evidence. One was collateral damage occurring to civilians and their property in the course of regular military operations, with sieges and bombardments posing the greatest danger. Second was civilian involvement in guerrilla activity—sometimes voluntarily and sometimes not. Third was the requisitioning and capturing of civilian property, sometimes on a very large scale. Finally—and most drastically—there was the deliberate and systematic destruction of civilian military infrastructure—a policy to which the ominous label "total war" is sometimes attached. We shall look briefly at each of these in turn.[170]

Civilians in the Line of Fire

When hostilities occur in areas where civilian populations are located, the risk of civilian casualties becomes an intrinsic attribute of war. As in so many areas, the guiding consideration is the principle of military necessity. On the one hand, it is not permitted to attack civilian areas when no military purpose whatsoever is served. At the same time, however, an armed force cannot acquire an immunity from attack by deliberately locating itself in or near a civilian area.[171]

This principle was illustrated in the Civil War by the problem of ambushes on Union forces. This problem was especially acute along the rivers in the western theater, where Union riverboats—sometime with purely civilian passengers and cargo—were fired on from secluded positions along the shores. Sometimes, however, the firing came from populated areas; and Union commanders made it clear that they would respond vigorously to such attacks. In June 1862, navy lieutenant Edward T. Nichols bluntly informed the local civilian authorities of Rodney, Mississippi, that "punishment . . . will be visited upon the town" if attacks were made from it.[172] His commander, David Farragut, followed up that warning by advising Confederate general Mansfield Lovell to take steps to ensure that innocent persons were not in harm's way when attacks were made against Union forces, "for rest assured that the fire will be returned, and we will not hold ourselves answerable for the death of the innocent."[173]

It is interesting to note that Lovell readily conceded that the presence of civilians nearby did not immunize his troops from attack. But he did caution the Union officers that they should not "hasten to the nearest collection of unarmed and peaceable women and children and wreak . . . vengeance upon them." Lovell explained that the sites for his batteries were selected on the basis of strictly military considerations. If a site within a town was chosen, then the Union forces were permitted to shoot back at it, notwithstanding the risk of collateral damage to civilian areas. It was not permitted, however, to destroy a town that was merely *near* an enemy firing site, unless "imperious military necessity" was present.[174]

On basic principles, then, the two sides were largely in agreement: that the siting of military weapons in civilian areas necessarily carried a risk of civilian casualties when hostile fire was returned. At the same time, however, the *deliberate* targeting of civilian areas as a reprisal for *bona fide* military operations was not allowed. Any deliberate destruction of civilian areas had to be justified separately on grounds of military necessity. The distinction between a reprisal and a *bona fide* military operation was not always easily drawn.

The most obvious situations in which civilian areas were targeted as a military operation—as distinct from a reprisal—were bombardments of towns. This issue arose at the very outset of the War. In April 1861, President Lincoln pondered whether, or how, to prevent the Maryland legislature from convening (the assumption being that, if it met, it would vote to take the state out of the Union and into the Confederacy). Lincoln decided to let the legislature meet. But he also expressed a determination to take drastic steps if it acted against the Union, "even, if necessary, to the bombardment of their cities."[175]

One of the most contentious questions concerned the giving of warnings to civilian populations prior to a bombardment. The Lieber Code reflected the competing considerations in this area. On the one hand, it stated, as a factual matter, that commanders generally did issue warnings before bombarding civilian areas. At the same time, however, it carefully refrained from holding this to be an inflexible requirement. "[I]t is no infraction of the common law of war," the code stated, "to omit thus to inform the enemy. Surprise may be a necessity."[176]

In a number of instances during the war, warnings prior to bombardments were given. In May 1862, for example, a twenty-four-hour warning was given to the town of Vicksburg, Mississippi, prior to a bombardment of the town's defenses by Union naval forces.[177] In November of that year, when a peremptory demand was made to the authorities of Fredericksburg, Virginia, to surrender to the Union army, a period of sixteen hours was allowed, following the surrender deadline, for the evacuation of civilians.[178] When Charleston was bombarded by Union forces in August 1863, twenty-four hours' prior warning was given.[179] That same year, General Ambrose Burnside, operating in Tennessee, also gave warnings prior to bombardments.[180]

One prominent occasion in which a prior warning was *not* given occurred in 1864, when General Sherman ordered an artillery attack on Atlanta in 1864 prior to his capture of the city. General Hood sharply criticized his Union opponent for firing without prior warning, as was "usual in war among civilized nations."[181] Sherman sharply denied that there was any duty to notify and that it was incumbent on the defenders to be on their own guard. "You were bound to take notice," he retorted to Hood. "See the books."[182] As it happens, "the books" are scarcely more definite on this subject today than they were in the 1860s. The laws of war, to the present day, contain no specific rules on bombardments in land warfare.[183] The matter is therefore left to be governed by the more general principle of military necessity, with its prohibition against "unnecessary suffering" and the like. It remains all too easy today, as it was in the 1860s, for military commanders stoically to accept the "necessity" of bombarding areas where civilians are present, without prior warning, in the interest of bringing a military operation to a successful conclusion.

Civilians and Guerrilla Activity

One of the most important—and often tragic—ways in which civilians were caught up in the conflict was in connection with guerrilla activity. This came about in various ways. Sometimes, it was on the basis that the civilians were at least partly complicit in sabotage, ambushes, and the like, even if only in comparatively indirect ways, such as providing information or shelter to guerrilla bands. In such cases, the civilians were regarded as wrongdoers in their own right. Sometimes, however, civilians were the targets of reprisals, without any real suspicion of actual wickedness on their part. In addition, civilians could be victims of indiscriminate policies aimed at extirpating guerrilla warfare— policies that would later receive such ominous labels as "area denial," involving such harsh practices as wholesale destruction of crops and even forcible population removal.

An example of an attempt to ferret out actual civilian collaborators with guerrillas was provided by Union action in Tennessee in 1862, ordered by Brigadier General Grenville Dodge. Civilians who sympathized with the guerrillas would be required to pay for the damage committed, by being "levied upon" (i.e., having their property taken). When Union pickets were shot at, local civilian sympathizers would be taken hostage and held until the actual guilty party was located. If a picket was injured, then disloyal citizens in the vicinity would be fined up to $10,000.[184]

In the Department of Southwest Missouri, a policy of imposing various disabilities onto disloyal persons was adopted in June 1862. All citizens in the department were required to take an oath of loyalty, for which they would be given a certificate. Those who did not do so were deprived of the right to vote or to be jurors or witnesses in trials. They were also denied the right to transact any business and, for good measure, were confined to house arrest. Union troops were to check all persons traveling outside their homes for possession of the certificates of loyalty.[185]

A case of rather less exacting discrimination occurred in August 1862, when Farragut ordered the town of Donaldsville, Louisiana, to be burned to the ground because of its employment as a rendezvous for Confederate snipers. He gave one day's warning of his action, to allow for (rapid) evacuation of the civilians, then made good his word. This was a particularly interesting incident because it had a legal repurcussion after the war, in the form of a French claim against the United States on behalf of a French national who happened to have been among those affected by the action. France contended that Farragut's act was a war crime (i.e., an illegal act of reprisal). The arbitral panel that heard the case disagreed and exonerated the United States, holding Farragut's action to have been a "lawful and justifiable act of war, caused by the firing of the Confederate military forces, with the complicity of the inhabitants of Donaldsville."[186]

Distinct from these cases of actual collaboration of civilians in unlawful forms of warfare—in principle at least if not always in practice—were situations of reprisal, that is, cases in which action was taken against civilians without actual proof of participation in the original wrongdoing. An example was the policy ordered in Virginia by General Pope. When Union troops were fired on from a house, the house would be razed to the ground and the inhabitants imprisoned.[187]

In a number of instances, the reprisal broom swept more widely. In September 1862, General Sherman burned the town of Randolph, Tennessee, to the ground, following guerrilla attacks on boats that were being unloaded there. Punishment for such action, he maintained, must be "speedy, sure, and exemplary"—although, at the same time, he disclaimed any intention to commit "wanton mischief or destruction." The particular town, in his opinion, was "of no importance, but the example should be followed up on all similar occasions."[188]

The following month, Sherman indicated a willingness to consider further measures affecting civilians. The problem of attacks on boats, he suggested, might be dealt with by landing troops "on unexpected points and devastat[ing] the country into the interior." He also considered a policy of expelling civilian families from occupied Memphis in response to such attacks.[189] By 1864, such measures had gone beyond the stage of mere contemplation. In his famous (or notorious) March to the Sea from Atlanta to Savannah in the autumn of 1864, Sherman showed a determination to punish civilians for supporting guerrilla activity. He ordered his subordinate commanders to "enforce a devastation more or less relentless, according to the measure of such hostility."[190]

Another strategy sometimes adopted was to make civilians collectively responsible for rectifying damage inflicted by guerrillas. Pope illustrated this approach when he announced, in his July 1862 campaign in Virginia, that, in cases of destruction of railroads, telegraphs, or wagon-roads, the entire civilian population in a five-mile radius would be turned out "in mass" for repair work. They would also be assessed the expenses incurred by the Union forces in the policing of this *corvée* duty.[191]

In Missouri, General Schofield devised an elaborate policy along this line. For each Union soldier or citizen killed, the county in which the act occurred would be assessed $5,000. For each one wounded, the tariff would be $1,000 to $5,000. In addition, the full value of property stolen by guerrillas would be repaid. The money would be allocated to the victims by an assessment board set up for each county. If the assessments were not paid within "a reasonable time," then property would be confiscated in the amount due.[192] A cruder and more direct application of this approach was exemplified by Sherman in Mississippi in 1864. In response to guerrilla attacks on steamboats, he seized a thousand bales of cotton, with (apparently) no discrimination between loyal and disloyal owners. He then turned the goods over to Treasury Department agents for sale, with the intention that the proceeds would be used to compensate the boat owners.[193]

Harshest of all were policies of "area denial," which included denuding an area of resources so as to make it impossible for guerrillas to operate there. That such policies had the sanction of the law was apparent from the writing of Vattel, who made it clear that civilians could not expect to be wholly exempt from the horrors of war. To "plunder and lay waste" to a country, he noted, is generally not unlawful, although it should only be done in cases of "evident necessity" or for "urgent reasons."[194] The Lieber Code took much the same position. "Military necessity," it stated, allowed "all destruction of property, and obstruction of the ways and channels of traffic, travel, or communication, and of all withholding of sustenance or means of life from the enemy."[195] At the same time, though, the code expressly prohibited "the wanton devastation of a district."[196] The line between the two types of action could easily become blurred in practice.

General Philip Sheridan was the principal exemplar of this severe approach when, in August 1864, he began a campaign of destruction and seizure of crops and livestock in the Shenandoah Valley. He explicitly instructed his officers to explain to the local population what the purpose of "this delicate, but necessary, duty" was: "to make this Valley untenable for the raiding parties of the rebel army."[197] That goal appears to have been accomplished with ruthless efficiency. His forces were estimated to have destroyed over two thousand barns and seventy mills, and also to have driven away some four thousand head of livestock.[198]

In November, Sheridan visited a similar fate upon Loudoun County, Virginia, near Washington, ordering his forces to "consume and destroy all forage and subsistence, burn all barns and mills and their contents, and drive off all stock." Here too, the purpose was to deprive the enemy of potential subsistence. The order, it was insisted, was to be "literally executed."[199] Sheridan did, however, caution his troops that no dwellings were to be burned and no personal violence committed against the citizens. It will be observed in due course that this order became the subject of litigation after war.[200]

It should be appreciated that the principle of military necessity, which was the basis for these destructive actions, made no distinction between friend and foe. When the goal was to deny sustenance and support to the enemy, then indiscriminate destruction was in order. The Confederates followed much the same policy in similar cases of necessity. In March 1862, the Confederate Congress authorized the military to destroy cotton, tobacco, and other forms of property in order to prevent them from falling into enemy hands.[201] The policy was soon put to practical use, when Secretary of War Randolph ordered the general destruction of cotton and tobacco in the New Orleans area in the face of the Union advance on the city.[202]

Similarly drastic were policies of forcible population movement. For the most part, these were directed against disloyal persons. In St. Augustine, Florida, in 1862, all local civilians were required to take an oath of allegiance—with those who declined then being driven out of the Union lines.[203] Authorities in New Orleans adopted a similar policy the following year, requiring persons who were registered enemies to leave the military department.[204] In Missouri, always the most troublesome area for the Union with respect to irregular warfare, General Thomas Ewing ordered that disloyal persons were to be forced to be leave the state, although they were to be allowed to take livestock, provisions, and household goods with them. Those who declined to leave on their own would be forcibly taken to Kansas City "for shipment south." Ewing did, however, expressly order his forces to "discriminate as carefully as possible" between those who were compelled, by threats or fears, to aid the rebels and those who aided them from disloyal motives.[205]

In Virginia, General Pope took similar steps. In July 1862, he announced that all disloyal male citizens within the lines of his forces were to be arrested. If they agreed to take an oath of loyalty (and to support it by providing security), then they could remain. Otherwise, they were to be expelled, specifically, left to wander over to the Confederate-held areas as best they could. Those who took oaths of loyalty and were later found to have violated them would be shot, and their property seized and applied to public use.[206] (It was in re-

sponse to this policy that the Confederates determined, as noted, to deny
prisoner-of-war treatment to Pope if he was captured.) General Grant, in 1864,
determined to subject Loudoun County, Virginia, to a similar treatment. He
urged Sheridan to adopt a policy of arresting *all* men under fifty years of age
in the county who were capable of bearing arms, and then holding them as
prisoners of war in order to keep them from joining (or being forced into) the
ranks of guerrillas.[207]

The most drastic of all the population-removal policies came in August
1863 in Missouri, when General Ewing ordered the *complete* evacuation of
three counties in Missouri (along with part of a fourth)—without regard to
the loyalty or disloyalty of the persons affected. Fifteen days were allotted for
the movement. Persons in possession of loyalty certificates could go to any
military station within the district (which was adjacent to the Kansas border).
Others had to leave the district and make their way as best they could. Grain
and hay were to be taken and delivered to the military, with an implied promise that loyal owners would receive compensation at some point.[208] The suffering caused by this wholesale expulsion order was immense; the affected area
was known for many years afterward as the "burnt district."[209]

A problem with these harsh policies was that they risked exacerbating the
very problem that they were designed to deal with. They caused vast outrage
in the Confederacy, making it easier for propagandists to portray the Union
forces as oppressive and cruel tyrants; and they risked alienating local populations by exposing innocent persons to harsh tactics. Halleck showed his sensi-
tivity to this consideration when, in September 1862, he gave his approval to
Schofield's population-removal measures. In so doing, however, he stressed
that "this power should be sparingly exercised, as it is not good policy to increase the ranks of the enemy by sending South all their friends and sympathizers." Consequently, no one should be molested "without good and
satisfactory evidence" that the person actually presented a danger to public
safety.[210] Because of considerations of this sort, drastic measures affecting
civilians were often not enforced to anything like the letter of their initial pronouncements.[211]

Taking Enemy Private Property

Requisition, capture, and destruction were the three basic forms of takings of
enemy private property. Requisitions (or "contributions" in the older parl-

ance) will be considered first, as these were the least controversial form of interference with private property. The basic principle here was simple enough
in theory, even if it was not always easily applied in practice. Private property
could be taken from enemy civilians in case of *actual* need by the armed forces,
for their *own* use.[212] Under American constitutional law, the Fifth Amendment requires that, when private property is taken "for public use" (such as the
sustenance of the armed forces), "just compensation" must be paid to the
owner. This compensation duty, however, only applies when the property is
taken in the exercise of the sovereign right of the government. It does not apply to property taking by way of belligerent right, which is the category into
which requisitions from enemy nationals fall.[213] Instead of a duty of compensation, there is a duty on the belligerent's part to exercise due restraint—to be
moderate in its demands, and to take no more than is actually required in the
specific circumstances at hand.[214]

This right of requisition was sometimes exercised on a significant scale,
chiefly in instances in which an army's military operations called for greater
mobility than its commissariat was capable of achieving. A good illustration
was the operation of Grant's armies in Mississippi in late 1862, in the early
stages of the Vicksburg campaign.[215] This would appear to have been a genuine military operation, dependent for its success on a high degree of speed
and mobility—greater speed and mobility, as it happened, than was possible
for a military supply train of the time.[216] More doubtful was the policy of
General Pope in Virginia, announced in July 1862, of having his troops live off
the countryside, with the local towns "laid under contribution" for this purpose.[217] Vouchers were to be issued, to enable loyal (but not disloyal) contrib-
utors to be compensated after the war. This policy may well have been
designed as a kind of collective punishment, since it appeared from the text of
the orders that a conscious choice was being made in favor of reliance on requisitions, even where commissary services were possible.[218] If this was so, then
Pope's policy amounted to a war crime.

The most notorious instance of an army deliberately living off the civilian
population in its area of operation was, of course, Sherman's March to the Sea
in the autumn of 1864. The explicit policy, ordered by Sherman himself, was
that the army was to "forage liberally on the country during the march." In
particular, horses, mules, and wagons were permitted to be taken "freely and
without limit." Persons whose animals were taken were to be issued with "certificates of the facts," but it was also specified that these would *not* constitute

receipts—i.e., that they would not entitle the holders to obtain compensation from the federal government. Some restrictions were imposed. Soldiers were instructed not to enter private dwellings or commit any personal violence against civilians. In areas where the army was not molested, the civilian property was to be altogether spared. Soldiers should "[e]ndeavor" to leave each family with "a reasonable portion for their maintenance." They were even to refrain from "abusive or threatening language."[219]

The other two forms of taking enemy private property—capture and destruction—are permissible, like requisition, under the heading of military necessity, that is, when they are done as part of a military operation designed to bring about the defeat of the enemy. Several important points should be noted about the traditional belligerent right of capture in land warfare, as it existed in the Middle Ages and subsequent centuries.[220] The first is that it was a right to appropriate any and all property belonging to enemy nationals, without limit and without any need to demonstrate that the capture, in particular cases, actually made a contribution to the war effort or was required for the army's own use. It should also be noted that ownership by *any* enemy national (or resident of enemy territory) sufficed to justify the capture. Whether the actual owner, in a given case, actually supported the enemy's war effort or not was entirely irrelevant.[221] Moreover, the act of capture *itself*—i.e., the taking of the property into the physical custody—automatically effected a transfer of legal title to the property from the original owner to the captor state.[222]

This traditional belligerent right to capture enemy private property was a sign of what might fairly be called a total-war mentality that prevailed in the law of war in the Middle Ages. The thesis was that *all* nationals of an enemy state, even civilians plying their ordinary trades, are automatically regarded as enemies and liable to be treated as such. The underlying thesis was that any citizen's property might, at any time, be put to use by his or her ruler in furtherance of the war effort. Even in the Middle Ages, however, this generous policy (to captors) began to be mitigated; and, at least in European land warfare, the view gradually took hold that private property should not be subject to capture.

International lawyers were hesitant, though, to institute an outright *prohibition* against the capturing of private property. Vattel, in the middle of the eighteenth century, held it to be still lawful.[223] The Lieber Code did not contain an explicit general prohibition against the capture of enemy private property on land.[224] The traditional belligerent right of capture therefore maintained a sort of vestigial existence. It is perhaps best to say that the circum-stances in which the right could be exercised were considerably narrowed over the course of time, but without the right *itself* being altogether abolished. In all events, by the nineteenth century, it was widely regarded as unlawful to *exercise* the traditional right of capture except in cases of military necessity (i.e., situa-tions in which its exercise made a genuine contribution to the war effort).

Midway through the conflict, Congress, in effect, made a determination that such an exceptional case of military necessity was present, by enacting a law popularly known as the Captured and Abandoned Property Act, in March 1863.[225] The principal effect of this legislation was to allow the capture of pri-vately owned cotton supplies in the South.[226] It has been estimated that cot-ton comprised as much as 95 percent of the property taken pursuant to the law.[227] The basic policy was that property covered by the act was to be taken into custody by the armed forces and then turned over to agents of the Trea-sury Department for sale, by auction, to private buyers in the Union states.[228]

There was some vacillation over the years on the part of the Supreme Court as to the legal justification for this departure from the usual practice of not tak-ing enemy private property. In 1865, the Court pronounced it to be well known "that cotton has constituted the chief reliance of the rebels for means to pur-chase the munitions of war in Europe. . . . The rebels regard it as one of their main sinews of war."[229] In a case in 1870, the Court held, somewhat vaguely, that cotton, by virtue of "its peculiar character and its uses," constituted an ex-ception to the general rule against the capture of private property on land.[230] Three years later, the Court delphically referred to captured and abandoned property as "a peculiar species of property," known only during the Civil War (and therefore, presumably, not covered by the existing laws of war).[231]

Later, however, the Court took a still different tack, by explicitly holding the taking of captured and abandoned property to be a remnant of the old general right to capture any and all enemy-owned property in war. That right, strictly speaking, remained in force, the Court held. There was merely a mod-ern *practice* on the part of declining to exercise it, as a matter of grace. As a result, states could lawfully reassert the traditional right in appropriate circum-stances such as the present one.[232] In all events, the captured-and-abandoned-property program became the principal vehicle for the confiscation of property belonging to disloyal Southerners.[233]

One important point about captured and abandoned property, which would loom large in the aftermath of the war, is worth stressing. As a remnant of the traditional general right to capture enemy property, the policy targeted property belonging to *any* enemy national (or resident), without regard to his or her personal sentiments. The act of capture *per se,* therefore, fell with equal harshness on both loyal and disloyal persons in the South. At the same time, however, and from the very outset, it was provided that a distinction would *later* be made between loyal and disloyal victims of the capture policy. This would be achieved by holding the proceeds of sale of captured and abandoned property in a special account separate from the general government funds in the Treasury. Loyal owners—but not disloyal ones—were given a statutory right to claim these proceeds of sale back from the government for a period of two years after the end of the war.[234] (The property *itself* could not be recovered, as it would have been sold at auction to a third party.) Disloyal owners, in contrast, would simply be left to suffer the loss. It will be seen in due course that this aspect of the policy would provide abundant employment for the federal courts for many years following the war.[235]

Destruction of Civilian Infrastructure

More extreme than either the requisitioning or the capturing of enemy-owned property was its outright destruction. One form that this policy assumed has been noted: the devastation of areas with a view to making it impossible for guerrillas to subsist. In addition, both sides engaged in the destruction of cotton supplies, to keep that valuable commodity from falling into the hands of the opposing party. Most drastic of all the practices of the Civil War, though, was the policy of extending this policy to encompass the deliberate and systematic destruction of civilian infrastructure and economic assets—a practice to which the label "total war" is sometimes applied (a term coined, it would appear, by Giulio Douhet, the Italian prophet of air power and strategic bombing, in 1921).[236]

Such a policy was, at least on its face, a flagrant departure from the fundamental principle that the sole purpose of war is the overcoming of the enemy armed force on the field of battle. The justification for this departure—as usual—was military necessity, in its permissive guise: the thesis that anything that actually contributed to military victory was permissible, provided that it was not actually *forbidden* by the laws of war. Moreover, in this area, much as in the case of capture, the grim history of the laws of war loomed heavily over the present. In the Middle Ages, it had been held that *all* nationals of the contending sides were automatically enemies of one another—hence fair game for hostile measures. That this traditional view of war was not regarded as wholly obsolete was apparent from the Lieber Code, which candidly stated that "[t]he citizen or native of a hostile country is . . . an enemy, as one of the constituents of the hostile state or nation, and as such is subjected to the hardships of war."[237]

Destruction of economic resources on at least a modest scale began quite early in the conflict. When Stonewall Jackson evacuated Harper's Ferry after the outbreak of the war, he took as much property of the Baltimore and Ohio Railroad with him as possible. But he also destroyed a great deal more, which he was unable to take. Forty-two locomotives were destroyed, along with some 386 cars. In addition, twenty-three bridges were burned and 102 miles of telegraph line pulled down. As a result of these depredations, it took some nine months for the Union to put the railroad back into working order.[238] More—much more—was to come.

A decisive step was taken in mid-1863, in the wake of the fall of Vicksburg, when Sherman began a program of systematic destruction in the vicinity of Jackson, Mississippi. Railroads were dismantled for ten miles on either side of the city. Factories and cotton stocks were burned, while foragers fanned out over the countryside, "absolutely stripping the country of corn, cattle, hogs, sheep, poultry, everything," as Sherman reported (with some obvious professional pride) to Grant. He confessed that the "wholesale destruction" being visited on the area was "terrible to contemplate"—but he also carefully pointed out that it was an unavoidable element of the conflict.[239] This marked the first major occasion in the conflict of deliberate, systematic, and large-scale destruction of civilian infrastructure.

At least by the later part of the conflict, the policy of destroying civilian economic infrastructure had the wholehearted approval of Halleck. He instructed Sherman, after Atlanta was taken, that "every mill and factory within . . . reach" should be destroyed (unless it was required by the Union forces for their *own* use). Even now, though, a line continued to be drawn—in principle if not always in practice—between the destruction of economic assets useful to the enemy war effort and the destruction of materials required by civilians for personal subsistence. Halleck expressly disapproved of any policy of burning private dwellings or "uselessly destroying private property." Such conduct, in his view, was "barbarous." But anything that "may serve as supplies to us or to the enemy's armies" could be taken or destroyed in good conscience.[240]

In his March to the Sea through Georgia after the capture of Atlanta, Sherman put Halleck's advice into practice on a large scale by embarking on a program of systematic destruction of civilian economic infrastructure. Rome, Georgia, was singled out most explicitly on this score. Sherman ordered that foundries, mills, workshops, wagon-shops, and tanneries be destroyed, along with any other factories "that may prove useful to the enemy."[241] On Sherman's own testimony, the destruction of economic assets far outweighed the "liberal foraging" component of the March. He estimated the damage inflicted at $100 million—with $20 million comprising property taken for the use of the Union forces themselves, and the remainder being, in that doughty soldier's frank admission, "simple waste and destruction."[242]

There was never a judicial pronouncement on the lawfulness of this particular campaign. Historians, rather than judges, have been left the task of answering this question. Much in the manner of lawyers, they evince a plurality of views. One has characterized the Georgia campaign as one of "deliberate terrorism."[243] Another has emphasized the degree of restraint that was exercised.[244] Without attempting a definitive conclusion on this point, it may be observed that Sherman's Georgia campaign was not, either in its intention or its execution, merely a blind, free-for-all pillage spree, as some stereotypes would have it. Nor was it particularly destructive of human life. In the entire march from Atlanta to Savannah, there was not a single white civilian casualty. It was, however—and ironically—otherwise in the case of blacks, who did suffer abuses from their supposed liberators.[245] It should also be remembered that the destruction of civilian property for war purposes was no monopoly of the Union forces. The Confederacy had an official policy of destroying property in areas that were about to fall under Union control—a policy that was much in evidence in the Carolinas in the face of Sherman's northward advance of early 1865.[246]

It was only in the northward phase of Sherman's campaign that abuses against began to occur on a very large scale. This was especially the case for South Carolina, which was widely seen, with some justice, as the fountainhead of secession and Southern intransigence generally. Here, discipline seriously deteriorated; and scandalous abuses of civilians became common. The single most notorious incident was the burning of Columbia, South Carolina, in February 1865. An arbitral decision after the war held the burning to have been accidental, but there was certainly serious negligence in evidence.[247] The special status of South Carolina in this regard became further evident when the "destructive orgy" (as it has been described) halted abruptly with the army's passage into North Carolina, which was perceived, again with reason, as being far less fanatically devoted to the Confederate cause than its southern neighbor.[248]

It would be comforting to suppose that the Civil War marked the start of a much-needed clarification of the laws of war and of greater protection for civilian populations. The sad reality is that it was the opposite: it was an early demonstration—and, by later standards, a distinctly moderate one—of how great is the scope for civilian suffering in time of war. The problem of civilian victimization by war operations escalated so dramatically in the twentieth century that it almost seems hardly worth while to worry unduly over what happened during the Civil War. It is a problem that, by the early twenty-first century, was as far from resolution as ever. Further developments are awaited in this area of the law—but perhaps with more trepidation than hope.

4

Occupying Territory and
Seizing Property

No great territory has been permanently reduced without depriving the
leaders of its people of their land and property. It is these that give power
and influence. Few men have the commanding genius and talent to exercise dangerous influence over their fellow-men without the adventitious
aid of money and property.

—Edwin Stanton

The Union War effort was prosecuted not only on the battlefields and siege
lines but also behind the scenes. In the one case, the target was the enemy's
armed forces; and in the other, the enemy's property. Two very different kinds
of property will be considered in this connection. First will be Southern territory occupied by the Union armies. A systematic and comprehensive study of
the Union government's occupation policy (or policies) will not be possible in
the present context. But some important general points will be offered, concerning the legal character of the Union presence in the Southern states, and
the various choices and dilemmas that faced the federal government in that
area. The other type of property that will be considered is the privately owned
property of disloyal persons and—more particularly—the confiscation measures that were deployed against them. These gave rise to a host of legal problems that clogged the federal courts for years after the war ended.

Sitting on Bayonets

Questions of how to deal with occupied—or recovered—territory began to
present themselves early in the conflict. In the period up to February 1862, the

Union gained control of coastal regions of North and South Carolina, as well as western Virginia. In that month, the first major city (Nashville) fell into Union hands in the wake of General Grant's victories at Forts Henry and Donaldson.[1] But the major feat of occupation, by a large margin, was that of New Orleans—the largest city in the Confederacy—in April of that year.[2] From the legal standpoint, the Union was spoiled for choice on the question of how to treat these occupations. There were three possible legal regimes, each with its own distinctive characteristics. First was straight resumption of the presecession situation. Second was belligerent occupation. Third was conquest. A brief overview of each of these, with their respective merits and demerits, is in order. A similar survey of actual Union policy will reveal that the federal government never committed itself, on a global basis, to any one of these three but ended up adopting a kind of untidy blend of belligerent occupation and martial law.[3]

Resumption of Prewar Status

The first possible legal model for the occupations was reversion to the prewar status quo. This amounted to the assertion that, in occupying Confederate territory, the federal government was simply regaining effective control of territory that had always legally been part of the Union. The situation was analogous, on this theory, to the recovery of stolen property from a thief, the consequence of which is simply an automatic resumption of the preexisting legal position. This way of looking at things had one very obvious attraction. It logically entailed the complete effacing of the Confederate experience from the legal and political life of the areas concerned. In particular, it implied that the secession measures enacted by the Southern states would be regarded as automatically void.[4]

An important implication of this continuity theory (as it has sometimes been termed) was that the recovered areas would automatically reacquire all of the autonomy that they had previously possessed. This meant that the federal government would have no significant power to interfere in the domestic political and social arrangements of the recovered areas. Most obviously, the Southern states could retain slavery if they so chose. In addition, it would not be possible for any significant penalties or disabilities to be inflicted on the Southern states (although disloyal *persons* could still be punished in various ways, such as by prosecution for treason). For those of a vindictive turn of mind, as well as for those who believed that the Southern social system was in need of some radical changes, the idea of resumption of prewar status was un-attractive in the extreme.[5]

This continuity theory also had the effect of giving to Congress an impor-tant, if somewhat indirect, role in the arrangements for the recovered territo-ries by virtue of its prerogative to determine whether would-be representatives and senators from the recovered Southern areas would be allowed to take their seats or not. This arose from the constitutional provision that "[e]ach House shall be the Judge of the Elections, Returns and Qualifications of its own Members."[6] By making use of this power, the two Houses of Congress (inde-pendently of one another) could effectively signal their approval or disap-proval of policies that the executive pursued in the occupied areas.

Congress was not shy about making use of this power, sometimes to the discomfiture of the executive. An early example occurred in the wake of a House of Representatives election held in the occupied part of North Carolina in November 1862. The winner was barred by Congress from sitting, largely on the ground that the electorate that had chosen him was derisorily tiny in number. In one "election" held in a district of Virginia that was virtually entirely in Confederate hands, the winning candidate had only twenty-five votes. He was not seated. Another Virginia representative was allowed initially to sit, only to be expelled when it was discovered that he had received a mere ten votes at his election.[7]

Representation in the Senate entailed different considerations, since sena-tors at that time were chosen not by popular vote but rather by state legisla-tures. (This remained the case until 1913, when the Seventeenth Amendment to the Constitution took effect.) It was therefore necessary for a senatorial elec-tion that there be a functioning and recognized legislature in the relevant state. On this count, Virginia was uniquely well positioned, since it—alone of all the Southern states—possessed what would later be referred to as a government-in-exile. This rival government had been formed from scratch by a convention of Union loyalists. In fact, the convention simply converted itself into (sup-posedly) the legislature of the state. This "Wheeling government," as it was known (after the town in which it was first located) obviously lacked any sem-blance of effective control over the state as a whole. But it was nevertheless recognized by the federal executive as the lawful government of Virginia, en-abling it to dispatch two senators to Washington, who were duly allowed to take their seats in July 1861.[8]

Louisiana was rather less successful than Virginia in obtaining representation in the Senate. A constitutional convention held in March 1864 chose two senators. The Radical Republicans in Washington, however, were unhappy with some of the provisions of the constitution the convention drafted (notably its failure to grant the right to vote to nonwhites). And they were able to muster sufficient strength to prevent the seating of their two would-be colleagues.[9]

Congress was disposed, however, to allow representatives to take their seats if the elections were more or less regularly conducted. For example, three representatives from Virginia, elected prior to the state's secession, were duly seated by the House, having been chosen in an entirely regular manner. Another Virginia person, chosen in a special election in January 1862, was also seated. Texas elected two representatives in August 1861, on the state's regular election day; and they were accepted by the House.[10]

On the whole, it may be concluded that the principle of straight reversion to prewar status did not receive wide support. The executive was wary of the role it gave to Congress in the seating or nonseating of representatives. In Congress, Radical elements were loath to forego opportunities to reconstitute Southern society along more egalitarian lines than before. On the judicial front, Justice Samuel Nelson of the federal Supreme Court pressed for it in a dissenting opinion in 1865, relating to the capture of New Orleans; but the Court did not decide the issue on that occasion.[11] Not until long after the war, in 1879, did the Supreme Court finally pronounce on the matter, by expressly rejecting the thesis that the occupation of New Orleans automatically brought about a restoration of normal relations with the Union.[12]

Belligerent Occupation

A second possible approach was to make use of the laws of war, which recognized the occupation of enemy territory—or *belligerent occupation* as it is commonly known—as a standard means of waging war.[13] Several of its most important features should be noted. Perhaps the most fundamental of these was its inherently temporary character. This stemmed from the fact that belligerent occupation is regarded as a stratagem for prosecuting and winning the war. It is a means of gaining and holding a *military* advantage of some kind.

Belligerent occupation, as the name clearly implies, is the exercise of a *belligerent* right. In fact, one of the most important of all belligerent prerogatives (or rights of war) is the right to occupy territory of the enemy. This naturally means that occupation, as a belligerent operation, can entail no claim to sovereignty over the area by the occupying power, since there is always the possibility that the fortunes of war will reverse and the area be recovered by its true sovereign. Transfer of full sovereignty over an occupied territory can only come about in two ways: by conquest (which will be considered presently) or by means of a peace treaty at the conclusion of the war in question. In essence, a belligerent occupier is best regarded not as a sovereign in its own right but rather as a substitute for the legitimate sovereign—with the implication that the occupier must maintain and administer the *existing* law of the territory rather than imposing its own.

More specifically, the arrival of an army in the territory of its enemy had two principal effects, one concerning the law governing the area, and the other concerning the relation of the inhabitants to the occupiers. First, regarding the governing law. The Lieber Code stated that a military occupation had the *automatic* effect of bringing what it called "martial law" into operation for the area. This meant that the law of the region could be overridden by command of the occupiers, to the extent that the occupying force deemed necessary for military purposes.[14] At the same time, however, it was envisaged that ordinary civil and criminal laws would continue to take their "usual course," and that there would only be actual suspension of the "governmental functions" of the sovereign (i.e., that the legislative, executive, and administrative tasks of the previous government would now pass into the hands of the occupying force).[15]

The second principal—and automatic—effect of a military occupation was that the occupants of the occupied area became subject to a duty of allegiance to their new rulers. The principal form which this took was a prohibition against the supplying of information by the residents of an occupied territory to the armies of their sovereign state—an act that was essentially the same as spying, but which was designated by the Lieber Code as "war-treason."[16] (The distinction between the two was that spying was the obtaining of information by serving soldiers, operating in civilian guise, while war treason was the obtaining and transferring of information by civilians in occupied areas.)[17]

Similar in some respects to war traitors were persons whom the Lieber Code called "war rebels."[18] This somewhat quaint term referred to inhabitants of an occupied territory who, not content with merely supplying information to their national armies, go further and "rise in arms" against the occupiers. These persons were regarded as a category of unlawful combatants, who are denied prisoner-of-war status and who were also subject to the death penalty for their operations.

It was not the intention of the laws of war, however, that belligerent occupation should weigh too onerously on the affected population. For one thing, as noted above, it was accepted that, at least in the usual cases, civil and criminal laws of the territory would continue to have their usual force. In addition, the Lieber Code stressed the imperative duty of occupiers to be "strictly guided by the principles of justice, honor, and humanity" in their administration.[19] On a more practical level, when property was requisitioned for the use of the Union armies from an occupied territory—as opposed to being taken from an enemy population while on the march—compensation had to be paid, on the ground that the population of the territory could no longer be regarded as enemies in the fullest sense.[20]

The modern law of occupation of territory, as it evolved after 1865, has rejected the position of the Lieber Code on the question of a duty of allegiance. Although the matter is not wholly free from doubt, the better view would seem to be that residents of an occupied territory do *not* have such a legal duty to the occupier. Residents can, to be sure, be punished for acts prejudicial to the occupation. But this is best seen as resting on the basis that the occupier possesses an inherent right of self-defense—a right that is grounded in necessity and is therefore *not* matched by a corresponding duty of obedience or loyalty on the part of the discontented resident.[21]

Belligerent occupation bears a very strong family resemblance to martial law, to the point that the Lieber Code uses the term "martial law" in reference to both.[22] They are similar in that both involve the rule of civilian areas by military commanders—in the one case, with a portion of the commander's *own* people being governed; and in the other case, with a portion of the enemy's population being ruled over. In terms of the prerogatives of the military rulers and the duties of obedience of the population, the two are much the same. The chief distinction between them lies in their permitted duration. Martial-law rule over a commander's own population must cease once the emergency that provoked it has passed.[23] Belligerent occupation, in contrast, can continue for as long as the belligerent has the strength to hold onto the territory. But in the Civil War, the two were not always very carefully distinguished in practice.

On several occasions, martial law was declared in occupied portions of the Confederate states. A formal proclamation of martial law was promulgated, for example, in St. Augustine, Florida, in April 1862.[24] That same month, General David Hunter grandly proclaimed the whole of South Carolina, Georgia, and Florida to be under martial law (even though there was actual Union control only of a few coastal enclaves in those states).[25]

The most notable example of a martial-law proclamation for an occupied area occurred in New Orleans, at the hands of General Benjamin Butler shortly after the Union taking of the city in 1862.[26] New Orleans, he announced, was now to be governed "by the law martial," promising at the same time that property rights would be regarded as "inviolate." Inhabitants were urged to go about their normal business. Misdemeanors, together with all civil actions, would be dealt with by the municipal authorities. More serious cases of disorder would be the concern of military courts. No publication would be allowed "tending in any way to influence the public mind against the Government of the United States." For publications that were allowed, there was censorship in the form of a requirement of prior submission to military authorities of all news stories and commentary. Municipal authority was suspended (except for the judicial functions that were expressly reserved for it). The fire department was permitted to continue in operation as before. Telegrams could only be sent under military supervision. Finally, the populace was warned that martial law would be "vigorously and firmly administered as occasion calls." The following month, an oath of loyalty was required of all persons performing any legal or judicial positions, such as sheriffs, attorneys, and notaries.[27]

The temporary or provisional character of belligerent occupation naturally made it a somewhat unattractive model for Union rule in the Southern states, since the natural preference was to view Union control as permanent. It may be noted that this was one important respect in which the Union's policy of pointedly not recognizing the Confederacy as a belligerent power in the full legal sense made a concrete difference. A full recognition of belligerent status would have meant (or at least strongly implied) that any territory taken by the Union armed forces could *only* be governed on the basis of belligerent occupation and not of full sovereignty. But the Union authorities were careful never to accept such a thesis. There was even some tendency to regard the *Confederate* government as a belligerent occupier of the Southern states—a theory to which the federal Supreme Court gave some support after the war, when it characterized the Confederacy as a "government of paramount force."[28]

Conquest

The third possible legal characterization of the Union presence in the South was *conquest*. This, as might readily be surmised, entailed the highest degree of control of the three available legal models, since it entails the acquisition of full sovereignty over the captured area by the occupying state. Conquest in the true legal sense, however, was (and continues to be) a somewhat obscure and misunderstood subject, even for lawyers. It is best seen as the real-property counterpart of capture, in which the very act of taking possession of an enemy's personal property automatically operates to transfer legal title.[29] The position is much the same with conquest, with the act of acquisition operating as a transfer of sovereignty.

A key point in this regard is that a very high degree of control is required for conquest—much higher than for mere belligerent occupation. Basically, conquest requires *complete* control of the acquired area, to the total exclusion of the previous sovereign, with the ingress and egress of all persons carefully policed. Hugo Grotius, the great natural-law and international-law writer of the seventeenth century, held that conquered territory must be "so surrounded by permanent fortification that the [enemy] will have no access to it."[30] Once conquest was effected according to this demanding standard, the conquering state acquired full sovereignty, including an unlimited right to determine the legal arrangements in the area.[31] It should also be appreciated that conquest, in the true legal sense, is different from the acquisition of territory by way of peace treaty at the end of a war. That is, strictly speaking, a transfer of legal title by way of cession. Conquest in the true legal sense is an acquisition of title to territory *during* a war, achieved by the unilateral effort of one of the belligerents.[32]

The American Constitution makes no explicit provision for conquest. It appears likely enough that the United States possesses the right of conquest as an adjunct of its war-waging power, although there is no clear instance in American history of an acquisition of title by this means.[33] One of the drawbacks—or, depending on one's view, advantages—of this legal vehicle for occupation is that the ruling of conquered territories is not exclusively a presidential prerogative, as belligerent occupation is. On the contrary, the Constitution expressly grants to Congress the power to make "all needful Rules and Regulations" regarding "Property belonging to the United States."[34] For that reason, there was a great deal of interest in regarding the Southern states as conquered territory in the aftermath of the conflict. But that contentious story belongs more to the history of Reconstruction than to that of the war itself.[35]

Union Policy in Action

The Union government did not ever commit itself with any decisiveness or consistency to any one of these three models. It is safe to say, though, that, in practice, belligerent occupation (with its close juridical cousin martial law) provided the dominant model for Union policy in the increasingly occupied Confederate states. There was judicial confirmation of this in several instances. For example, in 1865 a federal court in Louisiana characterized the situation in that state as one of "armed belligerent occupation," carried out by the President under his powers as commander-in-chief.[36] Several years after the war, the federal Supreme Court expressed a similar view.[37] It has been observed that, many years after the war, the Supreme Court rejected the theory of reversion of prewar status.[38] Conquest played an important part in federal dealings with the Southern states, but chiefly after the war, in the context of Reconstruction, rather than during it.

One clear virtue of the belligerent-occupation model was that it fell unambiguously within the President's prerogatives as commander-in-chief of the armed forces, thereby conveniently allowing Congress to be kept at arm's length.[39] Some of the dispositions made by President Lincoln during the struggle accordingly did bear at least a resemblance to measures of belligerent occupation. Foremost among these was the appointment of military governors for the acquired areas, who were quite distinct from the field commanders of the forces. The first such appointment was of Senator Andrew Johnson, who was appointed military governor of his home state of Tennessee in March 1862. Later that same year, military governors were appointed for North Carolina, Louisiana, and Arkansas, as well as for the Sea Islands off the coast of South Carolina and Georgia.[40]

At the end of 1863, President Lincoln attempted to bring a much-needed element of coherence into policies toward the occupied areas, in the form of what came to be known as the 10 Percent Plan.[41] The essence of this proposal was that, once 10 percent of the voting population had taken an oath of loyalty to the Union and the federal Constitution, a regular state government could be reestablished—with only loyal persons allowed to participate in it. It

was expected that any states so reestablished would provide for the emancipation of slaves, although that was not expressly stated to be a prerequisite to
readmission to the Union.

An opposition proposal was then put forward by Benjamin Wade in the
Senate and Henry Winter Davis in the House. This Wade-Davis proposal was
considerably more stringent, most notably in requiring 50 percent to swear allegiance instead of only 10 percent, as in Lincoln's plan. Emancipation of
slaves was stated as another explicit condition. In the interest of gaining conservative support in Congress, the Wade-Davis bill specified that the suffrage
would be limited to whites, as in the Lincoln plan.[42]

This measure was approved by Congress, but then pocket-vetoed by Lincoln.[43] Although the Constitution does not require a President to state reasons
in such a case (as it does in the case of ordinary vetoes), Lincoln did so anyway.
He maintained that Congress had no power to abolish slavery in a slave state,
in the absence of a constitutional amendment. In addition, Lincoln objected
to the fact that the Wade-Davis proposal implicitly conceded that the Southern states had been successful in seceding from the Union, something he was
not prepared to admit. Finally, Lincoln was opposed to the inflexibility of the
plan, preferring that the government not be legally locked into a particular reconstruction plan at the very outset of what was clearly going to be a delicate
process.[44]

The first test of Lincoln's 10 Percent Plan for reconstruction came in
Arkansas, when three persons were elected in late 1863 and early 1864 to the federal House of Representatives. In an ominous sign of a growing rift between the
executive and Congress on the reconstruction question, the three were not allowed to sit—although, curiously, the House permitted them to draw their
salaries, on the ground that they had presented persuasive claims to their
seats.[45] The Senate also refused to seat two would-be members from Arkansas.
In these votes, there was an interesting alliance of Radicals and conservatives—
the Radicals being unhappy about the dominant role being played by the President at the expense of Congress, and the conservatives upset at the narrowness
of the electorate (i.e., the exclusion of too many slavery-inclined Democrats).
One conservative senator derided Arkansas as "a rotten borough government
established by Abraham Lincoln, and not by the people of Arkansas."[46]

Some special attention is in order regarding Virginia, which was unique in
two noteworthy (and related) respects. One was its possession of a government-
in-exile, in the form of the Wheeling government. The other unique feature

was that, also alone of all the Confederate states, Virginia suffered a reduction in size, when a new state—West Virginia—was carved out from its territory.[47] This process brought some awkward legal questions to the fore. The Constitution has a provision on the matter, albeit one of a rather negative character. "[N]o new State," it provides, "shall be formed or erected within the Jurisdiction of any other State . . . without the Consent of the Legislatures of the States concerned as well as of the [federal] Congress."[48] In other words, the consent of the Virginia legislature would be required for this step to take place. The *de facto* state government in Richmond naturally would not cooperate. So the consent was sought instead of the Wheeling government, which was distinctly more cooperative.

There was sharp division within the Lincoln cabinet over whether to proceed with the admission of West Virginia. Attorney General Edward Bates was strongly opposed, scornfully asserting that the Wheeling government "does not and never did, in fact, represent and govern more than a small fraction of the State." The so-called consent of Virginia was, in Bates's opinion, "a mere abuse, nothing less than attempted *secession,* hardly veiled under the flimsy forms of law."[49] Lincoln's own thoughts on this question ran very differently (as he set them down in a memorandum at the end of 1862). He was well aware that the Wheeling government had been elected by only a minority of the potential voters of Virginia. But he contended that the views of nonparticipants in elections were simply to be disregarded—and all the more so when the nonparticipants were engaging in open rebellion against the federal Union.[50]

A quite distinct question, in Lincoln's view, was whether it was expedient, on political and strategic grounds, to proceed with the admission of West Virginia as a new state. In essence, this was a cost-benefit issue: whether there was more to be lost by offending Virginians in the Confederate-dominated areas, or to be gained by acceding to the wishes of the westerners to form their own state. He inclined to believe, on this point, that the balance lay in proceeding with admission. He acknowledged the division of a state to be "dreaded as a precedent." But he expressed confidence that, as a "measure made expedient by war," the partitioning of Virginia could not be held to create any precedent for times of peace. If this was an act of secession—and it was—then comfort could be taken that it was, in Lincoln's words, "secession in favor of the Constitution" rather than secession against it. On this basis, he signed the legislation on December 31, 1862.[51] (Actual admission was consummated in April 1863.)[52]

After the war, the Virginia legislature made no attempt to recover the lost area, although it did contest sovereignty over two counties. This dispute was resolved by the federal Supreme Court in 1871, in a closely divided judgment, in West Virginia's favor.[53] There was another matter remaining between the two states, however: the question of the equitable division of the debts of prewar Virginia between the two states. Legal contests over this question continued into the twentieth century, reaching the Supreme Court on two occasions.[54]

Confiscating Property

Less conspicuous than the occupation of Confederate territory—but every bit as problematic legally—was the federal government policy of taking the *private* property of individual persons who supported the rebellion. It has been observed, in the context of requisition, that there are two quite distinct bases on which private property can be taken: by sovereign right, and by belligerent right. Perhaps no other subject area shows the difference between sovereign and belligerent right into such sharp relief as this one. For that reason, the topic is particularly instructive.[55]

Regarding the taking of property by belligerent right, there has already been a discussion of the two principal methods involved: requisition and capture, both of which were carried out by the Union armies in the course of their military operations.[56] The taking of private property by way of sovereign right involves (as will be seen) the forfeiture of property on the ground of some form of misconduct by the owner, or alternatively, some improper use of the property in question.

In addition, there is a type of property seizure that lies, somewhat uneasily, on the borderline between sovereign-right action and belligerent-right action. This is the confiscation of private property which belongs to enemy aliens and is located in the territory of the confiscating state. This would chiefly apply to property held by merchants and investors and the like for use in business activities. The taking of this type of property had generally been treated by lawyers as a belligerent right—that is, as simply one form of exercise of a *general* belligerent right, recognized since at least the Middle Ages, to take any property belonging to any national of an enemy state. In the case of enemy property located in the territory of the confiscating state, though, such a taking could equally be regarded as a sovereign-right measure, since any sovereign has jurisdiction automatically over any territory located physically within its bounds.

By the nineteenth century, however, the erstwhile general *belligerent* right to confiscate any and all property of enemy nationals had been considerably reduced. By the time of the Civil War, it was universally accepted that only *public* property, belonging to the enemy government, could be lawfully taken without limit and without any other justification. Private property was to be left undisturbed, except for the special case of requisition.

This alteration in the law left the question of confiscation of enemy property located within a state's territory in a kind of limbo. Looked at from the standpoint of belligerent right, it would seem to fall within the rule that private property of enemy nationals should not be taken. Looked at from the standpoint of sovereign right, however, the prerogative of the sovereign was unaffected—specifically, the government continued to possess its general sovereign right to determine the disposition of property located within its territory. Furthermore, there was a good reason to support the continued exercise of this right: to prevent the property from being exported by the enemy national to his home state and then put to use in the war effort. To deal with this problem, the general practice of states in the nineteenth century (and continuing in the twentieth) was a sort of practical compromise: property located in a belligerent state and belonging to enemy nationals would be sequestered but not actually confiscated. That is, it would be frozen during the state of war, to prevent its exportation to the enemy country, and then returned to its owners after peace was made.

The South resorted to this right from the very outset of the conflict. In May 1861, the Confederate Congress decreed the sequestration of debts owed by Confederate nationals to Union nationals.[57] This meant that, if a Confederate citizen owed money to a Union national, then the debt would be paid into a fund held by the Confederate government instead of being duly paid over to the creditor. That payment would constitute a discharge of the debt, with the effect that, if the Union creditor sued for payment in the courts of the relevant Southern state (private indebtedness being a matter of state rather than of federal law), then the action would fail. The money would be held by the Confederate government for the duration of the war, and then paid over to the Union creditor when peace came.[58] As will be seen presently, the Confederate government later went further down this road, to full confiscation—but that was on the ground of reprisal, rather than of either sovereign or belligerent right.

The Union, in contrast to the Confederacy, never resorted to a general sequestration of Confederate property. It did, to be sure, engage in property seizure—and on a substantial scale at that—but it was always in the context of some kind of improper usage of the property, or of misconduct on the owners. Seizure was never resorted to by the Union simply on the sole ground of Confederate nationality of the owner. The reason is not difficult to discern: the reluctance of the Union authorities to concede belligerent status to the Confederacy, even implicitly, in any context beyond the actual conducting of the hostilities themselves.

The Union measures, therefore, were targeted not against enemies as such—i.e., not against Confederate-state citizens or residents *per se*—but rather against *disloyal* persons. These could only be carried out by way of judicial proceedings. Such proceedings came in two basic forms, which should be carefully distinguished from one another. The first type involved the taking of property as a criminal penalty, analogous to fine or imprisonment. In this situation, the legal proceedings in question are primarily directed against the persons themselves, in the form of criminal prosecutions for some form of *personal* misconduct (such as treason). The confiscation of the property then follows (as it were) in the wake of the criminal proceedings, as an automatic and mechanical consequence of them. In such a case, "due process of law" must be accorded to the person whose guilt has been pronounced. This means that the accused person must receive a trial by jury, with a right to counsel, a right to cross-examine witnesses, a presumption of innocence, and so forth. Regarding this first form of confiscation, it is important to note two key points. The first is that this type of proceeding unquestionably fell into the category of sovereign-right measures rather than that of belligerent-right actions. The second point is that, in this type of case, there is no requirement that the property that is taken have any actual connection with the criminal act that was committed. It is only required that the property belong to a party who has been duly convicted of a crime (i.e., of a crime for which property confiscation is a stipulated penalty).

The other form of confiscation proceeding will be less familiar to laypersons. This is the situation in which the legal action is taken against the property *itself* rather than against the owner. Personal misconduct may well be present. In fact, it commonly would be. But it lurks, so to speak, in the background, in that the proceedings against the property are justified on the ground that the particular property in question was closely associated with some kind of wrongdoing. The classic example is smuggled goods. In such a case, the goods are, as it were, themselves "at fault," in the sense that they are an integral component of the smuggling operation. In such an instance, a condemnation proceeding can be instituted against the property as such, even if the smuggler himself is not prosecuted. (For example, the smuggler may have successfully eluded capture but left the smuggled goods behind.)

Such a proceeding against property as such is known to lawyers as an *in rem* action—meaning, simply, a legal proceeding against a thing or object, rather than against a person. This contrasts with a criminal prosecution of a person, which is known to lawyers (reasonably enough) as an *in personam* action. An *in rem* action against smuggled goods is not, of course, a criminal prosecution because inanimate objects cannot commit crimes. By the same token, inanimate objects do not possess the myriad constitutional rights of due process, in the way that humans do when they are accused of crimes. At the same time, it is apparent that *in rem* proceedings will typically be, in reality, very tightly connected with criminal conduct. This point was to cause a great deal of difficulty to the federal courts during and after the Civil War, chiefly because of the great uncertainty (as will be seen) over whether this category of proceeding should be regarded as a sovereign-right or as a belligerent-right measure.

With these general points about confiscation in mind, we may proceed to observe that, during the Civil War, the Union side devised four different confiscation programs, giving rise to varying legal issues. Two were adopted early in the conflict—the first dealing with property traded in violation of the Nonintercourse Act of July 1861, and the second (more controversially) applying to property actually employed in the rebellion. A third program consisted of confiscation in connection with the direct tax of 1861. The fourth—and by far the most legally contentious—was a (potentially) wide-sweeping confiscation program aimed at Confederate supporters generally.

Before looking at each of these in turn, and the legal issues to which they gave rise, it is only necessary to recall that the most important property-taking measure of all, in material terms—the policy on captured and abandoned property—was not strictly a confiscation measure but rather (as noted earlier) an exercise of the belligerent right of capture.[59] The distinguishing point about confiscation measures in the true sense is that they involve proceedings in a court of law, rather than at the hands of campaigning soldiers in the field.

Confiscation under the Non-intercourse Act

The first of the Union confiscation measures need be considered only briefly. It concerned property taken in the process of enforcing the Non-intercourse Act of July 1861.[60] This law, together with the President's proclamation pursuant to it on August 16, 1861, essentially made it an offense for persons in the Union states to trade with the eleven Confederate states.[61] But it prescribed no *personal* punishment for violation. Instead, it stated that, in case of violation, the property that was employed in illegal transaction was to be forfeit to the United States. That is to say, the act provided for *in rem* proceedings against the property itself but not for criminal prosecution of the person involved. Suspected property was to be brought before a federal court for adjudication. If it was found to have been employed in unlawful trading, then it was to be pronounced as confiscated, with legal title passing to the federal government, which would then auction it off to private bidders and deposit the proceeds of sale in the Treasury.

In practice, this legislation resulted in very little in the way of actual confiscation; so it need not be dwelt on at length. Its most important characteristic, for present considerations, was that it was regarded legally as an exercise of Congress's normal legislative prerogatives and *not* as a belligerent measure. Specifically, the law was viewed as an exercise of Congress's ordinary constitutional power to "regulate Commerce . . . among the several States."[62] Shortly after its enactment, a federal district court in New York confirmed this position, holding the Non-intercourse Act to be "sovereign in character" and "not intended as a declaration or establishment of the belligerent rights or powers of the government."[63]

This legislation, it should be appreciated, chiefly affected disloyal persons in the Union states, rather than in the Confederate ones—"disloyal" persons, that is, in the rather loose sense of persons who disobeyed federal laws on trading. As a result, the law did not, in any significant way, take property belonging to Southerners. For this reason, it aroused no great controversy. The position was quite otherwise, however, with the other three confiscation enactments.

The First Confiscation Act

The second confiscation measure, enacted in August 1861, aroused considerably greater legal concern than the nonintercourse policy had. The First Confiscation Act (as the law became widely known) concerned property that was

actually employed in the furthering of the Confederate war effort.[64] It was
to be liable to condemnation in much the same way as property taken for violation of the Non-intercourse Act: by way of *in rem* proceedings in federal
district or circuit courts, with title to the property passing to the federal
government, for later resale to private buyers at auction. As in the Non-
intercourse Act, there was no provision for criminal prosecution of the *persons*
who wrongfully employed the property. Informers were to receive half the
proceeds from condemnation.[65]

The controversy over this new measure arose for several reasons. One was
that the law was naturally expected to affect property located *in* the Southern
states. In particular, slaves could be confiscated from their owners under this
provision, if the slaves' labor was put at the service of the Confederacy (by, say,
employment on the building of fortifications). In fact, the adoption of the law
was sparked by just such considerations—that is, by the escape of slaves to en-
campments of Union troops in Virginia, followed by their owners demanding
the return of their property. Union general Benjamin Butler refused to comply with these demands, on the ground that the slaves, even considering them
to be mere property, amounted to contraband of war, thereby becoming subject to confiscation. The legal aspects of this "contraband" theory will be considered later.[66] For the present, it is only necessary to note that Butler's action
was the impetus for the enactment of the First Confiscation Act, which had
the effect of placing his policy onto a sound statutory footing.

For present purposes, the chief point of interest lies in the fact that the law
was widely perceived—and resented—as being penal in substance, if not in
form. This was on the thesis that the law would operate, at least in its practical effect, to take property from persons engaged in rebellion—i.e., to penal-
ize persons engaging in disloyal conduct by taking their property from them.
Some support was lent to this thesis by the Kentucky Court of Appeal, when
it held, in 1866, that property which was employed in the rebellion against its
owner's will would *not* be forfeit under the act.[67] Two years later, the federal
Supreme Court lent even stronger support to this assertion by candidly stating
that property was taken under the act as a consequence of the owner's consent
to its use in support of the rebellion.[68]

This criminal-law flavor (as it might be described) attaching to the First
Confiscation Act was objectionable to Southerners in two quite distinct ways.
First, the act provided nothing in the way of due-process guarantees to the
persons affected. It is true that, in the confiscation proceedings, there had

to be proof of the use to which the property had been put. But *if* the real purpose of the law was to inflict punishment on the owner—as appeared to be the case—then the owner should be entitled to the full range of constitutional rights of due process, such as a presumption of innocence, a right to trial by jury, a right to counsel, and so forth. The act provided for none of these.

The response to this objection was that the proceedings were, legally speaking, *only* against the property itself (i.e., were *in rem* rather than *in personam*)—and moreover, that the property in question was the instrument of wrongdoing. That meant (it was contended) that the situation was precisely analogous to the case of confiscating smuggled goods when the smugglers themselves were absent. In due course (although not until 1882), the federal Supreme Court endorsed this thesis. Misconduct by the owner of the property, the Court explained, was only relevant to the question of whether proceedings should be *instituted.* But the proceedings *themselves,* once under way, were *in rem* and not *in personam*—with the result that the due-process guarantees attaching to criminal proceedings were not applicable.[69]

The second, and distinct, objection to the First Confiscation Act as a *de facto* (if not strictly *de jure*) criminal measure was the thesis that the law amounted, in practical terms, to an unlawful method of waging war. This was because the act, in effect, made it a criminal offense for Confederate-state citizens and residents to support their *own* government's cause in their *own* territory. The Union government was conceded to be entitled, as a matter of *belligerent* right, under the laws of war, to capture enemy property as war booty on the field of battle, when it was in the *very* act of being employed in the Confederate cause. But the laws of war did not permit one belligerent to make it a criminal offense, under its national law, for nationals of the opposing state to contribute their labor or their property to their own government's war effort. The essence of this objection, it may be noted, was the insistence that opposing states, in time of war, must wield only belligerent-right weapons against one another (such as the right of capture), and not sovereign-right weapons (such as criminal legislation).[70]

The Union disagreed on this point. It consistently maintained that the conflict was a case of rebellion and not of true war and that, consequently, it was always entitled to operate in *both* a belligerent and a sovereign mode, entirely as it chose. The courts in the Union—most notably the Supreme Court in the Prize Cases—expressly endorsed this position.[71]

The importance of the First Confiscation Act was therefore not the fear that it would actually lead to large-scale confiscations of property. Nor did it. Neither President Lincoln nor Attorney General Bates had any real enthusiasm for enforcing the law. In addition, the difficulty of proving that property had actually been employed to further the rebellion made enforcement difficult.[72] The act was therefore important not in material terms or in practical effects, but rather in its demonstration of the federal government's willingness to wield the *sovereign* weapon of the criminal law, as well as the *belligerent* weapon of capture, against the Confederacy.

The Confederate Congress quickly demonstrated its depth of feeling about the Confiscation Act by extending its policy of sequestration of property owned by Union nationals. It will be recalled that original sequestration measure of May 1861 had only applied to debts owed to Union creditors. In new legislation enacted in August 1861, the sequestration was extended to cover *all* kinds of property owned by Northerners.[73] This property was to be held as a fund, for the payment of compensation to victims of the Union legislation. It was therefore in the nature of what lawyers sometimes call a "clawback" measure—one designed to cancel out losses caused by the action of some foreign government. This action was justified *not* on the basis of general belligerent rights, but rather as a reprisal measure, in response to the allegedly unlawful First Confiscation Act (unlawful, that is, under the international law of war).

Then, in February 1862, the Confederacy took the further step of actually confiscating this property.[74] The sequestered property was now to be sold, with the proceeds paid into the Treasury. This step too was expressly justified as a reprisal measure against the First Confiscation Act. In contrast to the position in the North, the Confederate confiscation legislation was vigorously and efficiently enforced, and it made a substantial contribution to the rebel war effort. It raised about $12 million for the Southern cause (as compared to $4 million provided by import and export duties).[75]

Confiscation for Arrears of the Direct Tax of 1861

The third avenue for taking property in connection with the rebellion arose out of the Direct Tax Act of 1861.[76] It will be recalled that this tax was apportioned among the states as required by the Constitution—with the disloyal states being duly assigned their share according to their population.[77] In June 1862, Congress decided to institute a land-confiscation policy as a means of bringing arrears of the tax into the Treasury.[78] It did this by placing the tax-collection machinery in the rebellious areas into federal hands (with the collection process in the loyal areas left in the hands of the states). Specifically, Congress provided that *individual* plots of land in the rebellious areas would be charged with the payment of a proportionate share of the tax moneys assessed for the state in question, with the owners then given sixty days in which to pay the tax to the federal government.

Failure to pay the assessed sum would result in confiscation of the land, by way of an *in rem* proceeding by the federal government. After being taken from the recalcitrant owner, the land would be leased or sold to loyal buyers, with title passing from the original owner upon sale. Tax commissioners were to follow the Union armies and implement the policy as the rebellious lands were reduced to submission. Similarly to the First Confiscation Act, this law contained no provision for criminal prosecution for nonpayment of the tax. It provided "only" for loss of land. The thrust of the law, in other words, was to make Southern lands stand surety for the payment of the tax.

This legislation was open to objection on various grounds. Considered as a belligerent-right measure, it was objectionable for being (at least arguably) a violation of the laws of war, which (as observed earlier) permit the taking of enemy-owned private property only in cases of military necessity, not as a routine policy.[79] Moreover, the right of capture, even when military necessity is present, only applies to personal property, not to land. Considered, on the other hand, as a sovereign-right measure, the law was vulnerable (like the First Confiscation Act) to the criticism that, in its practical impact, it inflicted a criminal penalty without any provision for the constitutional due-process guarantees to which accused persons are entitled.

The objection to the tax policy as a belligerent stratagem was, in effect, conceded. The objections from the due-process standpoint, however, were not found to be persuasive—at least not in the Union. The position taken was that the law was a nonpenal, sovereign-right measure applying to territory that was fully within the jurisdiction of Congress. Specifically, the law was purely a revenue-raising mechanism, employing entirely *in rem* proceedings, with a view to ensuring that tax revenues that were owing actually arrived safely in the federal Treasury. Since the law was nonpenal by nature, there was no need for such due-process considerations as trial by jury. Evidence for the nonpenal character of the policy was provided by the fact that questions of loyalty played no part. What made the land subject to confiscation was not disloyalty but simple nonpayment of the tax. By the same token, what rescued the land from confiscation was payment of the tax—also without regard to loyalty.

It is not surprising that this tax-arrears policy was widely resented in the South. Notwithstanding its technical legal character as a combination of revenue-raising measure and bribe, Southerners commonly viewed it as a thinly disguised property-confiscation engine. A judge on the Virginia Supreme Court, for example, voiced the powerful suspicion, in a case in 1868, that the direct-tax forfeitures were "designed really to get the land, and not to get the tax."[80] The policy amounted, on this view, to a crude pronouncement of a criminal penalty *en masse* against supporters of the Confederacy. It was regarded as a brazen attempt by one belligerent power to extend its domestic laws into the territory of its enemy, contrary to all laws and usages of war, and as a palpable sign of the active malice harbored by the Union authorities against the Southern way of life.

As the Union armies advanced southward, the tax commissioners duly followed in their path. By the end of the war, they had made assessments of the taxes owing on each parcel of land in about half the counties of the erstwhile Confederacy. There were many examples in which lands of considerable value were sold for the payment of quite small sums of tax. In one instance, a house in Little Rock, Arkansas, was taken for the collection of some $70 owed, and then sold for $3,000.[81] In another case, property in South Carolina was sold for tax arrears of some $91, with an additional $5,000 realized at sale for the benefit of the federal government.[82] It was, however, held by the Supreme Court—though only long after the war—that the erstwhile owner was entitled to be paid the balance of the sum realized over the arrears due.[83] Even so, it remained the case that the owner lost the land and was compelled to rest content with the monetary surplus from the sale.[84]

As matters unfolded, the material effect of the policy proved to be considerably less than it might have been. Only a small percentage of assessed properties were actually sold in the manner provided. One difficulty was that proceedings under this legislation were slow, with foreclosure and sale taking place on a parcel-by-parcel basis. In addition, a number of the sales were held invalid by the courts, on the ground that the tax money actually had been tendered to the federal government but wrongly refused. The federal government adopted a policy of refusing to accept offers of payment prior to sale if they were made after the expiry of the sixty-day payment deadline following assessment, and also of refusing payments that were tendered by agents rather than by the owners in person. The Supreme Court held that neither of these grounds of refusal was permissible.[85] As a result, all sales of property in those cases were invalid—that is, they passed no legal title to the buyers, so that the original owners could reclaim the property.

The most famous demonstration of this situation in action concerned the property of Robert E. Lee, located in Arlington, Virginia. The tax assessed on the Lee property was some $92, with land then sold for $26,200, to the federal government itself, which planned to transform the estate into a national cemetery. When it was established, however, that the Lee family had tendered the tax money prior to sale through an agent, and that the government had refused it, the courts duly held the sale to have been invalid. As a result, the Lee family continued to hold legal title to the property. The family then brought civil proceedings to eject federal armed forces from the property—taking their case successfully to the federal Supreme Court in 1882.[86] The federal government was thereby reduced to taking the property in the normal manner, by way of eminent domain, with an agreed figure for payment of compensation eventually arrived at with the Lee family. And Arlington National Cemetery was duly founded.

The Second Confiscation Act

The greatest problems, by a wide margin, in the confiscation area arose from the fourth of the property-taking measures, which became known as the Second Confiscation Act, of July 1862.[87] This measure was decidedly more drastic than the ones just discussed. It also raised, in more acute form than before, the vexing question of distinguishing a sovereign-right measure that was designed, in its practical effect, to punish wrongdoers from a belligerent-right measure that was directed only against property as such.

There is no doubt that certain portions of the legislation were penal. The first two sections of the law altered the law of treason and created a (purportedly) new criminal offense of engaging in rebellion.[88] These were clearly penal provisions, with the punishments duly set out in the same sections that created the offenses. Convictions for these offenses could only occur by way of normal criminal proceedings, complete with the full set of constitutional due-process guarantees. But these criminal-law sections did not contain the confiscation measures.[89]

The confiscation sections of the act bore, at least in form, no direct connection to the treason provisions. They provided for the confiscation of *all* prop-

erty that belonged to persons falling into six designated categories. Four of
these categories were predictable enough: Confederate political and military
leaders, plus important state government officials of the Southern states, together with all holders of governmental office in the Confederacy (whether
Confederate, state, or local). A fifth category comprised any persons who had
previously held "an office of honor, trust, or profit" in the federal government
(such as a cabinet office or an ambassadorship). The sixth conprised *any* persons who assisted in the rebellion *and* who owned any property in the loyal
states.[90]

These six categories clearly did not cover anything like the entire population of the Confederacy. The act, however, provided a mechanism for extending the confiscation policy to all *disloyal* persons in the South. The President
was empowered to issue a general proclamation giving all supporters of the rebellion sixty days to halt their disloyal activity. If they persisted in supporting
of the Confederate cause after that sixty-day grace period, then their property
too would become subject to the confiscation measures. The policy was designed to give Confederate supporters a concrete material incentive to desert
the Southern cause. By going over to the Union side, persons in the designated
statutory categories could ensure the retention of their property.[91]

The debate over this law in the Congress was acrimonious; and President
Lincoln contemplated vetoing it, for two principal reasons. One was a worry
over the lack of due-process guarantees in the confiscation proceedings. The
bill, Lincoln opined, was, in substance, a forfeiture "for the ingredients of treason, without a conviction of the supposed criminal, or a personal hearing
given him in any proceedings."[92] Lincoln's other chief objection was a fear that
the law fell foul of the constitutional provision on treason, which expressly
gives Congress the power "to declare the Punishment of Treason," but subject
to a key proviso: that "no Attainder of Treason shall work Corruption of
Blood, or Forfeiture except during the Life of the Person attainted."[93] In Lincoln's view, this restriction prevented Congress from taking the *whole* legal
title to property of disloyal persons. It was only permissible, in his view, to take
the property for the duration of the offender's *own* life, leaving his descendants
unaffected. The sins of the fathers, in short, must not be visited on the children. Lincoln's misgivings on this score were probably unfounded, for reasons
too technical to explore here; but they were sincerely held.[94]

Congress sought to deal with at least some of these objections by the unusual means of adopting an interpretive resolution to accompany the law.[95]

This resolution had three provisions. One stated that the act was not to be retroactively applied (i.e., it would apply only to persons who fell into the designated categories *after* its enactment).[96] A second provision stated that the law was intended to effect a forfeiture only for the natural life of the person concerned (and was therefore not to affect the person's heirs). Third, it was pronounced that *state* legislators or judges who had *not* taken an oath to support the Confederacy would not fall into any of the categories of persons immediately subject to confiscation. Armed with these assurances, Lincoln signed the act and, within a week, duly issued the public warning to all persons to cease supporting the rebellion.[97]

The side resolution did not, however, resolve the fundamental question of whether the confiscation provisions were penal in character. As with the other confiscation measures, this one was certainly nonpenal in *form,* in that it provided only for *in rem* proceedings against the property itself, independently of any criminal prosecution of the persons. But the question of whether the confiscations were penal in *substance* was a far closer question than it was in the other cases. The reason is that, in the case of the Non-intercourse Act and also of the First Confiscation Act, the property that was confiscated was *itself* closely connected to the wrongdoing in question. In the nonintercourse case, the property was employed in violation of the act itself. The First Confiscation Act dealt with property used to further the rebellion. In both cases, therefore, it was easy to hold that the property itself had (so to speak) committed the wrongful acts and consequently that the property could be proceeded against.[98]

This new law was very different. Here, there was no requirement that the property *itself* have any connection with any form of wrongdoing. Therefore, this new confiscation program, as President Lincoln had expressly pointed out, appeared to the naked eye to be a penalty inflicted purely for *personal* misconduct on the part of the owners. As such, it appeared to be an egregious violation of the due-process rights of the owners. There was only one way of countering this seemingly insurmountable objection: to contend that the law was an exercise of belligerent right, rather than of sovereign right. If that were so, then normal due-process considerations would not be applicable.

Not until several years after the war had ended did the federal Supreme Court finally resolve this crucial question definitively—and not without a deep division of opinion among its justices.[99] In the leading case on the subject, decided in 1871, the Court held the Second Confiscation Act to have been

an exercise of belligerent right rather than of sovereign right.[100] The confiscations were a means of carrying on the armed struggle, a tactic of war, rather
than a punishment of individuals for personal acts of guilt. In so holding, the
Court referred to the preamble of the act, which expressly stated the purpose
to be "to insure the speedy termination of the rebellion." In addition, the
Court pointed out that the act "defined no crime. It imposed no penalty. It
declared nothing unlawful."[101] The Second Confiscation Act was therefore
held to be a measure directed against enemies rather than criminals. As such,
it was outside the purview of the due-process guarantees of the Constitution,
which only applied to cases of crime and punishment.[102]

There was a strong dissent from this conclusion by Justice Field, who contended that the confiscations were in reality criminal penalties imposed on the
persons falling into the various categories of wrongdoer set out in the Act. It is
true, he conceded, that *in rem* proceedings could, in some circumstances, be
taken against property alone without any corresponding personal action
against an individual. But this was allowed only in severely restricted cases—
basically, cases in which the property concerned was itself closely connected to
wrongdoing (as in the case of smuggling). The Second Confiscation Act, in
sharp contrast, provided for the taking of property *solely* by virtue of the misconduct of the owners. The confiscations consequently must be regarded as
punishment for crime and not as a war measure.[103]

This division of opinion between the majority and the dissent is a classic illustration of a perpetual dilemma in cases of statutory interpretation: between
an emphasis on external form (favored by the Court's majority), as opposed to
an emphasis on substance (favored by Field). Field's position was endorsed by
only one other justice (Clifford).[104] In the longer term, however, it gained the
upper hand, at least in cases of property forfeiture. This is apparent from a federal Supreme Court case in 1993, which held that forfeiture proceedings could
be (and in this case were) penal in reality, even though they were civil in
form.[105]

For all of the debates and dilemmas associated with the confiscation laws,
it turned out that their material contribution of the policy to the Union war
effort was tiny. In the immediate aftermath of the adoption of the Second
Confiscation Act, the War Department took steps to have the armed forces
implement it.[106] Attorney General Bates, however, opposed military involvement in what he regarded as civilian legal affairs. In November 1862, President
Lincoln acceded to his view and expressly assigned the enforcement of the act

to the attorney general.[107] If vigorous implementation was the intention, then a drastic error was made, since Bates strongly disliked the legislation and positively obstructed its enforcement.[108] The result was that the Second Confiscation Act produced for the Union more controversy and resentment than material gain. It has been estimated that less than half a million dollars was brought into the federal Treasury by it—far less than was yielded by the captured-and-abandoned-property program. As a result, the chief effect of the Confiscation Acts, on the assessment of one historian, was to produce "a feeling of irritation and injury on the part of a few despoiled owners."[109]

There was, however, another form of property-taking during the Civil War that aroused far more resentment, and legal controversy, than even the Second Confiscation Act did. This was the taking of property in human beings. And it involved more than merely a transfer of ownership. It attacked the very concept of this species of ownership. To this momentous act of juridical transformation—of chattels into persons—we may now turn our special attention.

5

The End of a Peculiar Institution

Slavery cannot exist without law, any more than property in lands and goods can exist without law.

—U.S. Supreme Court

There is a venerable tradition in Western jurisprudence of regarding slavery as a local and exceptional matter, with the general and residual position being that all persons are free. This was clearly stated in the *Institutes* of Justinian in the sixth century A.D.[1] This position found an echo in the U.S. Supreme Court in 1825, when it stated slavery to be contrary to the law of nature—while immediately going on to hold that it was nonetheless permitted by the custom or *practice* of nations.[2] The Lieber Code followed in this tradition, stating matter-of-factly that slavery "exists according to municipal or local law only. The law of nature and nations has never acknowledged it."[3] That municipal law recognized and protected the practice of slavery in some portions of the United States was accepted by virtually everyone in the years prior to the Civil War—if often with disapproval.

In the legal system of the United States, slaves were property. More specifically, they were *chattels,* which simply means personal or moveable property (as opposed to *real property,* which is land)—hence the common expression "chattel slavery." The respect for, and protection of, private property was sewn deeply into the fabric of American law; and this was fully applicable to property in slaves. Explicit confirmation on this score was provided by the federal

Supreme Court in 1842, when it held that the Constitution accorded "a positive and unqualified recognition of the right of the owner in the slave."[4]

Moreover, slavery, as in inherent part of the law of property, was virtually entirely governed by *state* rather than by federal law. The Constitution, to be sure, acknowledged the existence of slavery in a variety of ways. But it did not, by any stretch of the imagination, *create* the institution of slavery. The states did that, in the exercise of their general sovereign prerogatives. Nor did the Constitution give to the federal government any authority to countermand or reverse the laws of the states, even if the federal government were so inclined, which it basically was not. There had certainly been many debates about slavery issues in Congress in the years leading up to the war. But these had always concerned marginal questions such as the expansion of slavery into newly acquired federal territories and the recovery of fugitive slaves from free states. The existence of slavery within the slave states had always gone virtually unchallenged.

As a result, those who sought to abolish the "peculiar institution" of slavery (as it was often rather quaintly and euphemistically known) faced a double legal hurdle: the absence of any explicit legal power on the part of the federal government to tamper with state laws; and the more general, but very powerful, respect for private property which was firmly embedded in the American juridical psyche. There were many in the free states who, while harboring little enough affection for slavery as such, were very loath to see the federal government interfere with the internal affairs of the states, or to trespass on private property rights. For if one species of property could be tampered with by the federal government today, then what could be guaranteed to be safe tomorrow?

An instinctive hesitation to mount a direct attack on slavery in the slave states was clearly apparent in the early period of the war. Even before hostilities broke out, in February 1861, the House of Representatives stated, without a dissenting vote, that the federal government had no right to interfere with slavery in the slave states.[5] Similar in character was the Crittendon Resolution, adopted by the two houses of Congress in July 1861, practically as the guns were firing at Bull Run. It stated the aim of the federal government in the struggle to be the restoration of the Union—"with all the . . . rights of the several States unimpaired"—and not the elimination of slavery.[6] Similar caution prevailed in the executive branch. President Lincoln, although personally opposed to slavery, carefully held back from attacking it directly, largely because of concern over alienating slaveholders in the border states from the Union cause.

The federal government, however, was not given the luxury of dealing with slavery questions according to its own convenience. The matter pressed itself upon the attention of the Union armed forces and government from (so to speak) the bottom up, as the slaves in the South began first to scent freedom and then to embrace it with a vigor that unpleasantly surprised their former masters—and their often-reluctant liberators as well. As was so frequently the case, the federal government had before it two legal modes of operation: belligerent powers and sovereign powers.

The belligerent powers of the federal government, it soon appeared, could make a substantial, if somewhat covert, contribution to the cause of emancipation, particularly if a degree of legal creativity was applied. It duly was, in the form of the treatment of runaway slaves as contraband of war. In addition, the plenary powers of martial-law administrators could extend, at least arguably, to the emancipation of slaves. But the greatest of all the belligerent-right measures against slavery was the Emancipation Proclamation of January 1863, in which the President invoked his commander-in-chief power to effect a sweeping (though not comprehensive) freeing of slaves. There were always grave doubts, however, as to whether belligerent-right measures such as these could lawfully be employed to effect permanent changes of a very fundamental nature in the legal and social system of the Southern states.

On the sovereign-right side, the prerogatives of the federal government were severely limited. Congress did, however, hold substantial powers over the District of Columbia and the territories, which it duly exercised in the cause of emancipation. Over the law of property within the slave states, however, the Congress was (as noted above) largely powerless. Consequently, for the definitive and absolute termination of slavery, a constitutional amendment proved the only solution.

Inching toward Freedom

It has been observed that the laws of war, since the seventeenth century, had evolved in the direction of making war ever more into a contest between professional armed forces on the field of battle, rather than a comprehensive struggle between whole populations. On this thesis, it was generally understood that warmaking should not involve subverting the legal and social system of the enemy state. This belief was most directly reflected in the rule that a belligerent occupier of enemy territory would leave the local law and institutions—including slavery—intact.[7] On the face of it, therefore, belligerent rights looked to be a fairly unpromising mechanism for the cause of emancipation.

In certain respects, however, it became apparent that belligerent prerogatives could be put to good use against slavery, on the thesis that the liberation
of slaves could be legally justified as a *bona fide* war measure, that is, as an integral part of the campaign to defeat the enemy armed force. When this theory was exploited to an ever greater extent, as it gradually came to be, and
combined with certain legislative measures that were clearly within Congress's
constitutional purview, it proved possible to make some very considerable legal
(or arguably legal) inroads into slavery. The steps taken in this direction were
often short and hesitant. But in the aggregate, they did much to undermine—
though not actually to abolish—the peculiar institution.

"Contraband" on the Move

The vexed question of slavery first impressed itself on the Union authorities
when slaves began to desert their masters and flee to nearby federal military installations.[8] This soon-to-be-familiar process first occurred in May 1861, at
Fort Monroe, Virginia. The numbers were modest at first; but by the end of
July, some eight hundred runaways were there, over half of them women and
children.[9] It is interesting to note that, after the conclusion of the hostilities,
Attorney General Speed expressly held that slaves had a legal *duty* to flee from
disloyal masters. A slave who was loyal to the Union cause, he held, must of
necessity "become the enemy of the man who was his master when the master
becomes a traitor." A slave, he reasoned, was subject to "the duty of upholding
and sustaining the government," meaning that he was obligated to refuse to
toil for a disloyal master. Speed even held that, once a slave fled from a disloyal
master, his status as a slave was terminated; and he became a free person.[10]

Early in the war, such bold thinking was not in evidence. It should be remembered that at that time the Fugitive Slave Act of 1850 was still in force, so
that in principle, at least, the owners had a right to reclaim their wayward
charges.[11] Attorney General Bates was insistent that the act continue to be enforced.[12] In addition, some Union commanders were determined to prevent
runaway slaves from entering their lines. In November 1861, Halleck, then
commanding the Missouri theater, issued an order to that effect, as did Sherman in Kentucky.[13] The general intention (or at least the hope) was for a policy of "absolute nonintervention" by the military in slavery questions.[14] A
Union soldier, in Halleck's crisp phraseology, should not act either as "negro
catcher or negro stealer."[15]

A more adventurous approach was taken by the local Union commander at

Fort Monroe, General Benjamin Butler (the later occupier of New Orleans). He was of a strongly abolitionist persuasion and also, in civilian life, a shrewd lawyer. His policy was to employ able-bodied runaway slaves in the service of his forces, while at the same time expressing himself willing to return slaves to any master who would first take an oath of loyalty to the Union.[16] The War Department approved of this policy and instructed that it be followed in Kentucky.[17]

This was the origin of the employment of the concept of *contraband* (or, in its fuller form, *contraband of war*) as a legal tool for dealing with the problem of escaped slaves. Contraband was a long-standing feature of the international law of armed conflict and neutrality, finding extensive expression in the bilateral treaty practice of the principal European maritime states from the seventeenth century onward.[18] Its basic meaning was quite simple. Contraband (of war) consisted of materials that were useful in the prosecution of war. Most obviously, this meant inanimate objects such as weapons and ammunition. It was established practice since the Middle Ages, and established *law* since the seventeenth century, that belligerents could capture and confiscate any contraband of war that was being carried to their enemies by merchants of neutral countries. This entailed, as in cases of capture generally, the acquisition of legal title to the captured goods. The captor state, in other words, now became the owner of the contraband goods and could turn them to use in its own war effort.

With a little imagination and a deft resort to analogy, this concept of contraband could be adapted to the purpose at hand. Very helpful in this regard was the fact that authority and precedent existing for the treatment of human beings as, in effect, a sort of animate contraband. This was the position of soldiers being transported on neutral ships, on the rationale that soldiers, like guns and ammunition, made a direct and obvious contribution to the enemy's war effort. In the treaty practice of the European countries—and of the United States itself—it was commonly provided that serving soldiers who were found by a belligerent on board a neutral ship could be removed from the neutral vessel at sea and made prisoners of war.[19]

This preexisting law of contraband proved to be a particularly attractive legal device for the Union authorities in the awkward situation of dealing with escaped slaves. For one thing, the right to confiscate contraband was clearly a war measure, falling within the belligerent powers of the United States. A contraband policy could therefore be activated and carried out on the sole initiative of the President, as the commander-in-chief of the armed forces, with no

THE END OF A PECULIAR INSTITUTION

need for congressional legislation. In addition, the law of contraband entailed the *permanent* dispossession of the original owners of the contraband goods, with full legal title being transferred to the captors. That meant that there would be no obligation to return the slaves to their owners after the war.[20] Nor was there any question of compensation being owed to the erstwhile owner, since (as noted earlier) the constitutional requirement of compensation for the taking of property only applied to property that was taken by *sovereign* right, not to property taken by belligerent right.[21]

Finally—and far from least—there was the important political consideration that the contraband theory enabled slaves (i.e., private property) to be taken from their owners without unduly frightening conservative elements in the Northern and border states, and also without committing the Union government to any general program of abolition. Secretary of War Simon Cameron was thereby able to assure Congress, in December 1861, that slaves in the custody of the Union forces "constitute a military resource" directly contributing to the war effort.[22] At the very same time, and without obvious inconsistency, Cameron could confirm to General Sherman that the *general* federal policy was to "avoid . . . all interference with the social systems or local institutions of every State beyond that which insurrection makes unavoidable."[23] As one journalist wryly put it: "The venerable gentleman who wears gold spectacles and reads a conservative daily prefers confiscation to emancipation. He is reluctant to have slaves declared freemen, but has no objection to their being declared contrabands."[24]

In certain other respects, though, it was clear that the law of contraband did *not* fit the situation at hand very smoothly. Most outstanding was the consideration that contraband-quality goods, in the legal sense, meant goods that were useful *solely* for war purposes; and it was obvious that slaves hardly qualified on that count. There was also the problem, as Butler appreciated at the outset, that slaves who were not in a condition to labor for his forces could not qualify as contraband, since they could not reasonably be regarded as war resources of the enemy.[25] In addition, there was the difficulty that, strictly speaking, the law of contraband did not bring about the *emancipation* of the slaves, but only their *confiscation*. That is to say, the law of contraband was a means of transferring legal title to contraband goods from the original owners to the captors (i.e., to the federal government). To those of an abolitionist persuasion, this was clearly a very serious shortcoming to the contraband approach. It may fairly be speculated that President Lincoln, of all people, can hardly have relished the thought of himself becoming, in a manner of speaking, a slave-owner on a gigantic, and constantly growing, scale.

Treating escaped slaves as contraband also involved a number of annoying practical problems, chiefly the question of proof. If a civilian slave-owner entered Union military lines in search of his property, how was it to be determined whether that property (i.e., the sought-after slave) had been employed in furtherance of the rebellion? For that was the issue that determined whether the owner would be allowed to retrieve his charge or not. Early in the conflict, there were instances in which Union troops allowed recovery of slaves simply because of the absence of any proof that the slaves had been used in the cause of rebellion. Increasingly, though, the burden of proof tended to drift, at least in practice, in the other direction, with an increasing tendency on the part of Union military officers not to allow recapture of escaped slaves.[26]

In all events, it would appear that the contraband policy never received the straightforward endorsement of the federal government. In fact, the term "contraband" appears to have been more prominent in popular than in official circles, referring in a loose manner to any runaway slave.[27] (For example, there was a lighthearted popular song among escaped slaves, "I's a Happy Contraband.") Nevertheless, various executive and congressional initiatives gradually emerged which were at least broadly consistent with the contraband theory. As early as July 1861, for example, the House of Representatives resolved that "it is no part of the duty of . . . soldiers . . . to capture and return fugitive slaves."[28] This policy was given full statutory force in March 1862, in legislation prohibiting the employment of the armed forces in the capturing or returning of escaping slaves—without any regard to the loyalty or disloyalty of the owner.[29] A further provision, to similar effect, in the Second Confiscation Act in July of that year, prohibited the military from pronouncing on the validity of claims to runaway slaves and also from delivering runaways to purported owners.[30] And in addition, a presidential order of July 1862 expressly authorized the employment of "so many persons of African descent as can be advantageously used for military and naval purposes," with "reasonable wages" to be paid to the workers.[31]

The subject, however, continued to be beset with uncertainty and ambiguity. In a minor masterpiece of legal diplomacy, the adjutant general of the Army of the Potomac explained his position on the matter in August 1862 by characterizing slaves as "occupying simply a peculiar legal status under State laws, which condition the military authorities of the United States are not required to regard at all in districts where military operations are made necessary by the rebellious action of the State governments."[32] The general cloudiness that beset this delicate subject would be some time in lifting.

Toward Emancipation—First Steps

Gradually, the federal government began feeling its way toward a bolder policy of outright emancipation. It naturally concentrated its attention first on disloyal slave-owners. The First Confiscation Act of August 1861 contained a special provision on the subject, stating (rather vaguely) that a disloyal owner who employed a slave in war-related service was to "forfeit his claim" to the slave's labor.[33] Judge Advocate General Joseph Holt, of the War Department, later maintained that this meant that a slave who was so employed became *automatically* free, without the need of any judicial condemnation proceedings (as were required for the confiscation of other types of property under the act).[34]

The Second Confiscation Act of July 1862 contained further blows against slavery, prescribing emancipation of slaves as a penalty attaching to two criminal offenses: the existing crime of treason and the newly created offense of engaging in rebellion.[35] In the case of treason, it was provided that the slaves belonging to a convicted person "shall be declared and made free." For engaging in rebellion, there was a similar, but not identical, provision for the "liberation of all slaves" of the guilty party. There would be, of course, no compensation, since the slaves were being taken as a measure of punishment for criminal misconduct and not for "public use."

President Lincoln, combining the exactitude of the lawyer with the wariness of the politician, chided Congress for employing what he called "an unfortunate form of expression" in these provisions. There could undeniably be confiscation of slaves as a penalty for crimes, but this must necessarily involve a transfer of ownership of the slaves from the convicted criminal to the federal government. There could not be a simple extinguishment of the property relationship *per se.* Fortunately, Lincoln was able to suggest a lawyerlike resolution of the matter. "[I]f it were said that the ownership of the slave had been first transferred to the nation," he suggested, "and that Congress had then liberated him, the difficulty would at once vanish."[36] In material terms, these provisions were of no real importance, given the absence of actual convictions of slaveholders for the specified offenses.

In addition, the act provided for the emancipation of three specified categories of slaves belonging to disloyal owners: those "taking refuge" in the Union military lines; those captured by Union forces; and those "found" in occupied territory. These three categories of persons were declared to be "captives of war." But they were also stated by the act to be "forever free of their servitude, and not again held as slaves."[37] In other words, these persons, like the ones covered by the First Confiscation Act, *automatically* became free, without need for court proceedings, as soon as they fitted into one of the three categories. Holt explained that their status as captives of war meant that they were under the military protection of the federal government and ought to be issued with certificates confirming their newfound free status.[38] The effect of this provision was to extend the contraband policy in two important ways: first, by providing expressly for outright emancipation rather than merely for a change of ownership; and second, by imposing no requirement that the labor of the slave have had any connection with the waging of the war.

At least some attempt was made to implement this policy. In the Missouri-Kansas border area, General Thomas Ewing ordered military commanders who had fugitive slaves at their posts to separate those who belonged to disloyal masters from the others. "[D]ue and public notice" would be given, to allow owners to establish their loyalty if they could. The act was not, however, followed scrupulously in this case, since the slaves of disloyal owners were not actually to be treated as prisoners of war, but instead were to be given passage to places of safety where they could begin to earn their livelihoods as free persons.[39]

The following year, the Lieber Code added its authority to this policy. It stated that,

> if a person held in bondage . . . come[s] as a fugitive under the protection of the military forces of the United States, such person is immediately entitled to the rights and privileges of a freeman. To return such person into slavery would amount to enslaving a free person, and neither the United States nor any officer under their authority can enslave any human being. Moreover, a person so made free by the law of war is under the shield of the law of nations, and the former owner or State can have . . . no . . . claim of service.[40]

This Lieber Code provision, it may be noted, went further than the Second Confiscation Act did, in that it referred to slaves held by *any* enemy national. In the context of the Civil War, this meant, of course, that any slave who fled to the Union army lines from *either* a loyal *or* a disloyal master in Confederate territory would become free.[41]

As the war progressed, and as Union military penetration of the South grew ever greater, the Union armies increasingly took on the character of a moving frontier of freedom.[42] But it was a chaotic process, involving much hardship and suffering. The collapse of slavery in the Confederate areas, in reality, owed more to the initiatives of the slaves themselves, who fled their erstwhile masters in large numbers as federal troops approached, often (and inevitably) with little knowledge of what sort of future really lay in store for them. The orderly procedures of the Second Confiscation Act remained, in this regard, lodged firmly in the statute books but with little, if indeed any, impact on events on the ground. It has been credibly estimated that virtually no slaves actually gained their freedom by way of the Second Confiscation Act.[43] More drastic measures would be required—and it was not long before they appeared.

Emancipation by Martial Law

Martial law, it will be recalled, is an emergency situation in which the ordinary law of a more or less tightly defined area is suspended, and the will of a commanding officer substituted for it as the basis of government.[44] With a modicum of imagination, it was not difficult for martial-law commanders to conclude that the freeing of slaves might be necessary in order to deal with the exigencies of the rebellion. Just such a conclusion was arrived at by the Union commander in Missouri, General John C. Fremont, who in August 1861 proclaimed martial law throughout the state. One of the measures imposed under this heading was the liberation of slaves in the district—although this was applicable only to slaves belonging to participants in the rebellion.[45] Lincoln responded by urging Fremont to withdraw the order.[46] When Fremont balked, asserting that he viewed his emancipation policy as "right and necessary," Lincoln took a firmer line and ordered it to be rescinded.[47]

A second noteworthy instance of emancipation by martial-law proclamation took place in South Carolina early the following year. In March 1862, General David Hunter began to issue certificates of emancipation to slaves who had been employed by the Confederacy. The following month, he issued an order, proclaiming slaves in the regions of Fort Pulaski and Cockspar Island, Georgia, who were held by "enemies of the United States," to be "already confiscated and declared free."[48] Hunter's most striking move, though, occurred in May 1862, after his declaration of martial law over the whole of South Carolina, Georgia, and Florida (the three states contained in his military department). He went on to pronounce slavery and martial law to be "altogether incompatible" with one another, with the result that slaves throughout the

three states were thereby "declared forever free."[49] This initiative of Hunter
went beyond his earlier one, or that of Fremont, in declaring *all* slaves to be
free, without regard to the loyalty of their owners.

President Lincoln had less patience with Hunter's initiative than he had
with Fremont's. He swiftly and publicly countermanded it, affirming by
proclamation that the general had no authority to take such a step and flatly
declaring the purported emancipation measure to be "altogether void." The
President further stated that any decisions on emancipation policies were reserved for himself.[50]

The problem with emancipation by martial law, though, lay deeper than
simply the inadvisability of exercising it in particular circumstances. The major difficulty lay in the limited nature of martial law itself, which (as observed
earlier) was, by its nature, a mechanism for dealing with short-term emergencies. It was not designed as a means of bringing about permanent and fundamental social change. Lincoln explained the position with characteristic clarity
in a private letter in 1861:

> If a commanding general finds a necessity to seize the farm of a private
> owner, for a pasture, an encampment, or a fortification he has the right to
> do so, and to so hold it as long as the necessity lasts; and this is within mil-
> itary law, because within military necessity. But to say the farm shall no
> longer belong to the owner or his heirs forever; and this as well when the
> farm is not needed for military purposes as when it is, is purely political,
> without the savor of military law about it. And the same is true of slaves. If
> the General needs them, he can seize them, and use them; but when the
> need is past, it is not for him to fix their permanent future condition. This
> must be settled according to laws made by law-makers, and not by military
> proclamations.[51]

The greatest care should be taken, Lincoln asserted, that the executive did not
"impliedly seize and exercise the permanent legislative functions of the government" under the guise of martial law—a concern that did not weigh so
heavily on Lincoln's mind in other, less sensitive areas.[52]

Emancipation in Federal Areas

It was possible for the federal government to strike directly at slavery by way
of legislation in two restricted geographical areas: the District of Columbia
and the territories. Regarding the District of Columbia, the Constitution ex-

pressly grants to Congress the power to "exercise exclusive Legislation in all Cases whatsoever."[53] Pursuant to this power, Congress enacted a law abolishing slavery in the Federal District in April 1862.[54] Since this was an exercise of sovereign, rather than of belligerent, power by the federal government, Congress included a provision for "just compensation" for loyal slave-owners, as required by the Fifth Amendment.[55] Up to $1 million *in toto* was appropriated for this purpose, with a maximum payment per emancipated slave of $300. Lincoln, still treading cautiously at this time on the slavery issue, expressed gratification at the payment provision.[56] It is doubtful, however, whether it really met the standard of "just" compensation, since $300 was well below the going market rate for slaves.

This first emancipation program was administered by a three-person board, whose chief tasks were twofold: determining the loyalty of claimants, and assessing the compensation in individual cases. On the loyalty question, a policy of extreme lenience was adopted. Compensation was refused only if the claimant had actually borne arms for the Confederacy, with mere sympathy for the Confederate cause posing no bar to payment. Over 95 percent of compensation applications were successful in whole or in part, with the maximum figure of $300 per slave awarded in most instances. In all, about a thousand owners claimed compensation, for the freeing of some 3,100 slaves.[57]

Regarding the federal territories, the power given by the Constitution to Congress is rather less sweepingly stated than is that given the Federal District. Congress is empowered to "make all needful Rules and Regulations" for the territories. In June 1862, two months after the enactment of the abolition measure for the District of Columbia, Congress, in a little-noticed action, exercised this power by abolishing slavery throughout the federal territories—this time *without* any compensation for the slave-owners.[58] Lincoln, as a staunch and long-standing opponent of the expansion of slavery into the territories, had no misgivings about putting his signature to this measure.

The Emancipation Proclamation

By the summer of 1862, President Lincoln had managed to overcome his earlier scruples about effecting permanent changes in fundamental laws and rights by way of martial-law action. He resolved to wield his power as commander-in-chief of the armed forces to proclaim slavery ended in the rebellious areas. One of the most potent considerations behind this decision was the attitude of foreign countries, and the fear that Britain and France, most notably, might extend formal recognition to the Confederacy as an independent country. Slavery in the Confederacy was naturally a factor militating against such recognition. But, so long as the Union persisted in refusing to make the war into a principled crusade against slavery, there was embarrassingly little scope for choice between the two rival sides on that question.[59]

In deciding how comprehensive to make his emancipation measure, Lincoln faced two key decisions. The first concerned, so to speak, how deeply the policy should go—whether the slaves of *both* loyal and disloyal owners would be freed. The second question was how broadly the policy should sweep geographically—i.e., whether to extend emancipation to *all* of the slave states, including the Union ones, or whether to confine it to the eleven rebellious ones. The decision reached was that emancipation would cover *all* slaves in the affected areas, without regard to the loyalty of their masters, but that the affected areas would *not* include the Union slave states.

The Emancipation Proclamation has been the subject of much attention elsewhere, so that it is only necessary here to comment on the specifically legal aspects of it.[60] It came in two installments: the Preliminary Proclamation on September 22, 1862, announcing that emancipation was impending; followed by a final one on January 1, 1863, actually effecting it (or at least purporting to). The Preliminary Proclamation was somewhat ambiguous as to the authority on which it was based.[61] There was much emphasis on the existing statutory ban on the return of slaves by military officers to their owners, as well as on other existing statutory provisions. The President exhorted the armed forces fully to enforce these laws.[62] The impression was thereby given (without being expressly stated) that the Preliminary Proclamation was issued pursuant to the President's constitutional duty to "take Care that the Laws be faithfully executed."[63] It is also worth noting that the Preliminary Proclamation expressly affirmed the aim of the Union war effort to be the restoration of "the constitutional relation between the United States and each of the states and the people thereof"—with *no* reference here to emancipation. The President even hinted at compensation for *loyal* slave-owners by including a vague promise that "in due time" they would receive compensation for *all* war-related losses suffered, including the loss of slaves.[64]

The final Proclamation of Emancipation, of January 1, 1863, was much more explicit as to its legal basis.[65] It was expressly described, in the text, as "a fit and necessary war measure" for suppressing the rebellion, issued under the President's power as commander-in-chief of the armed forces. It was therefore

fitting that the final proclamation, like its preliminary counterpart, was simultaneously issued as a military order to the armed forces.[66] Significantly, the
suggestion of compensation for loyal slave-owners was *not* included in the final proclamation. As ever, boldness was tempered with caution. The final
proclamation did *not*, at least on its face, state emancipation to be an actual
war aim. It was presented instead, in strictly instrumental terms, as a means of
bringing the war to a successful conclusion. A concern over the fostering of
disorder—or even, in the worst-case scenario, racial warfare—was evident in
the urging of all freed persons "to abstain from all violence, unless in necessary
self-defense." The Final Proclamation also expressed the hope that, "in all
cases when allowed," they would "labor faithfully for reasonable wages." The
chains of servitude were being broken, it is apparent, by lawyers and not by
revolutionaries.

The Proclamation of Emancipation resembled the presidential proclamations of September 1862 on disloyal practices, in that it effectively created, by
executive fiat, a new criminal offense of slaveholding. In at least one instance,
in Arkansas in 1864, a person was actually prosecuted for dealing in slaves in
violation of the Proclamation. He was tried by a military commission, convicted, and sentenced to five years' imprisonment. That the Proclamation did
not explicitly provide for prosecution or punishment of slaveholders was of no
great moment in the eyes of Adjutant General Holt. The abolition of slavery,
in his view, must necessarily and universally be understood to imply that persons engaging in that odious practice would be subject to punishment.[67]

There was room for grave doubt as to whether the President had the power
to make so momentous a change in the internal laws of the states under the
guise of his commander-in-chief power.[68] It was even highly doubtful (to say
the least) whether the Proclamation could fairly be regarded as a martial-law
measure, since it purported to apply to areas that the Union armies did not
even control. Confederate secretary of war James Seddon, ironically echoing
Lincoln's own earlier misgivings, objected that martial law measures were, by
their nature, temporary in duration, dealing only with "the events of a sea-
son." The Proclamation, however, in sharpest contrast, purported to have permanent force, effectively making it (again in Seddon's words) "an imperial
edict, determining arbitrarily [the] civil, social, and domestic institutions and
relations" of the affected areas "for all time."[69] Seddon was hardly an unbiased
commentator, but he was right to point out that the Proclamation went stun-
ningly far beyond the bounds of "ordinary" martial law.

The Emancipation Proclamation has sometimes been said to have been a great watershed, marking the point at which the federal war effort ceased to be a law-enforcement operation, directed against disloyal individuals, and began instead to be a true war directed against the entire territory of the Confederacy without regard to the sentiments of individual persons. The most concrete sign of this change was, of course, the decision that *all* slaves in the affected areas would be declared free, without distinction between loyal and disloyal owners. In the terminology employed in the Prize Cases of 1863, the Proclamation may be asserted to mark the point at which the conflict ceased to be "personal" in character and became "territorial" instead.[70]

There is much to be said for this thesis. At the same time, it should be borne in mind that the federal government continued, to the very end of the war, to distinguish between loyal and disloyal persons in a variety of ways. This was most clearly apparent with regard to two policies: requisitions and the captured-and-abandoned-property program. In the case of requisitions, it was envisaged that loyal property owners would receive compensation (eventually) on the basis of receipts issued by the armed forces at the time of taking. And in the case of captured and abandoned property, loyal persons were given a statutory right to claim the proceeds of sale of the property.[71]

Nevertheless, it is fair to say that, with the issuing of the Emancipation Proclamation, the federal government committed itself, as never before, to waging war not merely against individual miscreants but rather—and far more broadly—against the Southern way of life itself. Seddon was clearly of this opinion. The promulgation of the Proclamation, in his view, starkly indicated that the Union now sought (if it had not previously) "an entire overthrow of [the] social order" of the Southern states. That could only mean, he darkly concluded, that the conflict was henceforth to be "a war of massacres and confusions" between rival ways of life, rather than merely—as wars were meant to be—a "trial of right" between rival sovereigns.[72] In short, the Proclamation *did* move the conflict into a new phase—but with many remnants of the previous one still present.

Unfinished Business

Nobody was under any illusion that the Emancipation Proclamation marked the definitive and complete end of slavery in the United States. There were two important respects in which it fell short of that ambitious goal. First, and most obviously, the Proclamation, by its terms, exempted large areas. Basically, the Union slave states (plus Tennessee) were excluded in their entirety from its reach, as were most of the Union-occupied areas in the South. In theory at least, loyal slaveholders in the border states retained all of their prewar rights over their slaves. That even included reaping the benefit of the Fugitive Slave Act of 1850, which remained on the statute books through most of the war.[73] Attorney General Bates made it clear that the act would continue to be enforced in the District of Columbia, even after the abolition of slavery there, with respect to slaves fleeing from Maryland.[74]

An important inroad into that notorious law was made, however, by the Second Confiscation Act, which effectively limited its benefit to *loyal* slaveowners, by providing that slaves would be returned only to owners who swore an ironclad oath of loyalty (i.e., an oath that they had been loyal to the Union cause throughout the conflict).[75] Eventually, the Fugitive Slave Act itself was repealed, although not until June 1864.[76] The delay resulted from opposition by a combination of border-state representatives, Democrats, and conservative Republicans. By that time, events on the slavery front had moved on to the more momentous question of outright emancipation; so the repeal attracted hardly any public attention.[77]

Even with the demise of the Fugitive Slave Act, it remained the case that escaping from a slave state into a free state did not, in itself, bring legal emancipation. The Constitution expressly so provided, by stating that a slave escaping across a state line was not thereby "discharged from [the] Service or Labour" which he or she owed.[78] The repeal of the act, in other words, deprived slaveowners only of their effective *remedy* regarding escaped slaves and did not terminate the master-slave relationship *per se*. In addition, it was still possible that state laws in the Union slave states could make it illegal to assist slaves in escaping from their masters. As late as 1865, a criminal prosecution was mounted in the Kentucky courts against a Union general for just such an offense.[79]

The other respect in which the Emancipation Proclamation fell short of definitively resolving the slavery question concerned the knotty question of the legal effect that august measure. Even within the Lincoln administration, there were doubts as to whether so vast and permanent a change in the American social and legal fabric could really be wrought by presidential pronouncement.[80] Since the Proclamation was presented exclusively as a military measure, there was a fear that it might *automatically* cease to have any applicability once the war was concluded, on the ground that no military justification could be held to exist any longer. More realistic was the contention that, as a military measure, the Proclamation could have validity only within areas actually controlled by the federal armed forces.

In the years immediately following the war, there were a number of Southern state supreme court decisions to this effect. In 1866, for example, the Arkansas Supreme Court held that, as a war measure, the Proclamation could only operate as a directive to the Union armed forces.[81] On this interpretation, it simply made a modest change to the existing policy, in the Second Confiscation Act, concerning slaves escaping to the Union military lines—by making *all* such persons free, even if they were fleeing from loyal owners.[82] Pursuing this line of reasoning to its logical conclusion, the Texas Supreme Court, in 1868, pointed out that full and permanent emancipation of all slaves could only come about by way of "a complete and thorough subjugation of the revolted states and districts"—but not by mere proclamation.[83] In the light of these many doubts about the legal effect of the Emancipation Proclamation—as well as for the ending of slavery in the Union slave states—further action was agreed to be necessary.

Permanent Solutions

In the light of the grave doubts as to the legal status of the Emancipation Proclamation, there was a general appreciation of the need to place the abolition of slavery onto a sounder legal footing. There was less of a consensus, however, on how best to go about this. There were two basic possibilities: legislation by Congress; or, more definitively, a constitutional amendment. It is interesting that, at first, abolitionist and Radical elements preferred statutory to constitutional action, apparently out of fears that the necessary two-thirds majority might not be attainable in the two houses of Congress, as well as concern over whether three-quarters of the states would ratify it. In this connection, there were worries over the implication of counting the eleven Confederate states in the ratification process.[84] In the end, however, it came to be agreed that only a constitutional amendment could bring a definitive legal end to slavery.

Ending Slavery by Constitutional Amendment

Even with this agreement reached, there was considerable scope for dispute as to what, precisely, such an amendment should actually contain. Some favored a minimalist approach, in which there would be simply an abolition of slavery as such, with no other changes made. Some said that emancipation should be coupled with a guarantee of certain basic rights, such as the right of access to courts, or the guaranteeing of citizenship. In the end, the minimalist view prevailed. The amendment as it passed Congress contained two basic provisions. First, it pronounced that "[n]either slavery nor involuntary servitude . . . shall exist within the United States" or its possessions (except as punishment for crimes). Second, it conferred onto Congress the power to enforce the amendment by "appropriate legislation." In this form, the amendment mustered the required two-thirds of each house of Congress on February 1, 1865.[85]

The question of how to count the states for the purpose of obtaining ratification from three-fourths of them was the next hurdle—one that had received remarkably little attention during the congressional drafting and adoption process. If the full complement of states, including the Confederate ones, were counted, then the total at the time was thirty-six—with twenty-seven ratifications needed. If the eleven confederate states were left out of the process, then nineteen ratifications would be needed. Congress adjourned in March 1865 without a firm decision having been made. Lincoln, in what proved to be his last public address, in April 1865, expressed the view that all thirty-six states should be counted, to ensure that there would be no lingering doubts as the validity of the amendment.[86] As events developed, this view prevailed.

It might be thought that the eleven Confederate states then had only to refrain from ratifying it, and the amendment would then be defeated, since they accounted for well over one-fourth of the thirty-six states. The political (and military) reality at the time, however, dictated otherwise. By the time the South had been militarily vanquished and the Confederate government effectively dismantled, it was abundantly clear that there was no possibility of salvaging slavery from the general wreckage. It was apparent to the Southern states that, if they were to be admitted back into the Union on their former footing, they would have to accept that slavery was now definitively finished. Ratification of the Thirteenth Amendment was therefore regarded, in effect, as a required passport to political rehabilitation.[87]

The major concern of Southerners, by the end of the war, was not the abolition of slavery *per se*. It was the more worrying possibility that Congress, when adopting "appropriate" enforcement legislation pursuant to the amendment, might enact a far-reaching program of political, legal, and social equality of the races. The Lincoln administration did its best to dispel these fears. When the postwar provisional (i.e., Union-appointed) governor of South Carolina protested to Secretary of State Seward that his state would never consent to an amendment that gave Congress the power to legislate about the race relations within its borders, Seward hastened to assure him that the amendment's enforcement clause was actually "restraining in its object," designed to restrict rather than to enlarge the powers of Congress.[88] Gradually, in the course of the debates in the states, it was agreed that the amendment could not reasonably be interpreted as granting (or allowing Congress to grant) the right to vote to ex-slaves. With this fear, and similar ones, allayed, the requisite number of state ratifications was forthcoming, and the amendment entered into force in December 1865.[89] Eight of the Confederate states ratified the amendment prior to its entry into force (thereby contributing to the formation of the necessary three-fourths majority of states), with two following later—and only Mississippi standing obstinately aloof.[90]

Some ratifying states appended interpretive declarations to their ratifications. South Carolina, for example, stated that "any attempt by [the federal] Congress toward legislating upon the political status of former slaves, or their civil relations, would be contrary to the Constitution of the United States, as it now is, or as it would be altered by the proposed amendment."[91] Alabama, in a similar vein, stated its understanding that the amendment did not "confer upon Congress the power to Legislate upon the political status of Freedmen in this State."[92]

The Thirteenth Amendment in "Action"

In one respect, the Thirteenth Amendment was a powerful instrument. It was what lawyers call *self-executing*. That meant that, by its own force, it made slavery legally impossible in the United States, without the need for any separate act of abolition from Congress.[93] What the amendment did *not* do, though, was to attach a specified criminal penalty to be visited on persons who attempted to keep slaves contrary to it. Congress was empowered, by the enforcement provision of the amendment, to enact "appropriate legislation" for this additional purpose, which it proceeded to do in May 1866.[94] That law made it a federal criminal offense to kidnap or carry away any person with the intention of holding him or her as a slave. The stipulated penalty was a fine of $500 to $5,000, or imprisonment for up to five years, or both. This legislation is effectively still in force, and is no mere historical relic. There were ninety-eight prosecutions under it in the period 1992–2005 alone, involving 284 defendants and resulting in nearly two hundred convictions. These cases most frequently arise from situations of oppressive domestic employment.[95] It has also been held by lower federal courts (though not, as yet, by the Supreme Court) that this enforcement statute operates to confer a private civil right of action onto the victims.[96]

The assurances given by the supporters of the amendment prior to its passage—that the enforcement clause could not and would not be used to bring about a broad-based situation of equality between the races—were largely borne out by judicial developments. The courts proceeded to interpret the clause in a literal and restrictive fashion. As the Kentucky Court of Appeal candidly put it in 1867, the amendment "gave the colored race nothing more than freedom. It did not elevate them to social or political equality with the white race."[97] In 1883, the federal Supreme Court expressed agreement, holding that the Thirteenth Amendment "simply abolished slavery" and went no further.[98]

The conservative tenor of the federal courts on this point was demonstrated by the way in which they treated various matters ancillary to the slave relationship. One example was the seemingly abstruse question of whether a person who had entered into a contract for the sale of a slave, at a time and place where such transactions were lawful, could sue the buyer under the contract for payment for the slave, *after* the abolition of slavery itself. Those who favored sweeping all traces of slavery from the federal judiciary, such as Chief Justice Chase, were of the opinion that any contract rooted in slavery could not be enforced by the federal courts. But majority of the Supreme Court held otherwise in 1872, holding the buyer legally liable to pay, on the ground that the contract had been lawful when made. As Justice Noah H. Swayne put it, speaking for the majority of the Court:

> Whatever we may think of the institution of slavery viewed in the light of religion, morals, humanity, or a sound political economy,—as the obligation here in question was valid when executed, sitting as a court of justice, we have no choice but to give it effect. We cannot regard it as differing in its legal efficacy from any other unexecuted contract.[99]

The South Carolina Supreme Court reached a similar conclusion in 1870, in striking down a postwar state constitutional provision purporting to bar the state's courts from entertaining suits on contracts for the sale of slaves.[100]

If courts were disposed to take a narrow view of the abolition of slavery, Congress showed itself willing to act considerably more boldly. In 1866 Congress, increasingly under the dominance of Radical elements, sought to employ the enforcement clause of the Thirteenth Amendment as the legal basis of a broad-ranging program of equality of civil rights for the freed slaves. The Civil Rights Act of 1866 guaranteed a wide range of civil rights to the ex-slaves, such as the right to conclude contracts, sue in courts, give evidence, own and inherit property, and, in general, to benefit from laws guaranteeing security of person and property.[101] It achieved this end by the somewhat indirect means of prohibiting the *states* from abridging these rights.

Not surprisingly, there were strong doubts as to the constitutionality of this law, which obviously went far beyond the bounds of the bare abolition of slavery as such. Nevertheless, the California Supreme Court had no difficulty holding the act constitutional under the Thirteenth Amendment; and there was later authority from the lower federal courts to the same effect.[102] (Not until 1968 did the Supreme Court add its endorsement.)[103] To dispel any doubts on the subject, Congress decided to place these equal-rights provisions onto a distinct and explicit constitutional footing, in the form of the famous provisions of the Fourteenth Amendment, requiring states to guarantee due process of law and also "the equal protection of the laws" to all persons within their borders. In the fullness of time, these provisions would bring about a profound constitutional and social transformation of American society. In the more immediate term, they rescued the constitutionality of the 1866 act.

These Fourteenth Amendment provisions, however, suffered from a key weakness: that they were, at least on their face, restrictions only on the powers wielded by the *states*. For those who sought equality between the races in the fullest sense, it was necessary to find some way of striking at *private* discriminatory action, such as refusals by private proprietors to serve blacks in hotels or restaurants. One way of achieving this, it was hoped by some (and feared by others), was to employ the Thirteenth Amendment, which clearly did strike at private action. Private discriminatory acts, it was suggested, could be reached by the enforcement clause of that amendment *if* they could somehow be regarded as falling within the concept of slavery. There was an attempt to achieve this by contending that discriminatory action by private parties should be regarded as what came to be called a "badge of slavery."[104] Congress put this theory to the test by enacting the Civil Rights Act of 1875, which prohibited a broad range of private discriminatory acts.[105]

For all of its ingenuity, this approach to equality between the races did not win the endorsement of the federal courts. In 1883, in the Civil Rights Cases, the Supreme Court, with Justice Joseph P. Bradley writing for the majority, held the 1875 act to be unconstitutional.[106] The Court did not, however, reject the badges-of-slavery argument in principle. It conceded that the Thirteenth Amendment had what it called "a reflex character" which reached out to encompass all "incidents" of slavery. But it took a cautious view of how far that reflex action actually extended, holding that "[m]ere discriminations" by private parties such as innkeepers did not fall within its compass. Consequently, the 1875 act was not authorized by the enforcement clause of the Thirteenth Amendment.[107]

There the matter lay for a very long time. When legislation was finally enacted to make private discrimination into a federal offense, in 1964, an entirely different constitutional vehicle was employed: the commerce clause, which allowed Congress to regulate interstate commerce.[108] Ironically, this was a part of the original Constitution of 1787, owing nothing to the Civil War amendments. Any provider of accommodation to the general public whose "operations affect commerce"—and that was acknowledged to be virtually everyone—was barred from engaging in racial discrimination.[109] With that legislation, private discrimination in public facilities died an instant death. The constitutionality of that legislation was duly upheld by the Supreme Court that same year.[110]

The story of the Thirteenth Amendment was not over, however. In a little-noticed development in 1968, the federal Supreme Court resurrected the badges-of-servitude theory as a vehicle for striking at private acts of discrimination.[111] The case concerned the refusal of a home-owner to sell a house to a black person, allegedly on racial grounds, in violation of the 1866 act. The Supreme Court finally—and rather belatedly—held that act to have been constitutional as an exercise of Congress's power, under the enforcement clause of the Thirteenth Amendment. At the same time, it held that the act applies not only to state actions but also to private acts which qualify as badges of slavery—a category now held to be capacious enough to include discrimination in the sale of houses.[112] This decision attracted hardly any attention at the time (and very little since).[113] It is possible, though, that too little regard has been paid to this development, since the critical difference between the Thirteenth and the Fourteenth amendments, identified above, remains that the Thirteenth Amendment clearly covers private action, while the Fourteenth Amendment covers only state action. It is therefore not impossible that the Thirteenth Amendment may harbor some surprises for the future.[114]

6

Taking Liberties on the Home Front

The substance must not be sacrificed to the form. Our first, great constitutional duty is to save the nation and the States; and, if possible, we must save them according to law. But, if the two duties conflict, still the greater must be performed and the lesser must yield, even as a conflicting act of Congress must yield to the Constitution.

—Edward Bates

The doctrine sometimes advanced by men, with more zeal than wisdom, that whenever war exists in one part of the country the constitutional guaranties of personal liberty, and of the rights of property, are suspended everywhere, has no foundation in the principles of the common law, the teachings of our ancestors, or the language of the Constitution, and is at variance with every just notion of a free government. Our system of civil polity is not such a rickety and ill-jointed structure, that when one part is disturbed the whole is thrown into confusion and jostled to its foundation.

—Justice Stephen J. Field

Liberty was a concern not only of slaves but also—though in different ways—of persons who were already free. Throughout the Civil War, there were grave doubts over the extent to which the normal rights of free persons encompassed the right to oppose the Union war effort. Opposition to the policies of the Lincoln administration and the Union war effort came from diverse parts of the ideological spectrum. There were some, such as the veteran firebrand (and pacifist) William Lloyd Garrison, who were so ill-disposed toward slavery and the Southern states as positively to advocate disunion. Conversely, some were sympathizers with the South, opposed to tampering with slavery.[1] Others had little strong opinion one way or the other about the Confederacy but were intensely unhappy with certain aspects of the Union war policy—such as conscription, high taxation, or the liberation of slaves.

The federal government was not overly disposed toward tolerance of dissent. But the arsenal of legal weapons at its disposal was rather limited. True, there were federal criminal laws against treason and related activities (bolstered by additional legislation during the war). But the criminal law was a cumbrous instrument, slow and uncertain (particularly with the risk that sympathetic juries might refuse to convict popular defendants even in the face of overwhelming evidence). With a certain imagination, however—liberally admixed with a willingness to go beyond the strict letter of the law—alternative means could be devised for dealing with disloyal (or sometimes merely obstreperous) opponents of the administration. One was the suspension of the right of habeas corpus, to prevent persons in detention from using the courts to gain their freedom. In addition, the military was extensively employed against dissenters, both for arrest and detention and even for the trial of civilians before military commissions.

If the legal tools available to the government were limited, those available to persons in detention were more restricted still. At the time of the Civil War, there was no significant body of Supreme Court case-law on the protection of civil liberties, whether in "normal" circumstances or in times of emergency. Nevertheless, persons affected by the various measures sometimes managed to fight back, by legal means—occasionally with notable success. In the process, the first major constitutional protections of civil liberties were hammered out. In some important respects, then, the modern law of civil liberties was born in the confusion and turmoil of the Civil War.[2]

Rooting out Disloyalty

Against enemies on the home front, the most obvious weapon that the government possessed for the suppression of disloyalty was the law of treason. Treason has the interesting distinction of being the only criminal offense that is defined in the text of the Constitution itself. It comprises *only* two activities: "levying War" against the United States; and "adhering to . . . Enemies [of the United States], giving them Aid and Comfort."[3] In the crisis of the 1860s, the giving of aid and comfort to enemies was not relevant, as it was agreed that that provision referred only to aiding *foreign* enemies in an international war. Adherence to the Confederate cause did, however, fall within the scope of levying war.

Since 1790, there had been a treason statute in federal law, carrying the death penalty.[4] In the Second Confiscation Act of July 1862, Congress made two alterations.[5] First, it eliminated the mandatory penalty, by authorizing the courts to inflict sentences of imprisonment and fine (along with liberation of slaves) instead of death. Second, it created (somewhat puzzlingly) what looked to be an overlapping offense, of engaging in or supporting rebellion against the federal government.[6] The following year, another related offense was created, of communicating with the Confederate government from a foreign country (without the consent of the Union authorities).[7]

A number of treason prosecutions were instituted during the war. In Virginia alone, there were some eight hundred indictments.[8] The number that were carried to a conclusion, however, was negligible. Chief Justice Roger Taney, who was in charge of the highly important Maryland circuit, certainly did his best to ensure that treason prosecutions would not come to trial there. He justified his policy, in a letter to Associate Justice Samuel Nelson, by holding that Maryland was, in reality if not in name, under martial law and that, in such an atmosphere, fair trials were not possible. Even if a defendant were to be acquitted, he or she would be promptly rearrested, and the courts would be powerless to provide any real protection.[9] As a result, the treason prosecutions in that state lingered until the end of the war and then were quietly dropped. It might be noted that John Merryman was in this category. Although his attempt to obtain release by way of habeas corpus had failed, he eventually was freed on bail and, in the event, was never tried.[10] A prosecution in California of some would-be privateers for the Confederate cause represents well-nigh the only actual use of the new 1862 legislation.[11]

In place of criminal prosecutions, the federal government adopted a broad range of other control devices. A comprehensive study of these is not possible here.[12] But those which gave rise to interesting legal issues will be briefly surveyed. These are habeas corpus issues, the widespread employment of loyalty oaths, military arrests, and the trial of civilians before military commissions.

Suspending Habeas Corpus

Consideration has already been given to the important question of who possessed the power of suspending habeas corpus.[13] Here, it is important to say a bit more about its nature as a vital instrument for the protection of civil liberties. Habeas corpus is actually quite narrow in focus, in that it is a remedy against only one specific wrong: unlawful detention. It enables a person held in detention to obtain, very expeditiously, a ruling from a court of law as to whether that detention is lawful. More specifically, the *writ* of habeas corpus is, in essence, an order from a court to the detainer to come before the court for the purpose of justifying the detention—and, in so doing, to "have the body" (*habeas corpus,* in Latin) of the detainee physically present with him. If the detention cannot be justified by the detainer, then the detainee will be ordered released forthwith. Narrowly focused as it is, habeas corpus is rightly regarded as one of the brightest lights in the firmament of Anglo-American legal systems, chiefly because the burden is placed on the *detainer* to establish that the detention is lawful. Moreover, the process is especially valuable for its swiftness. Habeas corpus proceedings, in sum, represent the presumption in favor of liberty in its most robust and effective form.

The suspension of this great remedy therefore constitutes a drastic inroad into the fundamental right of liberty. It should be appreciated, however, what suspension of habeas corpus does *not* entail. Most outstandingly, suspension of habeas corpus effects no change whatsoever in the substantive law of the land. Suspension, that is to say, is the withholding of a *remedy* and not an alteration of the law itself. Suspension therefore does not transform an unlawful detention into a lawful one—although it does, of course, make it impossible to *contest* the lawfulness expeditiously. Nor does suspension of habeas corpus have any effect whatever on the due-process rights to which accused persons are entitled when they are actually tried. A presumption of innocence, a right to trial by jury, a right to representation by counsel, a right to a speedy and public trial—all of these vital guarantees are entirely untouched by a suspension of habeas corpus.[14] The Lincoln administration did abridge those other rights as well, but by other means, which will be explored presently.

It has been observed that, with the enactment of the Habeas Corpus Act in March 1863, suspension of the writ was finally given a statutory basis.[15] More specifically, the act provided that military officers who held persons in detention were not required, as they ordinarily would have been, to bring detained persons physically before the court. It also provided that a statement made by a military officer that a person was being held pursuant to the authority of the President was to be conclusive, thereby forestalling any judicial inquiry into the matter.

It should also be noted that the act contained some safeguards for persons in detention. For example, it required the secretaries of state and war to submit to federal judges lists of persons held under their auspices. If the persons on these lists were not formally indicted for crimes by grand juries in the normal manner by the end of the grand jury session following their arrest, then federal judges were to order their release on the taking of an oath of allegiance. In practice, however, these safeguards did not prove to be very effective.[16]

Loyalty Oaths

One of the most unusual (even somewhat bizarre) aspects of the legal scene during the Civil War was the extraordinary obsession with oaths of loyalty.[17] For present purposes, the principal point about them will be the manner in which they gradually altered their character—from reasonably defensive measures designed to keep disloyal persons out of sensitive positions, to a broad-sweeping system of control that had the practical effect of saddling large numbers of people with criminal-style disabilities without due process of law. It is one of the major, and less known, stories of the war.

The use of loyalty oaths started out modestly enough. At the outset of the hostilities, in April 1861, members of the federal government were required, by executive order, to retake the oaths that they had sworn on assuming their posts. For good measure, a law of August 1861 required heads of executive departments to compel their employees to take yet another oath of loyalty.[18] The various department heads were left to decide on their own just what this oath would consist of. Generally, the cabinet heads required no more than an affirmation of intention to be loyal to the Union cause in the future.

Other categories of persons were gradually subjected to oath requirements. A law of March 1862 required loyalty oaths of all masters of ships clearing from United States ports to foreign destinations.[19] The Habeas Corpus Act of 1863 required a loyalty oath of released political prisoners (a practice that had already been in place in any event).[20] Loyalty oaths were also required in connection with a host of federal government services, such as the obtaining of passports and visas. In the South, loyalty oaths were even more ubiquitous than in the North, although they came more from the initiatives of the state governments than of the Confederate one.[21]

The great innovation was the devising of what became known as the iron-clad oath.[22] This oath differed from an "ordinary" one, in that it entailed swearing as to one's past activities as well as to one's present intentions. It required a person to swear not only that he or she was loyal at the time of swearing, and intended to remain so, but also that he or she *had always been* loyal

in the past. The effect—which of course was fully intended—was that an
ex–Confederacy supporter who had resumed loyalty to the Union could not
take an ironclad oath without committing perjury.

This ironclad oath was first imposed on persons seeking compensation for
slaves emancipated in the District of Columbia by the law of April 1862.[23] After that, it spread steadily. Would-be voters in the District of Columbia municipal elections of May 1862 were required, again by federal statute, to swear
an ironclad oath.[24] The following month, it became a condition of eligibility
for federal jury service.[25] In July 1862, the Second Confiscation Act required
an ironclad oath from putatively loyal slave-owners seeking to reclaim their
runaway slaves in the Union states.[26] That same month, it became a condition
for the holding of "any office of honor or profit" under the federal government—
thereby applying to the entire federal executive workforce with a lone exception made for the President.[27] Early in 1865, the ironclad oath was extended to
all lawyers practicing in the federal court system.[28] Some states spread the
ironclad oath into even more varied walks of life, with Missouri having the
doubtful honor of going the furthest. It adopted a law barring persons from
holding a wide array of positions—including teachers, lawyers, and ministers
of religion—unless they could swear to their past innocence of as many as
eighty-three identified activities.[29]

In certain respects, these oaths were unobjectionable. It was clearly reasonable, for example, to use them to prevent disloyal persons from occupying sensitive war-related posts, such as employment in the War Department. It may
be objected that a disloyal person would probably have few scruples about
swearing falsely in such a case. That may be so. But if such a person was subsequently discovered to be disloyal, he or she could be prosecuted for perjury
on the basis of the oath, without the need to prove the commission of any *specific* act of wrongdoing, which might have been well concealed. The general
principle that loyalty oaths may be required, *if* loyalty is a *bona fide* qualification for the post in question, is firmly accepted in American constitutional
law, reaffirmed by the Supreme Court in 1951.[30]

It is equally, and oppositely, clear that a loyalty-oath requirement that has
the effect of stripping persons of fundamental rights will not be constitutional.
A clear (if rather extreme) illustration may readily be offered. Suppose that a
law were adopted requiring defendants in criminal cases to swear an ironclad
loyalty oath—with the provision that, if they refused to do so, they would not
be granted a presumption of innocence or a right to counsel in their trials.

Such a law would clearly be unconstitutional for the simple reason that it operated as a vehicle for depriving persons of basic, inalienable civil rights.

The difficulty, in legal terms, with loyalty oaths lies in the fact that there is a gigantic gray area between these two extremes. At what point, precisely, does a loyalty oath stop being a genuine job qualification and start becoming an infringement of basic rights? That sensitive issue was posed, for the first time, during and after the Civil War, with results that will be considered presently.

Detention without Trial

It would be difficult to name as egregious a violation of basic civil rights as a policy of detention at the pleasure of the executive, without the benefit of judicial hearing. The most notorious example of it was the French practice, prior to the Revolution of 1789, of issuing *lettres de cachet,* or "sealed letters."[31] These were orders for the arrest and detention of named individuals, who were then held at the monarch's pleasure. There is no explicit constitutional authority for so striking an interference with liberty in the United States. From the very outset of the Civil War, though, it became apparent that the federal authorities were willing to take drastic action against persons suspected of disloyalty, without regard to whether specific infringements of the existing criminal law could be established.

The practice of executive detention began when a Treason Bureau was set up in the Department of State, staffed by a large force of detectives. Secretary Seward appears to have positively relished his role as the government's chief ferreter-out of disloyalty. He is alleged to have boasted to the British ambassador to Washington, Lord Lyons, that, at the mere ringing of a "little bell" on his desk, he could have any citizen in the United States arrested.[32] It was a somewhat ill-judged boast, since stories of Seward's "little bell" soon began to figure prominently in antiadministration propaganda.[33]

Ironically, Seward's claims contained a rather high element of braggadocio. Relatively few persons were arrested on Department of State orders in the early months of the conflict. During that period, over half of all the detentions in the early months of the war were at the hands of state or local authorities; and many of the State Department's efforts were directed toward trying to discover why these other arrests had taken place. In the period from the outbreak of the hostilities until February 1862, the total number of arrests ordered by the Department of State was 864.[34]

The position changed significantly in February 1862, when the chief responsibility for internal security was transferred from the State Department to the War Department. This change was accompanied a public announcement that all political prisoners were to be released on parole—but, significantly, with exceptions made for spies and also for persons "whose release at the present moment may be deemed incompatible with the public safety."[35] The reality was that the War Department proved itself more zealous, as well as more efficient, in the pursuit of disloyal elements than the State Department had been, leading to a very sharp increase in the number of detentions.[36]

The typical pattern was that a person would be arrested on some kind of suspicion and then held in detention for a period varying from some weeks to several months. During this period, special investigating commissions would look into the detainee's activities, with these commissions typically comprising a senior military officer and a civilian lawyer. If evidence of actual disloyalty was inadequate, the person would be released.[37] These arrests were essentially preventive in nature, as President Lincoln himself candidly stated.[38] Consequently, in his view, there was no need for the sorts of formalities and safeguards that the Constitution provided for cases of actual criminal prosecution.[39] Release was typically conditioned on the taking of a nonironclad loyalty oath.[40]

The result was a dualistic system for the maintenance of law and order, consisting on the one hand of ordinary law enforcement, under the auspices of the attorney general, and on the other hand of executive detentions by the War Department. Attorney General Bates characterized the distinction as one between "judicial arrests" and "political arrests." A judicial arrest was one "whose object is to secure the presence of the accused so that he may be tried for an alleged crime before a civil court." A political arrest, in contrast, was "usually executed by the military arm—whose object is to secure the prisoner and hold him subject to the somewhat broad and as yet undefined discretion of the President as the political chief of the nation."[41]

The most intense period of executive detention—hence, from the civil-liberties standpoint, the darkest days of the entire war—occurred in August and September 1862. This was the time in which the initial steps toward conscription were taken, and the Preliminary Proclamation of Emancipation was issued. It was also (as noted above) the time of the first nationwide suspension of habeas corpus, and of the martial-law measures which provided for the imprisonment of persons who interfered with enlistments or who engaged in "disloyal practices" in general.[42] The crackdown on disloyal practices, in particular, led to a veritable orgy of detentions.[43]

The closest study of the Lincoln administration's civil-liberties record has concluded that the picture was, in some important respects, less alarming than many have supposed—and than many at the time alleged. The policy never, not even in the autumn of 1862, reached the point of wholesale arrests on an utterly arbitrary basis. It is true that the number of persons detained was actually considerably larger than traditional estimates have supposed—with recent research concluding that the traditional figure of some 13,000 political arrests in the whole of the war period was a woeful underestimate of the true numbers.[44] At the same time, though, the short-term nature of most of these detentions must be borne in mind. Moreover, the brunt of the measures was concentrated on the border states, where pro-Confederate sympathies actually were present to a substantial degree, as well as in the occupied areas of the South itself. In large parts of the Union, military arrests were little in evidence.[45]

Civilian Trials by Military Commissions

As just observed, most of the political detentions during the Civil War were preventive in nature and did not lead to trials. In a number of cases, however, civilians were not merely arrested by the military. They were tried by military commissions as well.[46] This practice began on an *ad hoc* basis early in the conflict, in Washington, when General John Dix and Judge Edwards Pierrepont set about examining prisoners arrested by the Department of State. They examined over eighty political prisoners, most of whom they discharged on oath or parole not to aid the enemy.[47] At about the same time, General Fremont provided for the trial of civilians by military commissions, if they were taken "with arms in their hands," as part of his martial-law administration of Missouri.[48] Little notice was taken of these measures at the time. But the use of military commissions escalated dramatically, particularly with the great crackdown of August and September 1862, when persons accused of disrupting enlistment and of "disloyal practices" became subject to military trials.[49]

It should not be assumed that military commission trials were mere drumhead affairs or instruments of oppression. The commission set up by Fremont, for example, expressed a clear and strong displeasure over the fact that many persons were being arrested on the basis of no evidence at all. Persons should only be detained, the commission insisted, on the basis of "some strong circumstantial proof of facts"—a stricture that met with Fremont's approval.[50] It is the case, however, that one of the most basic safeguards of civilian trials— trial by jury—was conspicuously absent in the military tribunals. Nor does it appear that any very exact definition of the term "disloyal practices" ever emerged. Basically, persons could be put on trial for *any* activity that impeded the war effort, regardless of whether it breached any specific criminal law.

The number of military trials of civilians during the war has, not surprisingly, proved difficult to estimate. One researcher has given a minimum figure of 4,271.[51] Another investigator, not inconsistently, has put the number of military trials at approximately 5,460.[52] On the whole, the geographical pattern of military trials of civilians was much the same as with detentions, with most of the activity occurring in the border states and the occupied territories of the South. It appears that nearly half of the these trials may have taken place in Missouri. The trials were commonly for acts such as sabotage and various forms of guerrilla warfare, thereby accounting for the prevalence of Missouri in the statistics, as that state was particularly beset with irregular warfare. Another offense commonly attended to by military tribunals was the violation of loyalty oaths. The nonborder states were apparently little affected by military commissions, possibly accounting for a mere one-twentieth of all of the military trials of civilians. In some loyal states, there was not a single such trial.[53]

Consequently, any suggestion of wholesale, nationwide displacement of civilian courts by military tribunals must be rejected as exaggerated. That broad fact was, however, scant comfort to the particular individuals who were caught up in the various federal initiatives for the suppression of disloyalty. Some of the political and military detainees sought to win back their liberty— a daunting prospect against a government with a war to win and a very limited tolerance for disruption. Some of these dissidents, however, did manage, against heavy odds, to achieve some success. In so doing, they laid the first significant foundations of federal civil liberties law.

The Dissenters Fight Back

The legal weapons ready to hand for dissenters from federal war policies were few in number, as Attorney General Bates candidly attested. "[A]rrests merely political or military," he opined, "are . . . beyond the reach of the judicial officers and subject only to the political power of the President, who may at his discretion dispose of the prisoners by orders addressed to his subordinate officers whether civil or military." The judiciary, in his view, "have no power or duties in regard to the prisoners merely political or military."[54]

Despite the daunting barriers to effective action, valiant attempts were made to obtain judicial redress for executive acts that strayed beyond the bounds of the law—although, in the most important cases, vindication only came after the conclusion of the hostilities. Two main avenues of relief were employed. First was state courts, in the form either of habeas corpus relief or the pursuit of ordinary civil actions. Second, and more important, were constitutional challenges in the federal courts, which involved, most notably, challenges to two of the Lincoln administration's weapons against dissidents: trials of civilians by military commissions; and the ironclad oath.

Habeas Corpus Relief from State Courts

Since the federal courts, as Bates candidly admitted, were inhospitable to dissenters, some attempts were made to obtain relief from state courts. One possibility was habeas corpus relief, on the thesis that state courts were not affected by the federal habeas corpus suspensions. The federal government, however, was determined to foil this strategy; and it largely succeeded. In particular, it insisted that state courts had no authority to order the release of persons held in federal custody. There was existing authority for that proposition, in the federal Supreme Court case of *Ableman v. Booth* in 1859, although that judgment, strictly speaking, had only explicitly covered one distinct type of federal detention (of fugitive slaves by commissioners under the Fugitive Slave Act).[55]

Whether state courts could interfere with other forms of federal detention was an unresolved question at the start of the war. Questions on the subject soon began to be presented to state courts, principally in the form of habeas corpus to secure the release of persons from service in the armed forces.[56] Interference in this area by federal judges had been halted (as observed earlier) by the suspension of habeas corpus relief of September 1863.[57] State courts were not covered by the federal suspensions. But the War Department's position was that they did not need to be because they had no power in the first place to inquire into detentions by federal authorities. On that thesis, the War Department's policy was that habeas corpus writs from state courts should simply not be obeyed. Federal officials served with writs from state courts should respond by denying the jurisdiction of the court in the matter and refusing to bring the detainee before the court.[58] After the war, in 1872, this position was vindicated by the federal Supreme Court, which held that state courts had no jurisdiction to grant habeas corpus relief in cases of federal detention.[59]

Constitutional Challenge to Military Trials of Civilians

During the hostilities, no successful challenge was mounted to the trial of civilians by military commissions. A valiant attempt was made, however, by one of the war's most famous, and vociferous, dissidents: an Ohio politician named Clement Vallandigham. In May 1863, he delivered a fiery antiwar speech, lashing out with gusto against the Union war effort as a "wicked, cruel, and unnecessary war, one not waged for the preservation of the Union, but for the purpose of crushing out liberty and to erect a despotism; a war for the freedom of the blacks and the enslavement of the whites."[60] He was promptly arrested by the army for violation of a military order which prohibited (among many things) "[t]he habit of declaring sympathy for the enemy."[61] For this offense, he was tried and convicted by a military tribunal.[62]

Vallandigham appealed to a federal circuit court in Ohio, contending that, as a civilian, he could not be subjected to trial by a military commission. The court ruled against him, holding the various measures of the federal government to be lawful on the ground that they were "necessary to the protection and preservation of the government and the constitution." It was not necessary that the particular acts of disloyalty fall within the definition of any particular criminal offense. It sufficed that they tended to undermine the war effort. The court conceded that it was possible that subordinates of the President might be excessively zealous in carrying out their commander-in-chief's policy. But the court expressed confidence that, in such an unhappy event, the President would himself take the necessary disciplinary action.[63] A subsequent application to the federal Supreme Court—this time for a ruling that the trial *itself* had been unfairly conducted—also brought no relief. The Court held that it had no jurisdiction to review the proceedings of military tribunals.[64] In the end, Vallandigham was disposed of, on President Lincoln's order, by being summarily delivered in the dead of night to a Confederate military encampment. Eventually, he returned to the Union territory by way of Canada.[65]

Not until after the war had ended was a successful challenge made to the trial of civilians by military commissions. This one was brought by an opponent of the Union war effort named Lambdin P. Milligan. Milligan's opposition to the war appears to have been of a rather more activist character than Vallandigham's—in the form of participation in what was called the "Northwestern Conspiracy," a shadowy affair involving the formation of a paramilitary group and the fomenting of rebellion in the midwestern states. The general plan appears to have involved launching an attack from Canada in the summer of 1864, seizing arsenals, and then releasing and arming Confederate prisoners of war. In all probability, Milligan had some role in this murky affair, although it is difficult to discern just what it was.[66] He was also active in discouraging enlistments into the military, and was thought by federal agents to be involved in the arming of draft resisters.

For his troubles, Milligan was arrested in October 1864 at his home in Indiana, tried some two weeks later by a military commission, and convicted of two offenses—inciting insurrection, and giving aid and comfort to the enemy.[67] He was sentenced to death, although this was commuted by President Andrew Johnson to life imprisonment. Interestingly, a local civilian federal grand jury considered indicting him on ordinary (i.e., statutory) criminal charges but elected against doing so.

Milligan challenged the right of a military commission to try him and took his case all the way to the federal Supreme Court in 1866. The result was the quashing of the conviction.[68] In so doing, the Court stressed the limitations on the martial-law powers of the President. These powers, it emphasized, were "confined to the locality of actual war"—an area that, most emphatically, did *not* include the portion of Indiana in which Milligan had been arrested. More generally, the Court pronounced that martial law "can never exist where the courts are open, and in the proper and unobstructed exercise of their jurisdiction."[69]

On this point concerning martial law—i.e., concerning *presidential* prerogatives under the commander-in-chief power—the Court was unanimous; and that portion of the judgment caused little controversy.[70] Another aspect of the case, however, caused a great deal of alarm and earnest debate: the separate question of whether *Congress* (as opposed to the President) possesses the power to subject civilians to military trials when civilian courts are in operation. On that point—which actually was not directly at issue in Milligan's case—the Court divided five to four, with the majority opining that Congress did *not* have such a power, any more than the President did. That holding aroused a storm of controversy because of its potential impact on the congressional program of Reconstruction.[71]

In the years following the Civil War, the federal courts became ever sterner in their insistence that military courts have no jurisdiction over civilians. In 1955, the Supreme Court held that a *former* serviceman could not constitutionally be tried in a military court, even if the alleged offense occurred during his period of service.[72] In 1960, the Court, in the same vein, disallowed the trial in military courts of civilian dependents of serving soldiers.[73] Government policy has generally accorded with this position. During the Vietnam War, for example, when there were numerous instances of civilian interference with the process of conscription, the government made no attempt, in the manner of Lincoln, to subject such persons to military trials. All such offenses were tried in civilian courts, as ordinary criminal offenses, pursuant to preexisting legislation by Congress.

Fighting the Ironclad Oath

The basic characteristics of the ironclad oath have been set out. It is necessary here to set out the two basic constitutional objections to it: first, that it was, in practical effect if not in strict form, a bill of attainder; and second, that it was, in its practical impact, an *ex post facto* law. It should be appreciated that one particular feature of the ironclad oath underlay both of these objections: the fact that the oath, by definition, entailed swearing not merely as to one's present state of mind and intentions for the future, but also—and crucially—swearing as to one's past deeds.

The first constitutional objection to ironclad oaths was that they constituted a *bill of attainder*. This is an expression that will be unfamiliar to many laypersons. In its purest form, it refers to the imposition by a *legislature* of a criminal penalty on a named individual. It is objectionable on the ground that it saddles the person in question with a criminal conviction, without any of the due-process protections which a judicial proceeding would have guaranteed—without a formal indictment, or a presumption of innocence, or the right to confront witnesses, or a trial by jury. For this reason the Constitution expressly bars both the federal and the state governments from enacting bills of attainder.[74]

A measure can still qualify as a bill of attainder if it departs somewhat from this pure form. For example, it is not necessary that a bill of attainder actually name the person or persons affected. A description of a class of persons will suffice, provided that membership in the class is reasonably determinable. In addition, a bill of attainder need not impose a criminal sentence of the obvious type, such as a fine or imprisonment or death. It will suffice that the measure imposes disadvantages or disabilities onto the persons affected which are sufficiently serious to be reasonably considered to be penal in nature—i.e., to constitute punishment for some previous conduct. It is in this broader sense that the ironclad oath of the Civil War era was vigorously argued to constitute a bill of attainder. It withheld various rights and advantages from persons who were unable to swear it (without committing perjury)—thereby making it (so it was argued) a penalty, imposed by a legislature, on a class of individual persons for their past conduct.

The second, and related, constitutional objection to ironclad oaths was that they amounted to *ex post facto* laws. In its pure sense, an *ex post facto* law is one which pronounces some action to be criminal (hence liable to punishment) *after* the action has been committed. The effect is that an act which was lawful at the time that it was committed becomes unlawful "after the fact" *(ex post facto).* This is objectionable for the obvious reason that the person concerned has no opportunity to bring his or her conduct into compliance with the law, since the acts being punished had already been committed when the law was enacted. So flagrantly unjust is such a measure that it is hardly surprising to find that the Constitution expressly prohibits it, along with a bill of attainder.[75]

As in the case of bills of attainder, the category of *ex post facto* laws contains more types of measure beyond the classic type just described. In particular, laws which increase the penalty attaching to an act after the act has been committed qualify as *ex post facto* laws.[76] It is not difficult to see that an ironclad-oath requirement would be vulnerable to challenge on this score, if it was imposed after the occurrence of the disloyal conduct at which it was aimed.

It should be noted that one common thread linked both of these constitutional objections to ironclad oaths: the thesis that the disadvantages that would flow from *failing* to swear an ironclad oath were penal in character or in substance, even if they were not formally denominated as such in legislation. More specifically, the essential issue was whether the ironclad oath, in a given context, functioned as a genuine qualification for the position or favor that was being sought or functioned in practice as what the federal Supreme Court called "a means for the infliction of punishment" for past misdeeds.[77] If an ironclad oath requirement operated in a punitive manner, then it would be unconstitutional as a bill of attainder or as an *ex post facto* law—or possibly as both.[78]

This issue lay at the heart of the consideration of the ironclad oath by the federal Supreme Court when, in January 1867, the Court handed down two closely related cases on the same day.[79] One of them concerned a former member of the Confederate House of Representatives and Senate for Arkansas named A. H. Garland. He objected to the federal law of January 1865, which required the taking of an ironclad oath as a condition for practicing law in the federal court system.[80] The other challenger was a Catholic priest from Missouri, Father John Cummings. He was challenging the (federal) constitutionality of a provision of the postwar Missouri state constitution, which required an ironclad oath as a condition for holding a bewildering array of ordinary civilian posts—including that of minister of religion.

The conclusion of the Supreme Court—by the narrowest of margins—was that, in the two situations under consideration, the oath requirement was punitive in substance. This was so, despite the fact that neither of the laws being challenged contained an express pronouncement of guilt; instead, these laws merely put the persons in the classes concerned to the choice of swearing the oath or engaging in some other line of work. Nevertheless, the Court held the ironclad-oath laws to be penal, on the ground that they were not designed to set *bona fide* qualifications for the jobs in question; instead, their purpose and effect was to deprive persons of their normal rights as punishment for past misdeeds.[81] Consequently, the two laws fell foul of the constitutional prohibitions against *both* bills of attainder and *ex post facto* laws. In addition, they were held to deprive persons of the fundamental right to a presumption of innocence. This was on the thesis that the two laws, in effect, presumed the guilt of persons seeking the employment in question and then imposed on them the burden of establishing that they were *not* guilty of the misconduct in question.

These two cases caused a public uproar, leading to bitter accusations of a pro-Southern bias on the Court's part reminiscent of the infamous prewar era of the *Dred Scott* decision. It was noted that all four of the dissenters in the two cases (with Justice Samuel Freeman Miller as their eloquent spokesman) were appointees of Lincoln, with four of the five justices on the majority side being prewar holdovers. The lone Lincoln appointee who sided with the majority—and who wrote both judgments—was Justice Stephen J. Field, who thereby won widespread vituperation as a traitor to the Union cause.[82]

Notwithstanding the controversy, the *Garland* and *Cummings* cases remain living law—the leading cases to the present day on the subject of bills of attainder, although the basic standards they set have been applied in some contentious ways.[83] But the key decision remains, now as then, the question of whether a given measure is punitive in character or not. This continues to be a difficult decision to arrive at in many instances. In 1898, for example, the Supreme Court considered a state law disqualifying persons convicted of felonies from the practice of medicine—even if the conviction had occurred prior to the enactment of the law. On the basis of the *Garland* decision, the measure was attacked as *ex post facto* legislation on the ground that (as in *Garland*) it imposed an additional penalty on an action after the act had taken place. The law, however, was upheld, on the ground that good character was found to be a legitimate qualification for a practicing physician—and consequently the law was not punitive in character.[84]

Also in the category of nonpunitive measures are laws that merely place conditions on favors or acts of grace. This point was illustrated by a Supreme Court case in 1984, concerning a federal law that required students, as a condition for receiving financial aid for higher education, to swear that they had registered for the draft as required by federal law.[85] Registration for the draft could hardly be regarded as a *bona fide* qualification for studying. The Court upheld the law, however, on the basis that financial assistance to higher education was a favor rather than a right—that the withholding of aid was nonpunitive and was therefore outside the scope of the Constitution's restrictions on bills of attainder and *ex post facto* laws. The law therefore amounted merely to the placing of conditions by Congress on recipients of its largesse, which it is fully entitled to do.[86]

This body of judicial decisions that arose from challenges to the various restrictions on normal liberties by the Lincoln administration marked, for all practical purposes, the inception of the constitutional law relating to civil liberties. Prior to the Civil War, civil liberties was a subject that scarcely troubled the Supreme Court. After the war, it would become one of the Court's major fields of activity—and even became, in the twentieth century, the subject area where the American Supreme Court earned its greatest renown (or, as the case may be, notoriety). Supreme Court case-law in the civil-liberties area often takes on the appearance of a continuous parade of defendants in criminal actions of some kind whose judicial challenges have conferred on them a kind of immortality, at least to lawyers. The first marchers in this parade were Milligan, Garland, and Cummings. Many more would follow them.

7

The World Watches

It is . . . unlawful to be concerned in putting in actual operation dangerous machines. He who is concerned in fitting out and arming a man-of-war for the purpose of preying on the commerce of a friendly state . . . is as much concerned in the attack as he who takes part in manufacturing and planting a torpedo in a frequented channel is responsible for the mischief done by the torpedo.

—Francis Wharton

Why should a nation without a navy, or with only a small navy, be harried and worried and oppressed with impunity by a great naval power, when, having money with which to purchase ships, it could defend itself if allowed to do so?

—William Beach Lawrence

One of the major ironies of the Civil War was the way in which the struggle catapulted the United States into a dramatic reversal of roles in the area of the international law of neutrality. Since its foundation in the late eighteenth century, the country had been a vigorous champion of the rights of neutrals and a stout resister of the demands of belligerents. It even had the dubious distinction of having gone to war, in 1812, in defense of the rights of neutrals.[1] In the 1860s, matters were far different. Now the United States was a belligerent, while the country that was traditionally the staunchest supporter of the prerogatives of belligerents—Great Britain—was in the highly unaccustomed position of being neutral. On both sides of the Atlantic, there were persons who worried that their respective countries, impelled by short-term considerations, might make major, and regrettable, departures from long-held positions.

The law of neutrality was applicable to the Civil War by virtue of what is called *recognition of belligerency* by various foreign countries, led by Great

Britain and France. This amounted, in essence, to a decision by those countries to treat the conflict on a legal par with an ordinary international war. As a result, *both* the Confederacy and the Union would be regarded as entitled, on a precisely equal basis, to exercise the full range of belligerents' rights, as those were known in international law. It also—and more importantly— meant that the recognizing country would observe a scrupulous neutrality in the struggle. In fact, so intimately associated are the status of neutrality and the recognition of belligerency that the very act of recognizing belligerency typically consists of the issuing of proclamations of neutrality. Britain took the lead in this regard on May 13, 1861, followed by France on June 10.[2] Some half-dozen other European states followed suit, as did several others such as Brazil and even the Kingdom of Hawaii.[3]

The law and practice of recognition of belligerency were not well settled in 1861. Largely as a result of the American Civil War, though, there came to be a consensus that foreign countries are allowed—but *not* compelled—to recognize belligerency when the insurgent side meets three basic criteria: first, the control of a certain portion of territory; second, the exercise, in that controlled area, of governmental functions (such as legislation and revenue collection); and third, the conducting of hostilities by means of organized armed forces adhering to the laws of war.[4]

The Union government took foreign recognition of belligerency seriously amiss, as it was deeply resentful of the idea that foreign countries, as neutrals, would treat it and the Confederacy on an equal footing.[5] It is true that Union itself treated the Confederates as belligerents, but only in the limited sense of conducting military operations against them on *land* in accordance with the laws of war. On the seas, matters were (in Union eyes) very different. Confederate attacks and captures at sea were regarded by the Union as mere piracy; and the federal government was affronted that foreign countries did not share its view.[6]

Careful note should be taken of the contrast between recognition of belligerency and the larger step of recognition of independent statehood. Recognition of belligerency means that, in the eyes of the recognizing state, the contending sides are precisely on a par with one another in the possession and exercise of the full range of *belligerents'* rights. Recognition of statehood, in contrast, is an acknowledgment, again by the recognizing state, that the insurgent side is entitled to the full range of *sovereign* rights. A concrete sign of this distinction concerns diplomatic relations. For one state to recognize a community as an independent state amounts, *ipso facto,* to a willingness to enter into formal and official diplomatic relations with that state. The lesser measure of recognition of belligerency, in contrast, does not have this consequence. Consistently with this distinction, the British and French governments received Confederate envoys only on an informal basis, taking scrupulous care to refrain from treating them on a par with diplomats from independent states.[7]

The principal legal consequence of recognition of belligerency is that the recognizing country thereby becomes neutral—meaning that it is fully entitled to all the rights of neutrals, and equally fully subject to all of the duties. In the 1860s, however, there was considerable room for dispute as to the precise ambit of these rights and duties. And the American Civil War provided the opportunity for a number of disputes about the law of neutrality to come urgently to the fore. In the course of the struggle, both the Union and the Confederacy became embroiled in disputes with foreign countries—chiefly Great Britain—over various aspects of the law of neutrality. The Confederate grievances chiefly concerned various questions about the impartiality of neutral states. The Union's dissatisfaction largely concerned issues of alleged British involvement in the conflict, chiefly for its failure to prevent the construction of Confederate warships in its territory. These allegations by the Union led, in 1872, to a famous international arbitral proceeding between the two countries.

Neutral Rights and Neutral Wrongs

Neutrality, in its legal sense, does not refer to an attitude or state of mind, that is, to mere indifference as to the outcome of a conflict. Rather, it refers to a body of specific rights and duties of third countries which, as it were, lie dormant in peacetime but which spring into action on the outbreak of a war. An exhaustive account of these is not possible here, but a general indication is in order. Regarding the *rights* of neutrals, two may be singled out for special notice: inviolability of territory; and the right to trade freely with either (or both) belligerents.

The *duties* of neutral states fall basically into two broad categories: *abstention* and *impartiality.* By abstention is meant that neutral countries (meaning neutral *governments*) must refrain from doing anything to further the war effort of either side, such as supplying armaments (i.e., supplying contraband of war).[8] Peaceful relations, such as trade or diplomatic ties, are allowed to continue. (In the case of the Civil War, this meant, of course, diplomatic ties with the Union *only*, since the Confederacy remained unrecognized as a state.) By impartiality is meant, simply, that any services supplied or favors granted to the belligerent countries must be extended evenhandedly to both, with no discrimination in favor of or against either warring party. The favors that are relevant here were sometimes known as "offices of humanity." This expression referred to routine services, or hospitality measures, which countries provided to the world at large, chiefly in the form of access by foreign ships to ports and to various services such as repairs, provisioning, or refueling (in the case of steam-powered vessels).[9]

In each of these areas, heated disputes arose in the course of the American Civil War. We shall look first at some noted problems of violations by the belligerents of the rights of neutrals, and then turn to allegations of violations by the neutrals of the rights of the belligerents.

Violations of Neutral Rights

It has just been noted that neutrals possess (for present purposes) two fundamental rights: inviolability of territory; and the right to trade freely with either belligerent, or with both. The right of freedom of trade was universally agreed to be subject to the right of belligerent countries to maintain and enforce blockades, a topic rich in legal controversy that will be discussed in due course.[10] For the present, consideration will be given briefly to the neutral right of inviolability of territory. This means, most obviously, that the belligerents are not allowed to conduct military operations in the territory of neutral countries. This principle encompasses not merely the land territory of neutral states but also territorial waters and (less obviously) neutral ships on the high seas.

Regarding belligerent acts in territorial seas, a notable incident occurred in October 1862, when a Union war vessel entered Cuban waters and destroyed a ship. Protests by the Spanish government (then sovereign over Cuba) led to a payment of $200,000 in damages by the United States to Spain, and also to a court-martialing of the naval commander responsible. The commander was convicted of the offense of violating neutral territory and sentence to dismissal (although also recommended for clemency).[11]

A similar incident occurred in October 1864, when a Union ship commander captured the Confederate commerce raider the *Florida* in Bahia harbor in Brazil and took it to Hampton Roads, Virginia. The Brazilian government protested against this "act of the most transcendent gravity" and demanded that the *Florida* be allowed to return to the place of capture.[12] Seward duly acknowledged the commission of an "unauthorized, unlawful, and indefensible exercise of the naval force of the United States" in Brazilian waters.[13] He ordered that the crew of the *Florida* be released from captivity and then given $20 apiece and ten days in which to absent themselves from Union territory. (The *Florida* itself could not be returned to Brazilian territory, as it was accidentally sunk shortly after the capture.) On this occasion, too, the Union commander was court-martialed for violation of the territorial jurisdiction of a neutral country, to which he pleaded guilty and was sentenced to dismissal (although Navy Secretary Gideon Welles disapproved the proceedings).[14] Later, the American navy submitted a letter of formal apology, accompanied by a twenty-one-gun salute in Bahia harbor to the Brazilian flag.[15]

The single most famous incident of transgression of neutral territory during the Civil War concerned "territory" that was, literally, afloat on the high seas, in the form of the British ship *Trent*. In November 1861, this soon-to-be-famous vessel was sailing from Havana to England, with four Confederate envoys on board (two of whom were going to Britain and two to France). A Union naval vessel stopped and boarded the ship, removed the four persons as prisoners, and then permitted the *Trent* to continue its journey. Sternly worded protests came from Britain and France (and from Austria and Prussia as well for good measure) over this incident, on the ground that, under international law, a ship on the high seas is regarded as substantially tantamount to territory of its country of registration.[16] That meant that the stopping and boarding of the *Trent* was regarded, in law, as the equivalent of an armed attack against Great Britain itself. Ruptures of diplomatic relations, and even war, loomed as genuine possibilities.

The crisis was soon resolved, although not very satisfactorily, since the two governments persisted in holding differing views as to precisely what the unlawful act had been. According to Secretary of State Seward, the visiting and searching of the *Trent* was lawful, as an exercise of the normal right of belligerent countries to board neutral ships on the high seas to search for contraband of war (i.e., for war-related materials being carried to enemy territory). Seward also insisted that the four envoys qualified as human contraband (somewhat in the manner of runaway slaves on land), since they were in the active service of the Confederate "government" at the time of capture.[17] The Union commander's only unlawful act, Seward maintained, was the removal of the four men at sea. He should, instead, have captured the *Trent* and brought it before a prize court in the United States, so that the question of the four men as human contraband could be duly adjudicated.[18] This failure on the commander's part was characterized by Seward as "simply an inadvertency . . . free from any wrongful motive."[19] On that basis, Seward duly set the four captives free.

The British were grateful for that outcome. They also readily conceded that belligerents had the right to visit and search neutral ships on the high seas for contraband. They differed from Seward, though, in their insistence that diplomatic envoys—even ones representing a "government" that was not recognized as a state—did not qualify as human contraband. To qualify as animate contraband, the persons in question must be in a military, rather than a civil, capacity. Moreover, it is an essential attribute of contraband (the British contended) that it be bound for an *enemy* destination, rather than, as here, for a neutral one.[20] Consequently, the unlawful act, in British eyes, was the American intervention with its sovereign right to conduct its diplomatic affairs without disruption. This underlying difference of opinion between the two countries was never officially resolved, although there is no serious doubt that the British view of the matter was the correct one.[21]

Duties of Neutrals—Impartiality

It has been observed that the basic legal duties of neutral countries are two: abstention and impartiality. These two deceptively simple principles became, in practice, fraught with controversy. Consider impartiality first. The Union naturally had a deep-seated objection to the very idea that foreign countries should treat the would-be Confederate "government" on a par with that of the United States. The Confederates, just as naturally, were happy with the principle of impartiality. They did, however, voice very great resentment over some alleged *violations* of that basic principle by various foreign governments. In three respects in particular, the Confederates strongly alleged unlawful conduct on the part of neutral countries—chiefly Britain—for perceived partiality to the Union side.[22] First was the failure to recognize the Confederacy as a fully independent state. Second was a restrictive policy on the bringing of prizes into British ports. Third was Britain's attitude toward the Union blockade. Each of these requires a brief explanation.

The first of the Confederacy's grievances against Britain was its failure to go beyond mere recognition of belligerency to the full recognition of the Confederacy as an independent country. The Confederates claimed to be legally entitled to such recognition, on the ground that their country was fully equipped with all of the accoutrements of state sovereignty—complete with a legislature, a judicial system, armed forces, and all other attributes of effective government.[23] The Confederate position on this point did not, however, rest on solid legal ground. It has never been generally accepted in international law that there is a legal duty on the part of foreign countries to recognize a secessionist entity as an independent state—even if it is clothed with most or even all of the outward trappings of sovereignty. The furthest that the law has gone is to *permit* recognition as a state in such circumstances, not to compel it—with the actual choice left to the foreign governments to exercise (or not) as a matter of policy.[24] As early as June 1861, a motion was put in the British House of Commons for the recognition of the Confederacy as an independent state; but it was withdrawn at the request of the foreign secretary, Lord John Russell.[25] Further discussions in Parliament of possible recognition, over the next two years, similarly came to nothing.[26]

The second major Confederate allegation of partiality on Britain's part concerned the British policy, announced in June 1861, of not allowing either belligerent to bring prizes (i.e., captured ships) into its territorial waters or ports.[27] This was the first time that a neutral state had adopted such a policy, but other neutral countries soon followed Britain's lead.[28] Although the measure was evenhanded on its face, it had a far more drastic effect in practice on the Confederacy than on the Union. Since the ports of the Union were open as usual throughout the war, it had no need of foreign facilities. The Confederates did need them—and ever more so, with the increasing effectiveness of the Union blockade.[29]

The inability of the Confederates to sequester captured ships in neutral ports had the direct effect of inducing them to adopt, as an alternative, some rather unorthodox techniques for dealing with captured Union ships. In particular, they devised two novel solutions: destruction of captured vessels at sea, and ransom bonding. Destruction at sea, the more robust of the two practices, was the common fate of ships whose cargoes were wholly owned by Union nationals. The practice began in the very early days of the conflict, when Captain Raphael Semmes—who was to become a sort of seaborne counterpart of

Robert E. Lee—commanded the ship *Sumter*, which captured a number of Union vessels in the West Indies and sought to bring them into Spanish ports in Cuba. On being refused permission to do so by the Spanish authorities, he burned the captured ships at sea. It should be emphasized that there was no loss of life, as the crews were taken onto the captor vessel. Semmes, who was a shrewd lawyer as well as an effective maritime raider, also took scrupulous care, throughout his career, to refrain from taking the private possessions of passengers or crew.[30] Still, there were mutterings from the Union side that Confederate officers and crews who destroyed merchant ships at sea should be prosecuted criminally for piracy when captured, although, in the event, that never happened.[31]

The alternative practice was *ransom bonding*, which was employed when part of a captured ship's cargo was owned by neutral parties. Destruction was not permissible in such cases, because of the Confederacy's policy of abiding by the rules of an international convention on maritime war known as the Declaration of Paris, concluded by the major European naval powers in 1856.[32] One of the rules set out in the Declaration was that neutral-owned cargoes were safe from capture even if they were being carried on belligerent vessels. The conclusion naturally followed that, if such goods were safe from capture, then they should be safe from destruction as well.

When captured Union ships were found to have neutral-owned cargoes in their holds, the Confederate practice, adopted early in the war, was to release the ships and allow them to continue their voyage, but subject to a key condition: that the Union master sign an agreement to pay the stated value of the *Union-owned* cargo to the President of the Confederacy after the conclusion of the hostilities.[33] The highest-value ransom bond of the war was for $261,000.[34] More commonly, values were in the range of $20,000 to $40,000. The enforceability of these bonds necessarily depended crucially on whether the South succeeded in its quest for independence. If it did not, then all concerned were well aware that the bonds would be useless—as proved to be the case. Neutral-owned cargo was, of course, not bonded (in the common expression), since it was not subject to capture.

The third contentious issue between the Confederacy and Great Britain concerned the important question of the effectiveness of the Union blockade. The question of the *material* effectiveness of the blockade—for example, the extent to which it contributed to the eventual Union victory—has naturally attracted much attention from historians (with diverse conclusions reached).[35]

Here, however, the concern is with the quite different question of the effectiveness of the blockade in the *legal* sense. In brief, a blockade is legally effective when the blockaded areas is enveloped by a squadron of ships sufficiently numerous to effect the systematic—as distinct from merely sporadic—capturing of vessels attempting to trade with the target region. The practice of simply proclaiming a port to be under blockade (or to be closed to neutral traders) and then engaging in sporadic captures was commonly referred to by lawyers, with some degree of contempt, as a *paper blockade* (i.e., one that existed by proclamation, or on paper, only) or alternatively as a *fictitious blockade*.

This legal requirement of effectiveness dates (as so much of the law of neutrality does) from European state practice in the seventeenth century, appearing in European treaty practice after 1725.[36] It was stated in its canonical form in the Declaration of Paris, as requiring a force "sufficient really to prevent access to the coast of the enemy."[37]

The Confederates continuously insisted that the Union blockade was *not* effectively maintained in this legal sense. This contention was based on a strict interpretation of the criteria for effectiveness set out in the Declaration of Paris. In a message to the Confederate Congress in January 1862, President Davis maintained that effectiveness required the *actual* prevention of ingress and egress by the blockading power, and that merely posing "an evident danger" of capture to ships entering or leaving was not sufficient.[38] The same point was forcefully made to the British government by Confederate commissioners in London.[39] The British, however, disputed this interpretation, adopting the less rigorous view that effectiveness only required that there be a high risk of apprehension of any ship attempting to cross through the line of the blockading squadron.[40]

The Confederates were particularly disheartened over the effectiveness issue because they thought (wrongly) that they had an implicit understanding with Great Britain: that, in return for the Confederates' carefully refraining from capturing or destroying British-owned cargoes on Union ships, Britain would cooperate on the blockade question.[41] When it became apparent that that cooperation would not be forthcoming, President Davis caustically denounced the British for, in effect, rendering assistance to the Union military effort. British neutrality, he fumed, "has been rather nominal than real, and . . . recognized neutral rights have been alternately asserted and waived in such a manner as to bear with great severity upon us, and to confer signal advantages on our enemy."[42] So bitter was the Confederate disappointment at

British acquiescence in the Union blockade that the Davis administration effectively broke its (rudimentary) ties with that nation in 1863, by expelling its consular representatives from the Southern cities.[43]

It may be noted parenthetically that the Confederacy, in one of its most striking blunders of the war, undermined its own case on the effectiveness issue by the ill-advised "cotton embargo" of the early period of the war. This was an informally agreed, but nonetheless largely effective, policy of refusing to ship cotton to Europe. The idea was that this embargo would lead promptly to a cotton famine, particularly in Britain, which would lead to serious economic distress in that country's textile industry. This would in turn (it was hoped) provoke public pressure for British intervention on the Confederate side. This belief proved very wide of the mark, as is well known. For present purposes, it is only necessary to note how inconsistent the cotton embargo was with the Confederate case on effectiveness of the Union blockade. By *itself* refusing to export cotton, the Confederacy managed to give the impression to the outside world that the Union blockade was more effective than it really was.[44]

Duties of Neutrals—Abstention

The other basic neutral duty was abstention. Like the duty of impartiality, it also became the subject of heated debate during, and after, the Civil War, although in this case, it was the Union rather than the Confederacy which regarded itself as the injured party. Its principal grievance concerned the alleged breach by Britain of what is sometimes called the *base-of-operations* rule. In principle, this is clear enough. A neutral country is universally agreed to be under a legal duty to ensure that its territory is not employed by either belligerent for the prosecution of its war effort. For example, a neutral country must not permit the armed forces of either belligerent to cross its territory en route to attacking its enemy. Nor must it allow either its land territory or its territorial waters to be used as a combination of launching pad and sanctuary by either belligerent.

Noteworthy disputes over the base-of-operations principle arose out of two attacks, launched against Union territory from the neighboring British possession of Canada, which became the subject of postwar arbitral claims by the United States against Britain. The first was a Confederate raid from Canada into St. Albans, Vermont, in October 1864 (the furthest north the Confederates ever carried their military efforts). The raiders slipped into United States territory on a one-by-one basis and then formed themselves into a military-style unit for the attack. The panel held there to have been no breach of law, because the degree of secrecy on the part of the attackers had been so great that no degree of diligence on Britain's part could have unmasked it.[45]

The second attack was the less-known Lake Erie raid of the previous month. A group of Confederates crossed from Canada into Union territory with a view to capturing a war steamer, which was intended to be used first to free some three thousand Confederate prisoners of war held on Johnson's Island (off the coast of Ohio in Lake Erie) and then to mount attacks on Union areas. The actual achievements of the expedition were considerably more modest, with only one Union ship sunk (a private steamer) and the rest of the plan abandoned. On this occasion, too, the arbitral panel found no liability on Britain's part, chiefly on the ground that the British authorities in Canada had notified Union officials of the plan as soon as they had information about it.[46]

The greatest controversy between the Union and Great Britain regarding the base-of-operations principle concerned the fitting-out of Confederate warships in British shipyards. In the Union's eyes, this amounted to the provision of support for the Confederate war effort. More specifically, the United States contended that the British government was under a legal obligation to police its shipyards with diligence, to ensure that private shipbuilding firms did not construct war vessels for the Confederacy.

As it happened, British law, as it stood throughout the Civil War, did prohibit British nationals from intentionally fitting out warships for belligerent countries.[47] The problem was that the Confederates, fully aware of this fact, went to great lengths to avoid violating at least the letter of this British law—while at the same time circumventing its spirit with impressive zeal and ingenuity. The basic technique was not complicated, although a good deal of skill and luck was required to make it succeed.

The idea was, in brief, to build warships in disguise. Ships would be commissioned in British shipyards on the representation that they were merchant vessels rather than warships. Once constructed, the putative merchant ship would sail, with a British master and crew, out of the port where it had been built; once it was clear of British territorial waters, it would metamorphose into a warship. It would rendezvous with a separate ship, also with a British crew, which would be carrying the armaments. At sea, or in some non-British-held area, the arms would be transferred onto the ship and the ship itself sold to the Confederate government. Inducements would also be offered to the

British workers and sailors present to become crew members on the new vessel (with the result that Confederate warships were largely foreign-crewed).[48]

The Union government was far from unaware of these machinations. The consul in Liverpool employed a small army of spies to gather evidence of violations of law by their wily Southern countrymen and to report them to British authorities.[49] The British government certainly made an effort to stop these practices, and the principal Confederate agent involved in the ship constructions was firmly convinced that the British government was highly partial to the Union cause.[50] On four occasions, the British authorities stopped ships from leaving the country's territorial waters. But they did not always succeed. One problem was that Britain's national law prohibiting the fitting-out of warships for belligerent powers was interpreted by the courts to apply only to cases in which a *complete* fitting-out occurred within British territory.[51]

In all, the Confederates succeeded in constructing four warships in British ports by the use of these devices. (Actually, the vessels were commerce raiders, since they had hardly any contact with Union warships.) The most famous one left British waters in July 1862 as "Gunboat No. 90." In the course of its construction, the local American consul became aware of developments and urged the British government to intern the vessel, providing a number of affidavits as evidence for his concern. The British customs authorities, however, held the evidence insufficient and permitted the unarmed vessel to depart. On arrival in Portuguese waters, it was armed by a ship from the West Indies and thereby transformed into a commerce raider named the C.S.S. *Alabama*.[52]

Under the captainship of Raphael Semmes, of *Sumter* fame, the *Alabama* had the most spectacular career of all the Confederate commerce raiders, capturing some sixty-two Union merchant vessels over a two-year period.[53] Two other British-built Confederate ships had impressive, if rather less famous, careers. The *Florida* captured some twenty-four ships before falling into Union hands (as noted above) in Brazilian waters in 1864.[54] The *Shenandoah* made about forty captures, mostly of whaling vessels in Pacific and Arctic waters.[55]

Ironically, the successes of Confederate commerce raiding, as costly and humiliating to the Union as they were, had scarcely any effect on the federal war effort, or even on the over-all flow of Union trade. What happened instead was a massive transfer of Union maritime commerce into foreign hands, since Union-owned property was safe from capture if it sailed under a neutral flag, pursuant to the rule in the Declaration of Paris (scrupulously observed by the Confederates) that "free ships make free goods."[56] This proved to be a

long-term effect, as much of the American carrying trade remained in foreign
hands long after the end of the war, seriously stunting the development of an
American merchant marine.[57]

The *Alabama* Sails to Geneva

In the United States, there was serious resentment against Great Britain over
the issue of Confederate warship construction. Most emotive of all was the
case of the *Alabama,* which was widely alleged to have involved serious negligence on Britain's part (at best) or outright collusion with the enemy (at
worst). This collective feeling of outrage translated readily into a determination to make an international claim against the British government for the
damage that these vessels caused. As it happened, Britain was receptive to the
idea of a judicial airing of the issues involved, since it had a very substantial
stake itself in seeing a clarification of the law in this area. The reason was that
there was every danger that, in some future conflict, Britain's enemies might
seek to augment their battle fleets from the safety of neutral countries in the
way that the Confederates had.

This coincidence of interest between the two countries enabled them, by
1871, to agree to the judicial resolution of a wide range of disputes that had arisen
during the war, of which the construction and escape of the *Alabama* was only
the most conspicuous. The Treaty of Washington, concluded in May of that year
(after years of arduous negotiations), provided for the establishment of two arbitration panels.[58] One, which sat in Geneva, was composed of five persons and
dealt chiefly with issues relating to the fitting-out of Confederate warships in
British territory. These were popularly known as the "*Alabama* claims," although there were claims relating to eight other ships in addition to that famous
one. One of the panel members was an American national (Charles Francis
Adams, who had been ambassador to Britain during the War). Another was
British (Lord Alexander Cockburn, an eminent judge), with the remaining three
from other countries. On the American legal team was an Ohio lawyer named
Morrison Waite, soon to be named chief justice of the Supreme Court.

The other arbitral panel, sitting in the United States, dealt with all other
claims arising out of the war (for example, for injuries to British nationals
from alleged violations of the laws of war by Union forces or by unlawful captures for blockade violation). For the present, we will consider only the Geneva arbitration. The other arbitration will be considered in due course.[59]

Agreeing to the Rules

The 1871 Treaty of Washington not only arranged for the setting up of the two arbitral panels but also set out the legal rules the Geneva panel was to apply in its deliberations. These "Washington Rules" (as they became known) were three in number. One of them was a statement of the base-of-operations principle in its most general form: that a neutral government must not "permit or suffer either belligerent to make use of its ports or waters as a base of naval operations" or for the recruitment of crews or for the "renewal or augmentation of military supplies or arms." A second rule—and the one that would cause the most controversy at the arbitration—applied this general principle to the specific problem of the fitting-out of warships. It stated that a neutral government must "use due diligence to prevent the fitting out, arming, or equipping" of vessels that it has reasonable grounds for supposing will be used for military purposes by a belligerent in an ongoing war. The neutral government was, furthermore, to use "like diligence" to prevent the departure from its territory of ships that had been "specially adapted" within its territory for military use. The third rule imposed on a neutral government the duty to exercise, once again, "due diligence" to prevent "all persons within its jurisdiction" from engaging in any of these activities.[60]

The Treaty characterized the legal status of these three Washington Rules with great precision. It contained an express denial on Britain's part that the Rules constituted part of *existing* international law. But it was then immediately added that Britain, in the interest of "friendly relations," would consent to the arbitration's proceeding on the assumption—i.e., the pretense or fiction—that Britain had made a prior undertaking, before the disputes arose, to act in accordance with these Rules. This was followed by the statement that, in their *future* relations, the two countries would regard the Rules as legally binding between the two of them—but that they would also invite all countries of the world to accede to them, thereby bringing about a change (or perhaps clarification) of international law on this subject.[61] It was envisaged, in other words, that the Treaty of Washington would blossom from a bilateral agreement into a multilateral one and become a successor to the Declaration of Paris.

The Arbitration in Geneva

The most contentious issue at the Geneva arbitration concerned the exact content of the "due diligence" requirement stated in the Treaty of Washington.

Specifically, the question was whether it sufficed that the neutral country conscientiously enforce its *own* laws on the subject, whatever their precise content happened to be; or whether, alternatively, there was an objective standard of due diligence to which the neutral country had to measure up, regardless of the state of its national law. The holding of the panel was that there was an objective standard, with the result that the prevailing state of the neutral country's national law was no defense against an *international* legal claim. If the neutral country's national law was insufficient for the task at hand, it was up to that country to make the necessary changes so that the objective international standard could be met.[62] (As it happened, Britain had already, in 1870, changed its law on the fitting-out of foreign warships, so it applied not only to a complete fitting-out but also to any shipbuilding activity in which there an intention or knowledge or even only probable cause to believe that the ship would be employed in military service in the future.)[63]

As to the actual contents of the due-diligence standard, the Geneva panel took a stringent line, holding that a neutral state is required to take action "in exact proportion to the risks" to which the belligerent state would be exposed by a breach of the duty.[64] The British member of the panel, Judge Cockburn, dissented, with much vigor, on the due-diligence issue, insisting that a due-diligence duty should only require of a neutral country that it "possess reasonable means to prevent offenses, and use such means honestly and diligently."[65] He sternly objected that the panel was placing too heavy a burden on neutral countries and was being too indulgent toward the interests of belligerents.[66]

Be that as it may, when the panel's standard of due diligence was applied to the five claims brought by the United States over ship construction, Britain was exonerated on three and held liable on two. The two were the *Alabama* and the *Florida*. In those two cases, the British government was faulted by the panel for failing to take any effective steps when they were notified of suspicious circumstances. Regarding the *Alabama,* for example, the British authorities were held to have been tardy in the issuing of a detention order.[67] Furthermore, the British government was held to be under a duty to make recompense for its prior negligence by interning those vessels in the event that either of them reentered British waters at any future time.[68]

A neutrality violation of a different nature was attributed to Britain regarding a third ship, the *Shenandoah*. When that vessel put into Melbourne in early 1865, the Confederates were permitted to recruit new crew members in the port. This was held to have been a violation of the general base-of-operations rule. The British authorities, it was ruled, should have interned the *Shenandoah* and thereby put a stop to its raiding career.[69] As it happened, these three ships were the ones that had caused the greatest damage to Union merchant and whaling shipping.

Although the due-diligence issue was the most conspicuous point of contention, there were other important disputes as well, chiefly relating to the damages owed in cases of violation. One of these concerned the duration of British liability in the cases of the *Alabama* and the *Florida*. Britain contended that, once a warship had received its commission from its government, or entered a home port, it became a lawful belligerent vessel from that point onward. The concrete result would be that Britain would then be liable *only* for the construction and escape of the vessels, and not for any of the damage that they caused in their raiding careers after their commissioning. Nor would Britain be under any obligation to intern the vessels if they entered its waters. The Americans contested this, insisting that, if an enemy war vessel had been unlawfully fitted out, then the neutral country that was responsible owed compensation for *all* damage done by the vessel throughout its *entire* belligerent career. On this point, the Geneva panel adopted the American position.[70]

There was considerable dispute as to what to include and exclude in the calculation of the damages, with the United States seeking reparation for various types of "indirect claims," as they came to be commonly termed. One of these was for the expenses incurred in tracking down the three unlawfully fitted-out vessels. On a three-two split among the arbitrators, these were held by the panel to be noncompensable, on the ground that they were simply general expenses of waging war.[71] The United States also sought compensation for losses of future profits from vessels destroyed. These were also rejected by panel, unanimously.[72] The most conspicuous of the "indirect claims" were the higher insurance premiums that shippers in general were compelled to pay by virtue of the general threat posed by the roving Confederate raiders. Britain fiercely resisted including these in the damages assessment. In the face of a British motion to adjourn the Geneva proceedings for further discussion of the matter, the United States grudgingly agreed to refrain from pressing these claims.[73]

The Aftermath

The damages against Britain were assessed as a single global figure—$15.5 million—with no allocation of specific amounts to each of the three ships for which legal violations had been found. (In legal terminology, this is known as a *lump-sum settlement*.)[74] As a matter of international law, this fund belonged to the American federal government, and not to the actual victims of the losses. This was on the thesis that, according to international law, the American government, and not the individual victims, had been the claimant party in the arbitration.[75] It was contended by some of the individual parties that the federal government held the fund as a trustee for the victims of the depredations— and that consequently it was under a legal obligation to disburse the monies to them. In due course (in 1891), the federal Supreme Court rejected that contention, holding that the money belonged absolutely to the federal government, which was accordingly under no more than a "moral obligation" to pay it over to the private parties.[76]

The federal government did, however, elect to discharge its moral obligation by setting up, in 1874, a body known as the Court of Commissioners of Alabama Claims, whose task was to consider claims by alleged victims of the Confederate warship raids and to allocate the fund among the individual victims as equitably as possible.[77] Claims were limited to direct losses caused by the three ships associated with the British neutrality violations, as found by the Geneva panel. These became commonly known as the "inculpated cruisers." If the aggregate value of the claims came to more money than was in the fund, then each claim would be reduced *pro rata*. As it happened, *pro rata* reduction was not necessary. It turned out that only about $9.3 million—less than two-thirds of the money paid by Britain—sufficed to pay all of the claims in full.[78] The Geneva panel, in short, had *over*estimated the total direct losses, leaving some $6.2 million of the award remaining.

The federal government's response to this *embarras de richesses* was to resuscitate the Court of Commissioners, by legislation in 1882, and to expand the opportunity for individuals to claim.[79] To this end, two new categories of persons were now allowed to make claims on the remaining fund, whose losses had *not* been held by the Geneva panel to be compensable. The first were the victims of Confederate cruisers in connection with which Britain had *not* been held liable. These were commonly referred to as the "exculpated cruisers." The second group were the principal indirect claimants—persons who had paid higher than normal insurance premiums during the war because of the dangers posed by the Confederate raiders. Direct losses (i.e., those caused by the exculpated cruisers) were to be paid preferentially, meaning that the whole of the remaining fund would be devoted to compensating those claimants, with any balance remaining then to be devoted to the satisfaction of the indirect claims. If there was any shortfall for either category, successful claimants would receive *pro rata*, or proportionate, payments. By the time of this second round of distribution, the size of the remainder of the award fund had grown to about $9.7 million, as a result of investments.

As it happened, the losses caused by the exculpated cruisers were adjudicated at a total of some $3.35 million. These were duly paid in full, leaving about $6.35 million for the indirect claimants. The total of their adjudicated claims, however, came to about $16.3million (covering over 3,600 successful claims), so that they received only *pro rata* payments, of somewhat more than one-third of the value of each adjudicated claim. The remainder of the fund was then distributed on this basis in 1886, bringing the process to a conclusion.[80]

By all appearances, then, the *Alabama* arbitration was a striking success for American diplomacy. But there were some who worried—or rejoiced—that appearances may have been deceptive. Some British observers maintained that, in the longer run, the arbitration was advantageous to them, since it placed so high a burden on neutral countries of policing their territories to prevent the augmentation of belligerent fleets in wartime. Britain's unmatched naval might, combined with the fact that it was less dependent than any other country was on foreign states for shipbuilding, meant that it was uniquely interested in making it difficult for *other* states to augment their fleets with neutral-state aid. The *Alabama* arbitration contributed very nicely to that long-term end. Small wonder, then, that Travers Twiss, a noted British admiralty lawyer, was reported to have drily commented that, with the Geneva arbitration, his country had purchased an extremely valuable precedent for the future at a bargain price.[81]

There were corresponding worries on the American side. William Beach Lawrence, for example, a noted international lawyer, expressed deep misgiving over the *Alabama* award, for much the same reasons that Twiss favored it. He feared that his government had improvidently lost sight of the fact that the its true long-term interest lay in promoting the rights of neutrals rather than those of belligerents—that is, of *not* placing excessive burdens onto neutral states by, in effect, requiring them to do the belligerents' work for them.[82]

Be that as it may, the longer-term aim of incorporating the Washington Rules into general international law did not bear fruit, largely because of British objection to the strictness of the arbitral panel's interpretation of due diligence. As a result, the plans for transforming the Washington Rules from a bilateral treaty into a multilateral one were stillborn.[83] In this, the British were basically in line with the general consensus of international lawyers, which has regarded the Geneva panel ruling as overly strict. In 1875, the newly founded Institute of International Law (a private organization of prominent persons, largely of a scholarly background) considered the matter and endorsed a moderate view of the due diligence principle—holding that a neutral state must "exercise vigilance" and take "the necessary measures" to prevent the fitting-out of war vessels in its territory—including the criminal prosecution of persons involved.[84] The current position on the question is stated in an international convention on maritime neutrality adopted by the Second Hague Peace Conference in 1907.[85] This requires a neutral state simply "to employ the means at its disposal" to prevent the fitting-out of warships by belligerents in its territory—essentially requiring neutral governments only to enforce their *existing* national laws conscientiously and evenhandedly.

In other words, the determining factor in whether the due-diligence duty has been met is the general efficiency and conscientiousness of the neutral government in the particular circumstances facing it, rather than (as in the Geneva panel's view) the level of material injury likely to emanate from a breach. Once a breach of the duty has been found to occur, however, it remains the case, as exemplified by the Geneva arbitration, that the negligent state is responsible for *all* of the damage that flows from its violation. This places states in substantially the same position as ordinary persons, who are responsible for the full material consequences of their negligent actions.

The Geneva arbitration did not cover, by any stretch of the imagination, the full range of controversies over the law of neutrality that the Civil War raised. In particular, it did not deal with questions relating to the law of blockade. These were many in number and high in controversy, representing the furthest reaches of international legal innovation arising from the American Civil War.

8

The Art of Blockade

Blockade running from neutral posts seems to have been organized as a business, and almost raised to a profession.

—U.S. Supreme Court

Successive voyages, connected by a common plan and a common object, form a plural unit. They are links of the same chain. . . . The ships are planks of the same bridge, all of the same kind, and all necessary to the convenient passage of persons and property from one end to the other.

—U.S. Supreme Court

The blockade of the Confederacy, mounted by the Union navy, was, to put it mildly, an ambitious enterprise. At its height, the blockade effort boasted some six hundred Union ships, patrolling around eight major seaports (along with something like 180 smaller outlets). In turn, the energetic efforts of the Confederates to breach the blockade were on an equally heroic scale.[1] To this end, they devised two basic ploys. One was to take goods *around* the blockade. This was done by the simple device of importing them into Mexico, which as a neutral country was unblockaded, and then taking them overland into the Confederacy.[2] The other stratagem was to run the supplies directly *through* the blockade, by means of craft that were purpose-built for the task and were based in various neutral ports in the West Indies. Cargoes bound for the Southern states would be taken to those neutral ports in regular merchant ships, for unloading and transshipment onto the blockade-running craft.

These two blockade-running devices were practiced on so large a scale as to bring about a major transformation in the traditional seagoing trading patterns of the region. The once somnolent Mexican port of Matamoros, for example, at the mouth of the Rio Grande River, mushroomed into a bustling trading center. Much the same was true of the various West Indian ports, such as Havana and Nassau, which underwent similarly explosive growth from backwaters to thriving shipping emporia.[3] As Chief Justice Chase sourly remarked in one of his Supreme Court judgments, blockade running from neutral posts "seems to have been organized as a business, and almost raised to a profession."[4]

Crucial to the viability of both of these blockade-running schemes was the *legal* inability of the Union navy to put a stop to them. The heavy involvement of neutral-state merchants in the trade lay at the root of the problem.[5] The law of blockade, as it then stood, did not allow the capture of neutral ships sailing to neutral (i.e., unblockaded) ports. That meant that neutral ships sailing to Matamoros or to the various blockade-running launchpads in the West Indies could not be apprehended, no matter how obvious it was that their journeys were part of a blockade-violation enterprise. In the course of time, the Union authorities and prize courts proved able to surmount this difficulty. They did so by breaking new—and controversial—legal ground, chiefly in the form of new applications of a mysterious-sounding principle known as the *continuous-voyage doctrine*. It provides one of the best illustrations that history can offer of how the law of nations is forged in the crucible of state practice at least as much as in the doctrines of treatise writers. Legal controversies would rage over the various American innovations long after the conclusion of the Civil War. They would play an important part in the later British policies of the First and Second World Wars, as well as in various more recent conflicts.

Tightening the Squeeze

Some of the more salient aspects of blockade law should be noted at the outset, since a number of aspects of that subject will be unfamiliar to laypersons (as well as to many lawyers). Perhaps the most fundamental point is that the expression "blockade" refers to several distinct, though densely interwoven, concepts. For one thing, it refers to the physical presence of a line of ships encircling an invested area—with the number of ships required to be large enough to satisfy the requirement of effectiveness (i.e., to make captures on a systematic, rather than merely a sporadic, basis).[6] A blockade is therefore a kind of fence or stockade— although composed not of posts and railings but of naval vessels.[7]

"Blockade" also refers, however, to the set of legal prerogatives which accrue to the belligerent power once the effectiveness threshold is met. The belligerent thereby acquires a legal right to capture neutral ships for violation of the blockade—with violation consisting, in essence, of the physical crossing or penetrating of the maritime fence (i.e., the line of the blockading vessels). These captured ships must be taken before prize courts (as in the case of the capture of contraband). A prize court is a somewhat curious legal phenomenon. It is a sort of hybrid entity which is national and international at the same time. It is a national court, in that it is established and staffed solely by a single state—specifically by a state which is at war at the time, since prize adjudication is a feature of a state of war. But it is an international court, in that the law which it applies is exclusively international law—most importantly, the law governing the capture and confiscation of enemy and neutral ships and goods on the high seas, and the visiting and searching of ships on the high seas.

Prize courts evolved gradually in the Middle Ages, among the major European maritime powers, but by the nineteenth century were a well-established institution.[8] A sizeable body of law governed their operation, though fortunately only a few salient points need be noted for present purposes. The basic function of a prize court was to adjudicate on the lawfulness of captures of ships and cargoes. More specifically, prize courts determined whether a given capture was a proper exercise of the captor's lawful rights as a belligerent. If it was, then the ship or cargo in question was duly pronounced condemned; and it was either confiscated and put to use by the captor state, or else sold at auction, with the proceeds going to the captor state (and sometimes shared out with the actual captors as prize money). If the capture was held to have been unlawful (i.e., to have exceeded the scope of belligerents' rights in the situation at hand), then the ship and cargo were set free. If the prize court held that there was not even probable cause for the capture, then the owner of the ship was even entitled to a payment of damages for the delay and expenses suffered.

Prize courts are not permanent bodies. They are created in time of war, and then disbanded when peace is made. They need not even have personnel distinct from those of ordinary courts, and indeed in the Civil War that was the case. Federal district courts actually operated (and continue to operate) in two capacities: as "ordinary" courts, but also, when called on, as admiralty courts.[9] Prize jurisdiction is, in turn, a subcategory of admiralty law. Federal courts, in other words, sat in a distinct capacity or role when acting in prize cases—the chief hallmark of that special role (for present purposes) being that the law applied was the international law of war and neutrality, and not the national law of the United States. Appeals could be taken to higher courts, including ultimately to the federal Supreme Court—which, in such appeals, itself sat as a prize court, applying international law.[10]

When a ship was captured on the high seas, or in enemy territorial waters, the procedure was that the captured vessel was "taken into prize," in the common expression. That meant that a prize crew from the captor ship was put on board, and it was physically escorted to the nearest location in which a prize court might be sitting. There, the adjudication of the lawfulness of the capture would proceed. The federal district court of New York was a frequent venue of prize cases. There were also Union prize courts in Key West and New Orleans after that city's capture in the spring of 1862.

The overwhelming majority of prize cases during the Civil War naturally concerned captures made for alleged blockade violation. The master of a ship that was captured on this ground might proffer any number of defenses. He might claim, for example, that he was merely sailing past the blockade, making no attempt to cross the line of the blockade. Or he might claim not to have had adequate notice of the existence of a blockade. Or he might contend that the so-called blockade was a legal nullity because it was not being effectively maintained at the time of the capture. Or he might claim the presence of an emergency (such as serious damage to his ship from a storm), which was recognized as a valid excuse for breaching a blockade. The task of the prize court was to adjudicate the validity of such proffered defenses. If the prize court held the capture to have been lawful—i.e., held that a blockade was legally in force and that the neutral vessel attempted to breach it without a valid excuse—the consequence was that the ship, together with all of its cargo, was confiscated, with legal title passing to the captor state.

Blockade running has many of the hallmarks of a criminal offense—as attested by the common label blockade *violation*—with loss of ship and cargo as the penalty.[11] It is not, however, a crime in the ordinary sense of being a violation of the *internal* criminal law of the blockading state. It is, instead, a violation of *international* law on the part of the blockade runner. More specifically, the essence of the "offense" of blockade running (or blockade violation) may be said to be the interference by the would-be blockade runner with the blockading power's belligerent right, under international law, to mount blockades around enemy ports or areas. It may readily be seen, then, that the enforcement of blockades is a matter of belligerent, rather than of sovereign, right. This fact is evident too from the fact that blockades are enforceable not only against nationals of the blockading state (and of the target state) but also against neutrals.

Blockade violation differs from "ordinary" criminal offenses in another important respect: that personal punishments, such as imprisonment, may not be inflicted on neutral-state nationals who violate blockades. The crews of neutral blockade-running ships cannot even be interned administratively as prisoners of war, but instead must be set entirely free.[12] In informal legal parlance, blockade violation was said to be an "offense of the ship," with the effect that any "punishment" could only be inflicted on the ship (and its cargo), rather than on the persons who manned it. Condemnation proceedings for blockade violation were therefore strictly *in rem* rather than *in personam*.[13] Throughout the war, the Union duly followed the policy of releasing neutral nationals who manned blockade-running vessels, although sometimes only with very palpable reluctance.[14]

With these basic attributes of the law of blockade in mind, it is possible now to explore the various ways in which the Union made some important and far-reaching innovations, of which three may be singled out as being of particular importance: the devising of something called the intention doctrine; the fortifying of the blockade by means of export controls; and the application of the continuous-voyage doctrine. Each of these calls for a brief explanation.

The Intention Doctrine

One of the Union's devices for extending the physical reach of the blockade was by applying a doctrine that has sometimes been called the *intention doctrine*. This odd-sounding expression may be very simply explained. It was the thesis that, in order to commit the offense of blockade running, it is *not* actually necessary to make a physical penetration of the cordon of ships making up the blockade. According to the intention doctrine, the offense of blockade violation is complete at the moment that a ship embarks from its home port with the *intention* of violating a blockade at its place of destination (hence the name of the doctrine). The act of blockade violation therefore encompasses (on this thesis) the *entire* process of sailing from the neutral home port to the blockaded area, and not merely the climactic act of slipping through the cordon of ships on arrival.

The practical effect of applying this doctrine is to allow a preemptive capture of blockade runners. In fact, it allows would-be blockade runners to be captured for the offense of blockade violation literally anywhere on the high seas all over the face of the earth—provided only that the master of the ship, at the time of the capture, harbored the intention of *eventually* running the blockade on arrival at the port of destination. Another feature of the intention doctrine is that it allows ships that were not even part of the blockading squadron to make captures for blockade violations.

The intention doctrine was not actually an innovation of the Civil War. It received its first notable endorsement in 1630, during the Dutch war of independence against Spain, from the Court of Admiralty of Amsterdam.[15] In the early eighteenth century, it had the support of the Dutch admiralty judge and international-law scholar Cornelius van Bynkershoek.[16] The principal support for it in state practice was provided by the British admiralty courts in the early nineteenth century.[17] The American Supreme Court, which tended to follow the British lead in neutrality cases, spoke approvingly of it as early as 1809.[18] It was approved by lower federal courts in the Mexican War.[19] Halleck also supported the intention doctrine in his treatise on international law.[20] By 1863, an acting attorney general of the United States could assert with confidence that it was "a well settled principle in the law of blockade."[21] Not until 1865, however, did the federal Supreme Court give it a clear and ringing endorsement, and even then it was with some reluctance. Its position was that the intention doctrine was a regrettably necessary tool of a blockading power, in the light of the sophistication demonstrated by the blockade runners.[22] In practice, though, the intention doctrine was not actually widely applied during the Civil War.

Among international lawyers and statesmen, the intention doctrine has been controversial, in general winning the support of Anglo-American commentators and courts while being rejected by continental European writers and governments. The objection to the doctrine rests on the thesis that a blockade violation is, by *definition,* the act of penetrating a cordon of patrolling vessels. To allow the capture of ships far from the line of the blockade must necessarily amount to a policy of mere sporadic capturing—i.e., to a "paper," or noneffective, blockade.[23] American courts, however, stood their ground, with the Supreme Court giving renewed support for the doctrine in the Spanish-American War.[24] It was also incorporated into the United States Naval Code of 1900. British and American commentators also endorsed it for the most part.[25]

The matter received a thorough airing at the London Naval Conference of 1908–1909, which was a gathering of the major maritime powers for the settlement of a range of disputes about the law of maritime war (including blockade). The Declaration of London (as the convention adopted by the Conference was called) stated that captures for blockade violation could only be made by the ships of the blockade squadron, and only within the squadron's "area of operations."[26] The intention doctrine was therefore basically rejected, although the Declaration stopped short of confining captures *strictly* to the line of the blockade, as advocated by continental European writers and governments.

As it happened, however, the Declaration of London never entered formally into effect, so the status of its "area of operations" provisions remains unclear. The United States continues to insist on validity of the intention doctrine to the present day. Instructions to naval commanders issued in 1989 specify that "[a]ttempted breach of blockade occurs from the time a vessel or aircraft leaves a port or airfield with the intention of evading the blockade."[27] The position in international law, however, continues to await definitive resolution.

Short Rations for the Neighbors

Another device for increasing the effectiveness of the blockade was a program of choking off supplies to the Confederacy at their source, by means of a program of export controls. In this case, that meant preventing supplies from flowing from the Union states themselves into the Confederacy through the blockade by way of the West Indies. This was no mere theoretical concern, as it became increasingly obvious that goods shipped from the northeastern ports in the United States to the West Indies had a disturbing history of finding their way onto blockade-running vessels for importation into the Confederacy. That the Union government wished to put a stop to this traffic would appear to be eminently reasonable. But the method adopted caused outrage on the part of the British government.

The idea was for the United States to establish controls over exports from the Northern ports. The power to do this was given to the President by statute in May 1862.[28] Regulations were then promulgated controlling trade to two categories of destination. One category comprised areas of the Confederacy that were no longer blockaded by virtue of their being in Union hands (Beaufort and newly captured New Orleans). The other group comprised *any* ports from which the goods "are probably intended to be . . . reshipped in aid of the existing insurrection."[29] This clearly referred to the various West Indies ports that had become notorious as blockade-running jump-off points or launchpads. The Department of State instructed consuls to refuse licenses to any American vessel whose *cargo* was believed to be ultimately destined for the Confederacy. Even for goods that were permitted to be exported, bonds had to be posted, that is, sums of money deposited as security. The money would then be forfeit if it was subsequently discovered that the goods went to Confederate territory.

This export-control policy caused considerable hardship in the West Indies. The British governor of the Bahamas, astonished at the American action, informed the Colonial Office that he could "hardly imagine" that the United States would take a step "so inconsistent with the principles which regulate the intercourse of nations at the present day."[30] There was a clear note of desperation in his communication—understandably so, since the Bahamas was heavily dependent on the United States for many of its basic items such as food and clothing. The British Foreign Office, in the same spirit, objected that the controls amounted to "a virtual admission that the blockade is not adequately or legally maintained."[31]

The United States' defense of its action in legal terms took two forms. One was to assert that the export-control measures were an exercise of *sovereign* rights by the United States rather than of *belligerent* rights. There could be no legal objection, in the Union government's eyes, to a state's controlling the flow of goods from its *own* soil, particularly when all governmental action—bonding, prohibition against sailing, and so forth—took place on American territory. (Nor was there any domestic constitutional objection to the policy, since Congress was expressly accorded the power to "regulate Commerce with foreign Nations.")[32] Seward's other defense was that the measures were imposed *not* for the regulation of trade *per se* but rather as "public safety" measures, justified by the general natural-law right of self-preservation.[33]

The issues raised in this dispute have not, even now, been resolved to anything like a full extent. But some perspective on them may be offered in the light of later developments. Ironically, the use of sovereign-right measures as an adjunct to—or even as a virtual substitute for—the traditional process of blockading was carried to a far greater extent by Britain itself during the First World War. During that conflict, in which a blockade of the Central Powers was one of the essential components, Britain adopted a vast range of restrictions on exports to neutral countries which bordered on the enemy states (the Netherlands, Switzerland, and the Scandinavian countries). The basic idea was simple—and in its essentials, the same as the American policy of the 1860s. British exporters were allowed to send exports from Britain itself to these neutral countries *only* in amounts sufficient for consumption *in* those neutral states, so as to ensure that there would be nothing to spare for re-exporting to the enemy. There were widespread complaints, echoing those of Britain during the Civil War, that the policy led to serious collateral damage (to use today's term) in the form of shortages and hardship within the affected neutral states.[34] This general subject—the use of sovereign-right measures as a device of waging economic warfare—has many interesting facets but remains, to the present day, largely untouched by judicial decisions.[35]

Continuous Voyages and Their Doctrines

The most striking, and controversial, of the innovations that the Union devised for tightening the blockade—and the one that struck most directly against the Confederate use of neutral ports to facilitate blockade violation—consisted of extensions of something known, somewhat cryptically, as the *continuous-voyage doctrine*. The doctrine is, in a nutshell, a kind of antifraud measure, employed to prevent some substantive rule of law from being circumvented in a bad-faith manner. It is not a stand-alone principle, but rather a sort of ancillary device for bolstering or reinforcing some *other* substantive rule of law.

The continuous-voyage doctrine was originally devised by Britain in the mid–eighteenth century to bolster a strange-sounding principle called the "Rule of 1756." That story, mercifully, need not be explored here.[36] It will suffice to say that the essence of the continuous-voyage doctrine (or simply "continuous voyage," for short) was that a prize court would take what *appeared* to be two separate voyages and treat them, for legal purposes, as constituting, in substance, one single integrated (or "continuous") voyage. During the American Civil War, the Union government and prize courts extended this device to new spheres of operation: to contraband and (most controversially) to blockade.

Continuous Voyage Applied to Contraband

The application of this doctrine to contraband was the means employed by the Union authorities for countering the strategy of carrying goods *around* the blockade by shipping them to Mexico (in neutral vessels) and then transporting them overland into the Confederacy. The carriage was in neutral (chiefly British) hands because Confederate vessels were automatically subject to capture and confiscation, as enemy property, wherever they were found and whatever their destination or cargo might be. (In addition, the Confederacy simply had no merchant navy to speak of.) The only way that the Union could counter this practice was to capture the neutral ships at sea, while they were en route to Mexico. The problem was that these ships could not be captured for blockade violation, for the obvious reason that the Mexican ports, being neutral, were not under blockade.

A partial answer to this challenge was duly devised: to capture neutral ships in the Mexican trade not for blockade violation *per se,* but instead on the different ground of carriage of contraband of war. For goods to qualify for capture (i.e., be *good prize,* in legal parlance) as contraband of war, they need only possess two basic features: first, that they consist of goods, such as arms and ammunition, which are useful solely for the carrying on of war; and second, that the goods be en route, at the time of capture, to enemy territory. There does *not* need to be any blockade in place at the enemy destination. It should also be appreciated that contraband cargoes can be captured anywhere in world, so long as the capture is made on the high seas (and so long as the two definitional requirements just identified are met). There is, accordingly, no requirement that captures of contraband be made near the coast of the country of destination, as there is for blockade. Nor is there any requirement of *effectiveness* in the law of contraband, as there is, crucially, in the law of blockade. That means that captures of contraband cargoes can be made on a purely sporadic basis, simply as opportunities present themselves.

The strategy of capturing Confederacy-bound cargoes on the basis of contraband, rather than of blockade, did, however, have some important drawbacks. For one thing, this device did not enable *all* goods in the Matamoros traffic to be captured—only those which were directly war-connected. A blockade, in contrast, allows *all* goods to be captured. The principal difficulty, though, concerned the second of the basic requirements for contraband: that goods such as arms and ammunition could only qualify as contraband if they are en route to an enemy destination *at the time of their capture.* The problem here was that Mexico—the immediate destination of the goods—was not an enemy destination, but a neutral one. It was on this obstacle that the Union blockaders and prize courts brought the continuous-voyage principle to bear, by contending that cargoes of contraband-quality goods could lawfully be captured on the basis that they were *eventually* going to be taken to enemy territory. The reasoning employed was straightforward: that the war-related materials being shipped to Matamoros were really being sent not *to* Mexico, but rather *through* Mexico *to* the Confederacy, in a two-stage process. The first stage consisted of carriage from a neutral port (e.g., Liverpool) to Matamoros. The second was the overland carriage from Matamoros to Texas.

In the view of the Union prize courts, these two journeys—one by sea and one by land—comprised, in reality, not two separate journeys but simply two separate stages of one single, integrated, continuous journey of the goods from Liverpool to Texas. On this reasoning, the goods *did* have an *ultimate* enemy destination, with neutral Matamoros being merely an intermediate stop or staging post. The Union prize courts held, however, that it was the eventual or ultimate destination, and not the intermediate one, that determined the legal character of the process as a whole. (For this reason, the continuous-voyage principle has sometimes been referred to as the *ultimate-destination* doctrine.)

The policy of systematically applying the continuous-voyage doctrine to contraband began in August 1862, when the Union Navy Department issued instructions to its blockade squadron to the effect that a neutral ship should be captured and taken into prize if it was "reasonable to believe that she is engaged in carrying contraband of war for or to the insurgents, and to their ports directly, or indirectly through transshipment."[37] The leading judicial pronouncement on the subject concerned a ship named the *Peterhoff,* which was captured en route from London to Matamoros in February 1863.[38] The New York prize court which considered the lawfulness of the capture ruled that it was "the ulterior destination of contraband goods," and not merely the intermediate one, which determined "the character of the trade, no matter how circuitous the route by which [the goods] are to reach that destination."[39]

On appeal, the federal Supreme Court agreed, although the case reached it only after the conclusion of the war, in 1866.[40] The crucial question, the Court agreed, was whether the contraband was "destined in fact" to the enemy, not whether the *immediate* port at which it would be landed was enemy or neutral.[41] In a follow-up case shortly afterward, however, the Court imposed an important limitation on the doctrine. The continuous-voyage principle, it held, could only be applied when the carrier of the contraband cargo on the first stage of the journey *knew* that the goods were ultimately destined for a belligerent country—i.e., the later transport (in the Court's holding) must have been the "known inducement" to the first voyage.[42]

The capture of the *Peterhoff* sparked a major outcry in the British press. The basis of the objection was that any condemnation of the goods prior to their arrival at the intermediate point must necessarily be justified on the basis of what was going to be done with those goods in the future, *after* their arrival in Mexico. The ship's papers would, of course, only identify the immediate port (Matamoros) as the destination—and properly so, since that unquestionably was the destination of the *ship* at the time of the capture. Consequently, the *only* evidence justifying condemnation would be inferences drawn from the general surrounding circumstances (i.e., the fact that Matamoros was notorious as a transshipment point, that Mexico itself had no use for such large imports of arms and ammunition, and so forth). But it is difficult to deny that these matters must inevitably involve a healthy—or perhaps unhealthy—degree of speculation, coupled with a complete absence of the kind of solid documentary proof that prize courts traditionally required for condemnation.

The reluctance of foreign courts to endorse the extension of continuous voyage to contraband was vividly illustrated by the subsequent consideration of the *Peterhoff* capture in British courts. This arose in a civil action brought by the cargo owners, who sought to claim for the value of the lost cargo from their insurers. The issue in the case was whether, at the time of the capture, the ship was trading with a belligerent state. The British court concluded that it was not. In so holding, it pointedly refused to take notice of what it delicately called "the situation" of Matamoros. Interestingly, the court was willing to concede not only that the cargo was actually destined for the Confederacy but also that the master of the *Peterhoff* was aware of the fact. Nonetheless, the two journeys—by sea to Matamoros and then by land to Texas—were still held to be separate, with the result that the carriage to Matamoros did *not* amount to participation in the later overland carriage to the Confederacy.[43]

One final point remains concerning the American action against the Matamoros traffic: that *only* contraband goods could be halted by the invoking of the continuous-voyage doctrine. Noncontraband goods had to be allowed through, and always were. The only circumstance in which *non*contraband goods could be captured on the high seas was when they were being run *through* a blockade.[44] As matters developed, the definition of what constituted going "through" a blockade turned out to be surprisingly elastic in the hands of Union prize courts. In that story, too, the continuous-voyage doctrine played a starring—and much contested—role.

Applying Continuous Voyage to Blockade

In terms of the halting of ships run directly *through* the blockade, the challenge for the Union was to find a way of lawfully stopping the various West Indian ports from being employed as launching pads for blockade-running expeditions. The goal of the Union blockade enforcers was simply enough stated: to

deal with blockade-violation enterprises in their earlier stages instead of confining their efforts to the very last phase of the process (i.e., the actual running of
cargoes through the cordons of ships at the Southern coastline). The ambition,
in other words, was to capture would-be blockade runners earlier in their adventure, while they were en route to the West Indies launching sites. The key to
accomplishing this goal was the continuous-voyage principle. The reasoning
was the same as in the contraband situation: that there was, in practical terms,
only one voyage, though it was comprised of two component stages.

It should be appreciated that this line of reasoning actually applied *two* departures from the traditional law of blockade in combination: the intention doctrine and the continuous-voyage principle. From the standpoint of continental
European lawyers especially—with their stern insistence on blockade violation
consisting *only* of physical penetration of the cordon of the blockade—this reasoning involved a stunning and egregious expansion of the normal rights of
blockading states. It was disturbing enough that a ship could be captured for
blockade violation a thousand miles from the line of the blockade, as the intention doctrine allowed. It was worse yet to hold that it could be captured for
blockade violation while it was unquestionably en route to a neutral port.

There was some hesitation in the Lincoln administration about taking this
large step. An acting attorney general worried about the lack of any precedent
for it from the British admiralty case-law.[45] But the Union prize court of
Southern Florida took the step of applying continuous-voyage doctrine to
blockade as early as 1862.[46] In the final year of the war, the federal Supreme
Court gave its clear and strong approval.[47]

But there was worse still to come (or better, depending on one's view). Suppose, as was commonly the case, that the ship from Liverpool was never intended *itself* to run the blockade—that it discharged its cargo in Nassau and
then departed for ordinary trading unconnected to the war. The discharged
cargo would then be transferred onto a custom-built blockade runner, which
would sail to the Southern coast and take its chances on outwitting the blockade squadron. The Union authorities and prize courts proved their mettle in
dealing with this stratagem of "cargo separation" (as it will be termed).

The solution, of course, was simply to apply the continuous-voyage principle to the cargo separately from the ship. This occurred in 1863 in the case of
a British vessel *Springbok*.[48] It was captured en route from London to Nassau;
and it was clear from the ship's papers that the cargo was to be discharged in
Nassau, with the ship then to go about other commercial business. The ship

and cargo were both condemned by the New York prize court for violation of the blockade. In 1867, the federal Supreme Court approved the condemnation of the cargo, although it insisted on the release of the ship, on the ground that there had been no intention that the *Springbok* itself was to run the blockade.[49] With the *Springbok* decision, there were now three respects in which the Union prize courts departed from traditional blockade law: the intention doctrine; the application of continuous voyage to blockades; and, finally, the application of continuous voyage to cargoes separately from ships.

Later Developments

It is hardly surprising that the various innovations in the blockade law generally—and the *Springbok* decision most of all—evoked a storm of objections abroad, both in the international legal community and by governments.[50] The French and Prussian governments both made their unhappiness clear. In Britain, there was an outcry in the shipping community.[51] The British international lawyer Travers Twiss (who was far from being unsympathetic to the rights of belligerents) maintained that no judicial decision in history had attracted such unanimous condemnation from international lawyers as the *Springbok* one.[52]

In the face of this flurry of criticism, it is interesting to note that at least one of the Supreme Court justices—the one who was most knowledgeable about prize matters—later expressed doubts about the *Springbok* decision. Justice Samuel Nelson, in a letter in 1873 to William Beach Lawrence, candidly confessed that "[t]he truth is that this feeling of the country was deep and strong against England, and the judges, as individual citizens, were no exceptions to that feeling. Besides, the court was not then familiar with the law of blockade."[53]

Condemnation of the American actions was not, however, unanimous.[54] The British government, most notably, proceeded cautiously. Its legal advisers clearly favored applying continuous voyage to contraband, even before the American cases on the subject appeared.[55] Regarding the application of continuous voyage to blockade, the British government held back from raising an official protest over the *Springbok* capture, on the ground that it had evidence that the owners of the *Springbok* were actually complicit in blockade-running schemes.[56] In fact, Britain's tradition as a strong upholder of belligerents' rights in maritime war inclined it positively to welcome the American innovations. Vernon Harcourt, for example, a prominent British Liberal politician and international lawyer, was openly grateful to the United States for blazing juridical trails in this area. "Let us . . . rejoice," he proclaimed with characteristic heartiness, "to see the boasted champions of neutrality building up impregnable bulwarks and fortifying by modern examples those belligerent rights for which we so long contended."[57]

In judicial circles, too, the American innovations received a degree of approbation. In the general war-claims arbitration established by the Treaty of Washington of 1871, Britain made a number of claims for wrongful condemnations of ships by Union prize courts. All challenges to the continuous-voyage principle, however, were rebuffed by the arbitrators. The rejection of a claim on behalf of the *Peterhoff* effectively affirmed the arbitrators' support for the application of continuous voyage to contraband.[58] A claim for the *Springbok* condemnation was also rejected.[59]

In general, international lawyers looked with greater tolerance on the extension of continuous voyage to contraband than on its extension to blockade. A noteworthy development on this score occurred in 1896, when the Institute of International Law considered various aspects of the law of contraband. It concluded—though very cautiously—that continuous voyage could be applied to contraband, provided that there were "incontestable proofs and indisputable facts" pointing toward a later overland journey, *and* provided that the two journeys were part of the "same commercial transaction."[60] The application of continuous voyage to blockade, in sharp contrast, was forcefully rejected by a panel of the Institute in 1883, as "a serious inroad upon the rights of neutral nations"—with the *Springbok* judgment expressly singled out for condemnation.[61]

The occasion for a thorough consideration by governments of these American innovations in the continuous-voyage doctrine arose at the London Naval Conference of 1908–1909, which (as noted above) drafted the Declaration of London. Regarding the application to contraband, a rather awkward compromise emerged. It was agreed that continuous voyage could be applied to what was called *absolute contraband,* but not to what was called *conditional contraband.*[62] It will suffice for present purposes to say that absolute contraband means goods which are useful *exclusively* for war purposes, whereas conditional contraband comprises what are now called dual-use items, that is, goods (such as communications or transport equipment) that are useful for both war and peace. These could be treated as contraband if (but only if) they were being carried to a military base or similar destination. According to this standard, the American Supreme Court judgment in the *Peterhoff* case was correct, since the cargo in question comprised absolute contraband.

On the more controversial question of applying continuous voyage to blockade, the conclusion of the London Naval Conference was flatly negative. "Whatever may be the ulterior destination of a vessel or of her cargo," the Declaration of London stated, "she cannot be captured for breach of blockade, if, at the moment, she is on her way to a non-blockaded port."[63] According to this rule, the condemnation of the *Springbok* would not be allowed, no matter how solid the evidence was that the journey in question constituted the first stage of a blockade-violation adventure. It should be remembered, however, that the Declaration of London never entered formally into effect.

In the First World War, the British government proceeded to demonstrate how useful the Civil War precedents could be to a determined belligerent. A crucial component of the Allied war effort in that conflict was the imposition of a blockade against the Central powers—and the continuous-voyage doctrine played a central part in it. Regarding contraband, the British and French governments discarded the distinction, set out in the Declaration of London, between absolute and conditional contraband, applying continuous voyage to both varieties, in both cases with the approval of their respective prize courts.[64] Even more controversially, Britain, like the United States before it, applied continuous voyage to blockade.[65]

Since 1945, the continuous-voyage principle has found several applications, most notably during the Iran-Iraq War of 1980–1988. In 1985, Iran began the systematic exercise of the traditional belligerent right of visiting and searching neutral ships for contraband goods being shipped to its enemy. It also applied the continuous-voyage principle to contraband, by capturing contraband goods being shipped to Kuwait, when it was suspected that they were intended for later overland transfer to Iraq.[66]

The current law on contraband and blockade is most authoritatively stated in the *San Remo Manual* of 1994, which is an authoritative summary of the law of maritime warfare prepared by a team of legal experts under the auspices of the Institute of International Humanitarian Law. The *Manual* effectively allows continuous voyage to be applied to contraband, although this is done by the somewhat indirect means of *defining* "contraband" as comprising war-related goods which are "*ultimately destined* for territory under the control of the enemy."[67] No distinction is made, as in the Declaration of London, between absolute and conditional contraband. It is therefore safe to say that, as the law now stands, the extension of continuous voyage to contraband, as pioneered by the Union prize courts in the Civil War, has been vindicated.

On the question of applying continuous voyage to blockade, however, the *San Remo Manual* is studiously silent. Nor is there any appreciable modern state practice on the point. The matter may therefore be regarded as being dormant, at least for the time being, although it is far from impossible the issue will arise in some future armed conflict. If it does, it seems likely to provoke as lively a debate as it did in the aftermath of the American Civil War. In this area, as in so many, there is still ample scope for further development of the law.

9

Ending a Rebellion

What was the precise character of [the Confederate] government in contemplation of law? It is difficult to define it with exactness. Any definition that may be given may not improbably be found to require limitation and qualification.

—U.S. Supreme Court

Laws made for the preservation of public order, and for the regulation of business transactions between man and man, and not to aid or promote the rebellion, though made by a mere *de facto* government not recognized by the United States, would be so far recognized as to sustain the transaction which would have taken place under them. But laws made to promote and aid the rebellion can never be recognized by, or receive the sanction of, the courts of the United States as valid and binding laws.

—U.S. Supreme Court

By the spring of 1865, the combined effects of the Union naval blockade and the victories of the federal land forces finally brought the armed struggle to a conclusion. Just as there had been no formal declaration of war (from the Union side at least), so there was now no treaty of peace. The federal government, as a matter of principle, refused to contemplate concluding a treaty with the Confederacy. More pertinently, the Confederate States of America effectively disappeared from history with the dispersal of its government after the evacuation of Richmond in April 1865, followed by the capture of its principal political leaders, including President Jefferson Davis.

It therefore remained for the Union to wind up the conflict by means of a series of unilateral measures. Because various aspects of the war were terminated at different times, it became difficult to say, with the precision so obsessively demanded by lawyers, exactly when the state of war actually terminated. This posed a number of practical problems, since various legal matters depended on the fixing of a termination date, including such matters as the running of statutes of limitation and the release of prisoners.

In addition, the disappearance of the Confederate States of America and its governmental apparatus immediately raised a host of new legal problems that clamored insistently for resolution. Broadly speaking, these problems fell into two categories. The first was what to do about the various governmental acts that had been carried out during the secession period. In this area, there was a need to consider matters relating to the Confederate *federal* government, and also (and separately) the actions of the *state* governments.

The second great category of legal issues concerned the fate to be meted out to *individuals* who had supported the rebellion. Some—but only a very tiny number—were prosecuted for war crimes. This select group included, however, the most prominent criminals of the entire war, the Lincoln assassins. In addition, there was the possibility of bringing ordinary criminal prosecutions in civilian courts for offenses such as treason, piracy, and the like. Here, too, only modest numbers of persons were targeted. In addition, civil actions could be brought by private parties; and these functioned as a sort of privatized version of war-crimes trials.

Ending a War

In certain respects, the end of the Confederate war effort came about in an orderly fashion, with the formal surrender of the various Southern armed forces to their Union foes. First, and most famous, was the surrender of Robert E. Lee's Army of Northern Virginia to General Grant at Appomattox on April 9, 1865. This was followed, over the next two months or so, by the surrenders of the various other land forces, concluding with the submission of a force of Cherokee Indians allied to the Confederacy on June 25. Some of the armies were less concerned with formalities. Mosby's force in Virginia, for example, simply disbanded without a formal submission. At sea, things lasted slightly longer, with the final submission—the very last of all—being that of the *Shenandoah,* which surrendered in Britain on November 6.

The question of determining when the Civil War *itself* came to an end—i.e., when the state of war between the two sides terminated—was distinct from the military surrenders. This was not merely an empty exercise for obscurantists. A number of important practical questions turned on it. For example, the right to mount blockades (and to capture neutral ships for violating them) terminated with the state of war.[1] Also, the release of prisoners of war became mandatory; and any parole conditions automatically ceased to be in force.[2] Military pay scales differed in time of war from time of peace. In addition, the two-year period for filing claims to the proceeds of sale under the Captured and Abandoned Property Act began running from the time of "the suppression of the rebellion."[3] A number of terms of imprisonment meted out to spies, war criminals, and the like were for the duration of the war, so that, from the date of termination, those persons had a legal right to be released. Most important of all, in terms of the number of people affected, were limitation periods (i.e., time periods within which claims had to be brought before courts). Regarding potential lawsuits between private persons on opposite sides in the war, the clock would typically not run (so to speak), on the thesis that, during a state of war, it was legally impossible for courts to hear cases involving enemy nationals.[4] To determine precisely when a limitation clock actually ran, it was necessary to know precisely when the state of war in question began and ended.

In practice, the war was brought to an end on a piecemeal basis, by way of a welter of specific measures by the Union government. The first concrete sign that the war was legally over occurred two days after Lee's surrender at Appomattox, on April 11, 1865. On that date, President Lincoln (as one of his last official acts) invoked the power, which the Congress had given him at the outset of the conflict, to close the Southern ports by proclamation, i.e., by exercise of *sovereign* right, as opposed to the *belligerent* method of blockade.[5] This closure of the Southern ports by proclamation was not of long duration, coming to an end on May 22.[6] The blockade, however, remained in force until June 23, when it was formally lifted.[7]

In a companion proclamation to the one on port closure, issued on the same day, Lincoln made it clear that the neutrality status of foreign countries was now expected to come to an end. Concretely, Lincoln stated that various restrictions on the treatment of Union ships in foreign ports, stemming from the application of foreign neutrality legislation, were expected to be discontinued—that the recognition of the Confederacy as a belligerent power by foreign states would no longer be tolerated. The United States, it was announced, would now claim the full range of traditional peacetime privileges in foreign ports and would retaliate if they were not duly granted.[8] On May 10, 1865, President Johnson followed this up with a warning to foreign countries to stop offering hospitality of any kind to Confederate cruisers, coupling this with a threat of retaliation (in the form of refusing access to American ports to government vessels of noncooperating countries).[9]

This proclamation of May 10—the very day of the capture of Jefferson Davis—also included an explicit statement that armed resistance was now "virtually at an end" and persons in revolt were now reduced to the humble status of "mere fugitives or captives."[10] Regarding persons who had been convicted of offenses by military tribunals and sentenced to imprisonment for the duration of the war, a general order of discharge was promulgated by the War Department on May 27, 1865.[11] A general release of prisoners of war followed on June 6.[12] The habeas corpus suspensions were lifted for all of the Northern and border states, except Kentucky and the District of Columbia, on December 1, 1865.[13]

The various property-confiscation programs were also wound down. On May 17, 1865, the secretary of the treasury ordered a halt in the sales of land confiscated for nonpayment of the direct tax of 1861.[14] Collection of the tax *itself,* however, continued until it too was suspended the following year, by statute.[15] In addition, the question of what to do about arrears remained in abeyance (as will be seen in due course) until 1891.[16] The nonintercourse policy (except for contraband goods) was terminated in two stages: for the states east of the Mississippi River by a presidential proclamation of June 13, 1865, and for the three western states by a proclamation of June 24.[17] This meant that, after those dates, property could no longer *become* liable to forfeiture for being traded to or from the Confederate states in question. Proceedings already under way, however, could continue; and fresh proceedings could even be brought regarding property that had *previously* been used in unlawful trading.[18] The collecting of captured and abandoned property was discontinued on the basis of a circular by the Treasury Department on June 27.[19]

The status of the Confiscation Acts was the source of some uncertainty. In May 1865, Attorney General Speed directed district attorneys to halt confiscation proceedings. That order, however, was shortly revoked; and Speed held that persons falling into any of the categories covered by the acts continued to be liable to proceedings until and unless pardoned.[20] It appears that President Johnson was minded to press on with confiscation proceedings—if anything, more vigorously than the government had done during the hostilities—as a ready means of inflicting punishment onto the defeated rebels.[21] In Virginia especially, new confiscation actions continued to be instituted after the cessation of hostilities. These were ended, though, by September of that year, as confiscation gradually became limited to the pursuing of a small number of prominent cases. By 1867, these too had stopped.[22]

This array of different termination measures and policies inevitably made it difficult to say with any confidence when the war *itself* actually ended in legal terms. Some, including Attorney General Speed, took the view that the presidential proclamation of June 13, 1865, terminating the main nonintercourse measures for the eight eastern Confederate states, marked the legal end of the conflict.[23] A federal circuit court in Connecticut agreed.[24] (It will be recalled, in this connection, that there had been a school of thought to the effect that the instituting of the nonintercourse policy in 1861 had similarly marked the true *commencement* of the state of war.)[25] The June 13 proclamation, however, expressly declared the insurrection to have been suppressed in only one state, Tennessee. Not until the following year was the war as such proclaimed to be ended in a comprehensive sense, in two stages. On April 2, 1866, President Johnson proclaimed "the insurrection" to be ended in all of the Confederate states except Texas.[26] Finally, on August 20, 1866, he pronounced it to be over in that state as well.[27]

In 1872, the federal Supreme Court, when considering the problem of fixing a termination date for purposes of statutes of limitation, ruled that, for each particular geographical area, the termination of the war would be the date of whatever executive act declared hostilities ended in the area in question.[28] That meant that there was a different termination date for different states. This was satisfactory for acts which had a specific geographical connection, such as a statutory limitation period. For certain purposes, however, it was necessary to settle on a single, global date. For the calculation of military pay entitlement, Congress, by statute, designated August 20, 1866, as the end of the conflict.[29] For the commencement of the two-year period for filing claims relating to the proceeds of sale of captured and abandoned property, the Supreme Court prescribed the same date.[30]

Dismantling a (Purported) Nation

In the terminology of international lawyers, the American Civil War ended by *subjugation.* This means not merely that one side in the conflict was utterly vanquished and occupied (in the manner of, say, Germany and Japan in the wake of the Second World War) but also that the defeated side wholly disappeared as a political and legal entity. Few tears were shed in the Union government over the evaporation of the Confederate States of America. But the question did arise of whether that would-be nation left any legal residues behind it. More specifically, the question was whether *all* of its acts, without distinction, should be regarded as complete nullities; or whether it might be necessary, or desirable, to accord some degree of recognition to measures it had taken.

The problem was similar, but not identical, regarding the Southern states. They did not vanish into the thin juridical air as the Confederate federal government did. But they had been, in President Lincoln's delicate phraseology, "out of their proper practical relation with the Union." He expressed the hope that it would not be necessary to arrive at a definite legal conclusion on the precise status of "the seceded States, so called" during their four years of waywardness.[31] Lincoln's wishes, in this respect, were not destined to be granted. Inevitably, questions about the position of the states, and the validity of acts which they had promulgated, did come before the courts; and the difficult legal questions raised could not be evaded.

The Confederate Federal Government

The liquidation of the Confederate federal government was a process for which no ready precedent was available. For one thing, it was by no means clear that the Confederate government possessed the power, under its Constitution, of self-liquidation. Shortly after Lee's surrender and the government's evacuation of Richmond, Confederate attorney general George Davis provided his presidential namesake with a legal opinion on that delicate subject.[32] After the recitation of a "melancholy array of facts," his opinion concluded that, according to the strict legal position, the Confederate government was, under its Constitution, "but the agent of the States." Consequently, President Davis did not possess the authority simply to dissolve it by unilateral proclamation. The opinion immediately went on, however, to note that the present circumstances were "so desperate as to over-ride all constitutional theories." In light of the fact that the Confederate government was already "virtually destroyed," the chief task left for President Davis to perform was "to provide as far as possible for the speedy delivery of the people from the horrors of war and anarchy." To this end, President Davis was advised to employ his power as commander-in-chief to disband the whole of the Confederate armed forces, and then to resign from his own office, while recommending to the Southern states that they meet in a convention to ratify terms of submission to their conquerors.

President Davis declined to follow this advice. He shortly left office in a manner rather less dignified than the one that his attorney general had proposed. On May 9, 1865, he was captured by Union forces in Georgia, along with several members of his cabinet. Most of the prominent figures of the Confederate government were also captured, although several escaped abroad.[33] Robert Toombs of Georgia, who had served briefly as Confederate secretary of state and also as a military general, escaped to Cuba, as did John C. Breckenridge, who was secretary of war at the conclusion of the struggle (as well as a general). Both of these eventually returned to the United States. The only Confederate leader who left the country permanently was Secretary of State Judah P. Benjamin, who went to England. He even became a prominent figure in his adopted country, as an eminent member of the English bar. To the present day, *Benjamin's Sale of Goods* continues to be a staple of English law offices (presently in its fifteenth edition), with most of its readers unaware of the original author's eventful life.

As an effective ruling apparatus, the Confederate federal government had now vanished. But, as noted, it remained to be decided what legal remnants, if any, it left behind, and in particular what degree of validity should be accorded to to various enactments. On May 9, 1865, President Johnson indicated his position by issuing an executive order flatly declaring the acts of the Confederate government to be "null and void."[34]

The federal courts took much the same stance. Chief Justice Chase (sitting on circuit in 1868), characterized the Confederacy as "a combination or unlawful confederacy organized for the overthrow of the national government."[35] In 1870, the full federal Supreme Court pronounced, in like manner, that "[t]he whole Confederate power must be regarded by us as a usurpation of unlawful authority, incapable of passing any valid laws."[36] In a later case, in 1874, the Court was even more emphatic that the so-called Confederate government was essentially nothing more than a vehicle for the commission of treason:

> The government of the Confederate States had no existence, except as a conspiracy to overthrow lawful authority. Its foundation was treason against the existing Federal government. Its single purpose . . . was to make that treason successful. So far from being necessary to the organization of civil government, or to its maintenance and support, it was inimical to social order, destructive to the best interests of society, and its primary object was to overthrow the government on which these so largely depended.[37]

The ineluctable conclusion was that no recognition could be accorded to acts promulgated by that great treasonous machine.

Such a policy of blanket nonrecognition of acts of the Confederacy carried some hardships for (relatively) innocent parties. Persons who had suffered injuries from the Confederate government had no avenue of legal redress, with that government no longer in existence—and with the Union government naturally accepting no liability for the acts of its Southern counterpart.[38] This meant that persons whose property had been requisitioned by the Confederate government and then consumed or lost were left without any hope of redress. In addition, persons who had purchased property confiscated by the Confederate government found, to their dismay, that they did not possess valid legal titles. This meant that the original owners could reclaim the property without owing any compensation to the buyer. The buyers were therefore treated as if they had simply purchased the property from a thief (i.e., the Confederate government).[39]

A comparable fate was in store for Southern debtors who owed money to Northern creditors. When the Confederate government confiscated these debts, the effect was to require the debtors to make their payments to it rather than to the erstwhile creditors. That is, the obligations of the debtors were not canceled, but merely redirected from the Northern creditors to the Confederate treasury. A federal court in North Carolina (with Chief Justice Chase sitting on circuit) held that payments to the Confederate government under this arrangement did *not* discharge the debtor *vis-à-vis* his or her original creditor.[40] The payments to the Confederate treasury were regarded instead as mere acts of extortion, to which the court would now pay no heed and give no credit. The unfortunate debtor was therefore required to make a second payment, this time to the original creditor.[41]

In a similarly unhappy position—if less sympathetically so—were persons who had voluntarily lent money to the Confederate government. The adoption of the Fourteenth Amendment to the Constitution in 1868 brought in a uniform and mandatory policy of nonpayment of Confederate-related debt. This policy also applied to any state debts that were "incurred in aid of insurrection or rebellion against the United States." Any such debt or obligation was pronounced to be "illegal and void." Holders of Confederate government bonds, therefore, simply lost any hope of repayment.[42] Energetic efforts were made over the years by the British Corporation of Foreign Bondholders to obtain payment, but these failed to produce any satisfaction.[43]

There were two caveats to this nonrecognition policy. One was that nonrecognition applied to *sovereign* acts of the would-be Confederate government but not to *belligerent* ones. This was confirmed by the federal Supreme Court in a case in 1868 which held that the Confederacy had indeed exercised the rights of belligerents—even if only by concession from the federal government.[44] A Supreme Court case in 1878 nicely illustrated the point. It concerned the destruction of cotton pursuant to orders issued by General Beauregard, whose authority in turn derived from a Confederate statute of March 1862.[45] The owner of the cotton later instituted a civil action against the person who had carried out the order. The destruction was held by the Court to have been lawful—not, however, on the basis of the validity of the Confederate statute *per se,* but instead on the more general ground that the destruction was a *bona fide* act of war permitted to belligerents by the *international* laws of war.[46]

The other caveat to the doctrinaire policy of nonrecognition of Confederate acts concerned the treatment of the Confederacy as what is called a *de facto* government. This expression refers to a government which, although not legitimate, nonetheless exercises effective control over a certain area of territory and, within that area, performs the normal functions of a government (such as legislation, administration of justice, and taxation). In the opinion of Chief Justice Chase, such a "government of paramount force" (as he described the Confederacy) was a sort of occupying power.[47] The consequence of having this status was that "governmental" acts performed by the power *within* the territory that it actually controlled would be recognized as valid by other governments—meaning that routine administrative measures would not be regarded as void.

In 1868, the federal Supreme Court subscribed to this idea of the Confederacy as a *de facto* government, thereby conceding legal validity to Confederate acts that concerned "transactions in the ordinary course of civil society."[48] Some justices, notably Justice Miller, had misgivings about this concession.[49] In 1878, however, the Court reinforced its support for the *de facto* government thesis by holding that persons living under the power of the Confederacy actually owed it a duty of obedience. This was not by virtue of the legitimacy of the Confederate government (for it had none) but wholly out of necessity, in the interest of the maintenance of some kind of order.[50]

The Southern States

The fate of the wayward Southern states and their governments was a quite distinct issue from that of the Confederate federal government. They had a long-standing legal existence, recognized in the federal Constitution and even predating the formation of the federal Union itself. So there was never any question of effacing them in the manner of the Confederate federal government. The struggle to determine *precisely* what their legal position was proved to be both arduous and drawn out. Moreover, it was intimately tied up with the bitter political divisions of the Reconstruction period. As a result, only a few of the important legal issues can be touched on here.

First and foremost was the problem of deciding whether the Southern states were members of the federal Union or not. The states themselves had a natural interest in resuming their prewar status as expeditiously as possible, once military defeat had become clear. The alternative was being treated as some kind of occupied or conquered territory, or even of being stripped of statehood status altogether and demoted (so to speak) to the status of federal territories.[51] In part to forestall such measures, the Southern states, under the auspices of presidentially appointed provisional governments, hastened to convene state conventions to reverse their secession ordinances. Some, such as Georgia, repealed them.[52] The majority, though, took the slightly different route of pronouncing them to be null and void.[53]

The fate of the Southern states' efforts to glide smoothly back into their accustomed positions in the federal Union is the story of Reconstruction rather than of the war. Here, the concern is over the question of what the legal position of the states was during the war era. Attorney General Speed set out the federal executive's view on that point shortly after the hostilities ended. Referring in immediate terms to Mississippi, he concluded that Mississippi, as a state, had always been legally part of the federal Union. The *citizens* of that state, however, "by their effort at revolution, . . . deprived themselves of all civil State government." As a consequence, "the Federal Government was bound to declare their late State organization a nullity, and all the State officials as without authority."[54] It was, however, open to the loyal citizens, as the ultimate sovereigns of the state, to establish a new and lawful government that would replace the illegitimate and treasonous one.

President Johnson took a similar position in his annual message to Congress in December 1865. Individual citizens in the Southern states may have committed treason; and, if they did, then they were subject to prosecution and punishment in the ordinary manner. The states *themselves,* however, had never left the Union. All of their "pretended acts of secession," Johnson maintained, were "from the beginning null and void." The result was that the states had placed themselves "in a condition where their vitality was impaired, but not extinguished; their functions suspended, but not destroyed."[55]

Judicial support for this stance soon came from the federal Supreme Court, in the famous (if somewhat opaque) case of *Texas v. White* in 1869.[56] During the period of the war, the state of Texas, Chief Justice Chase stated on behalf of the Court, "did not cease to be a State, nor her citizens to be citizens of the Union." The secession ordinance it had purported to adopt was, from the constitutional standpoint, "absolutely null." During the Confederate period, the rights of the state and its citizens were held to have been "suspended," with the consequence that the government and citizens of Texas "assumed the character of enemies," at least for the duration of the crisis.[57]

As with the Confederate federal government, however, it did not prove possible to sustain an inflexible stance of nonrecognition of the validity of state acts during the secession period. The most common position adopted by courts, both state and federal, was a pragmatic one—that the ordinary or routine acts of the state governments and courts during the secession period would be recognized as valid, but that any measures which had the purpose of furthering the rebellion would not be. The federal Supreme Court, in the *Texas v. White* judgment itself, gave its blessing to this approach, candidly conceding that, even though the acts of secession were legally void, it was necessary to accord legal recognition to at least some state acts of the secession period. In particular, the Court pronounced,

> acts necessary to peace and good order among citizens, such for example, as acts sanctioning and protecting marriages and domestic relations, governing the course of descents, regulating the conveyance and transfer of property, real and personal, and providing remedies for injuries to person and estate, and other similar acts, which would be valid if emanating from a lawful government, must be regarded in general as valid when proceeding from an actual, though unlawful government.[58]

The effect of this approach was to treat the state governments of the secession era as, effectively, *de facto* governments.

In 1873, the Supreme Court went somewhat further in this direction, by holding that, *in general,* the acts of the states during the secession were to be regarded as valid—subject only to the proviso that measures that were hostile in purpose (i.e., designed to further the rebellion) would not be accorded validity.[59] In the words of Justice Miller:

These laws, necessary in their recognition and administration to the existence of organized society, were the same, with slight exceptions, whether the authorities of the State acknowledged allegiance to the true or the false Federal power. They were the fundamental principles for which civil society is organized into government in all countries, and must be respected in their administration under whatever temporary dominant authority they may be exercised. It is only when in the use of these powers substantial aid and comfort was given or intended to be given to the rebellion, when the functions necessarily reposed in the State for the maintenance of civil society were perverted to the manifest and intentional aid of treason against the government of the Union, that their acts are void.[60]

The effect of this ruling (though not stated in so many words) was to establish a *general* rule of validity of state laws, with invalidity as the exception.

In some cases, it was easy for courts to make this crucial distinction between transactions that were routine acts of civil society and those that were tainted by support for the rebellion. A neat illustration was a case in 1867 before the Virginia Supreme Court concerning a criminal prosecution for bigamy. In his defense, the accused person contended that his second marriage should be entirely disregarded by the court, since it had been contracted under the auspices of the Confederate-supported state government. The argument was rejected.[61]

Sometimes it was not so easy to distinguish routine measures from acts that promoted rebellion. On this point, courts tended to hold that the determining factor was not the intrinsic nature of a given transaction, but rather the context in which it took place or the intention behind it. That meant that acts which were routine on their face might nonetheless be void by virtue of surrounding circumstances. This was illustrated by a case in the South Carolina Supreme Court, raising the question of whether an organization called the Chicora Importing and Exporting Company of South Carolina possessed legal personality or not—specifically, whether it had standing to sue in courts for moneys owed to it. The Company had been chartered by the state legislature during the war—something that the legislature was clearly authorized to do under its constitution. The problem was that the *purpose* of the company was to import and export goods in breach of the Union blockade. This illegality of purpose was held to render the legislative act creating the company void, so that the company had no standing to sue in the courts.[62]

In a similar vein, the Georgia Supreme Court, in a draft-related case, held that a person who contracted to serve in the Confederate military as a substitute for a conscript was not entitled to sue his principal for money owing on the contract. The reason was that the purpose of the agreement—providing manpower for the rebellion—rendered the arrangement unlawful.[63] On some occasions, however, courts were decidedly lenient toward the Confederate-era state governments, as in a controversial case concerning the issuing of state legal-tender banknotes by Tennessee during the war. Remarkably, and in the face of strong dissents, the federal Supreme Court held the note issue to have been valid, despite the fact that it was, to at least some extent, a war measure.[64]

One of the more difficult questions in this area concerned how to treat acts which made only very slight and indirect contributions to the cause of secession. An excellent illustration was the question of contracts that provided for payment in Confederate currency. The Alabama Supreme Court held that contracts which had only a "remote tendency" to promote the rebellion should be given effect.[65] Consequently, a mortgage given in exchange for Confederate notes would be held valid, even though the notes admittedly had been issued by the Confederate government as a war measure. (It may be observed that, in this case, unlike the Georgia one about the substitute, the subject matter of the contract *itself* was entirely unrelated to the war effort.) Some Southern states enacted legislation after the war revaluing contracts that had been made in Confederate currency. Legislation in Florida, for instance, provided that, in any lawsuit on a contract which had provided for payment in Confederate dollars, the damages awarded by the court should be the gold equivalent of the Confederate-money amount, as of the date of the making of the contract.[66]

The question of how to treat the Confederate state and federal governments was not the only issue urgently demanding the attention of the Union executive and courts. There was also the rather more emotive problem of how to deal with the individual persons whose actions had led to the shedding of so much blood.

Prosecuting Wrongdoers

The position of the federal government, throughout the crisis, was to reserve the right to prosecute the leaders of the rebellion for criminal offenses, once the hostilities had ceased. Vattel expressly allowed this, as did the Lieber Code.[67] So, for the most part, did later international-law commentators.[68] Moreover, there was a strong disposition in some federal government circles to prosecute the leaders of the Confederacy. Attorney General James Speed advised President Johnson that it was his "plain duty," as chief executive of the country, to prosecute persons responsible for the rebellion.[69] In his executive order of May 9, 1865, Johnson carefully reserved the right to take this course, stating that all persons who had exercised powers of any kind under color of Confederate law "shall be deemed and taken as in rebellion against the United States, and shall be dealt with accordingly."[70] Chief Justice Chase, sitting on circuit, provided judicial authority for this position, as did the supreme courts of Tennessee and Arkansas.[71]

Prosecutions fell, broadly speaking, into two categories: war crimes (i.e., violations of the laws of war); and "civilian" crimes such as treason or piracy. There was a clear institutional division of labor on this score, with war crimes tried by military tribunals and treason and piracy by the civil courts.[72] In addition, there was the possibility of civil actions by aggrieved private parties. We shall look at each in turn.

War Crimes

Bona fide acts of war, falling within the scope of the laws of war, could not be the subject of criminal prosecutions.[73] The commission of war crimes, in contrast, could be. These took place before military tribunals, convened either by the accused person's own armed force or that of the enemy if the suspect fell into their hands. In this regard, there was continuity from the war, since Union military tribunals, even during the conflict, had prosecuted Confederate prisoners of war in cases in which war crimes were suspected. This included cases of spying and sabotage, collusion with guerrillas, and the like. The scope for bringing prosecutions vastly increased with the end of the hostilities, however, since the surrenders of the various Confederate armies brought nearly the whole of the enemy armed force into Union hands. The actual number of war-crimes prosecutions was, however, very small.

One of the most noted ones was mounted against a notoriously homicidal Confederate guerrilla leader named Champ Ferguson. He was chiefly responsible (it is now clear) for the murdering of black Union soldiers in October 1864 after the Battle of Saltville.[74] He was apprehended by Union forces and placed on trial before a military commission in Nashville in the summer of 1865 for a range of violations of the laws of war. He was found guilty of being a "border rebel, guerrilla, robber and murderer," including the murder of no fewer than fifty-three men. As it happened, he was acquitted of the Saltville killings, though he was hanged for the other offenses in October 1865.[75] As observed earlier, Confederate general Felix Robertson, who was in overall command of the Confederate forces in that engagement, escaped capture and punishment, even though the Confederates themselves had sought to have him tried.[76]

More famous was the trial of Commander Henry Wirtz for the conditions at Andersonville Prison Camp in Georgia. This had become a sensational *cause célèbre* in the North when lurid photographs of conditions in the camp were published in *Harper's Weekly* in June 1865. Two charges were brought against Wirtz. The first was conspiracy "to impair and injure the health and to destroy the lives" of prisoners by various specified means, including "subjecting to torture and great suffering," exposure to the elements, confinement in unhealthy conditions, and provision of insufficient food and impure water. The second charge was the murder of thirteen individuals by various gruesome means, including beating, chaining to an iron ball, and tearing by bloodhounds.

The trial of Wirtz, presided over by Union general Lew Wallace (later the author of the best-selling novel *Ben-Hur*), began in August 1865. It resulted in a finding of guilt on the first charge, even though it was revealed at the trial that Wirtz had complained to his superiors about food shortages. There was also a finding of guilt for ten of the thirteen deaths alleged in the second count. Wirtz was executed by hanging in November 1865.[77] One of his subordinates was also tried, for robbery and for various violations of the laws of war. He was acquitted of the robbery charge but convicted of some of the war-crimes accusations and sentenced to fifteen years' imprisonment at hard labor.[78]

Conviction was not the invariable fate of Confederates who were put on trial for war crimes. Confederate brigadier general Hugh W. Mercer was prosecuted on two charges of murder but was acquitted of both.[79] A Confederate major—described as "barbarous, brutal, and avaricious"—was put on trial for mistreatment of Union prisoners at a prison camp in North Carolina, only to be acquitted.[80] In several other cases, contemplated prosecutions were not pursued.[81]

A particularly interesting case was that of Raphael Semmes, of C.S.S. *Alabama* fame. He worried about being prosecuted for piracy for the numerous instances in which he had destroyed Union ships and cargoes at sea.[82] But when he was arrested in December 1865, he was charged only with three comparatively minor violations of the laws of war: misuse of a white flag in the *Kearsarge* battle (by raising a white flag and then reopening fire); perfidiously running away after making surrender overtures; and reentering Confederate service without being encompassed within a prisoner exchange. Significantly, there was no charge of piracy, and even the three lesser charges, as matters developed, were not pressed. In due course, Semmes came within the terms of one of President Johnson's pardon proclamations and thereby became safe from any prosecution.[83]

The most prominent postwar trial, for obvious reasons, was of that of the Lincoln assassins. In the present context, it is only necessary to mention certain of the more salient points about it. The accused parties were tried by a military tribunal, on the thesis that their foul deed was not an ordinary criminal homicide, but was instead was a military operation, directed against the commander-in-chief of the Union armed forces. This trial of the accused assassins by a military tribunal did not meet with universal approval. Edward Bates, for example, though no longer in office as attorney general, was strongly opposed to a military trial. Nonetheless, the trial proceeded, with eight defendants, all of whom were found guilty. Four were hanged; three were given life sentences; and one was sentenced to six years imprisonment.[84]

Some hope for the imprisoned conspirators (if not for those who had been hanged) came some six months after the proceedings, in April 1866, when the Supreme Court handed down the *Milligan* decision.[85] This held out—or appeared to hold out—the possibility that the military trial might be held to have been invalid. Just two days after the *Milligan* judgment, Dr. Samuel Mudd, one of the prisoners, applied for a writ of habeas corpus and challenged the jurisdiction of the military tribunal on the ground that, as a civilian rather than a soldier, he was entitled to a civil rather than a military trial. The matter was argued orally before Chief Justice Chase; but the writ was not issued, probably on the basis that Chase had no authority to issue one outside the circuit on which he sat.[86]

It may be noted parenthetically that one of the persons accused of involvement in the Lincoln murder did receive a civilian trial—John H. Surratt, Jr. He avoided the trial by escaping abroad and entering the service of the Swiss Guard at the Vatican. In 1866, he was discovered and extradited to the United States, and then tried before a civilian court. The trial, however, miscarried because of a hung jury; and the charges against him were then quietly dropped.[87]

Crimes of Peace

The principal peacetime crime for which supporters of the Confederacy were at risk of prosecution was treason. It has been observed that, during the hostilities,

the extensive program of military arrests and detentions, first by the State Department and then by the War Department, was largely preventive in nature and
seldom led to prosecutions.[88] Some treason indictments, though, were handed
down during the war. There were a large number in Maryland in the early days
of the war. In September 1864, Nathan Bedford Forrest was indicted for treason,
along with some eighty of his followers, in connection with a guerrilla-style raid
that they had carried out against Union-occupied Memphis in August 1864.[89]

Once the hostilities were over, there appeared to be a very real possibility of
further large-scale treason prosecutions. In the federal district court of East
Tennessee alone, some nineteen hundred indictments were on the court dock-
ets by the end of 1865.[90] In March 1866, Attorney General Speed was notified
of over two hundred treason indictments in Kentucky. By April of that year,
over fifty treason indictments were pending in Knoxville alone.[91]

A policy of prosecution inevitably forced the federal government to take a
position as to what actually constituted the key offense of engaging in rebellion (as set out in the Second Confiscation Act of 1862).[92] In 1867, the Adjutant General's Office of the War Department gave an indication of the federal
government's stance, which strongly inclined toward leniency.[93] The offense,
it was stated, only occurred when there was "an overt and voluntary act, done
with the intent of aiding or furthering" the rebellion. The harboring of "[d]is-
loyal sentiments, opinions, or sympathies" did not amount to rebellion, although incitement of others to join the Confederate cause did. Acts performed
under conscription or "under paramount authority" would not constitute rebellion.[94] Nor would "[f]orced contributions in the form of taxes or military
assessments." In addition, "[m]ere acts of charity" would not qualify as rebellion, although "organized contributions of food and clothing" designed to aid
the Confederate war effort would. Even Confederate or state government service would not count as rebellion, provided that it was "not incident to war"
and involved only the performance of peaceful duties "necessary to the preservation of order and the administration of law."

In all events, most of the treason prosecutions were not pursued to their
conclusion. For example, in Maryland, Chief Justice Taney, who sat on the
federal circuit containing that state, pointedly kept them from coming to trial
during the war. Forrest also was never placed on trial, either on the treason
charges (which were dropped in 1868) or for war crimes connected to the Fort
Pillow Massacre. Even the leading Confederate government figures, for the
most part, were not prosecuted. Most were held for some six months after capture, as prisoners of war, and then released without criminal charges.[95]

A very few indictments were procured against Confederate government officials. Clement Clay (a former senator from Alabama and then a Confederate agent in Canada) was charged with complicity in the Lincoln murder and also with organizing terrorist bands. Senator David Yulee of Florida was charged with treason (for retaining his seat in the Union Senate while plotting the capture of federal installations in his home state), and with inciting war and rebellion. His fellow Floridian Stephen Mallory, the Confederate secretary of the navy, was charged with treason and with organizing piratical expeditions.[96] None of these prosecutions, however, was pursued.

The only Confederate leader whom the federal government made a serious effort to prosecute was, not surprisingly, Jefferson Davis. A number of charges against him were contemplated, including complicity in the Lincoln assassination and conspiracy to violate the laws of war.[97] But treason was the only accusation that was actually pressed, and even that effort was beset with problems. For one thing, there was uncertainty as to where a trial could take place, in light of the constitutional requirement that a federal criminal prosecution must be held in the state where the crime was committed.[98] Some contended that this would allow Davis to be tried in *any* state in which any Confederate military action had taken place. On this thesis, Governor Oliver Morton of Indiana generously volunteered his state as a trial venue, since there had been some Confederate raiding there—helpfully assuring President Johnson that there would be "no difficulty in getting a jury that will do justice" to the famous defendant.[99] The decision was made, though, that Davis should be prosecuted in Virginia (where he had been physically based during his time of disloyalty). But that naturally gave rise to doubts as to whether a jury in that state would convict its erstwhile head of government.[100]

The prosecution then became something of a comedy of errors. The original indictment (of May 1865) was lost; so a second one had to be procured the following year.[101] Congress became impatient over the delays.[102] Davis himself sought an early trial. But in May 1867, when he was finally brought to the Richmond courthouse and transferred from military to civilian custody, on the prosecution's confession that it was not yet prepared to proceed to trial, Davis was released on bail of $100,000. Eventually, in December 1868, the proceedings were definitively discontinued because of Davis's inclusion in the terms of an amnesty granted by President Johnson (which will be considered presently). Davis went on to become a businessman in Memphis, where he lived unobtrusively until his death in 1889.[103]

On the whole, the outstanding feature of the legal winding-up of the Civil War was not the imposition of either criminal or civil liability for the events of the conflict. On the contrary, the most conspicuous feature was mercy, in the form of executive clemency on the part of President Johnson. It soon became apparent, though, that mercy gave rise to many legal problems of its own.

10

Forgiving but Not Forgetting

The law always recognizes facts as they exist after the state of war has passed, and . . . it never attempts to undo or change what war has done.

—U.S. Court of Claims

In the wake of the hostilities, the policy of prosecution was far overshadowed by one of clemency. There had never been much doubt that ordinary Confederate soldiers and civilians would not, in practice, be subject to prosecution. This expectation was borne out in May 1865, when President Johnson issued the first of what proved to be a series of pardon proclamations. Considerable problems soon arose, though, as to what effects the pardons actually had. In addition, a reaction set in; and the Radical Republican Congress made concerted attempts to limit the impact of the pardon policy. The result was an ongoing struggle between the executive and the legislature, with the courts as adjudicators.

Pardons protected persons against criminal prosecution, but they did not protect against civil actions by aggrieved (or vindictive) private parties. Where executive clemency could not penetrate, however, other forms of protection were available. The laws of war, for example, conferred wide immunities onto soldiers. For civilians, there was the possibility of statutory protection from lawsuits, in the form of what is now called impunity legislation. The principal beneficiaries of this form of generosity were persons who had acted for, or at the behest of, the Union government, in execution of dubious practices such as military detentions and trials by military commissions. Both the federal and the state governments entered into this morally murky area—not surprisingly, with controversial results.

If erstwhile disloyal persons had an interest in receiving pardons, and former jailors in being protected from lawsuits by their charges, there were also large numbers of people who sought something more positive in the aftermath of the war: compensation for the losses sustained during the conflict. Many persons succeeded in obtaining recompense of some kind, principally persons whose property had been requisitioned by the Union forces. But many others—especially, of course, former Confederate supporters—were left to suffer their losses with as good a grace as they could muster. It might be too much to say that justice was done in any thoroughgoing way in this regard. But at least a genuine attempt (or rather a series of them) was made to heal wounds in a material way, which is all that the law—for all of its majesty—can accomplish.

Mercy and Its Pitfalls

The power to issue pardons is explicitly granted to the President by the Constitution.[1] Somewhat confusingly, the power was placed on a statutory footing as well by the Second Confiscation Act of July 1862.[2] The Supreme Court later characterized this statutory grant as merely a "suggestion of pardon" rather than as actual "authority" for it.[3] The basic legal nature of a pardon is clear enough. It is the effacing of all *penal* consequences flowing from the commission of a criminal act.[4] As the federal Supreme Court put it in 1867, a presidential pardon

> releases the punishment and blots out of existence the guilt, so that in the eye of the law the offender is as innocent as if he had never committed the offence. If granted before conviction, it prevents any of the penalties and disabilities consequent upon conviction from attaching; if granted after conviction, it removes the penalties and disabilities, and restores him to all his civil rights; it makes him, as it were, a new man, and gives him a new credit and capacity.[5]

The policy of offering of pardons began in the very midst of the war itself. In December 1863, President Lincoln issued a proclamation offering an amnesty to any Confederates who would resume their former loyalty to the Union by taking an oath of loyalty—an oath, that is, promising *future* loyalty to the Union cause, as opposed to an ironclad oath.[6] The proclamation promised the restoration of any property that had been taken but had not yet been sold on to a third-party purchaser. It was later estimated that, by May 1865, about 10,500 persons had taken advantage of this amnesty offer.[7] It was after the conclusion of the hostilities, however, that pardons assumed a much higher profile—and also began to be steeped in controversy.

The Johnson Pardon Policy

In the course of his administration, President Johnson issued a total of four general pardon proclamations, each one wider in scope than the last. The most important of them was the first one, issued on May 29, 1865, since it stood alone for over two years.[8] As a general condition, pardon beneficiaries had to swear an oath promising future loyalty, as well as obedience to proclamations abolishing slavery. The pardon grant also expressly excluded from its scope confiscation proceedings that were currently in progress. More important was the exclusion of no fewer than fourteen designated categories of persons from its ambit. Most of these were fairly obvious, comprising the principal military and political leaders of the Confederacy. One excluded category, however, was particularly troublesome and controversial: all persons with a net worth of $20,000 or more—clear evidence of an intention to strike at the Southern planter class as a body.

The various persons excluded from this amnesty proclamation were not, however, altogether without hope of forgiveness. They could still apply specially to the President for *individual* pardons. Apply they did, and in droves, with very high success rates.[9] President Johnson granted about nine-tenths of the requests. In all, he gave out some 13,500 individual pardons, over half of them to persons who had been excluded by the $20,000 provision. There were reports of hundreds of pardon petitions being granted in single days. Some of these applicants were noteworthy persons. By January 1867, eighty-six members of the Confederate House of Representatives had received individual pardons, together with a smaller number of senators and perhaps a dozen Southern state governors.[10] Robert E. Lee was an applicant—with the explicit support of General Grant—although his request was denied because of a failure to include an oath of loyalty along with it.

The other three postwar pardon proclamations may be mentioned more briefly. The second one, issued in September 1867, significantly narrowed the excluded classes, while retaining the requirement of a loyalty oath.[11] The only

persons now left out were "chief executive officers" of the Confederate government, military persons above the rank of brigadier general (or captain in the
navy), persons who had treated Union prisoners "otherwise than as prisoners
of war," and persons currently in confinement (with those involved in the Lincoln murder expressly singled out). Probably only some three hundred persons
fell into these excluded groups. Moreover, this proclamation, like its predecessor, was supplemented by the continued granting of individual pardons. Eventually, nearly all of the civilian leaders of the Confederacy received pardons,
with two notable exceptions: Jefferson Davis and Secretary of War John C.
Breckenridge (who was living abroad at the time), both of whom obstinately
refused to request individual pardons.[12] This second proclamation also went
beyond its predecessor in not excluding confiscation proceedings from its
reach.

The third proclamation, in July 1868, was a full and unconditional pardon,
this time with *no* requirement of a loyalty oath of any kind and only one excluded category—persons presently facing charges of treason or other felony,
such as Jefferson Davis.[13] This left only a minute number of persons excluded.
The fourth and final pardon was issued on Christmas Day 1868, granting a
"full pardon and amnesty," plus full restoration of rights, to all persons.[14] This
finally put a stop (as noted above) to the Davis treason trial. Practically the
only persons now remaining outside the circle of mercy were the convicted
Lincoln murderers—and even three of them were given individual pardons, in
Johnson's final days in office in March 1869, for services performed for their
fellow inmates and jailors during an outbreak of disease in their prison.

The Reach of a Pardon—Confiscation Proceedings

It has just been noted that a pardon has the effect of eliminating all *penal* consequences of past wrongdoing. It should be carefully appreciated, though, that
*non*penal effects of past acts are not affected by a pardon. Some of the most
important of these may be mentioned briefly. It remained possible for *civil*
proceedings to be instituted against pardon holders for specific unlawful acts
that they might have committed. Pardons also did not affect *in rem* proceedings, since those were regarded as noncriminal (i.e., situations in which, so to
speak, the *property*, rather than the pardoned person, had committed the
crime). For this reason, property lost as a result of prize proceedings was not
recoverable.[15] In addition, any proceedings for confiscation of property were

not reversible once title had passed by court adjudication.[16] A pardon also did not enable its holder to benefit from an act of grace or favor from the government, since the withholding of a favor could not be regarded as penal. More generally, the Supreme Court stated (though only as dictum) that pardons also did not affect any measures that the federal government might have imposed under its *belligerent,* as distinct from its *sovereign,* powers.[17]

In determining the practical effect that a pardon would have, it is therefore crucial to determine whether a given disability or disadvantage is classed as penal or not. If it is penal, then it is curable by a pardon. If not, not. But this determination is not always easy to make. In no area was it more problematic than that of confiscations and captures of property. Of particular importance and interest in this area were issues arising in three areas: the direct tax of 1861; the two Confiscation Acts; and the captured-and-abandoned property program.

Consider first the confiscations for nonpayment of the direct tax of 1861, in which Southern lands were burdened with specified tax liabilities and sold off for nonpayment.[18] Confiscations under this heading were regarded as nonpenal, that is, as a mechanism for the gathering in of the taxes due and not as a criminal punishment for their nonpayment.[19] Therefore, these proceedings were not affected by a presidential pardon. It may be noted, though, that in 1872 Congress provided a measure of statutory relief, by granting to ex-owners a right to *redeem* their property, specifically, to reacquire it from the federal government—though not from a private buyer—on payment of the tax owed (plus costs and interest).[20]

Regarding the Confiscation Acts, there were three distinct questions to be resolved: first, whether a pardon precluded the *instituting* of proceedings; second, whether a pardon mandated the discontinuing of ongoing proceedings; and third, whether, on the strength of a pardon, a person could claim the proceeds of sale of confiscated property *after* disposition. The second of these categories, ongoing proceedings, was the easiest to deal with. It will be recalled that President Johnson's first pardon proclamation, of May 1865, expressly stated these would not be affected by a pardon. The courts reached essentially the same conclusion, chiefly by way of the key Supreme Court ruling of 1871, that proceedings under the Second Confiscation Act were exercises of belligerent, rather than of sovereign, right. As such, they were *in rem* (i.e., against the property *itself*) rather than *in personam* (against the owners).[21] On that basis, it would appear likely that, even without the express exception in the Johnson pardon, ongoing confiscation proceedings would not be terminated by a pardon.[22]

It was otherwise, however, regarding both the commencing of confiscation actions and the claiming of proceeds of sale afterward. After some considerable litigation and uncertainty, the conclusion seems to have been reached that personal misconduct was, in effect, a condition precedent for the instituting of confiscation proceedings, even though the proceedings *themselves* were *in rem*. On that thesis, a pardon would preclude the commencing of confiscation, on the ground that a pardon effectively precluded the necessary condition precedent from being legally present. This conclusion was clearly articulated with regard to the First Confiscation Act and may be (cautiously) taken to apply to the Second Confiscation Act as well.[23]

Finally, there was the question of whether pardon holders could claim the proceeds of sale of confiscated property on the strength of their pardons.[24] In 1873, the federal Supreme Court allowed such a claim, though without any detailed discussion.[25] In a similar case in 1876, the Court was somewhat more forthcoming on the subject. In the context of claims to the proceeds of sale, the Court appeared to be willing, if only implicitly, to treat confiscations under the Second Confiscation Act as penal, hence as falling within the reach of the pardon power.[26] This conclusion may appear at first glance to be seriously inconsistent with the 1871 decision, which was never explicitly overruled. Later developments, however, have clarified the picture by establishing that proceedings that are not inherently criminal in nature can nonetheless have *consequences* which are penal.[27] And those penal consequences can be expunged by a pardon.

The Reach of a Pardon—Captured and Abandoned Property

In this area as in others, captured and abandoned property stood on a different footing from confiscation. It will be recalled that property in this category was turned over to officials of the Treasury Department for sale.[28] The erstwhile owners of the property were given a statutory right to claim the proceeds of sale in proceedings in the Court of Claims—*if* they could establish their loyalty, and *if* they filed their claims within two years of the conclusion of the war (i.e., of August 20, 1866).[29] The question naturally arose as to whether a presidential pardon had the effect of relieving claimants of the burden of proving loyalty. The answer, given by the Supreme Court, was that it did, on a generous interpretation of the Captured and Abandoned Property Act. In 1872, the Court ruled that the capture and sale of property was not intended actually to divest the owners of their title. Instead, it merely altered the *nature* of the property, transforming it from goods or chattels into a sum of money—a sum of money which the federal government then held on behalf of the ex-owner as a sort of trustee.[30] On this theory, the inability of formerly disloyal persons to recover their *own* property (as it effectively was) must be regarded as a penalty. As such, it was curable by a presidential pardon.[31]

Holders of pardons were not so fortunate, however, with respect to the other key restriction on the claiming of proceeds of sale of captured and abandoned property: the requirement that claims be filed within two years after the end of the war (i.e., within two years of August 20, 1866). The Supreme Court held that pardons did not have the effect of extending this deadline—so that the two-year period ran inflexibly from August 20, 1866, and *not* from the date of the receipt of the pardon. Consequently, any pardon received after August 20, 1868, conferred no effective right to recover the proceeds of sale of captured and abandoned property.[32]

In opposition to this holding, it was strenuously argued that disloyalty ought to be considered a disability, analogous to, say, infancy or insanity, and also that the two-year condition ought to be treated as an ordinary limitation period—as a restriction on the right of would-be claimants to approach the courts for relief. The effect of this approach would be that time would not begin to run against the two-year limitation period until the disability was lifted—so that pardon holders would then would have two years *after the receipt of the pardon* to file their claims. In 1875, however, the federal Supreme Court held that this disability-and-limitation theory was not correct. The true position, it pronounced, was that the two-year requirement was not a limitation period. Rather, it was a *jurisdictional* constraint on the Court of Claims *itself,* rather than a condition imposed on aspiring litigants as individuals. The effect of this judgment was that the Court of Claims lacked the *power* to grant relief on any claim filed after August 20, 1868.[33] The result was that the two-year limit was rigidly fixed, unless Congress elected to extend it.[34]

Placing Shackles on Mercy

The Johnson policy of widespread clemency did not (to put it mildly) meet with universal approbation. To many Radical Republicans, the President's pardon power had been used so profligately as to undermine the achievements of the war itself. During the Johnson impeachment proceedings of 1868, Congress even considered adding abuse of the pardon power as one of the grounds of impeachment, although in event it elected not to do so.[35] Nonetheless, with the growing political weakness of President Johnson and the increasing confidence and influence of the Radical faction in Congress, efforts were made to place restraints on the President's pardon power.

A first attempt took the form of a law enacted in January 1867 (over Johnson's veto), in the wake of the Radical gains in the 1866 midterm elections.[36] It repealed the earlier statutory grant of a pardon power, contained in the Second Confiscation Act. The law never had a real effect, though, since, just a week before its enactment, the Supreme Court ruled, in the *Garland* case, that the President's pardon power, being rooted directly in the Constitution, could not be curtailed by statute.[37]

Congress soon adopted different approaches to limiting the effects of presidential pardons, with the process evolving into something of a juridical cat-and-mouse game between executive and legislature. In 1870, Congress took an intriguingly indirect approach to the matter, in a little-noticed provision deeply buried in a complex appropriations bill.[38] Rather than purporting to limit the President's right to *grant* a pardon, the law sought to restrict the ability of courts to give it full effect. Specifically, the provision purported to bar the Court of Claims from considering evidence of the receipt of a pardon by the claimant party—with the result that past disloyalty would continue to operate as an effective bar against claims, even to pardon holders. Two years later, however, the Supreme Court struck the law down as unconstitutional, with a combination of scorn and disbelief.[39] The Court ruled that, since Congress was precluded from abridging the President's pardon power directly by statute, it was similarly precluded from doing the same thing by a covert, back-door device such as this evidentiary rule.

The principal challenge to legislators of a vindictive turn of mind—and these were not in short supply—was to devise disabilities that were nonpunitive in nature and would therefore lie outside the legal reach of the pardoning power. The basic plan was simple enough: to exploit the subtle, but important, distinction between, on the one hand, true legal right and, on the other hand, mere grace or favor, or act of discretion. The denial of a right would be penal (hence within the reach of a pardon); the denial of a favor would not be. It happened that Congress was dealt a strong hand in this game, because *any* appropriation from the general revenues of the Treasury was necessarily a matter of discretion on Congress's part, by virtue of the constitutional provision that no money could be drawn from the Treasury except "in Consequence of Appropriations made by Law."[40] This included the payment of most categories of claims against the federal government, since the payments came out of the Treasury.

In March 1867, Congress began to flex its muscles in this direction, by enacting a law concerning the payment of *pre*war claims against the federal government.[41] No payments of these claims, it was stated, were to be made to anyone who had supported the rebellion. It was even expressly stated that a pardon would *not* entitle an ex-rebel to payment. In the early 1880s, the Court of Claims upheld the legislation as nonpenal, on the ground that it created no crime. It merely placed a condition on the payment of moneys from the federal Treasury—something that Congress was fully entitled to do, as part of its exclusive power over Treasury outlays.[42] The federal Supreme Court upheld this decision in 1886.[43] In doing so, it went so far as expressly to point out that the law need not have mentioned pardons at all because a pardon, by its own intrinsically limited character, cannot abridge the constitutional prerogative of Congress to control appropriations from the Treasury.

Congress employed this prerogative again in 1874, when it established the Court of Commissioners of Alabama Claims, to disburse the money from the 1872 Geneva arbitral award. Would-be claimants were required to prove that they had borne "true allegiance" to the Union cause throughout the war.[44] This requirement was found to be beyond the curative reach of a pardon, since (as observed earlier) these disbursements were regarded as a matter of grace by the federal government rather than of entitlement on the part of the claimants.[45]

The beneficial effects of pardons could also be limited by the exploitation of another prerogative of Congress: its constitutional power to fix the jurisdiction of federal courts and tribunals.[46] By this means, Congress could carefully withhold from a court the *power* (i.e., the jurisdiction) to grant a benefit of some kind to a disloyal person. Congress's power to limit the practical of pardons in this manner was taken to the Supreme Court. In 1894, in a case concerning a statutory denial of jurisdiction to the Court of Claims to approve payments to persons who had been disloyal during the war, the Court ruled in Congress's favor.[47] The President's clemency power, it pronounced, could not operate as a limitation on Congress's constitutional right to determine the jurisdiction of federal courts which it created. "To whom the privilege of suit should be accorded was for Congress alone to determine."

This jurisdictional stratagem was employed in various contexts. For example, Congress occasionally enacted special extensions of the two-year time limit for claims under the Captured and Abandoned Property Act in individual cases.[48] When doing so, Congress pointedly withheld from the Court of Claims the power to make an award to a formerly disloyal person. Jurisdictional limitation was also deployed (as will be seen) to limit payments for requisitioned property. In fact, Congress, armed with its jurisdictional power, effectively had a sweeping authority to withhold *any* kind of federal largesse from erstwhile disloyal persons.

Barred from Office—and Readmitted

There were special provisions concerning ineligibility for federal service. In July 1866, Congress enacted legislation barring army service by anyone who had served the Confederacy in any capacity.[49] More comprehensive ineligibility provisions were included in the Fourteenth Amendment to the Constitution, which entered into force two years after that. It applied to former federal and state officeholders who had taken oaths of office to support the Constitution, and who had subsequently "engaged in insurrection or rebellion." They were barred from holding any state or federal office, civil or military.[50] As this provision was set in constitutional concrete, it was beyond the reach of the presidential pardon power to cure. (It was later held, though, by opinion of the attorney general, that persons who had received presidential pardons *before* the Fourteenth Amendment took effect were not subject to the disability.)[51] In 1870, further measures were instituted against persons disabled by the amendment. A law enacted that year provided a specific legal process for the removal from office of persons who were holding governmental positions despite the legal disability. It also subjected those persons to criminal prosecution, including penalties of up to $1,000 in fines or one year of imprisonment, or both. (The removal mechanism did not apply to members of the federal or state legislatures, but the criminal provision did.)[52]

The Fourteenth Amendment did, however, hold out a hope of relief for persons affected by it. Congress—as opposed to the President—was empowered to remove disabilities, by way of a two-thirds vote of both houses. Legislation enacted in 1868, just prior to the entry into force of the Fourteenth Amendment, offered some clarification concerning this relief process. It provided that, when disabilities were removed by the requisite two-thirds vote, only an ordinary oath of loyalty to the Constitution would be required of the beneficiaries, and not an ironclad oath.[53]

In the event, Congress proved itself to be a match for President Johnson in the liberality of its exercise of this legislative disability-removal power. It did not even wait for the Fourteenth Amendment to enter formally into force. The first beneficiary of congressional forgiveness was a certain Rodrick R. Butler of Tennessee, whose disability was lifted in June 1868, to allow him to sit in the federal House of Representatives.[54] Within a week, the pace picked up very considerably, as many hundreds of persons from North Carolina, Alabama, and Georgia (plus two from Arkansas and five from South Carolina) had their disabilities similarly lifted.[55] The following month (still prior to the formal entry into force of the Fourteenth Amendment), hundreds more had their disabilities (or impending disabilities) removed at one fell swoop.[56]

These acts which preceded the entry into force of the Fourteenth Amendment were on the basis of mere majority votes of the two houses of Congress; but once the amendment was in effect, the stipulated two-thirds votes had to be mustered in both houses. That proved to pose no insurmountable hurdle. Congressional action in December 1869 benefited another large batch, followed by a particularly large number (into the thousands) in March 1870, bringing the total number of relieved persons to some forty-five hundred.[57] After this, the pace of individual disability removals slowed down considerably.[58]

In May 1872, Congress went a long step further by granting a mass lifting of disabilities to ex-Confederates in general, though with some pointed exclusions: persons who had served in the federal Congresses of 1859–1863; persons who had been officers (as opposed to enlisted men) in the United States armed services; and ex-ambassadors.[59] Despite this less-than-comprehensive coverage, many thousands of persons benefited from this act of collective generosity.[60] Immediately after the enactment of this law, President Grant directed the discontinuance of civil and criminal proceedings against disqualified persons who had been unlawfully holding offices.[61]

Those who remained excluded from this 1872 legislation, estimated at about 750 in number, could continue to hope for individual disability removals. Further action by Congress in this vein benefited about one-third of this group.[62] In June 1872, for example, five persons (including Zebulon Vance, former governor of North Carolina) had their disabilities lifted, in three separate pieces of legislation.[63] The final individual disability removals were granted, somewhat belatedly, in 1897, the very last beneficiary being a certain Colonel William E. Simms of Kentucky.[64] The following year, while the Spanish-American War was under way, Congress made the final gesture of removing, by unanimous vote, all remaining Fourteenth Amendment disabilities *en bloc*—if indeed there were any left by then.[65]

Nevertheless, one final act of individual generosity surfaced, much later, in the 1970s, in favor of no less a personage than Robert E. Lee. In 1975, Congress, expressly invoking the relevant provision of the Fourteenth Amendment, restored to Lee "the full rights of citizenship" retroactively to June 13, 1865 (i.e., to the date of Lee's original application for a pardon).[66] The 1975 law recited the reason for the action. Although (as noted) Lee had failed to include an oath of loyalty along with his original pardon application, recent research disclosed that he had rectified that shortcoming several months later, in October 1865, but that the federal government had somehow lost track of his oath. With that difficulty now removed, there seemed to be no compelling reason for the pardon request to have been denied. Congress could not grant the pardon—but nor was a pardon now needed, since Lee fell within the terms of President Johnson's fourth pardon proclamation of December 1868 (prior to his death in 1870). As a sort of substitute measure, Congress voted to remove Lee's Fourteenth Amendment disabilities. It might be pointed out that Lee had already fallen within the terms of the final collective lifting of the disabilities in 1898. But there is perhaps room for doubting whether that legislation applied to deceased persons, who would be ineligible for government service on, so to speak, other grounds. Be that as it may, Congress demonstrated an impressive combination of magnanimity, legal technicality, and long memory.[67]

Civil Suits and Impunity Laws

No cleverness on the part of Congress was required with regard to one of the principal shortcomings of pardons (from the standpoint of their holders). This was the inability of pardons, by their nature, to give any shield against civil liability. Even if pardons gave no protection against civil suits, defendants sometimes possessed immunities from suit which had other sources, two of which call for some attention. The first of these was the law of war—more specifically, the key principle that lawful belligerents possess immunity from *both* civil and criminal suits for *bona fide* acts of war. This principle was confirmed, in very sweeping terms, by the federal Supreme Court in 1880.[68] The second possible source of immunity from civil suit was legislation, either state or federal, expressly barring civil suits for various specified activities—typically for acts done pursuant to, or in actual execution of, official government policies. These are now commonly known as "impunity laws," although that expression was not used in the Civil War era. We shall look at each of these types of immunity in turn, and the legal problems to which they gave rise.

Immunity Conferred by the Laws of War

There was never any question that Union soldiers were immune from both civil and criminal actions for any acts done pursuant to the laws of war The position of members of the Confederate forces, however, was more doubtful. In 1867, the West Virginia Supreme Court held that Confederates did *not* possess such an immunity. It ruled that the Confederate troops were mere lawbreakers and that the concession of belligerents' rights to them operated only *during* the hostilities. Once the war was over, the full force of the law could take effect; and Confederates had to suffer the legal consequences of their unauthorized conduct.[69] The state legislature, however, stepped in and reversed this holding. In 1871, it enacted a law conferring legal immunity from civil actions onto soldiers on *both* sides in the recent conflict.[70] In addition, the federal Supreme Court, in 1868, ruled, in effect, that members of the Confederate armed forces qualified for legal immunity on the same basis as their Union counterparts.[71]

The principal legal challenge in an action against an ex-Confederate military person, therefore, was whether the act in question fell within the compass of the laws of war, or whether it was a war crime. Only war crimes could be the subject of civil suits. In a postwar case in Kentucky, for example, a judgment was obtained against a Confederate soldier for the taking of some $5,400 from a bank.[72] This was held to have been pillage, with the alleged authorization of a superior officer being no defense. In West Virginia, an ex-detainee sued a former Confederate provost marshal in the local courts for trespass (meaning illegal arrest and false imprisonment) and was awarded $600 in damages.[73]

That it was not always easy to distinguish war crimes from *bona fide* acts of war is nicely illustrated by a case that arose out of the raiding activities of Confederate general John Hunt Morgan. The Louisville and Nashville Railroad sued a member of Morgan's band for damages inflicted by Morgan's forces and was awarded $15,000 at the trial. On appeal, however, that award was held by the Kentucky Court of Appeal to be a "radical error" on the ground that the raid, and the damage to the railroad, was not an act of "wanton waste" but instead was a "stroke of Southern policy" qualifying for "the protective sanction of belligerent right."[74] For losses caused by *bona fide* acts of war, a person's only remedy was against the government, not the individuals involved, a matter to be considered presently.

Persons who had held political or judicial—as opposed to military—positions with Confederate federal or state governments were in a more exposed position, since the shield of the laws of war did not extend to them (i.e., their activities did not fall into the category of acts of war). This was illustrated by an action brought by a person who had been criminally prosecuted for treason (against the Confederacy) by Alabama officials. He brought a civil suit for malicious prosecution against the man who had been the judge at his trial. In this case, which went all the way to the federal Supreme Court, the ex-judge was held to be subject to suit, since the conviction over which he had presided had to be regarded as a legal nullity.[75]

Immunity Conferred by Statute (Impunity Laws)

It was not only Confederate government officials who were potentially exposed to civil lawsuits for their activities. Union ones could be as well—provided, of course, that the plaintiffs in question could actually establish that a wrong had been committed. As it happened, there was a substantial pool of persons with a possible interest in precisely that direction. These chiefly comprised persons who had been imprisoned by the military without charge or trial, or who (like Milligan) had been tried by a military commission which proved not to possess lawful jurisdiction over them. The particular individuals who had been in charge of the detentions or trials were potentially liable in damages to their former detainees.

As early as March 1863, with the Habeas Corpus Act, the federal government began taking steps to prevent private lawsuits from being pressed against its officials. That law provided that obedience to orders of the President would be a defense to any civil *or* criminal action for any searches and arrests.[76] The shield provided was fairly limited in scope, though, since it applied only to detention and search situations, and only during the continuance of the war. In the postwar years, Congress took several steps to strengthen the protection. In May 1866, it expanded the defense granted in the 1863 act, by providing that obedience to the orders of *any* superior military officer (not merely the President) would be a defense.[77] The protection still applied, however, only to questions of search and detention.

In the wake of the *Milligan* judgment of April 1866, the fear loomed in Congress that persons who had been detained and tried by military commissions might sue their former captors and judges for damages.[78] A law enacted in March 1867 was designed to foreclose this danger.[79] It provided that all acts of military tribunals were "approved in all respects, legalized and made valid," meaning that they must be treated as if they had been carried out pursuant to prior authorizing legislation. It covered the time period from Lincoln's first inauguration to July 1, 1866. As an added precaution, federal courts were stripped of jurisdiction to hear any claims in this regard. By interpretation, this protection was held by a federal court in New York to extend to cases of alleged theft.[80]

Some states enacted similar immunity legislation. Missouri, for example, provided in its postwar constitution that there could be no civil or criminal immunity for acts performed "by virtue of military authority."[81] This provision was held by the Missouri Supreme Court to be broad enough to protect civilian private parties who simply acted in obedience to martial-law orders.[82] North Carolina also enacted an Amnesty Act in 1866 to this end, as did Kentucky.[83]

The most difficult legal question concerning these impunity measures was whether the state or federal governments could constitutionally strip persons of all forms of legal redress for acts which had actually been unlawful at the time that they were committed. In the event, the federal Supreme Court answered this question in the affirmative. In 1870, for example, it upheld the Missouri state constitutional provision on impunity, which was challenged as a bill of attainder and an *ex post facto* law, on the thesis that it revoked citizens' rights to sue for civil wrongs *after* the right to sue had accrued. The Court upheld the measure, on the ground that it was not penal in character.[84] Indeed, its very purpose was to *preclude* any imposition of penalties.

In 1884, the Supreme Court considered the constitutionality of the various federal impunity laws and ruled that it was permissible for a statute to ratify *prior* acts—i.e., to halt the pursuit of an accrued right to sue—provided that the prior action could have been authorized by Congress to begin with.[85] Justice Field was an eloquent and vigorous dissenter from this conclusion. In a powerful opinion in an 1879 case, he excoriated the federal impunity laws, insisting that neither the President nor Congress could confer immunity for acts committed in violation of the rights of citizens.[86] The furthest Congress could go, he maintained, was to reimburse government agents for any judgments that might be assessed against them, so as (in effect) to transfer ultimate responsibility from the individual defendants to the government itself. But legal responsibility *per se*, he contended, could not simply be effaced by legislative fiat.

Field's views did not carry the day at the time. Nor, it may be added, have his views fared very well in later legal history. Courts have, admittedly, become receptive to the idea that a right to sue is a species of property which, as such, is entitled to constitutional protection.[87] It has also been held that immunity laws *do* constitute an inference with that right.[88] Immunity laws have not been held, however, to be an *unconstitutional* interference. That is to say, they have not been held to constitute either a taking of property "for public use" (contrary to the Fifth Amendment) or a taking of property "without due process of law" (contrary to the Fourteenth Amendment). It is not impossible, however, that certain types of immunity provisions might not be held, at some future point, to infringe one or the other of these principles.

To return to the post–Civil War position, it may be remembered that there was a very important proviso to the Court's approval of impunity legislation: that retroactive immunity could only be conferred onto acts which *could have been* constitutionally authorized prior to their commission.[89] This proviso was effectively exploited in a civil action brought by (appropriately enough) the irrepressible Lambdin P. Milligan. In the wake of his earlier triumph, he instituted a civil action in a federal circuit court in Indiana against his military jailors, for wrongful imprisonment. The court held that the later federal impunity laws could not provide an effective shield to the defendants, on the thesis (established by the Supreme Court in the *Milligan* judgment) that his trial by military commission could not have been constitutionally provided for by *any* means, not even by act of Congress. What Congress could not do directly beforehand could not be done indirectly afterward by way of a *post hoc* immunity grant.[90] (Milligan was only awarded nominal damages, though, by a clearly unsympathetic jury.)

A similar conclusion was reached by the Illinois Supreme Court in 1867, in a case concerning a detainee who had been held for three months and released without trial, and who, like Milligan, then brought a civil action against his jailors.[91] The defendants duly pleaded the orders of the President in their defense, but the Court rejected the plea. Again on the authority of the *Milligan* case, it held that, despite the immunity statute, the President's orders were no defense because the President had no lawful authority to make such an order. The furthest the Court was willing to go was to allow a plea of presidential orders to be used as evidence of good faith on the wrongdoer's part, so as to moderate the level of damages that would be awarded. The Kentucky Court of Appeal, in the same vein, ruled that that state's Amnesty Act could not have the effect of canceling *existing* rights of action.[92]

The United States is fortunate that impunity laws have not been an important feature of its political or legal history. So it is difficult to be confident as to how such cases would be treated by the courts today. Justice Field's position— that Congress can indemnify defendants for damages assessed against them but cannot strip plaintiffs of an accrued right to sue—would appear to make good sense, on the thesis that an impunity law is a measure of public policy done on behalf of the community as a whole, in the interest of promoting reconciliation. As such, it would seem fair that the economic burdens which flow from it ought to be discharged from general public funds, and should not fall exclusively on the particular individuals whose claims are cut off. Against this approach, though, it could be contended that the very *process* of litigation can legitimately be held to be undesirably divisive and contrary to the wider public interest of reconciliation. In that event, it could be held that the private interests of would-be claimants could justifiably be sacrificed in the larger public interest.[93] The definitive position of the law on this interesting, and disturbing, issue continues to be awaited.

Compensation for (Some) Victims

Four years of intense war that ranged over a large portion of the land territory of the United States can hardly have failed to disrupt ordinary lives in manifold respects. The most obvious forms of disruption included service in the armed forces (voluntary or otherwise), inflation of the paper currency, and high taxation. Other incidents of war included requisitions, capture and destruction of property, businesses either ruined or bolstered by war (as the case may be), and, perhaps most dramatically of all, a sudden and dramatic transformation, for millions of people, from a condition of servitude to one of freedom (if hardly of comfort). It was natural for many of those who suffered losses to seek compensation from the federal government. An indication of the variety of possibilities in this regard was afforded by a book published, in timely fashion, in 1866, by a certain George W. Raff, entitled *The War Claimant's Guide*. Its subtitle was perhaps more revealing as to the range of topics dealt with: *A Manual of Laws, Regulations, Instructions, Forms, and Official Decisions, Relating to Pensions, Bounty, Pay, Prize Money, Salvage, Applications for Artificial Limbs, Compensation for Steamboats, Cars, Horses, Clothing, Slaves, and Other Property Lost or Destroyed, Commutation of Rations, Travel, Etc.*

One important form of compensation comprised payment for property requisitioned for the Union war effort—although there were important differences as between Northerners and loyal Southerners in this area. There were other categories of compensation too. For captured and abandoned property, most notably, there was the possibility of recovery of the proceeds of sale by the owners. For injuries to foreigners, there was the possibility of the pursuit of claims by their governments for compensation. Finally, there was the possibility of individual grants of relief by Congress. Each of these paths had its own distinctive legal features.

Requisitions and War Damage

The principal area in which there was a legal entitlement to compensation for war-related losses was in cases of requisition. This refers to requisition by a belligerent government of the property of its *own* nationals, not those of the enemy. It has already been observed that, for goods requisitioned by armed forces in unoccupied enemy territory, there was no duty of compensation. The only duty on the part of the military was to be moderate in its demands and to take no more than was actually necessary for the purpose at hand.[94] Moreover, since this principle was a feature of the laws of war, it was a question of the government operating in a belligerent, rather than in a sovereign, capacity. Concretely, that meant that residents of the insurgent states had no right of compensation for requisitions, even if they happened to be personally loyal to the Union. This limitation was given explicit statutory force in February 1867.[95]

Requisitions in the loyal states, in sharp contrast, were matters of sovereign right—and, as such, were subject to the normal strictures of the Constitution. Most pertinently, that meant the Fifth Amendment, which requires that, when property is taken for a public purpose, "just compensation" must be paid. In 1864, a statute was enacted for the discharging of this duty.[96] It provided that claims to compensation for requisitions (or "stores," in the parlance of the time) be made to the quartermaster general of the United States. Interestingly, the possibility that a person resident in a loyal state might be personally disloyal was considered and provided for by Congress, as the law required that the military commissary had to be "satisfied" of a claimant's loyalty before it could make a compensation payment. In due course, jurisdiction over these claims was transferred, first to specially appointed commissioners and eventually to the Court of Claims.[97]

In this area, as in others, the question of the effect of a presidential pardon arose in due course. In 1875, the attorney general ruled that the holding of a pardon would discharge the requirement of satisfaction of loyalty.[98] (It will be recalled that, since the underlying right of requisition was limited to residents of the loyal states, citizens of the ex-Confederate states who held pardons could not benefit from this generous interpretation.) But Congress—ever vigilant on the subject of executive clemency—successfully counteracted this liberality, by its basic strategy of curtailing the jurisdiction of the Court of Claims to make awards to formerly disloyal persons. It explicitly provided, in a law of 1883, that the Court had no jurisdiction to approve awards to claimants who had not been loyal throughout the war.[99]

Requisition in the true sense must be distinguished from various other activities for which it might readily be mistaken—and for which there is no constitutional entitlement to compensation. For example, requisitions are quite distinct from *unauthorized* depredations by individual soldiers on their own initiative. These are war crimes, for which the soldiers responsible are subject to court-martial and punishment by their superior officers. But they give rise to no claim for compensation by the victim from the soldiers' *government*.[100] Nor did captured and abandoned property fall within the category of requisition, since that property was not taken for actual *use* by the Union armed forces themselves. Rather, it was taken as a war measure for the purpose of weakening the enemy side.

Finally—and most important—property that is requisitioned must be distinguished from property that is damaged or destroyed in the course of belligerent operations. It was a long-standing principle of the laws of war that incidental losses flowing from military action were merely, in the words of Vattel, accidents or "misfortunes of war," for which the losses should merely be left as they happened to fall.[101] In many cases, it was easy enough to distinguish requisitions from war damage. It was clear enough, for example, that the taking of tobacco for use as rations for the Union army fell into the category of requisition rather than of incidental war damage.[102] But in borderline cases, some delicate judgmental decisions needed to be made. For example, when General

Lew Wallace ordered the trees on a person's private property to be cut down, in order to provide his guns with a free range of fire, his action was held to constitute taking for use (i.e., requisition) rather than destroying in action. Therefore, compensation was owed.[103] The burning of cotton, to prevent it from falling into enemy hands, was also held to require compensation, on the basis that it was a preventive action rather than an actual belligerent operation.[104]

The deliberate destroying of civilian infrastructure, in contrast, was generally held to be a belligerent act and hence to be noncompensable. For example, compensation was denied for the destruction of a sawmill by Sherman's forces in Mississippi, on the ground that the mill was, at that very time, employed in the sawing of railroad ties for the Confederate government—hence that its destruction was, legally speaking, tantamount to a military action on the field of battle.[105] Compensation was also refused to farmers in Virginia whose property had been deliberately destroyed by General Sheridan's forces as an "area denial" measure against guerrillas.[106]

Inadvertent destruction of property was treated on a par with property destroyed by acts of war—as a mere accident, with no compensation owing. An illustration of this point arose from a claim before the British-American arbitral panel for damage from the burning of Columbia, South Carolina, in 1865. The panel held that, given the absence of either "intention or default" on the part of Union officers, the burning must be regarded as a mere accident for which compensation was not owing.[107]

Cases concerning claims for compensation for property requisition coursed through the federal courts for many decades after the war. It would appear that no one has, as yet, made a calculation of the aggregate amount that was actually paid out. Eventually, the federal government's patience was exhausted. In 1915, a little-remarked piece of legislation called the "Crawford Amendment" finally removed from the jurisdiction of the Court of Claims all cases of this kind.[108] Piece by piece, the great conflict was winding down.

Rewarding Southern Loyalists

It was observed above that the constitutional right of compensation for requisitions was reserved to residents of the loyal states, and consequently denied, *en bloc,* to residents of the Confederate states—even to Confederate-state residents who were personally loyal. There nevertheless was a general expectation that the federal government would, in due course, devise some kind of ar-

rangement for the relief of loyal Southerners for the suffering they had under-
gone for the Union cause. President Lincoln gave express (if somewhat vague)
voice to this sentiment in September 1862 in the Preliminary Proclamation of
Emancipation.[109] Only in 1871, however, did the federal government begin to
make good on this moral commitment, with the creation, by statute, of a body
known popularly as the Southern Claims Commission.[110] The basic task of
this body was to compensate loyal Southerners for requisitions on a par with
loyal Northerners. The principle of no compensation for damage caused by
belligerent operations was adhered to, though, so that no compensation was
provided for emancipation of slaves. Moreover, it was clearly understood from
the outset that this generosity to the stalwart Union folk of the South was a
matter of moral and not of legal obligation. As the Court of Claims later put
it, compensation claims for requisitions made by loyal persons in the Confederate states possessed "no merit in law, but . . . appealed to the equity and justice of Congress."[111] This of course reflected the fact that, as Confederate
residents, even loyal Southerners were in the legal category of enemies according to the laws of war.

    This lack of legal entitlement to compensation on the part of Southerners
had a subtle—but important—effect. It meant that the requirement that
claimants prove their loyalty was *not* a restriction of a legal right, but rather a
condition attached to the generosity of Congress. That had the key consequence of placing the loyalty requirement outside the reach of a presidential
pardon (i.e., a pardon did not absolve the holder from the duty of proving loyalty, as it did in claims to the proceeds of captured and abandoned property).
Not only did the possession of a pardon not absolve the holder of the duty of
proving loyalty. It could also, ironically, actually make the proof more difficult.
This became apparent when the Court of Claims came to regard the possession
of a pardon as *prima facie* proof that the holder had *not* been loyal during the
struggle—otherwise, why would he or she have or need a pardon?[112]

    In the sometimes arduous process of proving loyalty, the most difficult mat-
ter, from the legal standpoint, was the question of whether mere passive or routine acquiescence in the prevailing Confederate law necessarily amounted to
disloyalty. It was generally agreed that support for the Confederate cause that
arose from what lawyers call duress should not be held against claimants.
Duress operates chiefly in the area of criminal law, to excuse a person from
criminal responsibility in the extreme situation in which the person is forced by
some outside agent to commit an offense—and in which the real responsibility

for the crime rests, accordingly, on the person who applies the compulsion rather than on the person who succumbs to it. Claims cases were not criminal, but the general question of duress as a lawful excuse for disloyalty involved essentially the same considerations. Some courts took a lenient position on this question. The Virginia Supreme Court, for example, held that obedience of the prevailing law could qualify as duress and excuse disloyal acts.[113]

The federal courts, however, inclined toward a sterner view. In the leading case on the subject, in 1873, the Supreme Court held that, to meet the standard for duress, it was necessary that the person in question to be a victim of "actual violence."[114] "Actual violence" did not (or not quite) mean physical beating. It would suffice if there was what the Court called "[m]oral compulsion"— meaning threats of violence—that was "sufficient in legal contemplation to destroy free agency." Alternatively, it looked for "such degree of constraint or danger . . . as is sufficient in severity or apprehension to overcome the mind and will of a person of ordinary firmness." In another case, the Court held that "threats of battery to the person or of destruction of property" would meet the test of duress.[115] But it was clear that mere acquiescence in the requirements of the local law would not.[116]

The Commission carried on its work until 1881, when it was wound up.[117] In all, it dealt with some 22,000 claims, some of which were very sizeable. About seven hundred were for amounts in excess of $10,000. In terms of the number of awards made, the claimants fared reasonably well. About 40 percent of applications led to awards. In terms of the amount of money sought, however, the final verdict looks rather different. About $4.6 million was disbursed to the successful claimants, but this represented only about one-twelfth of the aggregate amount claimed.[118]

Captured and Abandoned Property

In the area of recovery of war losses, as in so many others, captured and abandoned property was in a distinct legal position. Its principal characteristic, for present purposes, was the trusteeship element—the fact that the federal government was regarded as a fund-holder on behalf of individual property owners for specific property sold. This had a number of important practical implications. One was that, as already observed, it meant that the holding of a pardon absolved a claimant from a duty to prove loyalty. In addition, the trusteeship element had an important effect on the amount of money that was recoverable by claimants. A claimant was entitled to whatever sum of money the federal government had *actually* realized from the sale of the particular goods taken—an amount that might be considerably less than the full market value at the time of the taking (which was the measure of "just compensation" in requisition cases). For this reason, it is not really correct to say that there was a right of *compensation* for the taking of captured and abandoned property. Rather, there was a property right in a specific fund comprising the proceeds of the sale.

By the mid-1870s, about $21 million was available *in toto* from the sales of captured and abandoned property. Eventually, about two-thirds of this was distributed to successful claimants, with the balance paid into the Treasury.[119] The claims process did not, however, go altogether smoothly. For example, there were grave suspicions of fraudulent claims, as well as concerns over money that might have been disbursed outside the prescribed procedures. These claims became a long-term presence in the federal courts for sundry technical reasons that need not be explored here. As late as the 1920s, the Court of Claims, and even the Supreme Court, could still be found grappling with aspects of them.[120]

Relief from the Direct Tax of 1861

A brief word may be said about the postwar history of the direct tax of 1861, which (as observed above) had been assessed on the insurgent states as well as on the loyal ones. At the end of the war, when collection was halted, over half of the tax (amounting to some $2.7 million) remained outstanding.[121] The awkward result was an inequitable situation in which persons in the loyal states had paid the tax, while those in the disloyal ones, in large part, had not.[122] The federal government therefore found itself facing a threefold dilemma: whether to "turn the clock back" by forgiving all arrears of the tax and also remitting the payments that had been made; or whether to complete the task by collecting the monies still due; or whether simply to let the matter lie where it was and do nothing in one direction or the other. It was a most intriguing public-policy conundrum.[123] For present purposes, it must suffice to note that the choice eventually made—but not until 1891—was for the first of these alternatives: to turn back the clock by forgiving all arrears and remitting the amounts paid.[124]

The reimbursement of the tax paid was not made directly to the individuals who had paid it, but rather to the states from which the payments had come. The states which received reimbursement monies were, however, obligated to keep these in trust for payment to the actual taxpayers—or to their legal successors, as the case may be. To this modest extent, then, there was some measure of federal relief to Confederate supporters. In all events, this tax finally disappeared from the American scene. On no occasion since 1861 has the federal government resorted to direct taxation, which may probably be safely regarded as a quaint footnote in American fiscal history.

International Claims Commissions

French and British nationals had the benefit of an avenue of redress that bore some resemblance to civil actions in United States courts. These were arbitral arrangements, in which the governments of the two countries would present claims on behalf of their nationals for alleged injuries.[125] These international arbitrations differed from domestic civil actions in that they provided relief *only* against wrongs committed by or on behalf of the federal government. That is to say, there was liability *only* for officially sanctioned actions and *not* for unauthorized acts of individuals.[126] There was no United States liability, however, for acts of the Confederate government.[127]

The British arbitration was agreed in the Treaty of Washington of 1871.[128] It functioned separately from the Geneva panel, which dealt only with issues relating to the construction of the Confederate warships. Some 420 claims were presented by Britain against the United States, concerning such matters as taking or destruction of property, wrongful arrests and detentions, and wrongful condemnation of ships. Over half the claims were for property requisitions. One hundred were for unlawful military arrests, of which thirty-four were successful, resulting in aggregate awards against the United States of some $167,000 in this area. Over half of this total ($116,000) was accounted for by a single claim, which involved business and profit losses. Many of the awards were for less than a thousand dollars.[129] In all, something over a third of all the British claims were successful, with total awards of about $1.9 million.[130] The largest single award made by the Commission, in a cotton-destruction claim, was for just over $197,000.[131] The panel was also empowered to adjudicate claims by the United States against Britain, but none of these was successful.[132]

The arbitration with France was agreed in a treaty of 1880.[133] Over seven hundred claims were filed by the French government for injuries to its nationals, resulting in aggregate damage awards of some $625,000.[134] The largest single award appears to have been $10,000 for the unlawful punishment of a detainee by General Butler in New Orleans.[135]

Relief from Congress

For those who had no regular means of obtaining compensation for losses sustained, there was the possibility of a direct appeal to Congress for the enactment of private relief legislation. This was a potentially fruitful source of funding, for those with the contacts or the determination to pursue it. Among those who were best placed on this score were the Union states, which in many cases sought, and obtained, compensation for expenditures they had undertaken in the war effort. There was precedent for this from the early days of the American republic, when, at the instigation of Treasury Secretary Alexander Hamilton, Congress made provision for the reimbursing of the states for expenditures made in the independence struggle against Great Britain.[136] This led to the payment of over $20 million.[137] The rationale for this was that the waging of the conflict had been a wholly federal responsibility, and that consequently state expenditures had been tantamount, at least in practical terms, to advances or loans made to the federal government, which Congress was bound, in honor if not in strict law, to repay.

In the years following that, and prior to the Civil War, there had been various payments by the federal government to states, on an *ad hoc* basis, generally for expenses incurred in Indian fighting. In 1817, Congress paid some $3.5 million to the states for their contributions to the War of 1812.[138]

In the Civil War, a similar policy was instituted at the outset of the conflict, in July 1861, when Congress made a general provision for the federal government to indemnify the states for various costs incurred in the suppression of the rebellion.[139] By a joint resolution of March 1862, Congress directed that the 1861 reimbursement statute be construed to apply to expenses incurred prior to its enactment, as well as subsequent to it.[140] By the end of 1862, the Treasury Department had advanced over $4.5 million to thirteen states, with a further $23 million of claims pending.[141]

After the war, Congress created a Select Committee on the War Debts of the Loyal States, to assess the claims. This Committee reported in February

1866, concluding that the loyal states had spent at least $468 million in the Union cause. A proposal put forward by Congressman James G. Blaine of Maine for a single comprehensive settlement of this obligation was not adopted. Instead, there was a series of *ad hoc* payments, over a number of years, to the various states. By 1884, nearly $45 million had been paid, with the largest amount (by far) going to Missouri (at some $7.58 million).

But the matter dragged on. In 1878, New York and Pennsylvania were voted approximately $113,000 (with nearly three-quarters of it going to New York).[142] In 1890, a further $35,000 was appropriated for the benefit of four states.[143] In 1902, West Virginia was given a reimbursement of just over $2,000 for services rendered by its state militia.[144] Three years later, Missouri received a further $475,000.[145]

A legal issue that arose concerned interest that states paid on money which they borrowed for war-related purposes. The actual expenditure (i.e., the amount borrowed) was of course reimbursable. But there was some question as to whether the interest paid to the lenders counted as war-related. In 1896, the federal Supreme Court resolved the issue in the states' favor, in a case involving bonds issued by New York state. The Court held that the interest payments fell within the terms of the 1861 reimbursement legislation.[146] This judgment led to a general reopening of the state claims process, by legislation (known as the Dash Act) enacted in 1902, to enable other states to take advantage of New York's judicial pioneering.[147]

Individuals, too, could obtain relief by way of congressional legislation. There were various reasons that this particular avenue of redress might be appropriate. Persons unable to satisfy loyalty requirements, for example, would typically have no other option for redress. The same was true of persons whose losses were caused by *bona fide* acts of war. An example of congressional relief was a grant, in 1871, to Kentucky University of $25,000 for the occupation of its buildings and use as a hospital.[148] A certain Otis P. Cutler did very well at the hands of Congress, successfully persuading it to appropriate $50,000 on his behalf in 1870 for the taking, by General Grant, of 268 bales of cotton (for equipping ships to run the Confederate artillery batteries of Vicksburg).[149] Much of this private legislation comprised awards of pensions to named individuals. Legislative relief was, of course, entirely a matter of discretion on Congress's part and not of legal right on the part of would-be beneficiaries.

Congressional action did not always entail direct cash payments. An alternate form of relief was a statutory waiver of the two-year time limit for filing claims for the proceeds of sale of captured and abandoned property.[150] These extensions did not, in themselves, guarantee that the beneficiary would actually receive a payment. A certain Sterling T. Austin, for example, was granted a time extension by Congress in 1883, only to have his claim fail on the ground of inability to prove loyalty.[151]

The legislative path to relief was not without its pitfalls. In addition to the effort of persuading a majority of both houses of Congress to act on a relief request, there was the possibility of derailment by a presidential veto, as the East Tennessee University could testify. Relief for this institution was voted by Congress, but then vetoed by President Grant.[152]

This method of compensation came to be very controversial. For one thing, there was clearly great scope for inconsistency of treatment, as some claimants would be more successful in their lobbying activity than others would be.[153] There were also grave suspicions that many formerly disloyal persons were obtaining compensation this way. The public concern on this point was enough to elicit a satirical proposal in the 1870s for the establishment of a "Grand Consolidated Rebel War Claims Collection Company of the Solid South," whose board of directors would include Jefferson Davis, Robert Toombs, Wade Hampton, and P. G. T. Beauregard. Its chief task would be to collect money from Northerners for their numerous acts of trespass in the Southern states during the war.[154]

The satirists may be begrudged their fun without undue loss. The impoverishment suffered by the South from the war was, however, a serious matter. Sympathy for dispossessed slave-owners may be severely limited (for various reasons), but there is no denying the magnitude of the losses they sustained. The Georgia Supreme Court, in 1869, estimated that emancipation alone had destroyed nearly half the taxable property value of the state.[155] When the effects of Sherman's "liberal foraging" policy are taken into account, along with the suffering caused by the evacuation of Atlanta, plus damage from actual battles, even the most rigid abolitionist heartstrings might be tugged (if only fairly gently).

Further economic hardship for Southerners arose from the fact that federal pension arrangements were reserved exclusively for Union veterans, to the total exclusion of former Confederate soldiers. Moreover, these pension rights became increasingly valuable as their terms were liberalized over the years. Most notable in this regard was a law of 1890 which extended pension rights to former Union soldiers to cover *any* kind of disability, whether war-related or not.[156] For favoring such measures, President Benjamin Harrison earned the sobriquet "the soldier's friend." So important and pervasive were these pension payments that they came to constitute a sort of *de facto* welfare program, accounting for over 40 percent of all federal expenditure by the 1890s.[157] It may be noted, though, that black veterans fared, on the whole, rather less well than their white counterparts did, largely because of bureaucratic obstacles. The legislation governing pension entitlements was formally race-neutral.[158]

It is hardly surprising that ex-Confederate soldiers were not awarded pensions by the federal government against which they had fought. In fact, legislation enacted in February 1862 had struck participants in the rebellion from the pension rolls, meaning that Confederate supporters (not merely serving Confederate soldiers) lost all pension rights that they had accrued in pre–Civil War service.[159] There was some relaxation of severity on this score, however. In the 1870s and 1880s, Confederate veterans who had also served for the United States in the War of 1812, the Mexican War, and the Indian wars had their pension rights relating to those conflicts reinstated.[160] In addition, a law of 1877 enabled Confederate veterans who joined the United States army *after* the war to receive pensions for disabilities incurred during that later service.[161] Eventually— although only very belatedly—the government altogether discarded the principle of refusing pensions to ex-Confederates. In 1958, in the run-up to the centennial of the Civil War, Congress enacted legislation granting pensions to Confederate veterans on a par with those for Union troops.[162] The material impact of this gesture of generosity can hardly have been very great, given the lapse of time since the conflict. But it appears that two Confederate veterans benefited, together with over a thousand widows of veterans.[163]

The compensation process, in sum, was heavily skewed in favor of the Northern states and against the Southern ones. Three factors (all of them discussed above) may be assigned the chief responsibility for this in the material sense. First was the disappearance of the Confederate federal government— and with it, all possibility of compensation from it for losses it had caused, chiefly in the way of property requisitions. Second was the principle that no compensation was owing for losses incurred by belligerent operations, from which the South suffered far more heavily than the North did. Third was the absence of pension rights for Confederate veterans. None of these, it should be appreciated, was in any way mitigated by the liberal pardon policy of President Johnson.

If it was any consolation to white Southerners, the situation could have been even worse. Radical proposals during the war for a program of systematic dispossession of the Southern planters of their lands had not been enacted.[164]

In addition, losses of captured and abandoned property were tempered by pardons, which (as noted above) absolved Confederate supporters from the onus of proving loyalty. More significantly, the material impact of the Second Confiscation Act and of the confiscations for default of the direct tax of 1861 proved, in the event, to be very modest in extent. The result was that the landed elite of the Southern states were, for the most part, left largely in place, even if they were also seriously impoverished.[165]

Far more serious suffering lay in store for the ex-slaves, whose freedom from bondage did not prevent them from being relegated to the status of distantly second-class citizens—a situation that endured, in legal terms, until the second half of the twentieth century. How that came about is a story of Reconstruction (and beyond) rather than of the war itself.[166] For the present, it must suffice to note that genuine efforts were made—highly imperfect and uneven though they were—to assuage the many and varied losses and injuries that had come in the train of America's greatest crisis.

Conclusion

The American Civil War remained a palpable presence in American social, political, and psychological life for many generations after the guns fell silent—even, to some extent, to the present day. A few remarks will be made here about the later fate of some of the legal issues that arose in that conflict. Two subjects in particular may call for some slight further attention: the fate of the compact theory of the federal government, and the question of the federal government operating simultaneously in a belligerent and a sovereign mode.

First, on the nature of the federal Union. It is probably fair to say that, as a result of the Civil War, the idea that the federal Union possesses only a sort of secondary reality, as compared to the constituent states—a conception lying at the heart of the compact theory—is no longer viable. No one would now see the United States as a kind of League of Nations, an artificial structure to be constructed or dismantled at the will of the sovereign states comprising its membership. The United States must therefore be regarded, in the wake of the Civil War, as a nation-state in its own right composed of one single body of citizens living under one single body of basic norms.

It is a melancholy fact that this issue cannot be said to have been settled by reason or persuasion or by judicial authority, but instead by force of arms. The rejection of the compact theory has been *acknowledged* by the federal Supreme Court on a number of occasions, rather than actually being *decided* by it. "The people of the United States," pronounced Chief Justice Chase on behalf of the Court in 1869, "constitute one nation, under one government."[1] In the second Legal Tender Case of 1871, the Court was more explicit on the subject, expressly holding that the Constitution "was intended to frame a government as distinguished from a league or compact."[2] Justice Bradley, in his concurring opinion in that case, was more forthright yet on the subject. The compact theory, he bluntly stated, "should be regarded as definitely and forever overthrown."[3]

The most concrete demonstration of this new—or newly established—fact of life was the Fourteenth Amendment to the Constitution, which took effect in 1868. It recognized, in a newly emphatic manner, the concept of citizenship of the United States as such—a subject on which the original Constitution had been silent.[4] More important yet was its articulation of two fundamental rights of all Americans—to due process of law and to the equal protection of the laws—which were carefully placed beyond the power of abridgement by the states. Admittedly, the pre–Civil War Constitution did contain a number of restrictions on the freedom of the states. They were barred, for example, from entering into treaties with foreign powers, from issuing commissions to privateers, from coining money, from granting titles of nobility, and—perhaps most important in practice—from impairing the sanctity of contracts.[5] But it was only with the adoption of the Fourteenth Amendment that the states became subject to federal standards of so wide-ranging a character as the due-process and, especially, the equal-protection provisions. Indeed, these would perhaps best be referred to as veritable universes of rights, for they have wrought, over the years, a legal and social revolution in American life—a process that is very far, even today, from having run its course.[6]

It remains to say a few words about the later status of one of the constant themes of this history: the operation of the federal government in two modes, sovereign and belligerent. To some (including some lawyers), it might have appeared that this theme was purely historical, with no relevance to later American life. Any confidence that may have lain behind such an assertion was shattered with great abruptness in September 2001, with the terrorist attacks on New York and Washington. The immediate effect was the launching of a "war against terrorism." In a manner in some ways eerily similar to the Civil War, this new conflict has been played out in the dual spheres of criminal law and belligerency.

In the manner of the Civil War, this new conflict was not inaugurated by a formal declaration of war by Congress, but rather by emergency action by the President. On September 13, 2001, President George W. Bush declared a state of national emergency, announcing that the country was now in a state of armed conflict, by virtue of those attacks.[7] The following day, he made provision, by executive order, for the mobilization of the armed forces for action.[8] This new crisis resembled that of the 1860s in involving simultaneous operation by the federal government on the military and civilian planes. For the hunting down of the leaders of the terrorist groups in foreign countries, the armed forces were employed, chiefly in Afghanistan in the autumn of 2001 (with explicit congressional authorization).[9] In parallel with this process has been the operation of ordinary criminal proceedings.

In the course of this new crisis, several issues from the 1860s came once again to the fore. Prominent among them was the question of unlawful belligerency. The Bush administration maintained that substantial numbers of persons who were captured in the course of its antiterrorist operations, particularly those captured in the Afghanistan conflict, did not meet the legal qualifications for belligerent status. Like their counterparts in the Civil War, these new guerrilla warriors were denied the status of prisoners of war—although spared the drastic response of summary execution. Also like their predecessors, they have not been treated wholly as civilians either because, when they were accused of specific offenses, they were subjected to trial not by civilian courts but instead by military commissions, where they would not be entitled to trial by jury.[10] (With the departure of the Bush adminstration there has been an increased willingness to conduct at least some of these trials in regular civilian courts.)

The Bush administration also took some care to ensure that these detainees would not have access to habeas corpus relief to challenge the lawfulness of their detention, although there was no attempt, as in the 1860s, on the President's part directly to suspend habeas corpus on his own initiative. Instead, two strategies were adopted. The first was to hold the prisoners outside the territory of the United States, at a military installation in Guantanamo Bay, Cuba. This was an executive action, which was intended, in part, to have the practical effect of making habeas corpus applications impossible. Second was an explicit suspension of habeas corpus by Congress in 2006, effectuated by the device of depriving courts of the jurisdiction to adjudicate over habeas corpus applications.[11] In 2008, the federal Supreme Court ruled that, at least in principle, these strategies were ineffective. Holding prisoners outside the terri-

tory of the United States, the Court held, does not automatically make constitutional constraints inapplicable. Moreover, even Congress does not possess
the power to suspend habeas corpus save in the two situations stated in the
Constitution: invasion and rebellion. Absent either of those (as in the case at
hand), Congress cannot deprive persons in custody of their habeas corpus
rights unless it provides an adequate alternative procedure—which it had
failed to do.[12]

The war on terrorism of the post-2001 era also resuscitated another practice
of the Lincoln administration: the arrest and detention of civilians on the home
front by the military, without judicial oversight. As in the case of habeas corpus,
the method employed was somewhat different. On this occasion, there was no
proclamation of martial law as in September 1862. Instead, the President asserted a power as commander-in-chief of the armed forces to make a determination that certain persons were members of an enemy armed force (i.e., of a
terrorist group). As such, the persons so designated were treated as belligerents
rather than as criminal defendants—though as *unlawful* belligerents.

The most notable instance of the exercise of this power occurred in 2002,
when an American national was arrested on American territory (at O'Hare Air-
port in Chicago) and then pronounced by President Bush to be no ordinary
criminal defendant, but rather an enemy combatant. As such, he was placed in
military custody in South Carolina. In 2005, a federal district court, explicitly
recalling the *Milligan* case, held the detention to be unlawful and ordered him
released.[13] On appeal, this order was reversed—not, however, on the ground
that the President's commander-in-chief power entitled him to imprison the
suspect, but rather on the ground that he had been granted that power by
statute.[14] Definitive resolution of the issue by the Supreme Court was, however,
thwarted by the executive's decision to transfer the suspect from military to
civilian custody for prosecution through the ordinary criminal courts.[15]

In sum, many of the legal experiences—"lessons" may be too strong a
word—of the Civil War remain relevant today—perhaps more so than many
of us would wish. So many issues that faced our forebears in the 1860s continue to be fully present and alive in the legal world of today—questions of the
powers of the executive, of the conduct of war and the rights of belligerents
(and of entitlement to those rights), due-process issues in cases of property
confiscation, race relations, access to habeas corpus remedies. It is of course
impossible to tell whether the country will again be put through so severe a
crisis as it was in the 1860s—and if it were to be, whether we would cope with

it as well as our ancestors did, with all of their imperfections. If nothing else, our nineteenth-century predecessors left us with an extraordinarily rich body of laws and precedents. For whatever comfort it might be worth, at least we face the future well armed juridically. To be sure, that is scarcely any guarantee of success. Indeed, if the past is anything to go by (a contentious question in itself), the tools of today will assuredly *not* be adequate for the tasks of tomorrow. They never have been.

But if the particular precedents and statutes and the like prove wanting in the face of future challenges, it may be that deeper patterns of legal thinking will prove more durable and more useful. That certainly is one of the lessons of the Civil War experience. It is remarkable, in many ways, how well the prior experiences of the judges and lawyers of the 1860s served them in the great crisis that fell upon them. That the American legal system—primitive as it was by our present lights—was robust enough to cope with so challenging a catastrophe says much for the maturity of the country at that time. The American Civil War therefore stands as something of a beacon for the world, proving that it is possible for the rule of law to cope—however imperfectly—with so daunting a challenge. It remains to be seen whether we will perform as well in future crises.

Glossary of Legal Terms

Abbreviations

Notes

Index

Glossary of Legal Terms

Absolute contraband: Goods, such as arms and ammunition, that are contraband of war in all circumstances, i.e., which are useful *only* for war-related purposes. *See also* Conditional contraband.

Abstention: One of the two fundamental duties of neutral states in wartime (along with impartiality). Broadly speaking, it requires neutral governments (though not private parties) to refrain from participating in *acts of war*. Defining acts of war for this purpose is sometimes fraught with controversy. *See also* Impartiality.

Acts of war: *See* Belligerent acts.

Adequacy-of-the-Constitution theory: The thesis that the Constitution grants to the federal government, even if only by implication, the full range of powers necessary to deal with any emergency situation, however grave. It was therefore opposed to theories which stressed the limits of powers accorded to the federal government by the Constitution.

Amnesty: Not a very precise legal term. It is best thought of as referring to a policy of nonprosecution for offenses committed, in the interest of promoting reconciliation. *See also* Pardon.

Base-of-operations principle: Rule of the international law of neutrality, forbidding a neutral country from permitting its territory to be used by belligerents as a launching pad for military operations, or as a sanctuary.

Belligerency, recognition of: A decision by a government to regard an internal conflict in a foreign country as being fully equivalent, in its eyes, to an interstate war. The effect of recognition of belligerency is to make the entire international law of neutrality applicable to the recognizing state and to entitle the insurgents to the full range of belligerents' rights, including (most importantly) permanent immunity from criminal prosecution for the commission of acts of war. *See also* Belligerent community.

Belligerent acts: Also known as acts of war. These are actions which are permissible according to the laws of war but not allowable in time of peace. Examples are killing and capturing in battle, mounting and enforcing blockades, taking prisoners, and occupying foreign territory. *See also* Military necessity.

Belligerent community (or belligerent power): A nongovernmental movement, such as a secession movement, which possesses full rights and powers under the laws of war, but which does not have the status of a sovereign, independent state. This was, effectively, the position of the Confederacy during the Civil War.

Belligerent occupation: Occupation of enemy territory during war, as part of the war-prosecution strategy, i.e., not pursuant to a claim to ownership of or full sovereignty over the territory in question. The area in question is governed by the armed forces of the occupying power. *See also* Conquest; Martial law; Military law.

Belligerent power: *See* Belligerent community.

Belligerent reprisals: Acts which, by their nature, are violations of the laws of war, but which are justifiable when committed in response to prior violations of the laws of war by the opposing side. The function of belligerent reprisals is to induce the original wrongdoing side to halt its unlawful conduct.

Belligerents' rights: Rights which belong to belligerents as such, i.e., rights which are available to states and persons only in a state of war, such as the killing and capturing of enemy troops or the occupation of enemy territory. *See also* Military necessity; Sovereign rights.

Bill of attainder: In its clearest form, refers to the imposition of criminal status (i.e., conviction for a crime) onto a named person by action of the legislature rather than by trial and conviction before a court. It is therefore a legislative usurpation of the functions of the judiciary. The Constitution expressly bars Congress from enacting bills of attainder (Art. I, sec. 9).

Blockade: The closing off of an area of coastal land during wartime from the seaward side, by means of a squadron of ships. A blockading power is legally entitled to capture and condemn ships (plus their cargoes) for attempting to cross a blockade line, either inward or outward. *See also* Effectiveness (of blockades).

Bond, ransom: *See* Ransom bonds.

Booty: Enemy property captured on the field of battle, such as weapons (but excluding the personal effects of enemy soldiers such as pocket money). Title to war booty passes automatically to the captor government on capture.

Capture: When referring to personal property, it means taking full possession and control of property owned by enemy nationals and located in enemy territory. Capture, by its own force, automatically effects a transfer of legal ownership of the goods to the state whose armed forces made the capture. For the position concerning real property, see Conquest.

Captured and abandoned property: Privately owned property in the disloyal states made subject to capture by the Act of Mar. 3, 1863, 12 Stat. 820. This property was therefore an exception to the general rule (or practice) that privately owned enemy property (on land) was not subject to capture.

Cartel: An agreement between two warring sides for the exchange of prisoners.

Chattel: An article of personal property, i.e., moveable property (as distinct from land, or real property). In the law of the slave states, slaves were regarded as chattels (hence the common expression "chattel slavery").

Civil war: In the very strictest sense, refers to an internal conflict of such a magnitude, and with the insurgent forces so highly organized, as to make the conflict fully equivalent to an interstate war, with the principal consequence being that both sides are required to conduct hostilities according to the international law of war. In less formal usage, "civil war" refers to any internal armed conflict in which the insurgents pose a particularly great challenge to the government.

Claimant (in prize law): The party whose ship or cargo was captured, and who is attempting to recover the property back from the captors in prize-court proceedings.

Common law: Unwritten (i.e., uncodified) law, which is elaborated on a continuing basis by judicial decisions. Contrasts with written law in the form of statutes or constitutions.

Combatant status: Membership of an armed force or, under certain circumstances, of a volunteer militia. Possession of combatant status entitles a person to commit acts of war without fear of legal consequences, such as criminal prosecution or civil suit.

Compact theory (of the Constitution): The theory that the Constitution is an ongoing contractual arrangement between the states as such, as opposed to an arrangement concluded by the people of the United States considered as an undifferentiated whole.

Conditional contraband: Goods (such as communications equipment) which have peacetime as well as wartime uses, i.e., dual-use goods in modern terminology. *See also* Absolute contraband.

Confiscation: Process of stripping, or divesting, a person of legal title to some kind of property, by way of judicial proceedings. *See also* Forfeiture.

Conquest: The acquisition of title to enemy territory by means of possession which is so tightly maintained as wholly to exclude any involvement in the territory by the former sovereign. It is to real property what capture is to personal property. *See also* Belligerent occupation; Capture.

Continuous-voyage doctrine: The thesis that two ostensibly separate voyages or acts of transport are, in reality, so closely connected with one another that they should fairly be regarded as two stages of a single voyage or transport.

Contraband of war: Goods which, by their nature, are useful in the prosecution of war, such as arms and ammunition. *See also* Absolute contraband; Conditional contraband.

Court-martial: Strictly speaking, not a judicial proceeding, but rather a disciplinary proceeding taken against a serving member of the armed forces. *See also* Military commission.

***De facto* government:** A government which, although not lawfully in power, is nonetheless in effective control of a portion of territory, to the point of being able to carry on governmental functions in that area. Foreign courts generally recognize the validity of measures taken by such "governments" in and concerning the territory so controlled.

Devastation: An obsolete term, referring to the deliberate destruction of civilian infrastructure under orders, as a means of bringing about victory in war. Regarded, in the 1860s, with grave misgivings but not actually prohibited by the laws of war.

Direct tax: A somewhat obscure term, referring basically to taxes on persons or property as such, as opposed to taxes on voluntary transactions or activities such as sales. The Constitution requires (Art. I, sec. 2) that direct taxes be "apportioned among the several States." *See also* Indirect tax.

Due-diligence principle: The rule, in the law of neutrality, that a neutral state must actively take reasonable steps to ensure that violations of the law of neutrality are not taking place in its territory.

Duress: A defense to a criminal charge, in the extreme case in which the defendant was forced, usually on something like pain of death, to commit a crime against his or her will.

Effectiveness (of blockades): The principle that a blockade does not exist in the legal sense unless there are sufficient ships on patrol to create a serious risk that ships attempting to enter the blockaded area will be captured. A noneffective (or "paper") blockade gives the belligerent power no right to capture or confiscate neutral ships or cargoes.

Enemy: National (or resident) of an opposing state in time of war.

Enforcement Clause (of the Thirteenth Amendment): Provision of the Thirteenth Amendment (abolishing slavery) which confers onto Congress the power to enact legislation necessary to enforce that amendment, such as the imposition of specified criminal penalties for slaveholding.

Executive power: An important (but undefined) set of powers which the Constitution vests in the President. These basically refer to the power to enforce laws.

Excise tax: A tax, in effect, on consumption or use of goods, usually consumer goods such as alcohol or tobacco.

Forfeiture: Liability to loss of legal title to property. The general rule is that *actual* loss of legal title (confiscation) only occurs after judicial proceedings. *See also* Confiscation.

Geneva Conventions: International treaties protecting victims of war, such as wounded persons, prisoners of war, or civilians. The current Conventions date from 1949, with two Additional Protocols adopted in 1977.

Good prize: Term of prize law, meaning that the property in question, generally a ship and/or its cargo, is lawfully subject to capture and confiscation. Enemy ships, whether warships or merchant vessels, are good prize per se. A neutral cargo will be good prize if it is contraband of war; and a neutral ship, together with its cargo, will be good prize if apprehended violating a blockade.

Guarantee Clause: Provision of the Constitution (Art. IV, sec. 4), stating that the federal government must "guarantee" to each state "a Republican Form of Government."

Guerrilla: Not a precisely defined term in modern international law, but referring basically to self-appointed fighters in a war who operate independently of the regular armed forces of the country for which they fight, who engage in armed action on a part-time basis, and who do not observe the laws of war in their operations. *See also* Partisan.

Habeas corpus: A remedial judicial proceeding that enables a person in some kind of detention to challenge the lawfulness of that detention before a judicial body, and to obtain an order for immediate release if the detention is found to be unlawful.

Hague Rules: The basic statement of the laws of war, initially drafted in 1899 by the First Hague Peace Conference. The present form of the rules dates from the Second Hague Peace Conference of 1907.

Impartiality: One of the two fundamental duties of neutral states in wartime (along with abstention). Simply stated, it requires that any service (such as port facilities or fuel supplies) which a neutral state affords to one belligerent must be afforded to the other on a strictly equal basis. What actually constitutes equal treatment is, in many areas, the subject of considerable disagreement. *See also* Abstention.

Indirect tax: A somewhat obscure term, referring basically to taxes on transactions or activities voluntarily entered into. Excise or sales taxes are the clearest examples. *See also* Direct tax; Excise tax.

***In personam* proceedings:** Legal proceedings (whether civil or criminal) brought against a person for some kind of misconduct. *See also In rem* proceedings.

***In rem* proceedings:** Legal proceedings which are taken "against" property as such, rather than against persons. Prize proceedings are a classic example in war. *See also In personam* proceedings.

Insurgency: Defined in older international legal writing as a situation of internal disturbance in which the rebel forces have a high degree of organization and have effective control of a portion of a state's territory. Insurgents (in this sense) do not possess the full range of belligerents' rights. In particular, they are not immune from criminal prosecution at the conclusion of the crisis.

Intention doctrine: A controversial doctrine holding that the act of violating a blockade commences not when the physical line of the blockade is crossed, but

instead at the very outset of the voyage of the ship in question, provided that, at
the time of sailing, the master of the ship intended to violate the blockade on
arrival at the invested area.

Ironclad oath: An oath that attests not merely to present and intended future loyalty
but also to past loyalty i.e., an affirmation of continuous, unbroken loyalty.

Law of nations: A somewhat archaic name for international law.

Laws of war: The rules of international law which govern the conduct of war. They
are presently codified chiefly in the Hague Rules of 1907, the four Geneva Conventions of 1949, the two Additional Protocols of 1977 to the Geneva Conventions, and
a number of treaties dealing with specific weapons and tactics. *See also* Military law.

Legal tender: If something has legal-tender status, then a debtor may offer (or "tender") it to a creditor in satisfaction of a debt. The debt is then discharged, even if
the creditor refuses to accept the tender.

Letter of marque: Written authorization by a government (or belligerent power) to a
private party to engage in privateering. *See also* Privateer.

Lieber Code: Summation of the laws of war, issued by President Lincoln as a general
order to the Union armies in April 1863. Highly influential in the later development and codification of the laws of war.

Limitation period: The length of time, prescribed by statute, within which a claim
(such as a suit for breach of contract or personal injury) has to be filed before a
court. Beyond that period, the court will not entertain the suit. Laypersons are
often inclined to use the expression "statute of limitations" to refer to this period.
It is common that times of war are not counted in the calculating of limitation
periods, regarding legal proceedings between individuals on opposite sides.

Marque, letter of. *See* Letter of marque.

Military commissions: Military courts. They are similar to courts-martial except
that the persons tried are either civilians or members of the enemy armed force.

Martial law: An emergency measure, in which the normal civil law in a given area is
suspended, and replaced by the orders of a military commander. *See also* Belligerent occupation.

Military law: Basically, the law governing the conduct of members of armed forces.
It is in partial or complete substitution for the regular civil law governing persons
in civilian life.

Military necessity: Basically, a situation in which the exercise of a belligerent right
makes a palpable contribution to the winning of the war. In the absence of such
necessity, belligerents should refrain from the exercise of the full range of their
legal rights. More specifically, certain belligerents' rights, such as the capture of
private property, should ordinarily not be exercised, in the interest of moderating
the suffering involved in war. In situations of military necessity, however, the
exercise of those rights will be allowed. It is important to appreciate that military
necessity *never* allows a belligerent to go *beyond* the ambit of belligerents' rights.

Militia: Refers to the entire population of a state that is capable of bearing arms and performing military service. Militias were the military arms of the states, although there is constitutional provision (in Art. I, sec. 8) for federal regulation and use of the militia in emergencies. The militia has now been supplanted by the state National Guard forces.

Natural law: Referred to fundamental, but uncodified, principles of law that were assumed to be of universal validity. Natural law applied between parties which had no common sovereign over them (i.e., which were in a state of nature *vis-à-vis* one another). It was an important source of international law.

Necessary-and-proper Clause: Provision of the Constitution (Art. I, sec. 8), empowering Congress to enact any laws that are "necessary and proper" for carrying any of the specifically enumerated powers into execution.

Necessity, general principle of: In international law, the principle that a breach of legal obligation is legally excusable in extreme emergencies. This is a subject fraught with difficulty, which is outside the scope of this work. It need only be stressed that this general principle of necessity is quite distinct from military necessity. *See* Military necessity.

Necessity, military: *See* Military necessity.

Neutrality: In the legal sense, it refers not to mere nonparticipation in a war or to indifference as to the outcome of a conflict, but rather to a detailed set of rights and duties applying to third states whenever any two countries are at war. Its fundamental principles are the duties of abstention and impartiality. *See also* Abstention; Impartiality.

Note: A written promise to pay money. Many notes are negotiable, meaning that the promise to pay is enforceable by whoever holds the note at any given time, thereby enabling such notes to pass from hand to hand as currency. Notes are not, however, in general, legal tender, meaning that creditors can refuse payment in notes and (in the Civil War era) insist instead on payment in specie.

Offices of humanity: An archaic term, referring to routine services offered by countries, as a matter of general custom, to foreigners. It chiefly referred to services offered to foreign ships, such as access to ports, repair services, assistance in emergencies (such as shipwreck), and the like.

Outlawry: A kind of secular and legal version of excommunication, in which the person outlawed loses all legal rights. All legal relations with other persons (such as contracts) are terminated; and the person can even be killed with impunity like a wild beast.

Paper blockade: A blockade that is not effectively maintained. So called because it exists only "on paper" and not in reality. Captures made in cases of paper blockades are illegal, and the ships captured are entitled to be released by prize courts. *See also* Effectiveness (of blockades).

Pardon: A power given to the President by the Constitution (Art. II, sec. 2), to remove all penal consequences flowing from conviction for a crime. The person is then legally in the position of never having committed the offense.

Partisan: An armed force operating independently of the regular armed forces of a belligerent; hence a kind of auxiliary force. Partisans are typically full-time soldiers, in uniform, observing the laws of war in their operations. As such, they are lawful combatants.

Pillage: The unauthorized taking of civilian private property in enemy territory for personal enrichment. It is a war crime. *See also* Booty; Devastation.

Piracy: Armed robbery on the high seas, committed for personal gain. *See also* Privateer.

Privateer: A private person who is given a commission (a letter of marque) by a government during war to engage in the capture of enemy merchant ships, and who fits out a ship at his own expense for that purpose. Typically, privateers are remunerated by being entitled to a share of the proceeds of any captures they make.

Prize law: The law relating to the capture of merchant ships (both enemy and neutral) during war.

Ransom bonds: Certificates drawn up by Confederates when capturing a Union ship containing neutral-owned, as well as Union-owned, cargo. Instead of destroying the ship and cargo, the Confederate captors would obtain a written promise from the master promising to pay to the Confederate government the value of the Union-owned cargo, after the conclusion of the war. The defeat of the Confederacy naturally rendered these bonds valueless.

Real property: Land. Distinguished from personal or moveable property (or chattels).

Redemption (of encumbered property): Refers, most commonly, to the right of a mortgagor of land to recover the land even *after* foreclosure and sale, by tendering the amount of money due on the mortgage to the purchaser of the land. It is therefore the right to reverse a foreclosure sale.

Reprisal: An action which, although unlawful in itself, is nevertheless excusable on the ground that it is committed in response to a prior unlawful act, with a view to ensuring that that original wrongdoing does not recur. Reprisals are nonpunitive in the sense that they are taken against someone other than the original wrongdoer.

Requisition: The taking of private property for public use in an emergency situation. The Fifth Amendment to the Constitution requires the payment of "just compensation" in cases of takings by the federal government.

Retaliation: A straightforward tit-for-tat response to a prior unlawful act, i.e., the inflicting on a wrongdoer of the precise wrong which he or she himself had committed. "An eye for an eye, and a tooth for a tooth" captures the essence of it all too well.

Rights of war: An alternative label for belligerents' rights.

Self-executing: Refers to a constitutional amendment (or a treaty) which is legally efficacious on its own, without requiring separate implementing legislation from Congress. The Thirteenth Amendment, abolishing slavery, was self-executing in this sense.

Sequestration: Process in which property is "frozen," i.e., in which the owner is deprived of the use of the property, without being divested of legal title (contrasting with confiscation, which entails loss of title).

Servitude, badges of: The theory that certain kinds of discriminatory treatment of freed slaves, such as relegation to segregated schools, may be banned by the federal government under the Enforcement Clause of the Thirteenth Amendment, on the ground that the treatment in question is an incident of slavery, which that amendment prohibited.

Sovereign rights: Refers basically to the corpus of rights which a government possesses in and over its territory. *See also* Belligerent rights.

Spy: In the legal sense, refers to a serving soldier who acts clandestinely (i.e., out of uniform) in enemy territory, to obtain information about the enemy. Spying is not a violation of the laws of war; but spies are not entitled to the normal privileges of belligerents, such as the according of prisoner-of-war status if captured.

Succession tax: What is now called an inheritance tax.

Suspension Clause: The provision of the Constitution (Art I, sec. 9) allowing the privilege of the writ of habeas corpus to be suspended in two prescribed emergency situations (rebellion and invasion). The clause fails to state explicitly who possesses the right to impose such a suspension.

Treason: The only criminal offense defined by the Constitution (Art. III, sec. 3), as "levying War against [the United States], or . . . adhering to [the] Enemies [of the United States]." The general opinion, during the Civil War, was that "enemies" referred only to foreign foes and therefore excluded Confederates. Treason prosecutions therefore focused instead on the first element, levying war.

Ultimate-destination doctrine: Another name for the continuous-voyage doctrine.

Unlawful combatant: A person who is not a member of his or her country's regular armed forces or of a regularly formed volunteer or militia group but who nevertheless engages in purported acts of war. Unlawful combatants do not possess the legal privileges of belligerents, such as entitlement to prisoner-of-war status when captured.

War, state of: A legal situation in which the contending sides are lawfully permitted to commit a range of violent acts against one another, such as killing, capturing, and occupying territory. These acts (known as belligerent acts or acts of war) would be unlawful in peacetime. *See also* Belligerent acts.

War rebel: According to the Lieber Code, a resident of an occupied territory who commits acts of violence against the occupying power. Such a person is regarded as a criminal and not as a lawful belligerent.

War treason: According to the Lieber Code, the conveying of war-related information by a resident of an occupied territory to the authorities of the displaced government. It is regarded as treason on the ground that it is a violation of the resident's legal duty of allegiance owed to the occupying power.

Abbreviations

A.C.	Appeal Cases (Great Britain)
Am. J. Int'l L.	*American Journal of International Law*
Am. L. Rev.	*American Law Review*
Basler, *Works*	Roy P. Basler (ed.). *The Collected Works of Lincoln.* 9 vols. New Brunswick. N.J.: Rutgers University Press, 1953
B.F.S.P.	British and Foreign State Papers (Great Britain)
Brit. Y.B. Int'l L.	*British Year Book of International Law*
CC	Circuit Court
Cd.	Command paper (Great Britain)
Ch.	Chancery Court (Great Britain)
C. Rob.	Admiralty Reports of Christopher Robinson (Great Britain)
C.T.S.	Consolidated Treaty Series
DC	District Court
Dep't of State Bull.	*Department of State Bulletin*
ED	Eastern District
Fed. Cas.	Federal Cases
FRUS	Foreign Relations of the United States
F. Supp.	Federal Supplement
H.C.	House of Commons (Great Britain)

H.L.	House of Lords (Great Britain)
I.C.J. Rep.	Reports of the International Court of Justice (World Court)
Int'l Legal Materials	*International Legal Materials*
Int'l L. Rep.	*International Law Reports*
Int'l L. Stud.	*International Law Studies* (U.S. Naval War College)
J. Am. Hist.	*Journal of American History*
La. L. Rev.	*Louisiana Law Review*
L.N.T.S.	League of Nations Treaty Series
Op. A-G	Opinions of the Attorneys General
OR	Official Records (*The War of the Rebellion: A Compilation of the Official Records of the Union and Confederate Armies.* 127 vols. Washington, D.C.: GPO, 1880–1901.)
OR-Naval	*Official Records of the Union and Confederate Navies in the War of the Rebellion.* 30 vols. Washington, D.C.: GPO, 1894–1922.
PCIJ Rep.	Reports of the Permanent Court of International Justice
PL	Public Law
Procs.	Proceedings
Prov. Ct. of La.	Provisional Court of Louisiana
S.C.R.	Supreme Court Reports (Canada)
Stat.	Statutes at Large
U.N.T.S.	United Nations Treaty Series
U.S.	Supreme Court Reports
U.S.C.	United States Code
U.S. Naval Institute Procs.	Proceedings of the United States Naval Institute
WD	Western District
Weekly Comp. Pres. Docs.	Weekly Compilation of Presidential Documents

Notes

Introduction

1. For a general history of war from the standpoint of law (i.e., international law), see Stephen C. Neff, *War and the Law of Nations: A General History* (Cambridge: Cambridge University Press, 2005).

2. For a thorough study of the legal aspects of the Confederacy, see William R. Robinson, Jr., *Justice in Gray: A History of the Judicial System of the Confederate States of America* (Cambridge, Mass.: Harvard University Press, 1941).

1. Breaking a Nation

Epigraphs: John C. Calhoun, *A Discourse on the Constitution and Government of the United States,* in Ross M. Lence (ed.), *Union and Liberty: The Political Philosophy of John C. Calhoun* (Indianapolis: Liberty Fund, 1992), at 212; Ford v. Surget, 97 U.S. 594 (1878), at 623.

1. On the lawfulness of secession, see J. G. Randall, *Constitutional Problems under Lincoln* (New York: D. Appleton, 1926), at 12–24.

2. For a lucid exposition of this thesis by the federal Supreme Court, see Williams v. Bruffy, 96 U.S. 176 (1878).

3. *See* Joel Parker, "The Right of Secession: A Review of the Message of Jefferson Davis to the Congress of the Confederate States," in 1 Frank Freidel (ed.), *Union Pam-*

phlets of the Civil War, 1861–1865 (Cambridge, Mass.: Harvard University Press, 1967), at 62–64. The author was a professor at Harvard Law School and former chief justice of the New Hampshire Supreme Court.

4. *See* N. Feinberg, "Unilateral Withdrawal from an International Organisation," 39 *Brit. Y.B. Int'l L.* 189–219 (1963). The Covenant of the League of Nations did contain a provision expressly allowing withdrawal.

5. Watts, Relation of Confederacy to Former Union, Dec. 27, 1862, in Rembert W. Patrick (ed.), *The Opinions of the Confederate Attorneys General 1861–1865* (Buffalo: Dennis, 1950), at 199.

6. *Federalist* (Madison), No. 39. On the origins of the compact theory, see Harold M. Hyman and William M. Wiecek, *Equal Justice under Law: Constitutional Development 1835-1875* (New York: Harper and Row, 1982), at 211–213.

7. *See,* in particular, Calhoun, *Discourse.*

8. *See* the relevant portions of Alexander H. Stephens, *A Constitutional View of the Late War between the States: Its Causes, Character, Conduct and Results* (2 vols., Philadelphia: National Publishing, 1868–70).

9. 1 *id.* at 500–501.

10. Act of Sep. 18, 1850, 9 Stat. 462. *See* Don E. Fehrenbacher, *The Slaveholding Republic: An Account of the United States Government's Relations to Slavery* (Oxford: Oxford University Press, 2001), at 231–248.

11. *See* Ableman v. Booth, 62 U.S. (21 How.) 506 (1859).

12. Constitution, Art. IV, sec. 2. For an exposition of the meaning and effect of this provision, see Prigg v. Pennsylvania, 41 U.S. (16 Pet.) 539 (1842).

13. Cobb, "Letter . . . to the People of Georgia," in Jon Wakelyn (ed.), *Southern Pamphlets on Secession, November 1860–April 1861* (Chapel Hill: University of North Carolina Press, 1996), at 90, 94.

14. 2 Stephens, *Constitutional View,* at 497.

15. *Id.* at 630.

16. Charge to Grand Jury—Treason, 30 Fed. Cas. 1032 (No. 18,270) (CC SD N.Y. 1861), at 1033.

17. Both found in Constitution, Art. IV, sec. 2.

18. Declaration of the Causes of Secession, Dec. 24, 1860; *reprinted in* J. A. May and J. R. Faunt. *South Carolina Secedes* (Columbia: University of South Carolina Press, 1960), at 76–81. *See also* Henry Steele Commager, *The Civil War Archive: The History of the Civil War in Documents* (New York: Black Dog and Leventhal, 1973), at 42–43.

19. Res. of Jan. 29, 1861, 1 (ser. 4) OR 81–85, at 84.

20. Webster, speech of Jan. 26, 1830, in 6 *The Writings and Speeches of Daniel Webster* (Boston: Little, Brown, 1903), at 65–66.

21. For opposition to the compact theory, see also Parker, "Right of Secession," at 64–71.

22. Ableman v. Booth, 62 U.S. (21 Howard) 506 (1859), at 516. Concerning this case, see Michael J. C. Taylor, "'A More Perfect Union': *Ableman vs. Booth* and the Culmination of Federal Sovereignty," 28 *J. Supreme Court History* 101–115 (2003).

23. For a general survey of contending ideas about the nature of the federal Union in the nineteenth century, see generally Paul C. Nagel, *One Nation Indivisible: The Union in American Thought* (New York: Oxford University Press, 1964).

24. *See,* for example, William C. Davis, *A Government of Our Own: The Making of the Confederacy* (New York: Free Press, 1994).

25. Constitution, Art. VII.

26. Mims v. Wimberly, 33 Ga. 587 (1863), at 592.

27. For the text of the Confederate Provisional Constitution of Feb. 8, 1861, see 1 (ser. 4) OR 92–99. For the text of the Confederate Permanent Constitution of Mar. 11, 1861, see *id.* at 136–147. On the Confederate Constitution, see generally Marshall L. DeRosa, *The Confederate Constitution of 1861: An Inquiry into American Constitutionalism* (Columbia: University of Missouri Press, 1991).

28. Watts,"Appointment during Recess of Senate," May 8, 1863, in Patrick (ed.), *Opinions,* at 265.

29. Watts, "Writ of Habeas Corpus," Aug. 8, 1863, in Patrick (ed.), *Opinions,* at 314.

30. Confed. Constitution, 1 (ser. 4) OR 136, Art. I, sec. 9(1).

31. On the question of secession in the Confederate Constitution, see DeRosa, *Confederate Constitution,* at 52–54.

32. *See* Randall, *Constitutional Problems,* at 48–73.

33. Enemies can, however, be prosecuted for specific violations of the laws of war committed during the hostilities. *See* Chapter 3 on this point.

34. Buchanan, Message to Senate and House, Jan. 8, 1861, in 5 James D. Richardson (ed.), *A Compilation of the Messages and Papers of the Presidents* (New York: Bureau of National Literature, 1896–99), at 657.

35. *See* Silvana R. Siddali, "'The Sport of Folly and the Prize of Treason': Confederate Property Seizures and the Northern Home Front in the Secession Crisis," 47 *Civil War History* 310–333 (2001).

36. Calhoun, *Discourse,* at 178.

37. Roger B. Taney, *Thoughts on the Conscription Law of the U[nited] States—Rough Draft Requiring Revision* (ed. Philip G. Auchampaugh; n.p., n.d.), at 3.

38. Black, "Power of the President in Executing the Laws," Nov. 20, 1860, in 9 Op. A-G 516.

39. *Id.* at 523.

40. Constitution, Art. I, sec. 8.

41. On the *Star of the West* incident, see Bruce Catton, *The Coming Fury* (Garden City, N.Y.: Doubleday, 1961), at 176–186.

42. For a fuller exposition of this point, see Stephen C. Neff, *War and the Law of Nations: A General History* (Cambridge: Cambridge University Press, 2005), at 247–254.

43. For the position in Roman law, see Ulpian, in Justinian, *The Digest of Justinian* (ed. Theodor Mommsen; trans. Alan Watson; Philadelphia: University of Pennsylvania Press, 1985), 49.15.24. For the position in the Middle Ages, see Neff, *War and the Law of Nations,* at 247–249.

44. Emmerich de Vattel, *The Law of Nations; Or The Principles of Natural Law* (trans. Charles G. Fenwick; Washington, D.C.: Carnegie Institution, 1916 [1758]), at 336–337.

45. *See* Chapter 7 on recognition of belligerency and its many implications.

46. Henry W. Halleck, *International Law; Or Rules Regulating the Intercourse of States* (New York: Van Nostrand, 1861), at 332–333. On the international law of war, see Chapter 3.

47. Constitution, Art. I, sec. 8.

48. Act of July 31, 1861, 12 Stat. 284. The purpose of this law was to fill a loophole left by the fact that, as a point of technical criminal law, the existing offense of treason only dealt with the actual *commission* of treasonous acts and not with conspiracies to commit them. *See* Ex p. Bollman, 8 U.S. (4 Cranch) 75 (1807). *See also* Charge to Grand Jury—Treason, 30 Fed. Cas. 1036 (No. 18,272) (CC SD Ohio, 1861), at 1037–1038; and Charge to Grand Jury—Treason and Piracy, 30 Fed. Cas. 1049 (No. 18,277) (CC D Mass. 1861), at 1051. For a prosecution under this act, see U.S. v. Scott, 27 Fed. Cas. 997 (No. 16,241) (DC D Ind. 1865).

49. Act of Aug. 6, 1861, 12 Stat. 317.

50. Act of Aug. 5, 1861, 12 Stat. 314; supplementary to main piracy statute, Act of Mar. 3, 1819, 3 Stat. 510.

51. Proc. No. 4, Apr. 19, 1861, 12 Stat. 1259. The blockade was extended to cover North Carolina and Virginia by Proc. No. 5, Apr. 27, 1861, *id.* at 1260.

52. Act of July 13, 1861, 12 Stat. 255, sec. 5, at 257; and Proc. No. 9, Aug. 16, 1861, 12 Stat. 1262.

53. Constitution, Art. I, sec. 8.

54. *See* The Sarah Starr, 21 Fed. Cas. 462 (No. 12,352) (DC SD N.Y., 1861).

55. Constitution, Art. I, sec. 8.

56. In support of the Union position, see the resolution of the Institute of International Law, "Rights and Duties of Foreign Powers and Their *Ressortissants* towards Established and Recognized Governments in Case of Insurrection," Sep. 8, 1900, in James Brown Scott (ed.), *Resolutions of the Institute of International Law* (New York: Oxford University Press, 1916), at 157–159, art. 4(2).

57. *See* Charge to Grand Jury—Treason, 30 Fed. Cas. 1032 (No. 18,270) (CC SD N.Y. 1861), at 1033.

58. *See* Chapter 4 for further exposition on this point.

59. *See* Chapter 9 on postwar prosecutions.

60. Constitution, Art. I, sec. 8; and Confed. Constitution, 1 (ser. 4) OR 136, Art. I, sec. 8(11).

61. Declaration of Paris, Apr. 16, 1856, 115 C.T.S. 1, art. 4.

62. On the legal issues that arose in connection with this blockading effort, see Chapter 8.

63. Act of Mar. 3, 1863, 12 Stat. 758.

64. Confed. Act of May 6, 1861, 1 (ser. 4) OR 281–285.

65. For various applications to the Confederate government for letters of marque, see 1 (ser. 2) OR 330–333. For the text of President Davis's instructions to private armed vessels, see *id.* at 340–342.

66. On Confederate privateering, see generally Robinson, *Confederate Privateers;* and Mark A. Weitz, *The Confederacy on Trial: The Piracy and Sequestration Cases of 1861* (Lawrence: University Press of Kansas, 2005), at 17–35.

67. Proclamation of a Blockade, Apr. 19, 1861, 12 Stat. 1259; *reprinted in* 4 Basler, *Works,* at 338–339.

68. *See* Chapter 1 on the criminal prosecution in Union courts of the Confederate "privateers."

69. A member of the prosecution team, incidentally, was Samuel Blatchford, a future federal Supreme Court justice.

70. U.S. v. Baker, 24 Fed. Cas. 962 (No. 14,501) (CC N.Y. 1861). *See also* Carl D. Swisher, *The Taney Period* (New York: Macmillan, 1974), at 866–872; and Weitz, *Confederacy on Trial,* at 71–83, 92–94, 163–190. For the Confederate perspective, see 2 Stephens, *Constitutional View,* at 430–435. Attempts by the prisoners to secure a new trial, and thereby to win their freedom, proved fruitless. For a request for a new trial by one of them, see Baker to Sullivan, May 16, 1862, 3 (ser. 2) OR 544–545.

71. U.S. v. Smith, 27 Fed. Cas. 1134 (No. 16,318) (CC ED Pa. 1861). On this prosecution, see Swisher, *Taney Period,* at 872–876. For a transcript of the trial proceedings, see 3 (ser. 2) OR 58–121. For a later case of prosecution for piracy, see Maureen Pearce, "The Old Navy: A Trial for Piracy," 118 *U.S. Naval Institute Procs.* 82–94 (1992). For a case in which purported privateers were indicted for treason rather than for piracy, in October 1861, see 1 (ser. 2) OR 144–146. It would appear, however, that no trial actually took place.

72. On this Philadelphia trial, see Weitz, *Confederacy on Trial,* at 83–91, 132–162.

73. *See* Chapter 3 on reprisals generally, and on this incident in particular.

74. 1 *Cadwallader's Cases* (Philadelphia: Rees Welsh, 1907), at 525; and Ashton to Seward, Feb. 3, 1862, 3 (ser. 2) OR 232.

75. For further consideration of the matter, this time by the Pennsylvania Supreme Court, see Fifield v. The Insurance Company of the State of Pennsylvania, 47 Pa. 166 (1864). On the disappearance of Confederate privateering, see Chapter 7. On the privateers' cases, see Randall, *Constitutional Problems,* at 92–94. On the exchange of the privateers for Union prisoners of war, see Whipple to Huger, June 2, 1862, 3 (ser. 2) OR 632.

76. Prize Cases, 67 U.S. (2 Black) 635 (1863), at 666. The name of the case is somewhat misleading, since no substantive issue of prize law as such was at stake. The cen-

tral issue in question was the date of commencement of the war. On other aspects of this case, see Chapter 2.

77. *Id.* at 666–667.

78. *Id.* at 667–668. The Court was here quoting unidentified "sages of the common law." Standards of citation were more lax in those times than they are at present.

79. Act of May 13, 1846, 9 Stat. 9 (emphasis added).

80. On the right of the President to wage defensive war of this kind, see Clinton Rossiter, *The Supreme Court and the Commander in Chief* (2d ed.; Ithaca, N.Y.: Cornell University Press, 1976), at 65–77.

81. On the application of the laws of war in the Civil War, see Chapter 3.

82. The Chapman, 5 Fed. Cas. 471 (No 2602) (DC ND Cal. 1864), at 473–476. Inconsistency with the early privateers' cases can perhaps be avoided on the thesis that the defense in those cases had *only* raised the claim of full independence and not that of belligerent status.

83. Act of July 13, 1861, 12 Stat. 255, sec. 4 and 5.

84. On the Prize Cases, see Robert Bruce Murray, *Legal Cases of the Civil War* (Mechanicsburg, Pa.: Stackpole, 2003), at 1–18; and Brian McGinty, *Lincoln and the Court* (Cambridge, Mass.: Harvard University Press, 2008), at 118–143.

85. On this somewhat abstruse and arcane issue, see Neff, *War and the Law of Nations*, at 178–186.

86. *See generally* Louis Fisher, *Presidential War Power* (Lawrence: University Press of Kansas, 1995).

87. The Supreme Court held consistently to this position. *See,* for example, the postwar case of Lamar v. Browne, 92 U.S. 187 (1876), at 195. *See also* Johnson v. Jones, 44 Ill. 142 (1867), at 149.

88. The Amy Warwick, 1 Fed. Cas. 799 (No 341) (DC D Mass. 1862), at 803. *See also* the later Supreme Court cases of Lamar v. Browne, 92 U.S. 187 (1876); and Young v. U.S., 97 U.S. 39 (1878).

89. For a strong assertion on this point, see 2 Stephens, *Constitutional View,* at 425–427.

90. Davis, Statement to Congress, May 8, 1861, 53 (ser. 1) OR 161–162.

91. Confed. Act of May 6, 1861, 1 (ser. 4) OR 281–285.

92. By 1887, the conflict was being referred to in statutes as "the late civil war." *See* Act of Mar. 3, 1887, 24 Stat. 505, sec. 1. For an early judicial use of the term "civil war" to refer to the conflict, see The Peterhoff, 72 U.S. (5 Wall.) 28 (1867), at 60.

2. Desperate Measures

Epigraphs: Ex p. Milligan, 71 U.S. (4 Wall.) 2 (1866), at 121; Tod v. Court of Common Pleas of Fairfield County, 15 Ohio 377 (Dec. 1864 term), at 390–391.

1. Constitution, Art. I, sec. 8.

2. *Id.,* Art. I, sec. 9.

3. Juilliard v. Greenman, 110 U.S. 421 (1884), at 457.

4. *See* Harold M. Hyman, *A More Perfect Union: The Impact of the Civil War and Reconstruction on the Constitution* (New York: Knopf, 1973), at 124–140; and Harold M. Hyman and William M. Wiecek, *Equal Justice under Law: Constitutional Development 1835–1875* (New York: Harper and Row, 1982), at 234–238. For the chief presentation of the thesis, see Timothy Farrar, "The Adequacy of the Constitution," 21 *New Englander* 51–73 (1862).

5. For an exposition of these categories of Presidential powers, see Bates, Suspension of the Writ of Habeas Corpus, July 5, 1861, 10 Op. A-G 74.

6. Constitution, Art. II, sec. 1.

7. Russell D. Buhite (ed.), *Calls to Arms: Presidential Speeches, Messages, and Declarations of War* (Wilmington, Del.: Scholarly Resources, 2003), at 43–44.

8. Act of Feb. 28, 1795, 1 Stat. 424. A law of 1807 authorized the President to employ the existing federal armed forces under the same circumstances. Act of Mar. 3, 1807, 2 Stat. 443.

9. Constitution, Art. I, sec. 9.

10. Act of Aug. 6, 1861, 12 Stat. 326.

11. *See* Chapter 5.

12. This came in two stages: Proc. No. 4, Apr. 19, 1861, 12 Stat. 1258, covering the coast from South Carolina to Texas; and Proc. No. 5, Apr. 27, 1861, *id.* at 1259, extending the blockade to the newly seceded states, Virginia and North Carolina.

13. Constitution, Art. I, sec. 8.

14. Act of July 13, 1861, 12 Stat. 255. For Lincoln's exercise of this power, see Proc. No. 9, Aug. 16, 1861, *id.* at 1262.

15. Proc. No. 9, Aug. 16, 1861, 12 Stat. 1262.

16. *See* Stanbery, Insurrectionary Status of Arkansas, Aug. 16, 1866, 12 Op. A-G 11, at 14.

17. Prize Cases, 67 U.S. (2 Black) 635 (1863).

18. *See* Chapter 1 for a discussion of this aspect of the case.

19. On the President's power to determine the existence of an emergency, see Martin v. Mott, 25 U.S. (12 Wheaton) 19 (1827); and Druecker v. Salomon, 21 Wis. 621 (1867).

20. For a current exposition of presidential war powers, see Louis Fisher, *Presidential War Power* (Lawrence: University Press of Kansas, 1995).

21. Prize Cases, 67 U.S. (2 Black) 635 (1863), at 682–698.

22. For similar, more recent pronouncements to this effect, see Rumsfeld v. Padilla, 352 F. 3d 695 (2d Cir. 2003), at 710–718; and Padilla v. Hanft, 389 F. Supp. 2d 678 (D.S.C. 2005), at 690–691, *reversed on other grounds,* 423 F. 3d 386 (4th Cir. 2005). These cases concerned the designation of a single named individual as an enemy combatant. The federal Supreme Court expressly declined to rule on the

question. *See* Rumsfeld v. Padilla, 542 U.S. 426 (2004); and Padilla v. Hanft, 547 U.S. 1062 (2006).

23. The Hiawatha, in 4 John Bassett Moore, *A History and Digest of the International Arbitrations to Which the United States Has Been a Party* (Washington, D.C.: GPO, 1898), at 3902, at 3908–3909. The *Hiawatha,* incidentally, was one of the very ships whose fate the Supreme Court was considering in the Prize Cases. On the British-American dispute over the Prize Cases, see Stuart L. Bernath, *Squall across the Atlantic: American Civil War Prize Cases and Diplomacy* (Berkeley: University of California Press, 1970), at 18–33.

24. Constitution, Art. I, sec. 9.

25. 3 Joseph Story, *Commentaries on the Constitution of the United States* (Cambridge, Mass.: Hilliard, Gray, 1833), at 208–209. *See also,* to the same effect, Rollin C. Hurd, *A Treatise on the Right of Personal Liberty and on the Writ of Habeas Corpus and the Practice Connected with It* (Albany, N.Y.: W. C. Little, 1858), at 555–556.

26. Lincoln to Scott, Apr. 27, 1861, in 4 Basler, *Works,* at 347.

27. Proc. No. 7, May 10, 1861, 12 Stat. 1261.

28. *See* 4 Basler, *Works,* at 364–365. Actually, suspensions had already been promulgated by the local commanders. So Lincoln's consent amounted, in reality, to a retrospective approval of the action.

29. Lincoln to Scott, July 2, 1861, *id.* at 419; and Lincoln to Scott, Oct 14, 1861, *id.* at 554.

30. Lincoln to Scott, June 20, 1861, *id.* at 414. The individual, a certain Major Chace, thereby attained whatever degree of immortality a footnote is capable of conferring. On the early suspensions of habeas corpus in the war, see Mark E. Neely, Jr., *The Fate of Liberty: Abraham Lincoln and Civil Liberties* (New York: Oxford University Press, 1991), at 4–11; and William H. Rehnquist, *All the Laws but One: Civil Liberty in Wartime* (New York: Knopf, 1998), at 22–25.

31. This contrasts with the position in ordinary civilian employment, in which a person is free to leave employment at will—subject to any damages that might be owed for breach of contract. But such damages are a civil remedy only. The employer has no right to force the person to work against his or her will. The position of the military is importantly different in this regard, where a person leaving the service without permission is punishable—and potentially severely at that—for the offense of desertion.

32. U.S. ex rel. Murphy v. Porter, 27 Fed. Cas. 599 (No. 16,074a) (CC D.C. 1861). On this case, see Carl D. Swisher, *The Taney Period* (New York: Macmillan, 1974), at 864–866.

33. On forceful Union action in Maryland, see generally 1 (ser. 2) OR 563–748.

34. For the text of which, see *id.* at 575.

35. Cadwalader to Taney, May 26, 1861, *id.* at 576.

36. Ex p. Merryman, 17 Fed. Cas. 144 (No. 9487) (CC D Md. 1861). On this case, see Clinton Rossiter, *The Supreme Court and the Commander in Chief* (2d ed.; Ithaca, N.Y.: Cornell University Press, 1976), at 18–26; Hyman, *More Perfect Union,* at 81–86; and Rehnquist, *All the Laws,* at 33–39. On the reaction to the *Merryman* decision, see Hyman, *More Perfect Union,* at 86–93. On Taney's attitudes during this period, see *id.* at 256–261.

37. On Lincoln's role in the Merryman affair, see Brian McGinty, *Lincoln and the Court* (Cambridge, Mass.: Harvard University Press, 2008), at 65–91.

38. 4 Basler, *Works,* at 430–431. For contemporary support for Lincoln's position, see Horace Binney, *The Privilege of the Writ of Habeas Corpus under the Constitution* (Philadelphia: C. Sherman and Sons, 1862); *reprinted in* 1 Frank Freidel (ed.), *Union Pamphlets of the Civil War, 1861–1865* (Cambridge, Mass.: Harvard University Press, 1967), at 199–252.

39. Bates, Suspension of the Writ of Habeas Corpus, July 5, 1861, 10 Op. A-G 74.

40. *See,* for example, Ex p. Benedict, 3 Fed. Cas. 159 (No. 1292) (DC ND N.Y. 1862); and McCall v. McDowell, 15 Fed. Cas. 1235 (No. 8673) (CC D Cal. 1867).

41. In re Kemp, 16 Wis. 359 (1863); and Griffin v. Wilcox, 21 Ind. 370 (1864).

42. Ex p. Field, 9 Fed. Cas. 1 (No. 4761) (CC D Vt. 1862).

43. *See* Opinion of Douglas in Parisi v. Davidson, 405 U.S. 34 (1972), at 47, which states the question still to be open. *See,* however, Opinion of Scalia in Hamdi v. Rumsfeld, 542 U.S. 1 (2004), at 111, that it is "understood" that Congress, rather than the President, possesses the suspension power. *See also* Padilla v. Hanft, 389 F. Supp. 2d 678 (D.S.C. 2005), at 692, which clearly states that the power belongs exclusively to Congress (although the question was not actually at issue in that case, and no authority was cited for the conclusion). *See also* William F. Duker, *A Constitutional History of Habeas Corpus* (Westport, Conn.: Greenwood Press, 1980), at 141–149; and Michael Stokes Paulsen, "The Merryman Power and the Dilemma of Autonomous Executive Branch Interpretation," 15 *Cardozo L. Rev.* 81–111 (1993). Even Congress's power to suspend habeas corpus is not unfettered. There must be a situation of "Rebellion or Invasion." If there is not, then the constitutionality of a suspension depends on the provision of an adequate alternative remedy. *See* Boumediene v. Bush, 128 S.Ct. 2229 (2008), for a case in which these standards were not met.

44. Act of Mar. 3, 1863, 12 Stat. 755. On this legislation, see Hyman, *More Perfect Union,* at 245–256. For further aspects of this law, see Chapters 6 and 9.

45. In re Murphy, 17 Fed. Cas. 1030 (No. 9947) (CC D Mo. 1867).

46. In re Oliver, 17 Wis. 681 (1864).

47. J. W. Hampton, Jr., and Co. v. U.S., 276 U.S. 394 (1928).

48. Mark E. Neely, Jr., *Confederate Bastille: Jefferson Davis and Civil Liberties* (Milwaukee: Marquette University Press, 1993), at 14–15.

49. Neely, *Fate of Liberty,* at 69. For a detailed exposition of judicial interference with conscription, see Fry to Stanton, Nov. 17, 1863, 3 (ser. 3) OR 1046–1062.

50. Proc. No. 7, Sep. 15, 1863, 13 Stat. 734.

51. Proc. No. 16, July 5, 1864, 13 Stat. 742. *See also* Neely, *Fate of Liberty,* at 90–92.

52. *See* Chapter 6.

53. On the habeas corpus suspension during the war, see generally Sherrill Halbert, "The Suspension of the Writ of Habeas Corpus by President Lincoln," 2 *American J. Legal History* 95–116 (1958).

54. 1 Edward Coke, *The First Part of the Institutes of the Laws of England, or, a Commentary upon Littleton* (13th ed., ed. Francis Hargrave; London: G. Kearsly and G. Robinson, 1775–1778 [1628]), sec. 412, at 249.

55. Johnson v. Duncan, 3 Mart. 530 (1815).

56. In re Kemp, 16 Wis. 359 (1863), at 395.

57. Griffin v. Wilcox, 21 Ind. 370 (1864), at 391.

58. *See* Jones v. Seward, 3 Grant 431 (1863).

59. Ex p. Milligan, 71 U.S. (4 Wall.) 2 (1866), at 127. *See also,* in this same vein, Johnson v. Jones, 44 Ill. 142 (1867); and McLaughlin v. Green, 50 Miss. 453 (1874). For other aspects of the Milligan case, see Chapter 6.

60. Proc. of Aug. 30, 1861, 1 (ser. 2) OR 221–222.

61. The Fremont Contract Cases, 2 Ct. of Claims 1 (Dec. 1866 term).

62. Halleck to McClellan, Nov. 30, 1861, 1 (ser. 2) OR 232–233.

63. Lincoln to Halleck, Dec. 2, 1861, in 5 Basler, *Works,* at 35.

64. General Orders No. 34, Dec. 26, 1861, 8 (ser. 1) OR 468.

65. General Orders No. 17, Feb. 8, 1862, *id.* at 547–548. For more detailed consideration of guerrilla warfare, see Chapter 3.

66. Proc. No. 16, July 5, 1864, 13 Stat. 742. *See also* Neely, *Fate of Liberty,* at 90–92.

67. For the texts of these, see Ex p. Field, 9 Fed. Cas. 1 (No. 4761) (CC D Vt. 1862), at 2.

68. General Orders No. 104, Aug. 13, 1862, 2 (ser. 3) OR 370.

69. Proc. of Sep. 24, 1862, in 5 Basler, *Works,* at 436–437; *also promulgated as* General Orders No. 141, Sep. 25, 1862, 2 (ser. 3) OR 587–588. Strangely, the text is not in *Statutes at Large.*

70. Benjamin R. Curtis, *Executive Power* (Boston: Little, Brown, 1862); *reprinted in* 1 Freidel, *Union Pamphlets,* at 450–473. For agreement with this assessment, see Neely, *Fate of Liberty,* at 65.

71. Ex p. Field, 9 Fed. Cas. 1 (No. 4761) (CC D Vt. 1862).

72. Ex p. Vallandigham, 28 Fed. Cas. 874 (No. 16,816) (CC SD Ohio 1863).

73. Griffin v. Wilcox, 21 Ind. 370 (1864), at 386.

74. *See* Chapter 6 on various methods by which dissidents attempted to challenge administration measures.

75. Constitution, Art. I, sec. 8.

76. *Id.,* sec. 9. This ban reflects the fear of Southerners in the 1780s that their staple exports, tobacco and cotton, might be burdened with the support of the federal government, with a corresponding reduction in marketing opportunities.

77. *Id.,* sec. 8.

78. *Id.,* sec. 2.

79. Act of Aug. 5, 1861, 12 Stat. 292, sec. 8–48, at 294–309.

80. *See* Chapter 4 on this subject.

81. Act of Aug. 5, 1861, 12 Stat. 292, sec. 49–53, at 309–312.

82. For an excellent account of the details and operation of the income tax, see Joseph Hill, "The Civil War Income Tax," 8 *Quarterly J. Economics* 416–452 (1894).

83. On the termination of the income tax, see Act of July 14, 1870, 16 Stat. 256, sec. 6, at 257.

84. For the suspension, see Act of July 1, 1862, 12 Stat. 432, sec. 119, at 489. For the definitive termination, see Act of June 30, 1864, 13 Stat. 223, sec. 173, at 304.

85. *Federalist,* No. 21 (Hamilton). *See also id.,* No. 36 (Hamilton).

86. Ware v. Hylton, 3 U.S. (3 Dall.) 171 (1796).

87. *See* Pacific Insurance Co. v. Soule, 74 U.S. (7 Wall.) 433 (1869); Veazie Bank v. Fenno, 75 U.S. (8 Wall.) 533 (1869); and Springer v. U.S., 102 U.S. 586 (1881). On the *Veazie Bank* case, see Robert Bruce Murray, *Legal Cases of the Civil War* (Mechanicsburg, Pa.: Stackpole, 2003), at 131–137.

88. Act of Aug. 27, 1894, 28 Stat. 509, sec. 27–36, at 553–560.

89. Pollock v. Farmers' Loan and Trust Co., 158 U.S. 601 (1895).

90. Davis Rich Dewey, *Financial History of the United States* (8th ed.; London: Longmans, Green, 1922), at 281–283; and Margaret G. Myers, *A Financial History of the United States* (New York: Columbia University Press, 1976), at 151–153.

91. For the complex story of the redemption of the greenbacks, see Myers, *Financial History,* at 189–196.

92. Redemption Act of Jan. 14, 1875, 18 Stat. 296.

93. Act of Feb. 25, 1862, 12 Stat. 345, sec. 1.

94. *See,* for example, the Kentucky case of Hord v. Miller, 63 Ky. 103 (1865), holding that greenbacks must be valued at their *market* price rather than at their face value. This was, in effect, a ruling against retroactivity. For the opposite conclusion, see the Massachusetts case of Wood v. Bullens, 88 Mass. 516 (1863).

95. Bronson v. Rodes, 74 U.S. (7 Wall.) 229 (1869). *See also* Butler v. Horwitz, 74 U.S. (7 Wall.) 258 (1869), decided two weeks later.

96. *See,* however, the postwar case of Adam v. U.S., in 3 Moore, *Arbitrations,* at 3066–3067, in which the British government unsuccessfully advanced a claim against the United States on this thesis. This claim was, however, on the basis of *international* law and not of American constitutional law.

97. In favor of allowing contracting-out, see the opinions of Judge Agnew, in Schollenberger v. Brinton, 52 Pa. 9 (1865), at 94–97; and the opinion of Chief Justice Chase in Butler v. Horwitz, 74 U.S. (7 Wall.) 258 (1869), at 267. For the opposing position, see opinion of Justice Bradley in Knox v. Lee, 79 U.S. (12 Wall.) 457 (1871), at 566.

98. For the California case, see Galland v. Lewis, 26 Cal. 46 (1864). For the Nevada case (which was explicitly critical of the California one), see Milliken v. Sloat, 1 Nev. 575 (1865).

99. Myers, *Financial History*, at 154.

100. *See,* for example, Metropolitan Bank v. Van Dyck, 27 N.Y. 400 (1863); Lick v. Faulkner, 25 Cal. 404 (1864); George v. Concord, 45 N.H. 434 (1864); Breitenbach v. Turner, 18 Wis. 139 (1864); Hintrager v. Bates, 18 Iowa 174 (1865); Van Husen v. Kanouse, 13 Mich. 03 (1865); Maynard v. Newman, 1 Nev. 271 (1865); and Schollenberger v. Brinton, 52 Pa. 1 (1865). The Indiana Supreme Court wavered on the issue. *See* Reynolds v. Bank of the State of Indiana, 18 Ind. 467 (1862); Thayer v. Hedges, 22 Ind. 282 (1864); and, finally upholding the legal-tender issue, Thayer v. Hedges, 23 Ind. 1421 (1864). On the Indiana cases, see Charles Fairman, *Reconstruction and Reunion 1864–1888,* pt. 1 (New York: Macmillan, 1971), at 692–693.

101. Hepburn v. Griswold, 75 U.S. (8 Wall.) 603 (1870).

102. Constitution, Art. I, sec. 8.

103. Bronson v. Rodes, 74 U.S. (7 Wall.) 229 (1869), at 251.

104. Constitution, Art. I, sec. 8. On the *Hepburn* decision, see Murray, *Legal Cases,* at 100–110.

105. Knox v. Lee, 79 U.S. (12 Wall.) 457 (1871). This is often referred to, somewhat confusingly, as *the* Legal Tender Case.

106. By way of contrast, one of the most striking reversals in Supreme Court history occurred in 2003, on the subject of the constitutionality of state laws against sodomy. Lawrence v. Texas, 539 U.S. 558 (2003), struck down such laws, and in the process reversed—in scathing terms—the previous case of Bowers v. Hardwick, 478 U.S. 186 (1986). Here, however, there was a seventeen-year gap between the two decisions. In another famous reversal—perhaps the most famous of all—concerning the constitutionality of racial segregation in public schools, there was a gap of fifty-eight years: from Plessy v. Ferguson, 163 U.S. 537 (1896), to Brown v. Board of Education of Topeka, 347 U.S. 483 (1954).

107. Knox v. Lee, 79 U.S. (12 Wall.) 457 (1871), at 534.

108. *Id.* at 546–547.

109. *Id.* at 540.

110. *Id.* at 543.

111. On the *Knox* decision, see Murray, *Legal Cases,* at 110–126. On the legal tender cases generally, see Fairman, *Reconstruction,* at 677–775; and McGinty, *Lincoln and the Court,* at 274–287.

112. Act of May 31, 1878, 20 Stat. 87.

113. Juilliard v. Greenman, 110 U.S. 421 (1884).

114. U.S. v. Curtiss-Wright Export Corp., 299 U.S. 304 (1936). *See* Louis Henkin, *Foreign Affairs and the United States Constitution* (2d ed.; Oxford: Clarendon Press, 1996), at 16–22. *See also* Missouri v. Holland, 252 U.S. 416 (1920), which, in effect, supports this thesis.

115. Constitution, Art. I, sec. 8.

116. *Id.*

117. Act of Feb. 28, 1795, 1 Stat. 424, sec. 2.

118. Proc. No. 3, Apr. 15, 1861, 12 Stat. 1258.

119. Proc. No. 6, May 3, 1861, *id.* at 1260.

120. Act of July 17, 1862, *id.* at 597.

121. Constitution, Art. I, sec. 8.

122. In re Griner, 16 Wis. 423 (1863).

123. Act of Mar. 3, 1863, 12 Stat. 731.

124. Constitution, Art. I, sec. 8. For Lincoln's own views on conscription, and the constitutional authority for it, see Lincoln, Opinion on the Draft, Sep. 14 (?), 1863, in 6 Basler, *Works,* at 444–449.

125. On the general history of conscription in the war, see Eugene Converse Murdock, *Patriotism Limited, 1862–1865: The Civil War Draft and the Bounty System* (Kent, Ohio: Kent State University Press, 1967). *See also* 1 Frederick Albert Shannon, *The Organization and Administration of the Union Army 1861–1865* (Cleveland: Arthur H. Clark, 1928), at 257–323; and 2 *id.* at 101–171. On the legal aspects specifically, see J. G. Randall, *Constitutional Problems under Lincoln* (New York: D. Appleton, 1926), at 239–274; and Swisher, *Taney Period,* at 946–951. On the historiography of conscription, see James W. Geary, "Civil War Conscription in the North: A Historiographical Review," 32 Civil War History 208–228 (1986).

126. Roger B. Taney, "Thoughts on the Conscription Law of the U[nited] States—Rough Draft Requiring Revision," copied by M. L. York from an unpublished manuscript in 1866 and edited by Philip G. Auchampaugh.

127. Kneedler v. Lane, 45 Pa. 238 (1863).

128. *Id.* Both judgments are printed together, with the same citation.

129. On conscription issues, see Randall, *Constitutional Problems,* at 239–274.

130. Act of Jan. 21, 1903, 32 Stat. 775.

131. It remained the case, however—and probably still remains—that the National Guard, as the successor to the militia, can only be employed by the federal government in the three situations identified by the Constitution: to execute federal laws, to suppress insurrection, and to repel invasion. Constitution, Art. I, sec. 8. *See,* to this effect, Wickersham, Acceptance of Office in National Guard of a State by Officer on Active List of Regular Army, Jan. 31, 1912, 29 Op. A-G 298.

132. The Selective Draft Law Cases, 245 U.S. 366 (1918), at 378.

3. Fighting by the Rules

Epigraphs: Dow v. Johnson, 100 U.S. 158 (1880), at 170; Halleck to Sherman, Sep. 28, 1864, 39(2) (ser. 1) OR 503.

1. The laws of war are formally known to international lawyers, somewhat more grandly, as "the laws and customs of war." There is no detailed, systematic treatment

of the history of the laws of war. *See,* however, Stephen C. Neff, *War and the Law of Nations: A General History* (Cambridge: Cambridge University Press, 2005), at 60–63, 107–110, 143–147, 182–187, for a brief account.

2. Constitution, Art. I, sec. 8.

3. Act of Apr. 16, 1806, 2 Stat. 359. The current rules are the Uniform Code of Military Justice, Act of May 5, 1950, PL 81–506, 64 Stat. 108; *codified at* 10 U.S.C. sec. 801 *et seq.*

4. Constitution, Art. I, sec. 8.

5. Justice Field was emphatically of the view that Congress has no such power. *See* his dissenting opinion in Miller v. U.S., 78 U.S. (11 Wall.) 268 (1871), at 316 (where the point was not actually at issue). Justice Story was of the same view in Brown v. U.S., 12 U.S. (8 Cranch) 110 (1814), at 153. For the opposite conclusion by the Kentucky Court of Appeal, see Norris v. Doniphan, 61 Ky. 385 (1863).

6. On Lieber's life and career, see generally Elihu Root, "Francis Lieber," 7 *Am. J. Int'l L.* 453–466 (1913); Ernest Nys, "Francis Lieber—His Life and Work," 5 *Am. J. Int'l L.* 84–117, 355–393 (1911); and Frank Freidel, *Francis Lieber, Nineteenth-century Liberal* (Baton Rouge: Louisiana State University Press, 1947).

7. Emmerich de Vattel, *The Law of Nations; Or The Principles of Natural Law* (trans. Charles G. Fenwick; Washington, D.C.: Carnegie Institution, 1916 [1758]).

8. Henry W. Halleck, *International Law; Or, Rules Regulating the Intercourse of States in Peace and War* (New York: van Nostrand, 1861). Subsequent editions were edited chiefly by the British writer Sir George Sherston Baker. The last was the fourth edition, published in 1908. On the life and career of Halleck, see generally John F. Marszalek, *Commander of All Lincoln's Armies: A Life of General Henry W. Halleck* (Cambridge, Mass.: Harvard University Press, 2004).

9. General Orders No. 100, Apr. 24, 1863, 5 (ser. 2) OR 671–682; *reprinted in* Richard Shelly Hartigan, *Lieber's Code and the Law of War* (Chicago: Precedent, 1983) at 45–71 (hereafter Lieber Code). *See also* Mark Grimsley, *The Hard Hand of War: Union Military Policy toward Southern Civilians, 1861–1865* (Cambridge: Cambridge University Press, 1995), at 145–151; and Theodor Meron, "Francis Lieber's Code and Principles of Humanity," in Jonathan I. Charney, Donald K. Anton, and Mary Ellen O'Connell (eds.), *Politics, Values and Functions: International Law in the Twenty-first Century* (The Hague: Martinus Nijhoff, 1997), at 249–260.

10. Kaspar Bluntschli, *Le droit international codifié* (trans. M. C. Lardy; Paris: Guillaumin, 1870), at 434–465.

11. Project of an International Declaration Concerning the Laws and Customs of War, Aug. 27, 1874, in 1 *(Supp.) Am. J. Int'l L.* 96 (1907).

12. Hague Convention II on the Rules of Land Warfare, July 29, 1899, 189 C.T.S. 429, 32 Stat. 1803.

13. Hague Convention IV Respecting the Laws and Customs of War on Land, Oct. 18, 1907, 205 C.T.S. 227, 36 Stat. 2277 (hereafter Hague Rules). The Hague Rules

have, however, been importantly supplemented by the four Geneva Conventions of 1949, as well as by the two Additional Protocols to the Geneva Conventions, drafted in 1977.

14. On Lincoln's selection of Chase as chief justice, see Brian McGinty, *Lincoln and the Court* (Cambridge, Mass.: Harvard University Press, 2008), at 229–235.

15. On Stanton's life and career, see generally Benjamin P. Thomas and Harold M. Hyman, *Stanton: The Life and Times of Lincoln's Secretary of War* (New York: Knopf, 1962).

16. Hyman, *A More Perfect Union: The Impact of the Civil War and Reconstruction on the Constitution* (New York: Knopf, 1973), at 190.

17. Lieber Code, art. 41. For later endorsement of this principle by the federal Supreme Court, see Coleman v. Tennessee, 97 U.S. 509 (1879); and Dow v. Johnson, 100 U.S. 158 (1880).

18. *See* Lieber Code, arts. 44 (on pillage), 70 (on poison), and 60 (on no-quarter policies).

19. *Id.*, art. 57. *See*, to this effect, the Tennessee Supreme Court case Hammond v. State, 43 Tenn. 129 (1866).

20. Lieber Code, art. 14 (emphasis added).

21. *Id.*, art. 16. *See also*, to the same effect, Vattel, *Law of Nations*, at 294–295; and Halleck, *International Law*, at 399. *See also* Burrus B. Carnahan, "Lincoln, Lieber and the Laws of War: The Origins and Limits of the Principle of Military Necessity," 92 *Am. J. Int'l L.* 213–231 (1998).

22. Military necessity, in this strict legal sense, is *not* the same thing as the *general* principle of necessity in international law. That general principle of necessity *does* justify transgressions of the law. For a classic example of the confusion, on the part of the Confederates, between these two distinct concepts see Seddon to Ould, June 24, 1863, 6 (ser. 2) OR 41–47, at 43 (commenting on the Lieber Code). This is a highly underexplored area of law, which must be left altogether outside the scope of this work. Those wishing to explore this fascinating subject may usefully consult Burleigh Cushing Rodick, *The Doctrine of Necessity in International Law* (New York: Columbia University Press, 1928). For the current statement of the general principle of necessity, see International Law Commission, Articles on Responsibility of States for Internationally Wrongful Acts, UN Doc. A/56/10 (2001), at 43–59, art. 25. For a highly lucid exposition, see Israeli Supreme Court, Judgment Concerning the Legality of the General Security Service's Interrogation Methods, Sep. 6, 1999, 38 *Int'l Legal Materials* 1491 (1999).

23. Lieber Code, art. 68.

24. Hague Rules, art. 22(e). For the current statement of the rule, in the more general form of a ban on "superfluous injury or unnecessary suffering," see Additional Protocol I to the Geneva Conventions of 1949, June 8, 1977, 1125 U.N.T.S. 3, art. 35(2) (hereafter Protocol I of 1977).

25. Special Field Orders No. 67, Sep. 8, 1864, 38(5) (ser. 1) OR 837–838. On this incident, see Grimsley, *Hard Hand*, at 186–190.

26. Hood to Sherman, Sep. 9, 1864, 39(2) (ser. 1) OR 415.

27. Mayor and two councilmen to Sherman, Sep. 11, 1864, *id.* at 417–418.

28. Sherman to Halleck, Sep. 20, 1861, *id.* at 414.

29. Halleck to Sherman, Sep. 28, 1864, *id.* at 503.

30. *See,* for example, Buell to Jones, Aug. 27, 1862, 16(2) (ser. 1) OR 428; and Butler to Taylor, Sep. 10, 1862, 15 (ser. 1) OR 565-567. *See also* Grimsley, *Hard Hand,* at 81–85, concerning the court-martialing of officers responsible for the sacking of Athens, Georgia, in May 1862.

31. *See,* for example, General Orders No. 50, Sep. 9, 1864, 39(1) (ser. 1) OR 405, on the prosecution (and acquittal) of Confederate brigadier general Richard L. Page for unlawful destruction. *See also* General Orders No. 36, May 31, 1862, 15 (ser. 1) OR 467, on the prosecution and conviction of six Confederates for parole violation.

32. At Nuremberg, there were two other sets of charges apart from war crimes: the planning of aggressive war (labeled "crimes against the peace"); and crimes against humanity. For the best book on the Nuremberg Trials from the legal standpoint, see Telford Taylor, *The Anatomy of the Nuremberg Trials* (Boston: Little, Brown, 1992).

33. On the Tokyo trials, see Neil Boister and Robert Cryer, *The Tokyo International Military Tribunal: A Reappraisal* (New York: Oxford University Press, 2008).

34. The word "vindictive," as it happens, differs in ordinary parlance from the legal term from which it derives. "Vindication," in Roman law, was a legal process for the confirmation of title to property. It is cognate to the word "wand" because a wand or stick was employed in the Roman legal procedure for the formal identification of, and claim to, the property in question.

35. Lieber Code, art. 28.

36. Lieber Code, arts. 27 and 28. The Code, somewhat confusingly, employed the term "retaliation" instead of "reprisal."

37. On these trials, see Chapter 1.

38. Davis to Lincoln, July 6, 1861, 3 (ser. 2) OR 5–6.

39. Confed. Cong. Res., Aug. 23, 1861, *id.* at 710; and Confed. Act of Aug. 30, 1861, *id.* at 714.

40. Mark W. Weitz, *The Confederacy on Trial: The Piracy and Sequestration Cases of 1861* (Lawrence: University Press of Kansas, 2005), at 195–196.

41. Office Commissary-general of Prisoners to Stanton, May 13, 1864, 7 (ser. 2) OR 150–151; and circular, Office Commissary-general of Prisoners, June 1, 1864, *id.* at 183–184.

42. On the treatment of the subject at the two conferences, see F. Kalshoven, *Belligerent Reprisals* (Leyden: Sijthoff, 1971), at 56–66.

43. Institute of International Law, "Laws and Customs of War on Land," Sep. 9, 1880, in James Brown Scott (ed.), *Resolutions of the Institute of International Law* (New York: Oxford University Press, 1916), at 25–42, art. 86.

44. In re List, U.S. Military Tribunal at Nuremberg, 15 *Int'l L. Rep.* 632 (1948), at 644–646.

45. Lieber Code, art. 58.

46. *Id.*, art. 59.

47. Geneva Convention Relative on Prisoners of War, July 27, 1929, 118 L.N.T.S. 343, art. 2. For the present prohibition, see Geneva Convention III on Prisoners of War, Aug. 12, 1949, 75 U.N.T.S. 135, art. 13 (hereafter Geneva Convention on Prisoners).

48. Protocol I of 1977, art. 51(6).

49. *Id.*, arts. 52–56. It may be noted that these various limitations on reprisals were one (but not the sole) reason the United States has declined to become a party to the 1977 Protocol. It is possible that these restrictions on reprisals have entered the general sphere of *customary* international law, in which case the United States is bound by them even without being a party to the 1977 Protocol. There is not as yet, however, clear judicial authority on this important point. On the modern law of belligerent reprisals, see generally Kalshoven, *Belligerent Reprisals.*

50. Mark E. Neely, Jr., *The Fate of Liberty: Abraham Lincoln and Civil Liberties* (New York: Oxford University Press, 1991), at 155–157.

51. For a useful history of hostage-taking incidents in the Civil War, see generally Webb Garrison, *Civil War Hostages: Hostage Taking in the Civil War* (Shippensburg, Pa.: White Mane, 2000).

52. Charter of the International Military Tribunal, Aug. 8, 1945, 82 U.N.T.S. 284, art. 6(b).

53. In re List, U.S. Military Tribunal at Nuremberg, 15 Int'l L. Rep. 632, at 641–644.

54. Geneva Convention IV on the Protection of Civilian Persons in Time of War, Aug. 12, 1949, 75 U.N.T.S. 287, art. 34.

55. Protocol I of 1977, art. 75(2).

56. Confed. General Orders No. 54, Aug. 1, 1862, 1 (ser. 2) OR 836–837. This order was rescinded after Pope was relieved of his Virginia command, by Confed. General Orders No. 84, Nov. 10, 1862, 4 (ser. 2) OR 938–939. *See also* Letcher to Randolph, Aug. 15, 1862, *id.* at 849–850, in which the governor of Virginia pressed for the criminal prosecution of some of Pope's officers.

57. Confed. General Orders No. 84, Nov. 10, 1862, 4 (ser. 2) OR 938–939.

58. Confed. General Orders No. 60, Aug. 21, 1862, 14 (ser. 1) OR 599.

59. General Orders No. 28, May 15, 1862, 15 (ser. 1) OR 426. On Butler's activity in New Orleans, see Peyton McCrary, *Abraham Lincoln and Reconstruction: The Louisiana Experiment* (Princeton: Princeton University Press, 1978), at 74–90.

60. Confed. General Orders No. 111, Dec. 24, 1862, in 1 James D. Richardson (ed.), *A Compilation of the Messages and Papers of the Confederacy* (Nashville: United States Publishing, 1905), at 269–274.

61. Lieber Code, art. 148.

62. Geneva Convention on Prisoners, art. 85.

63. *See,* for example, Report of Casey, May 8, 1862, 11(1) (ser. 1) OR 557–558.

64. Rains to Hill, May 14, 1862, 11(3) (ser. 1) OR 516–517.

65. McClellan to Stanton, May 4, 1862, *id.* at 134–135.

66. Sorrell to Rains, May 11, 1862, *id.* at 509.

67. Endorsement of Rains, on Sorrell to Rains, *id.* at 509–510.

68. Endorsement of Randolph, on Sorrell to Rains, *id.* at 510. Randolph essentially took Longstreet's side, but apparently only on the basis of Longstreet's higher rank. For substantially the same conclusion, see J. M. Spaight, *War Rights on Land* (London: Macmillan, 1911), at 81–83. *See also* Mark E. Neely, Jr., "Was the Civil War a Total War?" 37 *Civil War History* 5 28 (1991): 12–13.

69. Davis to Browne, Nov. 22, 1864, 44 (ser. 1) OR 880–881.

70. Report of Huntington, Dec. 25, 1864, *id.* at 79–80. Some twelve soldiers were killed by them, and eighty wounded.

71. Report of Sherman, Dec. 22, 1864, *id.* at 787–793, at 791.

72. Convention on Certain Convential Weapons. Protocol II on Mines, Booby-traps and Other Devices, Oct. 10, 1980, 1342 U.N.T.S. 137.

73. Convention on Anti-personnel Mines, Sep. 18, 1997, 2056 U.N.T.S. 211.

74. 1 Anonymous, *A General Collection of Treatys, Declarations of War, Manifestos, and Other Publick Papers, Relating to Peace and War* (London: J. J. and P. Knapton, 1732), at 167–168.

75. Vattel, *Law of Nations,* at 318.

76. Sherman to Hindman, Sep. 28, 1862, 13 (ser. 1) OR 682–683.

77. *See,* to this effect, Hugo Grotius, *On the Law of War and Peace* (trans. Francis W. Kelsey; Oxford: Oxford University Press, 1925 [1625]), at 653–656; Samuel Pufendorf, *On the Law of Nature and Nations* (trans. C. H. Oldfather and W. A. Old-father; Oxford: Clarendon Press, 1934 [1672]), at 1308; and Vattel, *Law of Nations,* at 287–288.

78. Vattel, *Law of Nations,* at 299–300.

79. The President was given statutory authority to enroll "persons of African descent" in the Union armies by the Second Confiscation Act, July 17, 1862, 12 Stat. 589, sec. 11, at 592.

80. Seddon to Ould, June 24, 1863, 6 (ser. 2) OR 41–47, at 45.

81. Seddon to Davis, Nov. 3, 1864, 3 (ser. 4) OR 756–771, at 769.

82. Cobb to Seddon, June 6, 1864, 7 (ser. 2) OR 203.

83. Indorsement of Seddon, *id.* at 204.

84. Confed. Cong. Joint Res., May 1, 1863, 5 (ser. 2) OR 940–941. On the Emancipation Proclamation, see Chapter 5.

85. *See* Walker to Jordan, apr. 20, 1863, 14 (ser. 1) OR 903.

86. Forrest to Washburn, June 25, 1864, 32(1) (ser. 1) OR 590–591.

87. Cartel of July 22, 1862, 4 (ser. 2) OR 266–268.

88. For the Union protest against the noninclusion of black prisoners in exchanges, see Ludlow to Ould, June 14, 1863, 6 (ser. 2) OR 17–18. For a thorough exposition of the Union's reasons for discontinuing prisoner exchanges, see Hitchcock to N.Y. Times, Nov. 28, 1863, *id.* at 594–600.

89. *See* Chapter 9.

90. Seddon to Beauregard, Nov. 30, 1862, 1 (ser. 2) OR 954.

91. *Id.*

92. Kirby Smith to Taylor, June 13, 1863, 6 (ser. 2) OR 21–22.

93. Bonham to Seddon, July 23, 1863, 6 (ser. 2) OR 145–146.

94. Grant to Taylor, June 22, 1863, 24 (ser. 3) OR 425–426; Taylor to Grant, June 27, 1863, *id* at 443–444; and Grant to Taylor, July 4, 1863, *id* at 469. On this battle, see Richard Lowe, "Battle on the Levee: The Fight at Milliken's Bend," in John David Smith (ed.), *Black Soldiers in Blue: African American Troops in the Civil War Era* (Chapel Hill: University of North Carolina Press, 2002), at 107–135.

95. Gregory J. Unwin, "'We Cannot Treat Negroes . . . as Prisoners of War': Racial Atrocities and Reprisals in Civil War Arkansas," 42 *Civil War History* 193–210 (1996), at 206.

96. For details of these incidents, see *id.* at 193–198.

97. United States Congress, Joint Committee on the Conduct of the War, "Fort Pillow Massacre, and Returned Prisoners," 38th Cong., 1st Sess., House Report No. 65 (1864); and Senate Report No. 63 (1864).

98. For the text of Forrest's ultimatum of surrender to the fort—containing a denial of responsibility for "the fate of your command" in the event of refusal—see Forrest to Booth, Apr. 12, 1864, 32(1) (ser. 1) OR 596. For Forrest's defense of his conduct, see Forrest to Washburn, June 23, 1864, *id.* at 591–593. The secondary literature on the incident is voluminous. *See,* for example, John L. Jordan, "Was There a Massacre at Fort Pillow?" 6 *Tennessee Historical Quarterly* 99–133 (1947); Albert Castel, "The Fort Pillow Massacre: A Fresh Examination of the Evidence," 4 *Civil War History* 37–50 (1958); John Cimprich and Robert C. Maintford, Jr., "Fort Pillow Revisited: New Evidence about an Old Controversy," 24 *Civil War History* 293–306 (1982); Gregory J. Macaluso, *The Fort Pillow Massacre: The Reason Why* (New York: Vantage, 1989); John Cimprich and Robert C. Maintford, Jr., "The Fort Pillow Massacre: A Statistical Note," 76 *Journal of American History* 830–837 (1989); and John Cimprich, "The Fort Pillow Massacre: Assessing the Evidence," in Smith, *Black Soldiers,* at 150–168. On the propaganda consequences, see Bruce Tap, *Over Lincoln's Shoulder: The Committee on the Conduct of the War* (Lawrence: University Press of Kansas, 1998), at 193–201, 203–206.

99. *See* Chapter 9.

100. Brisbin to Thomas (n.d.), Inclosure No. 6 of Report of Gardner, Oct. 26, 1864, 39(1) (ser. 1) OR 556–557. The Confederate report of the battle mentioned no such incidents. *See* Dibrell to Burford, Oct. 19, 1864, *id.* at 496–497.

101. On the Saltville Massacre, see Thomas D. Mays, *The Saltville Massacre* (Abilene, Kan.: McWhiney Foundation Press, 1995); and Thomas D. Mays, "The Battle of Saltville," in Smith, *Black Soldiers,* at 200–226.

102. Lieber Code, arts. 47 and 48.

103. Hunter to Davis, Apr. 25, 1863, 14 (ser. 1) OR 448–449.

104. Order of July 30, 1863, in 6 Basler, *Works,* at 357. This then became General Orders No. 252, July 31, 1863, 6 (ser. 2) OR 163.

105. Forrest to Washburn, June 14, 1864, 22(2) (ser. 1) OR 586–587.

106. *See* Bates, Fort Pillow Massacre, May 4, 1864, 11 Op. A-G 43. The opinion was sombre in tone and moving—a notable departure from normal legal style.

107. Marshall to Breckenridge, Oct. 21, 1864, 7 (ser. 2) OR 1020.

108. *See* Chapter 9.

109. A comprehensive account of irregular combat in the Civil War is lacking, but there are a number of studies of the phenomenon in specific areas. On the situation in Missouri, for example, see Jay Monaghan, *Civil War on the Western Border, 1854–1865* (Boston: Little, Brown, 1955); Albert Castel, "Quantrill's Bushwhackers: A Case Study in Partisan Warfare," 13 *Civil War History* 40–50 (1967); and Michael Fellman, *Inside War: The Guerrilla Conflict in Missouri during the American Civil War* (New York: Oxford University Press, 1989). On Tennessee, see Stephen V. Ash, *Middle Tennessee Society Transformed: War and Peace in the Upper South* (Baton Rouge: Louisiana University Press, 1988), at 147–157. On various forms of irregular warfare in the eastern theater, see Virgil Carrington Jones, *Grey Ghosts and Rebel Raiders* (New York: Galahad, 1956). For an informative survey of the historiography of guerrilla warfare in the Civil War, see Daniel E. Sutherland, "Sideshow No Longer: A Historiographical Review of the Guerrilla War," 46 *Civil War History* 5–23 (2000).

110. *See* Francis Lieber, *Guerrilla Parties: Considered with Reference to the Laws and Usages of War* (New York: Van Nostrand, 1862); *reprinted in* Hartigan, *Lieber's Code,* at 31–44. For correspondence between Lieber and Halleck in this connection, see 2 (ser. 3) OR 301–309. On Lieber's views on this subject, see Courtney S. Campbell, "Moral Responsibility and Irregular War," in James Turner Johnson and John Kelsay (eds.), *Cross, Crescent and Sword: The Justification and Limitation of War in Western and Islamic Tradition* (New York: Greenwood Press, 1990), at 104–108.

111. Lieber Code, art. 81.

112. Lieber, *Guerrilla Parties,* at 36.

113. *Id.* at 35–36.

114. *Id.* at 39.

115. *Id.* at 36.

116. Confed. Act of Apr. 21, 1862, in James M. Matthews (ed.), *Statutes at Large of the Provisional Government of the Confederate States of America* (Richmond: R. M. Smith, 1864), at 48; *reproduced in* Confed. General Orders No. 30, Apr. 28, 1862, 1 (ser. 4)

OR 1094–1095. For provision for payment to partisans for arms and ammunition captured from the enemy and turned over to the Confederate government, see Confed. General Orders No. 47, Apr. 21, 1863, 2 (ser. 4) OR 498–499.

117. Jones, *Gray Ghosts,* at 313.

118. David J. Eicher, *The Longest Night: A Military History of the Civil War* (New York: Simon and Schuster, 2001), at 560–563, 695.

119. Lee to Cooper, Apr. 1, 1864, 33 (ser. 1) OR 1252.

120. Ould to Mulford, Jan. 19, 1865, 8 (ser. 2) OR 93.

121. Ould to Lee, Mar. 25, 1865, *id.* at 431–432.

122. Sheridan to Grant, Aug. 17, 1864, 43(2) (ser. 1) OR 822.

123. Lee to Cooper, Apr. 1, 1864, 33 (ser. 1) OR 1252.

124. *See* Sedden to Taylor, Sep. 27, 1864, 3 (ser. 4) OR 688–690.

125. Confed. Act of Feb. 17, 1864, 6 (ser. 2) OR 194.

126. *See* Hague Rules, art. 29.

127. For a contemporary discussion of spying, see Halleck, *International Law,* at 406–409.

128. This statement assumes, of course, that the captor state makes spying a criminal offense under its national law. *See also* General Orders No. 52, June 27, 1865, 8 (ser. 2) OR 674–681, at 680–681, where it is said that the *employment* of a spy by a belligerent power is not a war crime, but that the spy's *own* conduct is. This contention is of doubtful validity.

129. Act of Apr. 16, 1806, 2 Stat. 359, art. 101(2), at 371.

130. Act of Feb. 13, 1862, 12 Stat. 339, sec. 4, at 340. *See also,* on the treatment of spies, General Orders No. 13, Dec. 4, 1861, 1 (ser. 2) OR 233–236.

131. *See* Fuqua to Ruggles, Sep. 22, 1862, 4 (ser. 2) OR 894–897. The only exception was the case in which the alleged spy was enrolled in the Confederate military. This position was not consistently adhered to. *See,* for example, the notable case of the Andrews raiders, discussed below, who were tried by a military tribunal for spying. Perhaps the element of sabotage in that case accounted for this departure from the general policy.

132. Lieber Code, art. 84.

133. *See* Chapter 4.

134. Lieber, *Guerrilla Parties,* at 40.

135. Halleck to Price, Jan. 22, 1862, 1 (ser. 2) OR 258–259.

136. *See* Holt to Stanton, Mar. 27, 1863, 10(1) (ser. 1) OR 630–634. The leader, Andrews, was hanged prior to the trial of the seven. As a civilian, he had not even a *prima facie* claim to treatment as a lawful belligerent.

137. Sedden to McCulloh, Jan. 19, 1864, 3 (ser. 4) OR 37–38. McCulloh was apparently part of a group that planned systematic arson of Union ships. Oldham to Davis, Feb. 11, 1865, *id.* at 1078–1079. As the plan included burning Union-bound ships leav-

ing foreign ports, it may be doubted whether the law of nations was being given much consideration. For similarly approved plans, see Authorization of Seddon to Courtney, Mar. 9, 1864, *id.* at 202–203; and Authorization of Seddon to Kay, Mar. 12, 1864, *id.* at 210. *See also,* for a similar proposal, Williams to Davis, Aug. 1864, *id.* at 581–583.

138. Confederate Act of Feb. 17, 1864 (secret session), *id.* at 139.

139. *See* General Orders No. 24, Mar. 20, 1865, 8 (ser. 2) OR 414–416.

140. Ex p. Quirin, 317 U.S. 1 (1943). On this affair, see David J. Danielski, "The Saboteurs' Case," 1996(1) *Supreme Court History* 61–82; and Louis Fisher, *Nazi Saboteurs on Trial: A Military Tribunal and American Law* (Lawrence: University Press of Kansas, 2003).

141. Mohamed Ali v. Public Prosecutor, [1969] 1 A.C. 430. This involved Indonesian forces planting bombs in a nonmilitary building, leading to the deaths of three civilians. The ambiguity lies in the fact that the court focused primarily on the fact that the perpetrators were out of uniform, rather than on the civilian character of the target.

142. Lieber Code, art. 82.

143. *Id.*

144. Sherman to Burbridge, June 21, 1864, 39(2) (ser. 1) OR 135–136.

145. Ruggles to Butler, July 15, 1862, 15 (ser. 1) OR 519–521.

146. *Id.*

147. Holmes to Curtis, Oct. 11, 1862, 13 (ser. 1) OR 726–728.

148. Benjamin to Carroll, Dec. 10, 1861, 1 (ser. 2) OR 854; and Benjamin to Crittenden, Dec. 13, 1861, *id.* at 855–856.

149. General Orders No. 32, Dec. 22, 1861, *id.* at 237. For records of trials of various persons for bridge-burning, railroad destruction, and related violations of the laws of war, see 1 (ser 2) OR 374–504.

150. Schofield to Kelton, June 2, 1862, 13 (ser. 1) OR 410–411.

151. General Orders No. 28, July 20, 1862, 4 (ser. 2) OR 246–247.

152. General Orders No. 13, June 26, 1862, 13 (ser. 1) OR 451.

153. General Orders No. 7, June 6, 1862, *id.* at 420. For an example of an order to shoot three captured guerrillas, see Merrill to Denny, Sep. 23, 1862, *id.* at 660–661. *See also,* in the same vein, Sherman to Hindman, Oct. 17, 1862, *id.* at 742–743.

154. General Orders No. 7, July 10 (?), 1862, 12(2) (ser. 1) OR 51.

155. Special Orders No. 41, July 7, 1862, 13 (ser. 1) OR 464–465.

156. Houston to Wirt, Oct. 19, 1862, *id.* at 750.

157. General Orders No. 10, Aug. 18, 1863, 22(2) (ser. 1) OR 460–461.

158. Randolph to Harris, June 29, 1862, 4 (ser. 2) OR 793–794. *See also* Seddon to Breckenridge, Nov. 11, 1864, 43(2) (ser. 1) OR 920.

159. Parkhurst to Whipple, Mar. 1, 1865, 8 (ser. 2) OR 324–328, at 325. This report of Forrest's views was, in legal terminology, hearsay.

160. Hague Rules, art. 1.

161. In re List (Hostages case), U.S. Military Tribunal at Nuremberg, Feb. 19, 1948, 15 Int'l L. Rep. 632, at 640.

162. *Id.*

163. Hague Convention IV, preamble.

164. Protocol I of 1977, art. 44.

165. Second Lateran Council (1139), canon 11, in 1 Norman Tanner (ed.), *Decrees of the Ecumenical Councils* (London: Sheed and Ward, 1990), at 199. On immunities of various noncombatants in the Middle Ages, see Maurice Keen, *The Laws of War in the Late Middle Ages* (London: Routledge, 1965), at 189–217.

166. Vattel, *Law of Nations,* at 283.

167. Declaration of St. Petersburg, Dec 11, 1868, 138 C.T.S. 297. The United States, as it happened, was not represented at the conference and did not ever become a formal party to the Declaration.

168. Lieber Code, art. 25.

169. *Id.,* art. 22.

170. For a thoroughgoing study of Union military policies toward Southern civilians, see generally Grimsley, *Hard Hand.*

171. For the modern statement of this rule, see Protocol I of 1977, art. 51(7).

172. Nichol to Authorities of the Town of Rodney, June 5, 1862, 15 (ser. 1) OR 475.

173. Farragut to Lovell, June 17, 1862, *id* at 484–485.

174. Lovell to Commanding Officer, June 12, 1862, *id.* at 474–475.

175. Lincoln to Scott, Apr. 25, 1861, in 4 Basler, *Works,* at 344.

176. Lieber Code, art. 19.

177. Lee to Lindsay, May 21, 1862, 15 (ser. 1) OR 13.

178. Sumner to Mayor and Common Council of Fredericksburg, Nov. 21, 1862, 21 (ser. 1) OR 783; and Sumner to Mayor , Nov. 22, 1862, *id.* at 788.

179. Gillmore to Spanish Consul, Aug. 22, 1863, 28(2) (ser. 1) OR 61. *See generally* W. Chris Phelps, *The Bombardment of Charleston, 1863–1865* (Gretna, La.: Pelican, 2002).

180. Burnside to Jones, Sep. 22, 1863, 30(3) (ser. 1) OR 786.

181. Hood to Sherman, Sep. 12, 1864, 39(2) (ser. 1) OR 419–422, at 420.

182. Sherman to Hood, Sep. 14, 1864, *id.* at 422.

183. There are rules, however, on naval bombardment. *See* Hague Convention IX on Naval Bombardment, Oct. 18, 1907, 205 C.T.S. 345, 36 Stat. 2351.

184. General Orders No. 11, July 26, 1862, 4 (ser. 2) OR 290–291.

185. General Orders No. 15, June 16, 1862, 13 (ser. 1) OR 435.

186. Meng v. U.S. France-U.S. Claims Comm'n, Nov. 2, 1883, in 4 John Bassett Moore, *A History and Digest of the International Arbitrations to Which the United States Has Been a Party* (Washington, D.C.: GOP, 1898), at 3689. *See also,* to the same effect, Jardel v. U.S., Nov. 2, 1883, *id.* at 3699. This was not a reprisal measure because the civilians were found to have been wrongdoers in their own right.

187. General Orders No. 7, July 10 (?), 1862, 12(2) (ser. 1) OR 51.

188. Sherman to Rawlings, Sep. 25, 1862, 17(1) (ser. 1) OR 144–145.

189. Sherman to Curtis, Oct. 18, 1862, 13 (ser. 1) OR 747–748.

190. Special Field Orders No. 120, Nov. 9, 1864, 39(3) (ser. 1) OR 713–714.

191. *Id.*

192. General Orders No. 3, June 23, 1862, 13 (ser. 1) OR 446–447.

193. Sherman to Chase, Mar. 11, 1864, 32(3) (ser. 1) OR 54–55. The records do not disclose whether Sherman's proposed policy was actually carried out.

194. Vattel, *Law of Nations,* at 295.

195. Lieber Code, art. 15.

196. *Id.,* art. 16.

197. Sheridan to Torbert, Aug. 16, 1864, 43(1) (ser. 1) OR 816.

198. For a report of the damage done, see Sheridan to Grant, Oct. 7, 1864, *id.* at 30–31. On this campaign, see generally Gary W. Gallagher (ed.), *The Shenandoah Valley Campaign of 1864* (Chapel Hill: University of North Carolina Press, 2006).

199. Order Sheridan to Merritt, Nov. 27, 1864, *id.* at 55–56.

200. *See* Chapter 9.

201. Confed. Act of Mar. 17, 1862, 1 (ser. 4) OR 1006.

202. Randolph to Lovell, Apr. 25, 1862, 6 (ser. 1) OR 883. *See also* Randolph to Jones, May 65, 1862, *id.* at 886–887, concerning similar destruction in case of evacuation of Pensacola.

203. Alpine to Bell, June 20, 1862, 14 (ser. 1) OR 356–357.

204. General Orders No. 35, Apr. 27, 1863, 15 (ser. 1) OR 710.

205. General Orders No. 10, Aug. 18, 1863, 22(2) (ser. 1) OR 460–461.

206. General Orders No. 11, July 23, 1862, 12(2) (ser. 1) OR 52.

207. Grant to Sheridan, Aug. 16, 1864, 43(1) (ser. 1) OR 811. It would appear that this particular instruction was not carried out. For a similar order applying to the West Virginia area, see Sheridan, Circular, Aug. 19, 1864, *id.* at 843.

208. General Orders No. 11, Aug. 25, 1863, 22(2) (ser. 1) OR 473.

209. This particular measure has received significant attention from historians. *See,* for example, Albert Castel, "Order No. 11 and the Civil War on the Border," 47 *Missouri Historical Review* 357–368 (1963); Ann Davis Niepman, "General Orders No. 11 and Border Warfare during the Civil War," 66 *Missouri Historical Review* 185–210 (1972); Charles R. Mink, "General Orders, No. 11: The Forced Evacuation of Civilians during the Civil War," 34 *Military Affairs* 132–136 (1980); and Mark E. Neely, Jr, "'Unbenownst' to Lincoln: A Note on Radical Pacification in Missouri during the Civil War," 44 *Civil War History* 212–216 (1998). It caught the attention also of the noted American artist George Caleb Bingham, who did a painting of the subject, with Ewing prominently placed in it. Niepman, "General Orders No. 11," at 208. Ewing pursued a political career after the war, in which the incident was used against him by his opponents.

210. Halleck to Schofield, Sep. 6, 1862, 13 (ser. 1) OR 616.

211. Bruce Catton, *Terrible Swift Sword* (Garden City, N.Y.: Doubleday, 1963), at 384–385.

212. *See,* for example, Vattel, *Law of Nations,* at 292–294; and Lieber Code, art. 15. *See also* Dow v. Johnson, 100 U.S. 158 (1880).

213. *See* Norris v. Doniphan, 61 Ky. 385 (1863); and Terrill v. Rankin, 65 Ky. 453 (1867). *See also* General Orders No. Oct. 11, 1864, 7 (ser. 2) OR 964–965. *See* Chapter 9 on compensation to Union nationals and loyal Southerners for requisitions.

214. *See,* for example, General Orders No. 8, Nov. 26, 1861, 8 (ser. 1) OR 280–281, issued by Halleck, relating to Missouri.

215. *See* Grant to Commanding Officers, Dec. 8, 1862, 17(2) (ser. 1) OR 393–394; and Special Field Orders No. 35, Dec. 29, 1862, *id.* at 505–506.

216. On this foraging policy, see Grimsley, *Hard Hand,* at 98–105.

217. General Orders No. 5 and 6, July 18, 1862, 12(2) (ser. 1) OR 50.

218. General Orders No. 5, *id.*

219. Special Field Orders No. 120, Nov. 9, 1864, 39(3) (ser. 1) OR 713–714.

220. Capture at sea was governed by a different set of rules. *See* Chapter 8.

221. In technical legal terms, it would be said that it was only necessary that the captured property *itself* have what lawyers call "enemy character."

222. Vattel, *Law of Nations,* at 307–308; and Halleck, *International Law,* at 451. *See also* Lamar v. Browne, 92 U.S. 187 (1876).

223. Vattel, *Law of Nations,* at 259.

224. It contained a restriction on the taking of private property (in art. 38), but this appears to be only in the context of occupation of territory, not of belligerent operations generally. *See,* however, the dissent of Justice Field in Prott v. U.S., 87 U.S. (20 Wall.) 459 (1874), which forcefully contended that the right of capture of private property was now obsolete. For a cautiously equivocal position on the subject, see Halleck, *International Law,* at 446–447.

225. Act of Mar. 12, 1863, 12 Stat. 820.

226. For the federal Supreme Court's endorsement of this view, see Mrs. Alexander's Cotton, 69 U.S. (2 Wall.) 404 (1865), at 419–420.

227. John Syrett, *The Civil War Confiscation Acts: Failing to Reconstruct the South* (New York: Fordham University Press, 2005), at 142.

228. *See,* to this effect, General Orders No. 88, Mar. 31, 1863, 18 (ser. 1) OR 580–582. On the role of the Treasury Department in this process, see Syrett, *Civil War Confiscation Acts,* at 107–113.

229. Mrs. Alexander's Cotton, 69 U.S. (2 Wall.) 404 (1865), at 420. On this case, see Robert Bruce Murray, *Legal Cases of the Civil War* (Mechanicsburg, Pa.: Stackpole, 2003), at 191–197.

230. U.S. v. Padelford, 76 U.S. (9 Wall.) 531 (1870), at 540–541. *See also* Lamar v. Browne, 92 U.S. 187 (1876).

231. U.S. v. Klein, 80 U.S. (13 Wall.) 128 (1872), at 136–138. *See also,* to the same effect, Bernheimer v. U.S., 5 Ct. of Claims 549 (1869).

232. Young v. U.S., 97 U.S. (7 Otto) 39 (1878). *See also,* to the same effect, Briggs v. U.S., 143 U.S. 346 (1892).

233. For other confiscation mechanisms, see Chapter 4.

234. Act of Mar. 12, 1863, 12 Stat. 820, sec. 3.

235. *See* Chapter 9.

236. *See generally* Stig Förster and Jörg Nagler (eds.), *On the Road to Total War: The American Civil War and the German Wars of Unification, 1861–1871* (Cambridge: Cambridge University Press, 1997).

237. Lieber Code, art. 21.

238. John E. Clark, Jr., *Railroads in the Civil War: The Impact of Management on Victory and Defeat* (Baton Rouge: Louisiana State University Press, 2001), at 37.

239. Sherman to Grant, July 14, 1863, 24(2) (ser. 1) OR 525–527.

240. Halleck to Sherman, Sep. 28, 1864, *id.* at 503. *See also,* to the same effect, Halleck to Sherman, Sep. 26, 1864, *id.* at 480.

241. General Orders No. 17, Nov. 10, 1864, 39(2) (ser. 1) OR 729–730.

242. Report by Sherman, Jan. 1, 1865, 44 (ser. 1) OR 7–16, at 13.

243. Russell F. Weigley, *A Great Civil War: A Military and Political History, 1861–1865* (Bloomington: Indiana University Press, 2000), at 393.

244. *See* Grimsley, *Hard Hand,* at 190–204.

245. For brief accounts of the March to the Sea, see Weigley, *Great Civil War,* at 387–96; and Grimsley, *Hard Hand,* at 190–200. For more detailed accounts, see Richard Wheeler, *Sherman's March* (New York: Crowell, 1978); Burke Davis, *Sherman's March* (New York: Random House, 1980); Joseph T. Glatthaar, *The March to the Sea and Beyond: Sherman's Troops in the Savannah and Carolinas Campaigns* (New York: New York University Press, 1986); and Anne J. Bailey, *War and Ruin: William T. Sherman and the Savannah Campaign* (Wilmington, Del.: Scholarly Resources, 2003).

246. *See* Cooper to Beauregard, Feb. 20, 1865, 47(2) (ser. 1) OR 1228; Lee to Johnston, Feb. 23, 1865, *id.* at 1256–1257; and Lee to Beauregard, Feb. 25, 1865, *id.* at 1272. For the statutory authorization of the policy, see Confed. Act of Mar. 17, 1862, 1 (ser. 4) OR 1006.

247. Brown and Sharp v. U.S., in 4 Moore, *Arbitrations,* at 3675–3677.

248. For a brief account of the Carolinas phase of Sherman's march, see Grimsley, *Hard Hand,* at 200–204. For a more detailed one, see John G. Barrett, *Sherman's March through the Carolinas* (Chapel Hill: University of North Carolina Press, 1956).

4. Occupying Territory and Seizing Property

Epigraph: Stanton to Lincoln, Dec. 1, 1862, 2 (ser. 3) OR 897–912, at 912.

1. On the early experiences of occupation of Confederate territory, see Mark Grimsley, *The Hard Hand of War: Union Military Policy toward Southern Civilians, 1861–1865* (Cambridge: Cambridge University Press, 1995), at 47–66.

2. Louisiana became the main laboratory for Union occupation and reconstruction policies. *See generally* Peyton McCrary, *Abraham Lincoln and Reconstruction: The Louisiana Experiment* (Princeton: Princeton University Press, 1978).

3. On the occupation of Confederate territory, see J. G. Randall, *Constitutional Problems under Lincoln* (New York: Appleton, 1926), at 215–238.

4. For further consideration of this point, see Chapter 9.

5. *See,* for example, William Sumner, "Our Domestic Relations; Or How to Treat the Rebel States," 12 *Atlantic Monthly* 507–529 (1863), at 518–519.

6. Constitution, Art. I, sec. 5.

7. Herman Belz, *Reconstructing the Union: Theory and Policy during the Civil War* (Ithaca, N.Y.: Cornell University Press, 1969), at 45–48.

8. On the Wheeling government, see *id.* at 29–32.

9. Bruce Tap, *Over Lincoln's Shoulder: The Committee on the Conduct of the War* (Lawrence: University Press of Kansas, 1998), at 223–224.

10. Belz, *Reconstructing,* at 45.

11. The Circassian, 69 U.S. (2 Wall.) 135 (1865), at 158–159. Also in favor of this approach was Henry Everett Russell, "Reconstruction," 4 *Continental Monthly* 684–689 (1863).

12. Dow v. Johnson, 100 U.S. 158 (1879). The Tennessee Supreme Court also expressly rejected the reversion theory. *See* Rutledge v. Fogg, 43 Tenn. 554 (1866).

13. On the law of belligerent occupation as it then stood, see Henry W. Halleck, *International Law; or Rules Regulating the Intercourse of States* (New York: Van Nostrand, 1861), at 775–809.

14. General Orders No. 100, Apr. 24, 1863, 5 (ser. 2) OR 671–682; *reprinted in* Richard Shelly Hartigan, *Lieber's Code and the Law of War* (Chicago: Precedent, 1983), at 45–71 (hereafter Lieber Code), arts. 1, 3.

15. *Id.,* art. 6.

16. *Id.,* arts. 90–92.

17. On spies and spying, see Chapter 3.

18. Lieber Code, art. 85.

19. *Id.,* art. 4.

20. *See,* for example, Buell to Thomas, Aug. 8, 1862, 16(2) (ser. 1) OR 290.

21. For a lucid discussion of this fascinating subject, see Richard R. Baxter, "The Duty of Obedience to the Belligerent Occupant," 27 *Brit. Y.B. of Inter'l L.* 235–266 (1950).

22. More properly, the term "military government" is preferable to "martial law" for describing belligerent occupation. *See* Opinion of Chase, in Ex p. Milligan, 71 U.S. (4 Wall.) 2 (1866), at 141–142.

23. On martial law imposed in Union areas, see Chapter 2.

24. *See* Bell to Benham, Apr. 15, 1862, 14 (ser. 1) OR 333–334, referring to the imposition of martial law three days earlier.

25. *See* General Orders No. 11, May 9, 1862, *id.* at 341, referring to the imposition of martial law on April 25.

26. Proc. of Gen. Benjamin Butler, May 6, 1862, 6 (ser. 1) OR 717–720.

27. General Orders No. 41, June 10, 1862, 15 (ser. 1) OR 483.

28. Thorington v. Smith, 75 U.S. (8 Wall.) 1 (1868). *See* Chapter 9 for a fuller discussion of this topic.

29. *See*, on this point, Emmerich de Vattel, *The Law of Nations; or The Principles of Natural Law Applied to the Conduct and to the Affairs of Nations and of Sovereigns* (trans. Charles G. Fenwick; Washington, D.C.: Carnegie Institution 1916 [1758]), at 307–308.

30. Hugo Grotius, *On the War and Peace* (trans. Francis W. Kelsey; Oxford: Clarendon Press, 1925 [1625]), at 667.

31. The right is unlimited, that is, in the eyes of *international* law. It is possible that the domestic constitutional arrangements of the conquering state could impose limits on rights over conquered territories.

32. For an excellent exposition of distinction between conquest and occupation, see U.S. v. Huckabee, 83 U.S. (16 Wall.) 414 (1873). *See also* Halleck, *International Law,* at 810–813.

33. The nearest example was probably the acquisition of West Florida by the United States during the War of 1812—the only territorial gain made by the country during the course of that struggle. That acquisition, however, is probably best regarded as an occupation of territory arising from a condition of necessity—as was, in effect, asserted by the American government itself—with actual title passing to the United States by virtue not of conquest but by cession, in the Adams-Onís Treaty of Feb. 22, 1819, 70 C.T.S. 1, 8 Stat. 252, art. 2. Similarly, territorial gains at the expense of Mexico in 1848 and Spain in 1898 came about by treaty (i.e., by cession) and not by conquest in the strict legal sense.

34. Constitution, Art. IV, sec. 3.

35. *See* Chapter 9 for further consideration of the question of conquest in the wake of the conflict.

36. U.S. v. Reiter, 27 Fed. Cas. 768 (No. 16,146) (Prov. Ct. of La. 1865).

37. The Grapeshot, 76 U.S. (9 Wall.) 129 (Dec. 1869 term). The immediate issue concerned the authority, if any, for the President's creation, by executive order, of a judicial body called the Provisional Court of Louisiana. *See also* the Tennessee Supreme Court case of Rutledge v. Fogg, 43 Tenn. 554 (1866); and the North Carolina Supreme Court case of Paul v. Carpenter, 70 N.C. 502 (1874).

38. Dow v. Johnson, 100 U.S. 158 (1879).

39. *See* Charles Russell, " 'Our Domestic Relations; or How to Treat the Rebel States,' " 5 *Continental Monthly* 511–516 (1864), at 512–514. *See also* U.S. v. Reiter, 27 Fed. Cas. 768 (No. 16,146) (Prov. Ct. of La. 1865).

40. On the experience with military governors, see Harold M. Hyman, *A More Perfect Union: The Impact of the Civil War and Reconstruction on the Constitution* (New York: Knopf, 1973), at 207–214.

41. Proc. No. 11, Dec. 8, 1863, 13 Stat. 737; *reprinted in* 7 Basler, *Works,* at 53–56.

42. James M. McPherson, *Battle Cry of Freedom: The Civil War Era* (New York: Oxford University Press, 1988), at 712.

43. A bill is "pocket vetoed" when it is passed by Congress within ten days prior to an adjournment and then simply not signed by the President. Ordinarily, a bill becomes law if the President goes for ten days (excluding Sundays) without either signing or vetoing.

44. Lincoln, Proclamation Concerning Reconstruction, July 8, 1864, in 7 Basler, *Works,* at 433–434. On the Wade-Davis proposal, see Belz, *Reconstructing,* at 198–243.

45. Ruth Caroline Cowen, "Reorganization of Federal Arkansas, 1862–1865," 18(2) *Ark. Historical Quarterly* 132–157 (1959), at 151–156.

46. Charles Fairman, *Reconstruction and Reunion 1864–1868,* pt. 1 (New York: Macmillan, 1971), at 97.

47. On the creation of the state of West Virginia, see Randall, *Constitutional Problems,* at 433–476; James C. McGregor, *The Disruption of Virginia* (New York: Macmillan, 1922); and George E. Moore, *A Banner in the Hills: West Virginia's Statehood* (New York: Appleton-Century-Crofts, 1963). *See also* Virginia v. West Virginia, 78 U.S. (11 Wall.) 39 (1871).

48. Constitution, Art. IV, sec. 3.

49. Bates, Act for the Admission of West Virginia into the Union, Dec. 27, 1862, 10 Op. A-G 426.

50. Lincoln, Opinion on the Admission of West Virginia into the Union, Dec. 31, 1862, 6 Basler, *Works,* at 26–28.

51. Act of Dec. 31, 1862, 12 Stat. 633.

52. *See* Vasan Kesavani and Michael Stokes Paulsen, "Is West Virginia Unconstitutional?" 90 *California Law Rev.* 291–400 (2002). The question is answered in the negative.

53. Virginia v. West Virginia, 78 U.S. (11 Wall.) 39 (1871). *See also* Fairman, *Reconstruction,* at 619–627.

54. *See* Virginia v. West Virginia, 206 U.S. 290 (1906); and Virginia v. West Virginia, 246 U.S. 565 (1918).

55. On constitutional aspects of confiscation, see Randall, *Constitutional Problems,* at 275–315.

56. *See* Chapter 3.

57. Confed. Act of May 21, 1861, in James M. Matthews (ed.), *Statutes at Large of the Provisional Government of the Confederate States of America* (Richmond, Va.: R. M. Smith, 1864), at 151.

58. *See* Daniel W. Hamilton, "The Confederate Sequestration Act," 52 *Civil War History* 373–408 (2006).

59. On captured and abandoned property, see Chapters 3 and 9.

60. Act of July 13, 1861, 12 Stat. 255.

61. For the President's proclamation, see Proc. No. 9, Aug. 16, 1861, 12 Stat. 1262.

62. Constitution, art. I, sec. 9.

63. The Sarah Starr, 21 Fed. Cas. 462 (No. 12,352) (DC SD N.Y., 1861), at 468. *See also,* to the same effect, U.S. v. 129 Packages, 27 Fed. Cas. 284 (No. 15,941) (DC ED Mo., 1862), at 287.

64. Act of Aug. 6, 1861, 12 Stat. 319. On the enactment of the law, see Silvana R. Siddali, *From Property to Person: Slavery and the Confiscation Acts, 1861–1862* (Baton Rouge: Louisiana State University Press, 2005), at 76–94.

65. On the First Confiscation Act, see generally Rufus Waples, *A Treatise on Proceedings in Rem* (Chicago: Callaghan, 1882), at 432–461.

66. *See* Chapter 5.

67. Porter v. Botts, 63 Ky. 365 (1866).

68. Armstrong's Foundry, 73 U.S. (6 Wall.) 766 (1868).

69. Kirk v. Lynd, 106 U.S. 315 (1882). *See* Chapter 9 for a fuller consideration of this case, in the context of the legal effect of pardons.

70. There were very marginal exceptions to this principle, notably the case of spying, in which states were permitted to invoke their criminal law against enemy soldiers. On spying, see Chapter 3.

71. Prize Cases, 67 U.S. (2 Black) 635 (1863), at 673.

72. On the operation, and practical ineffectiveness, of the First Confiscation Act, see generally John Syrett, *The Civil War Confiscation Acts: Failing to Reconstruct the South* (New York: Fordham University Press, 2005), at 1–19.

73. Confed. Act of Aug. 30, 1861, 1 (ser. 4) OR 586.

74. Confed. Act of Feb. 15, 1862, *id.* at 932.

75. Fairman, *Reconstruction,* at 779; William C. Davis, *Look Away! A History of the Confederate States of America* (New York: Free Press, 2002), at 380–381; and Clement Eaton, *History of the Southern Confederacy* (New York: Macmillan, 1954), at 234. There is a slight discrepancy in the figures given by these sources. Imports and exports were of course severely hampered by the Union blockade.

76. Act of Aug. 5, 1861, 12 Stat. 292, sec. 8–48, at 294–309.

77. On the apportionment of direct taxes among the states, see Chapter 2.

78. Act of June 7, 1862, 12 Stat. 422.

79. *See* Chapter 3 for a fuller discussion of this question.

80. Opinion of Justice Jones, in Martin v. Snowden, 59 Va. 100 (1868), at 131–132.

81. *See* Taylor's Administrator v. U.S., 14 Ct of Claims 339 (1878).

82. *See* McKee v. U.S., 164 U.S. 287 (1896).

83. U.S. v. Taylor, 104 U.S. 216 (1881).

84. On the policy of confiscations for arrears of the direct tax, see Randall, *Constitutional Problems,* at 317–323.

85. *See,* for example, Bennett v. Hunter, 76 U.S. (9 Wall.) 326 (1870); and Tracy v.

Irwin, 85 U.S. (18 Wall.) 549 (1873). The sixty-day period in the legislation was therefore interpreted, in effect, as simply a period of grace, during which the federal government would not act against the land, rather than as a restriction on the right of the
taxpayer to pay the tax. For persuasive doubts as to the constitutionality of any requirement of personal payment, see Lee v. Kaufman, 15 Fed. Cas. 204 (No. 8192) (CC ED
Va., 1879). On the *Bennett* case, see Robert Bruce Murray, *Legal Cases of the Civil War*
(Mechanicsburg, Pa.: Stackpole, 2003), at 137–143.

86. *See* U.S. v. Lee, 106 U.S. 196 (1882). On the Arlington Cemetery matter, see
Randall, *Constitutional Problems,* at 320–322.

87. Act of July 17, 1862, 12 Stat. 589.

88. *See* Chapter 6.

89. It may be noted that confiscation proceedings were provided for in the marginal case in which a convicted person had insufficient cash on hand to pay fines that
might be imposed. In such instances, property could be levied on, to the amount of
the fine owing.

90. The creation of the sixth category enabled the federal government to confiscate the property of *disloyal* Confederate residents, located in Union territory. It will be
recalled, in this regard, that the Union never adopted a policy of either sequestering or
confiscating property of Confederate residents generally.

91. On the adoption of the Second Confiscation Act, see Fairman, *Reconstruction,*
at 780–784; Patricia M. L. Lucie, "Confiscation: Constitutional Crossroads," 23 *Civil
War History* 302–321 (1977); Grimsley, *Hard Hand,* at 68–70, 75–78; Siddali, *From
Property to Person,* at 120–144; and Syrett, *Civil War Confiscation Acts,* at 20–50.

92. *See* Lincoln, Message to the Congress, July 17, 1862, 5 Basler, *Works,* at 328–331.

93. Constitution, Art. III, sec. 3. It is somewhat odd that this provision, dealing
with a power of Congress, appears in the article of the Constitution concerning the judicial branch of the government.

94. For a useful exposition of this obscure subject, see Max Stier, "Corruption of
Blood and Equal Protection: Why the Sins of the Parents Should Not Matter," 44
Stanford Law Rev. 727–57 (1992).

95. Res. No. 63, July 17, 1862, 12 Stat. 627.

96. The Supreme Court confirmed this in Conrad v. Waples, 96 U.S. 279 (1878).

97. Proc. No. 15, July 25, 1862, 12 Stat. 1266; *reprinted in* 5 Basler, *Works,* at 341–342.

98. In the case of the tax-arrears program, the policy from the beginning—applicable both North and South—had been that real property was to be charged with payment of the tax, meaning that there was a prior association between land and tax
payment. The confiscation policy built on that preexisting association.

99. On the postwar confiscation cases in the Supreme Court, see generally Daniel
W. Hamilton, "A New Right to Property: Civil War Confiscation in the Reconstruction Supreme Court," 29 *J. Supreme Court History* 254–285 (2004).

100. Miller v. U.S., 78 U.S. (11 Wall.) 268 (1871). The case concerned the confiscation of shares of stock. On this decision, see Murray, *Legal Cases,* at 205–213; Harry N. Schreiber, "Property Rights versus 'Public Necessity': A Perspective on Emergency Powers and the Supreme Court," 28 *J. Supreme Court History* 339–369 (2003), at 350–352; and Syrett, *Civil War Confiscation Acts,* at 169–174.

101. As noted above, the act did create criminal offenses. But these were separate from the actual confiscation provisions.

102. On the principal confiscation cases, see Fairman, *Reconstruction,* at 800–812; and Syrett, *Civil War Confiscation Acts,* at 169–184.

103. For opinions in a similar vein, see Field's dissenting opinion in Tyler v. Defrees, 78 U.S. (11 Wall.) 331 (1871). *See also* Conrad v. Waples, 96 U.S. 279 (1878), at 285.

104. *See* Randall, *Constitutional Problems,* at 307, for the cautious conclusion that the proceedings had "at least a quasi-criminal character."

105. *See* Austin v. U.S., 509 U.S. 602 (1993), where the specific issue was the applicability of the Eighth Amendment ban on "excessive fines." In this case, unlike the Civil War ones, the forfeiture proceedings were in conjunction with an actual criminal prosecution, although technically distinct from them. Also, this case gave no consideration to questions of belligerents' rights. But it appears likely that stand-alone forfeiture proceedings, such as the Civil War ones, would similarly be held to be penal at least in part.

106. *See,* for example, Stanton to Schofield, Sep. 5, 1862, 13 (ser. 1) OR 614, referring to the Missouri theater of war; followed by General Orders No. 19, Sep. 11, 1862, *id.* at 624–625. *See also* General Orders No. 34, Sep. 17, 1862, 50(2) (ser. 1) OR 125–126, concerning the Pacific Department; and General Orders No. 73, Sep. 18, 1862, 15 (ser. 1) OR 572–573, relating to the Gulf Department. *See also* General Orders No. 30, Apr. 26, 1864, 33 (ser. 1) OR 989–990, on property sequestration in Maryland.

107. Executive Order, Nov. 13, 1862, 2 (ser. 2) OR 765–766.

108. Hyman, *More Perfect Union,* at 177–181. *See,* for example, Bates to Wallace, May 25, 1864, 4 (ser. 3) OR 407–409, in which Bates asked General Lew Wallace to stop his sequestration efforts in Maryland. *See also* Stanton to Wallace, June 11, 1864, *id.* at 431. For a direct chiding of Bates by General Wallace for laggardly enforcement, see Wallace to Bates, Aug. 30, 1864, 4 (ser. 3) OR 413–415. On the enforcement of the Second Confiscation Act, see generally Syrett, *Civil War Confiscation Acts,* at 55–72.

109. Randall, *Constitutional Problems,* at 291. Echoing this conclusion is Siddali, *From Property to Person,* at 245–250.

5. The End of a Peculiar Institution

Epigraph: Civil Rights Cases, 109 U.S. 3 (1883), at 20.

1. *Institutes of Justinian* (ed. J. B. Moyle; Oxford: Clarendon Press, 1889), 1.2.2; and 1.3.2. *See also The Digest of Justinian* (ed. Theodor Mommsen; trans. Alan Watson; Philadelphia: University of Pennsylvania Press, 1985), 1.5.4.1; and 12.6.64.

2. The Antelope, 23 U.S. (10 Wheaton) 66 (1825).

3. Lieber Code, art. 42. The terminology here was somewhat imprecise, with the expression "law of nature and nations" referring to natural law. Chief Justice John Marshall, in the 1825 *Antelope* judgment, distinguished between the two, holding slavery to be contrary to the law of *nature* (i.e., to eternal principles of morality) but allowed by the law of *nations,* which was an expression of the custom or practice of states.

4. Prigg v. Pennsylvania, 41 U.S. (16 Pet.) 539 (1842), at 612–613. Concerning this case, see Paul Finkelman, "*Prigg v. Pennsylvania:* Understanding Joseph Story's Proslavery Nationalism," 1997(2) *J. Supreme Court History* 51–64 (1997).

5. *See* The Emancipation Proclamation Cases, 31 Tex. 504 (1868), at 525.

6. Michael Vorenberg, *Final Freedom: The Civil War, the Abolition of Slavery, and the Thirteenth Amendment* (Cambridge: Cambridge University Press, 2001), at 24.

7. *See* Chapter 3 on occupation of territory.

8. For material on the Union military experience with fugitive slaves, see generally 1 (ser. 2) OR 749–822.

9. For an account of the kind of conditions runaway slaves faced, see Cam Walker, "Corinth: The Story of a Contraband Camp," 20 *Civil War History* 5–22 (1974).

10. Speed, Bounty to Colored Troops, Oct. 17, 1865, 11 Op. A-G 365.

11. Act of Sep. 18, 1850, 9 Stat. 462.

12. Bates to McDowell, July 23, 1861, 1 (ser. 2) OR 761.

13. General Orders No. 3, Nov. 20, 1861, 1 (ser. 2) OR 778. Fugitive slaves who were taken on as personal servants by Union officers could be retained. Halleck to Asboth, Dec. 26, 1861, *id.* at 796. *See also* Curtis to Bassett, Mar. 1, 1863, 22(2) (ser. 1) OR 134–135. For Sherman's order, see Sherman to Turchin, Oct. 15, 1861, 1 (ser. 2) OR 774; and Sherman to McCook, Nov. 8, 1861, *id.* at 777.

14. Holt to Stanton, Aug. 17, 1863, 6 (ser. 2) OR 209–211, at 211.

15. Halleck to Asboth, Dec. 26, 1861, 1 (ser. 2) OR 796. For a fuller explanation of this policy, see Halleck to Farrar, Dec. 18, 1861, *id.* at 788–789. On military attitudes and policy toward slavery, see Mark Grimsley, *The Hard Hand of War: Union Military Policy toward Southern Civilians, 1861–1865* (Cambridge: Cambridge University Press, 1995), at 121–129.

16. Butler to Scott, May 24, 1861, 1 (ser. 2) OR 752. For approval of this policy by Secretary of War Simon Cameron, see Cameron to Butler, May 30, 1861, *id.* at 754–755; and Cameron to Butler, Aug. 8, 1861, *id.* at 761–762.

17. Cameron to Sherman, Oct. 11, 1861, *id.* at 773.

18. For early development of the law of contraband of war, see Stephen C. Neff, *The Rights and Duties of Neutrals: A General History* (Manchester: Manchester University Press, 2000), at 19–21, 32–34.

19. This practice of treating humans as contraband played a central role in the *Trent* Affair, which is discussed in Chapter 7.

20. *See* The Emancipation Proclamation Cases, 31 Tex. 504 (1868).

21. *See* Chapter 4.

22. Cameron, Report of Dec. 6, 1861, 1 (ser. 2) OR 783.

23. Cameron to Sherman, Oct. 11, 1861, *id.* at 773.

24. Edward L. Pierce, "The Contrabands at Fortress Monroe," 8 *Atlantic Monthly* (1861), at 627.

25. Butler to Scott, May 27, 1861, 1 (ser. 2) OR 754.

26. Allen C. Guelzo, *Lincoln's Emancipation Proclamation: The End of Slavery in America* (New York: Simon and Schuster, 2004), at 78–79. The problem of proof was substantially the same as it was for the First Confiscation Act, which in effect was a following-up of General Butler's contraband policy. On the First Confiscation Act, see Chapter 4.

27. For an early reference to "colored persons called contrabands," see Special Orders No. 72, Oct. 14, 1861, *id.* at 774, issued by Major General John Wool, commanding at Fort Monroe, Virginia. *See also* McCook to Sherman, Nov. 5, 1861, *id.* at 776; Saxton to Meigs, Nov. 9, 1861, *id.* at 777; and Hunt to Totten, Jan. 12, 1862, *id.* at 799–802.

28. House Res. of July 9, 1861, *id.* at 759.

29. Act of Mar. 13, 1862, 12 Stat. 354.

30. Act of July 17, 1862, 12 Stat. 589, sec. 10, at 591. The March 1862 act barred the military from actively engaging in the capture and return of slaves. The later act barred the "passive" surrendering of slaves who fled into the Union military lines.

31. General Orders No. 109, Aug. 15, 1862, 2 (ser. 3) OR 397, quoting a presidential order of July 22, 1862.

32. General Orders No. 154, Aug. 9, 1862, 11(3) (ser. 1) OR 362–364.

33. Act of Aug. 6, 1861, 12 Stat. 319, sec. 4.

34. Holt to Stanton, Aug. 17, 1863, 6 (ser. 2) OR 209–211.

35. Act of July 17, 1862, 12 Stat. 589. For further detail on these offenses, see Chapter 6. On the main features of this legislation see Chapter 4.

36. Lincoln, Message to Senate and House, July 17, 1862, in 5 Basler, *Works,* at 329.

37. Act of July 17, 1862, 12 Stat. 589, sec. 9, at 591.

38. Holt to Stanton, Aug. 17, 1863, 6 (ser. 2) OR 209–211.

39. General Orders No. 9, Aug. 8, 1863, 22(2) (ser. 1) OR 460. The act was not explicitly named in the orders; but the operative date from which disloyalty was judged was July 17, 1862, the date the act became law.

40. Lieber Code, art. 43.

41. It should be borne in mind that, by the time the Lieber Code was issued, in April 1863, the Emancipation Proclamation had been promulgated, which (as will be explained) had discarded the policy of distinguishing between loyal and disloyal slaveowners in the affected area. It should also be noted that the Lieber Code provision only

applied to slaves from the enemy side, thereby excluding slaves from the border states, and possibly from occupied Confederate areas.

42. *See* Guelzo, *Emancipation Proclamation,* at 77–81.

43. *See,* for example, Kenneth M. Stampp, *The Era of Reconstruction, 1865–1877* (New York: Vintage, 1965), at 42.

44. On martial law generally, see Chapters 3 and 6.

45. Proc. of Aug. 30, 1861, 1 (ser. 2) OR 221–222. *See also* two deeds of manumission of individual slaves issued by Fremont, *id.* at 769–770. On this affair, see Guelzo, *Emancipation Proclamation,* at 42–54; and Silvana R. Siddali, *From Property to Person: Slavery and the Confiscation Acts, 1861–1862* (Baton Rouge: Louisiana State University Press, 2005), at 99–109.

46. Lincoln to Fremont, Sep. 2, 1861, 3 (ser. 1) OR 469–470; *reprinted in* 4 Basler, *Works,* at 506.

47. Fremont to Lincoln, Sep. 8, 1861, 3 (ser. 1) OR 477–478; and Lincoln to Fremont, Sep. 11, 1861, *id.* at 485-486, *reprinted in* 4 Basler, *Works,* at 517–518.

48. General Orders No. 7, Apr. 13, 1862, 1 (ser. 2) OR 815.

49. General Orders No. 11, May 9, 1862, *id.* at 818.

50. Proc. No. 13, May 19, 1862, 12 Stat. 1264; *reprinted in* 5 Basler, *Works,* at 222–224. On this incident, see Guelzo, *Emancipation Proclamation,* at 72–75.

51. Lincoln to Browning, Sep. 22, 1861, in 4 Basler, *Works,* at 531–533.

52. *See* Chapter 2 for a discussion of Lincoln's assertion, in effect, of broad legislative powers under the commander-in-chief power.

53. Constitution, Art. I, sec. 8.

54. Act of Apr. 16, 1862, 12 Stat. 376.

55. It was at least arguable that the Fifth Amendment duty of compensation was not applicable, since the slaves were not being "taken for public use." This interesting point was not, however, pressed.

56. Message to Congress, Apr. 16, 1862, in 5 Basler, *Works,* at 192.

57. Michael J. Kurtz, "Emancipation in the Federal City," 24 Civil War History 250–267 (1978). This is a very informative article, based on a close study of the records of the board. On emancipation in the District of Columbia, see also Guelzo, *Emancipation Proclamation,* at 81–91.

58. Act of June 19, 1862, 12 Stat. 432.

59. On questions of foreign recognition of the Confederacy, see Chapter 7.

60. On the Emancipation Proclamation generally, see John Hope Franklin, *The Emancipation Proclamation* (Edinburgh: Edinburgh University Press, 1963); and Guelzo, *Emancipation Proclamation.*

61. Proc. No. 16, Sep. 22, 1862, 12 Stat. 1267; *reprinted in* 5 Basler, *Works,* at 433–436.

62. The Preliminary Proclamation was also issued in the form of military orders

directly to the armed forces. *See* General Orders No. 139, Sep. 22, 1862, 15 (ser. 1) OR 621–623.

63. Constitution, Art. II, sec. 3.

64. On compensation issues in the aftermath of the war, see Chapter 10.

65. Emancipation Proclamation (Proc. No. 17), Jan. 1, 1863, 12 Stat. 1268; *reprinted in* 6 Basler, *Works,* at 28–31.

66. *See* General Orders No. 1, Jan. 2, 1863, 3 (ser. 3) OR 2–3.

67. Holt to Stanton, May 25, 1864, 7 (ser. 2) OR 159–162.

68. *See,* for example, Schofield to Stanton, July 17, 1863, 3 (ser. 3) OR 525–526.

69. Seddon to Davis, Nov. 3, 1864, 3 (ser. 4) OR 756–771, at 769.

70. Opinion of Justice Samuel Nelson in The Prize Cases, 67 U.S. (2 Black) 635 (1863), at 693–696.

71. For the details of these policies, see Chapter 3. On the compensation arrangements as they actually worked out after the war, see Chapter 9.

72. Seddon to Davis, Nov. 3, 1864, 3 (ser. 4) OR 756–771, at 770.

73. Act of Sep. 16, 1850, 9 Stat. 462.

74. Bates to Bradford, May 10, 1862, 1 (ser. 2) OR 817.

75. Act of July 17, 1862, 12 Stat. 589, sec. 10, at 591. On ironclad oaths and the legal issues to which they gave rise, see Chapter 6.

76. Act of June 28, 1864, 13 Stat. 200.

77. On the repeal, see Don E. Fehrenbacher, *The Slaveholding Republic: An Account of the United States Government's Relations to Slavery* (Oxford: Oxford University Press, 2001), at 248–250.

78. Constitution, Art. IV, sec. 2. The provision even went on to add that the escaped slave "shall be delivered up on Claim of the Party to whom [his] Service or Labour may be due."

79. *See* Commonwealth v. Palmer, 65 Ky. 570 (1866). The prosecution appears to have been discontinued.

80. For a vigorous exposition of the thesis that the President's commander-in-chief power did not extend so far, see Benjamin R. Curtis, "Executive Power," in Frank Freidel (ed.), *Union Pamphlets of the Civil War, 1861–1865* (Cambridge, Mass.: Harvard University Press, 1967), at 456–469. For a *riposte* to Curtis, see Grosvenor P. Lowrey, "The Commander-in-chief: A Defense upon Legal Grounds of the Proclamation of Emancipation," *id.* at 474–502.

81. Dorris v. Grace, 24 Ark. 326 (1866).

82. For other decisions to this effect from Southern state supreme courts, see McMath v. Johnson, 41 Miss. 439 (1867); Slaback v. Cushman, 12 Fla. 472 (1869); Harrell v. Watson, 63 N.C. 454 (1869), at 458–459; McElvain v.Mudd, 44 Ala. 48 (1870); and Henderlite v. Thurman, 63 Va. 466 (1872).

83. The Emancipation Proclamation Cases, 31 Tex. 504 (1868), at 532.

84. On the misgivings concerning ratification, see Vorenberg, *Final Freedom,* at 222–226.

85. Res. No. 11, Feb. 1, 1865, 13 Stat. 567. On Congress's adoption of the Thirteenth Amendment, see 1 B. Schwartz, *Statutory History of the United States—Civil Rights* (New York: Chelsea House, 1970), at 25–96; Charles Fairman, *Reconstruction and Reunion 1864–1888,* pt. 1 (New York: Macmillan, 1971), at 1136–1159; Vorenberg, *Final Freedom,* at 176–210; and Alexander Tsesis, *The Thirteenth Amendment and American Freedom: A Legal History* (New York: New York University Press, 2004), at 37–48.

86. Lincoln, Public Address, Apr. 11, 1865, 8 Basler, *Works,* at 399–405, at 404.

87. *See,* to this effect, Johnson, Message to Congress, Dec. 4, 1865, in 8 James D. Richardson (ed.), *A Compilation of the Messages and Papers of the Presidents* (New York: Bureau of National Literature, 1896–99), at 3556.

88. Vorenberg, *Final Freedom,* at 229.

89. Certified by Proc. No. 52, Dec. 18, 1865, 13 Stat. 774.

90. The eight states that ratified prior to entry into force were: Virginia, Arkansas, both Carolinas, Alabama, Georgia, Tennessee, and Louisiana. The two ratifying after entry into force were Florida and Texas. On the ratification of the Thirteenth Amendment by the states, see Vorenberg, *Final Freedom,* at 212–233.

91. *Id.* at 230.

92. *Id.* at 231.

93. Civil Rights Cases, 109 U.S. 3 (1883), at 21.

94. Act of May 21, 1866, 14 Stat. 50. For the current version of the legislation, see 18 U.S.C. 1584.

95. Third Periodic Report of the United States to the UN Human Rights Committee, U.N. Doc. CCPR/C/USA/3 (2005), at 40–41. *See,* for example, U.S. v. Alzanki, 54 F. 3d 994 (1st Cir. 1995).

96. Manliguez v. Joseph, 226 F. Supp. 2d 377 (E.D.N.Y. 2002). The case did not hold that the Thirteenth Amendment itself confers a private right of action.

97. Bowlin v. Commonwealth, 65 Ky. 5 (1867), at 8.

98. Civil Rights Cases, 109 U.S. 3 (1883), at 23. *See also* U.S. v. Harris, 106 U.S. 629 (1883), at 643.

99. Osborn v. Nicholson, 80 U.S. (13 Wall.) 654 (1872), at 663.

100. Calhoun v. Calhoun, 2 S.C. 283 (1870). The state constitutional provision was "trumped" by the *federal* constitutional provision forbidding the states from impairing contracts. Constitution, Art. I, sec. 10.

101. Act of Apr. 9, 1866, 14 Stat. 27.

102. *See* People v. Washington, 36 Cal. 658 (1869). From the federal courts, see In re Turner, 24 Fed. Cas. 337 (No. 14,247) (CC D Md. 1867); and U.S. v. Cruikshank, 25 Fed. Cas. (No. 14,897) (CC D La. 1874). When the latter case was appealed, however,

the federal Supreme Court declined to consider the issue. U.S. v. Cruikshank, 92 U.S. 542 (1876).

103. Jones v. Alfred H. Mayer Co., 392 U.S. 409 (1968).

104. For an early use of this expression, by Justice Joseph P. Bradley of the Supreme Court in a dissenting opinion, see Blyew v. U.S., 80 U.S. (13 Wall.) 581 (1872), at 599.

105. Act of Mar. 1, 1875, 18 Stat. 335.

106. Civil Rights Cases, 109 U.S. 3 (1883).

107. *See also,* to the same effect, U.S. v. Harris, 106 U.S. 629 (1883). On the Civil Rights Cases, see Tsesis, *Thirteenth Amendment,* at 68–74.

108. Constitution, Art. I, sec. 8.

109. For the Civil Rights Act of 1964, see Act of July 2, 1964, PL 88–352, 78 Stat. 241, sec. 201, at 243.

110. Heart of Atlanta Motel v. U.S., 379 U.S. 241 (1964).

111. Jones v. Alfred H. Mayer Co., 392 U.S. 409 (1968L).

112. The Court stopped just short of overturning the Civil Rights Cases explicitly, in deference to the fact that the decision in those cases had accepted the badges-of-servitude argument in principle. The *Jones* case departed from the Civil Rights Cases in taking a far more expansive view of what actually qualifies as a badge of servitude. On the *Jones* case, see G. Sidney Buchanan, "The Quest for Freedom: A Legal History of the Thirteenth Amendment," 12 *Houston L. Review* 844–889 (1974–75), at 844–854; and Tsesis, *Thirteenth Amendment,* at 82–87. On the question of what constitutes a badge of servitude, see City of Memphis v. Greene, 451 U.S. 100 (1981), which held that the closure of a street leading into a predominantly black area by way of a predominantly white one was a mere "routine burden of citizenship" and not a violation of the Thirteenth Amendment.

113. On the later development of the Thirteenth Amendment, see Vorenberg, *Final Freedom,* at 244–250. For thorough histories of the Thirteenth Amendment experience, see generally Buchanan, "Quest for Freedom," 12 *Houston Law Review* 1–34, 331–378, 592–639, 844–889, 1070–1085; and 13 *id.* at 63–83 (1974–76); and Tsesis, *Thirteenth Amendment.*

114. On this possibility, see Alexander Tsesis, "Furthering American Freedom: Civil Rights and the Thirteenth Amendment," 45 *Boston College Law Review* 307–391 (2004).

6. Taking Liberties on the Home Front

Epigraphs: Bates, Act for the Admission of West Virginia into the Union, Dec. 27, 1862, 10 Op. A-G 426; Dissenting opinion in Beckwith v. Bean, 98 U.S. 266 (1879), at 294.

1. For studies of organized disloyalty in the North, see Frank L. Klement, *Dark Lanterns: Secret Political Societies, Conspiracies, and Treason Trials in the Civil War* (Ba-

NOTES TO PAGES 151–153

ton Rouge: Louisiana State University Press, 1984); and Jennifer L. Weber, *Copperheads: The Rise and Fall of Lincoln's Opponents in the North* (Oxford: Oxford University Press, 2006). These reach rather different conclusions on the question. On party political conflict in the North during the war, Mark E. Neely, Jr., *The Union Divided: Party Conflict in the Civil War North* (Cambridge, Mass.: Harvard University Press, 2002); and Adam I. P. Smith, *No Party Now: Politics in the Civil War North* (Oxford: Oxford University Press, 2006).

2. For thoughtful general studies of the civil-liberties record of the Lincoln administration during the war, see generally Mark E. Neely, Jr., *The Fate of Liberty: Abraham Lincoln and Civil Liberties* (New York: Oxford University Press, 1991); and Herman Belz, *Abraham Lincoln, Constitutionalism, and Equal Rights in the Civil War Era* (New York: Fordham University Press, 1998).

3. Constitution, Art. III, sec. 3. The Thirteenth Amendment, in effect, makes slaveholding a crime; but it provides no definition of the terms "slavery" or "involuntary servitude."

4. Act of Apr. 30, 1790, 1 Stat. 112, sec. 1.

5. Act of July 17, 1862, 12 Stat. 589 sec. 1 and 2, at 589–590.

6. It seems likely that this new offense of engaging in rebellion was actually a type of treason, in that it constituted levying war against the United States—but with this subcategory of treason distinguished from other forms of the offense by *not* allowing for the death penalty. For a discussion of this point, see U.S. v. Greathouse, 28 Fed. Cas. 18 (No. 15,254) (CC ND Cal. 1863).

7. Act of Feb. 25, 1863, 12 Stat. 696.

8. J. G. Randall, *Constitutional Problems under Lincoln* (New York: Appleton, 1926), at 85.

9. Carl Brent Swisher, *American Constitutional Development* (Boston: Houghton Mifflin, 1943), at 300.

10. Brian L. McGinty, *Lincoln and the Court* (Cambridge, Mass.: Harvard University Press, 2008), at 87–88. On Merryman's attempt at release by way of habeas corpus, see Chapter 2.

11. U.S. v. Greathouse, 28 Fed. Cas. 18 (No. 15,254) (CC ND Cal. 1863). The defendants were prosecuted for attempting to set sail with possession of a Confederate letter of marque. On legal problems connected with treason prosecutions, see Randall, *Constitutional Problems,* at 74–95; and Carl B. Swisher, *The Taney Period* (New York: Macmillan, 1974), at 951–959. On the treatment of Confederate privateers, see Chapter 1.

12. For a thoroughgoing study of the various measures, with great emphasis on the numbers of persons actually affected by them, see generally Neely, *Fate of Liberty.*

13. *See* Chapter 2.

14. Concerning infringements of some of these basic rights during the Civil War, see Chapter 6.

15. Act of Mar. 3, 1863, 12 Stat. 755. On the act, see generally Randall, *Constitutional Problems,* at 186–214; and Harold M. Hyman, *A More Perfect Union: The Impact of the Civil War and Reconstructiion on the Constitution* (New York: Knopf, 1973), at 245–256.

16. Randall, *Constitutional Problems,* at 163–168.

17. For an invaluable study of this phenomenon, on which this account draws heavily, see generally Harold M. Hyman, *Era of the Oath: Northern Loyalty Tests during the Civil War and Reconstruction* (Philadelphia: University of Pennsylvania Press, 1954). *See also* Harold M. Hyman, *To Try Men's Souls: Loyalty Tests in American History* (Berkeley: University of California Press, 1959), at 139–266.

18. Act of Aug. 6, 1861, 12 Stat. 326.

19. Act of Mar. 6, 1862, *id.* at 354.

20. Act of Mar. 3, 1863, *id.* at 755, sec. 2, at 755–756.

21. For a vivid description of the situation in the Confederacy, see Hyman, *Try Men's Souls,* at 219–250.

22. *See generally* Hyman, *Era of the Oath,* at 21–32.

23. Act of Apr. 16, 1862, 12 Stat. 376, sec. 2–3, at 376–377. *See* Chapter 5 for the lenient view taken of what actually constituted disloyalty.

24. Act of May 20, 1862, *id.* at 403. The oath was actually required only of voters whose loyalty was suspect, i.e., whose loyalty was challenged by any lawful voter.

25. Act of June 17, 1862, *id.* at 430, sec. 2.

26. Act of July 17, 1862, *id.* at 589, sec. 10, at 591.

27. Act of July 2, 1862, *id.* at 502. The President was excluded on the ground that the Constitution itself prescribes the text of the oath that he is to take. Constitution, Art. II, sec. 1.

28. Act of Jan. 24, 1865, 12 Stat. 424.

29. Eric Foner, *Reconstruction: America's Unfinished Revolution 1863–1877* (New York: Harper and Row, 1988), at 42.

30. Garner v. Los Angeles Board, 341 U.S. 716 (1951).

31. The word *cachet* means an official seal or stamp. Apparently by coincidence, the verb *cacher* means "to hide." Persons detained by *lettres de cachet* were indeed hidden away; but the expression actually referred to the noun rather than to the verb.

32. Neely, *Fate of Liberty,* at 19.

33. For example, it figured prominently on the frontispiece of the most influential attack on federal civil-liberties policy, the book *American Bastille* by John A. Marshall, which appears to have gone through a remarkable twenty-seven editions. For a reproduction of this frontispiece, see Harold M. Hyman and William M. Wiecek, *Equal Justice under Law: Constitutional Development 1835-1875* (New York: Harper and Row, 1982), plate 19, at 290.

34. On arrests in this period of the war, see Neely, *Fate of Liberty,* at 19–29.

35. Exec. Order No. 1, Relating to Political Prisoners, Feb. 14, 1862, 2 (ser. 2) OR 221–223.

36. Neely, *Fate of Liberty,* at 62, 75.

37. Hyman, *More Perfect Union,* at 254–255.

38. *See* Lincoln's Albany Response to E. Corning and Others, June 12, 1863, in 6 Basler, *Works,* at 260–269.

39. Lincoln to Birchard and Others, June 29, 1863, *id.* at 303.

40. Swisher, *American Constitutional Development,* at 283.

41. Bates to Cameron, Dec. 30, 1861, 2 (ser. 2) OR 182–183.

42. For the martial-law measures, see Proc. of Sep. 24, 1862, in 5 Basler, *Works,* at 436–437; *also promulgated as* General Orders No. 141, Sep. 25, 1862, 2 (ser. 3) OR 587–588. *See* Chapter 2 on these measures.

43. On this period, see Neely, *Fate of Liberty,* at 51–65.

44. For a thorough discussion of the numbers question, with its many nuances and uncertainies, see *id.* at 113–138.

45. *See,* generally, on this subject, *id.* at 75–92.

46. On the experience with military commissions generally during the war, see Neely, *Fate of Liberty,* at 160–175. For a detailed look at a specific case, see Joseph George, Jr., "The North Affair: A Lincoln Administration Military Trial," 33 *Civil War History* 199–218 (1987). For a general survey of military-commission trials in American history, see Louis Fisher, *Military Tribunals and Presidential Power: American Revolution to the War on Terrorism* (Lawrence: University Press of Kansas, 2005).

47. Margaret Leech, *Reveille in Washington 1860–1865* (Chicago: Time-Life, 1941), at 190–191.

48. Proc. of Aug. 30, 1861, 1 (ser. 2) OR 221–222.

49. Proc. of Sep. 24, 1862, in 5 Basler, *Works,* at 436–437; *also promulgated as* General Orders No. 141, Sep. 25, 1862, 2 (ser. 3) OR 587–588.

50. *See* General Orders No. 10, Sep. 12, 1861, *id.* at 282.

51. *Id.* at 167–169.

52. Thomas P. Lowry, *Confederate Heroines: 120 Women Convicted by Union Military Justice* (Baton Rouge: Louisiana State University Press, 2006), at 270.

53. Neely, *Fate of Liberty,* at 167–175.

54. Bates to Cameron, Dec. 30, 1861, 2 (ser. 2) OR 182–183.

55. Ableman v. Booth, 62 U.S. (21 Howard) 506 (1859). On other aspects of that case, see Chapter 1.

56. Service in the armed forces was not, of course, detention comparable to imprisonment. It was amenable to habeas corpus action on the basis that a conscripted soldier was not free to leave the service at will, in the way that a person is free to leave private employment at will (subject only to a possible civil action for breach of contract). For a comprehensive and scholarly consideration of the issue of state courts and federal detention, see In re Reynolds, 20 Fed. Cas. 592 (No. 11,721) (DC ND N.Y. 1867), concluding that state courts can issue habeas corpus writs regarding federal detentions.

57. Proc. No. 7, Sep. 15, 1863, 13 Stat. 734; *reprinted in* 6 Basler, *Works,* at 451–452. *See* Chapter 2 on this point.

58. *See* Circular No. 36, July 1, 1863, 3 (ser. 3) OR 460–461, drafted by William Whiting, the War Department solicitor.

59. Tarble's Case, 80 U.S. (13 Wall.) 397 (1872). The judgment was written in such broad terms as clearly to encompass *all* forms of federal detention, not merely military service.

60. Swisher, *American Constitutional Development,* at 286.

61. General Orders No. 38, Apr. 13, 1863, 23(2) (ser. 1) OR 237.

62. For the report of the trial proceedings, see 5 (ser. 2) OR 633–646.

63. Ex p. Vallandigham, 28 Fed. Cas. 874 (No. 16,816) (CC SD Ohio 1863).

64. Ex p. Vallandigham, 68 U.S. (1 Wall.) 243 (1863). His appeal to the Ohio court had been on the basis of absence of jurisdiction by the military court, rather than on the basis of unfairness of the proceedings themselves.

65. On the Vallandigham affair, see generally Randall, *Constitutional Problems,* at 176–179; Frank L. Klement, *The Limits of Dissent: Clement L. Vallandigham and the Civil War* (Lexington: University Press of Kentucky, 1970); Neely, *Fate of Liberty,* at 65–68; William H. Rehnquist, *All the Laws but One: Civil Liberty in Wartime* (New York: Knopf, 1998), at 59–74; Robert Bruce Murray, *Legal Cases of the Civil War* (Mechanicsburg, Pa.: Stackpole, 2003), at 58–74; and McGinty, *Lincoln and the Court,* at 182–192.

66. For a detailed report on this group, known as the Knights of the Golden Circle, see Holt to Stanton, Oct. 10, 1864, 7 (ser. 2) OR 930–953. Milligan was identified, at 933, as holding the rank of "major general" in this group. *See also* Allan Nevins, "The Case of the Copperhead Conspirator," in John A. Garraty (ed.), *Quarrels That Have Shaped the Constitution* (New York: Harper and Row, 1962), at 101–104.

67. For the report of the trial, see General Orders No. 27, May 9, 1865, 8 (ser. 2) OR 542–549. For the trial of one his coconspirators, see General Orders No. 1, Jan. 2, 1865, *id.* at 6–11.

68. Ex p. Milligan, 71 U.S. (4 Wall.) 2 (1866).

69. *Id.* at 127.

70. For an illustration of the executive's acquiescence in the *Milligan* decision, see Stanbery, Devlin's Claim, Mar. 9, 1867, 12 Op. A-G 128.

71. The *Milligan* decision has had mixed reviews from historians and lawyers. Clinton Rossiter, *The Supreme Court and the Commander in Chief* (2d ed.; Ithaca, N.Y.: Cornell University Press, 1976), at 30–39, for example, regards the decision as being of little or no significance. On the *Miligan* case, see Randall, *Constitutional Problems,* at 179–183; Nevins, "Copperhead Conspirator," at 90–108; Charles Fairman, *Reconstruction and Reunion 1864–1888,* pt. 1 (New York: Macmillan, 1971), at 185–239; Frank L. Klement, "The Indianapolis Treason Trials and *Ex Parte Milligan,*" in

Michael R. Belknap (ed.), *American Political Trials* (Westport, Conn.: Greenwood Press, 1981), at 101–127; Rehnquist, *All the Laws,* at 75-137; Michael R. Belknap, "Alarm Bells from the Past: The Troubling History of American Military Commissions," 28 *J. Court History* 300–322 (2003), at 313–315; Murray, *Legal Cases,* at 75-84; and McGinty, *Lincoln and the Court,* at 248–260. On the public response to the case, see McGinty, *Lincoln and the Court,* at 262–264. For an informative survey of the historiography of the *Milligan* case, see Neely, *Fate of Liberty,* at 179–184.

72. Toth v. Quarles, 350 U.S. 11 (1955).

73. Kinsella v. U.S., 361 U.S. 234 (1960). An earlier case had held such trials unconstitutional for capital offenses. *See* Reid v. Covert, 354 U.S. 1 (1957).

74. Constitution, Art. I, secs. 9, 10.

75. *Id.*

76. *See,* in this regard, the leading case of Calder v. Bull, 3 U.S. (3 Dall.) 386 (1798).

77. Ex p. Garland, 71 U.S. (4 Wall.) 333 (1867), at 370.

78. The Georgia Supreme Court, the previous year, had held the federal law of January 1865 to be a bill of attainder. *See* In the Matter of the Oath to Be Taken, 35 Ga. 286 (1866).

79. Cummings v. Missouri, 71 U.S. (4 Wall.) 277 (1867); and Ex p. Garland, 71 U.S. (4 Wall.) 333 (1867).

80. Act of Jan. 24, 1865, 13 Stat. 424.

81. This conclusion was not uniformly reached. *See,* for example, the West Virginia Supreme Court case of Ex p. Hunter, 2 W. Va. 122 (1867), which held an ironclad-oath law similar to that in the *Garland* case not to be punitive.

82. On the Garland Case, see Hyman, *Era of the Oath,* at 107–110; and Murray, *Legal Cases,* at 245–252. On the Cummings Case, see Hyman, *Era of the Oath,* at 110–114; and Murray, *Legal Cases,* at 239–245. *See also* McGinty, *Lincoln and the Court,* at 251–262. On the role of Justice Field in these two cases, see Hyman, *Era of the Oath,* at 113–114; and Paul Kens, *Justice Stephen Field: Shaping Liberty from the Gold Rush to the Gilded Age* (Lawrence: University Press of Kansas, 1997), at 113–117. Incidentally, Justice Field's brother was the counsel for Cummings.

83. *See* Chapter 9 for the application of these cases to situations of franchise restrictions in the wake of the Civil War.

84. Hawker v. New York, 170 U.S. 189 (1898).

85. Selective Service System v. Minnesota Public Interest Research Group, 468 U.S. 841 (1984).

86. *See also,* to this effect, Flemming v. Nestor, 363 U.S. 603 (1960), which held the denial of certain social-security benefits to aliens who were deported because of Communist Party membership not to be a bill of attainder. For a useful summation of federal case-law on bills of attainder, see Welsh, "Bill of Attainder."

7. The World Watches

Epigraphs: 3 Francis Wharton, *A Digest of the International Law of the United States* (2d ed.; Washington, D.C.: GPO, 1887), at 525; William Beach Lawrence, *Neutral Relations and the Treaty of Washington* (Washington, D.C.: McGill and Witherow, 1872), at 8.

1. For the most detailed accounts of the disputes over neutral rights leading up to the War of 1812, see Anna C. Clauder, *American Commerce as Affected by the Wars of the French Revolution and Napoleon 1793–1812* (Philadelphia: University of Pennsylvania Press, 1932); Bradford Perkins, *The First Rapprochement: England and the United States 1795–1805* (Berkeley: University of California Press, 1955); and Bradford Perkins, *Prologue to War: England the United States 1805–1812* (Berkeley: University of California Press, 1961).

2. For the text of the British declaration, see 1 Francis Deák and Philip C. Jessup (eds.), *A Collection of Neutrality Laws, Regulations and Treaties of Various Countries* (Washington, D.C.: Carnegie Endowment for International Peace, 1939), at 161–162. For the text of the French proclamation, see *id.* at 590–592. The British declaration encompassed Canada, since Britain at that time controlled Canadian foreign relations. On the controversy over the British policy, see Montague Bernard, *A Historical Account of the Neutrality of Great Britain during the American Civil War* (London: Longmans, Green, Reader, and Dyer, 1870), at 151–170. On the French recognition of belligerency, see Lynn Marshall Case and Warren F. Spencer, *The United States and France: Civil War Diplomacy* (Philadelphia: University of Pennsylvania Press, 1970), at 45–76.

3. For the texts of these proclamations, see Deák and Jessup, *Collection.*

4. *See,* to this effect, Institute of International Law, "Rights and Duties of Foreign Powers and Their *Ressortissants* towards Established and Recognized Governments in Case of Insurrection," Sep. 8, 1900, in James Brown Scott (ed.), *Resolutions of the Institute of International Law* (New York: Oxford University Press, 1916), at 157–159, art. 8. On recognition of belligerency in this period, see Stephen C. Neff, *War and the Law of Nations: A General History* (Cambridge: Cambridge University Press, 2005), at 254–264.

5. For the Union government objection to the British action, see Adams to Seward, May 21, 1861, in FRUS 1861, at 74–80. *See also* Bernard, *Historical Account,* at 151–170.

6. On the Union's treatment of Confederate activity at sea as piracy, see Chapter 1.

7. For reports of such informal meetings, see Yancy, Rost, and Mann to Toombs, June 1, 1861, in 3 (ser. 2) OR-Naval 219–221 (concerning Britain); and Report to Hunter, Oct. 28, 1861, *id.* at 287–288 (concerning France). On Confederate "diplomatic" relations, see generally James Morton Callahan, *The Diplomatic History of the Southern Confederacy* (Baltimore: Johns Hopkins University Press, 1901); Frank

Owsley, *King Cotton Diplomacy* (Chicago: University of Chicago Press, 1959); James Morton Callahan, *The Diplomatic History of the Southern Confederacy* (Westport, Conn.: Greenwood Press, 1968); and Charles M. Hubbard, *The Burden of Confederate Diplomacy* (Knoxville: University of Tennessee Press, 1998).

8. Neutral private parties, however, as opposed to neutral *governments*, are not covered by this prohibition. They run the risk, however, that any arms that they ship will be captured and confiscated by the opposing side as contraband of war.

9. Bernard, *Historical Account*, at 263–282. On similar policies by Spain and the Netherlands, see *id.* at 249–263. On the French policy, see Case and Spencer, *United States and France*, at 481–515.

10. *See* Chapter 8.

11. On the incident, see 19 (ser. 1) OR-Naval 267–281; and Stuart L. Bernath, *Squall across the Atlantic: American Civil War Prize Cases and Diplomacy* (Berkeley: University of California Press, 1970), at 100–107. Great Britain also sought damages, on the ground that the ship was British, but the Department of State rejected that claim. *See* Lyons to Seward, Aug. 1, 1863, FRUS 1864(1), at 680–682; and Seward to Lyons, Aug. 4, 1863, *id.* at 685–687. The Confederate government attempted, apparently without success, to induce Spain to pay the damages over to it, on the contention that the ship was Confederate. *See* 19 (ser. 1) OR-Naval 282–286.

12. Barloza da Silva to Seward, Dec. 12, 1864, 3 (ser. 1) OR-Naval 282–285. For the modern statement of the duty of the belligerent to release such a capture at the request of the aggrieved neutral country, see Hague Convention XIII Concerning the Rights and Duties of Neutral Powers in Naval War, Oct. 18, 1907, 205 C.T.S. 395, 36 Stat. 2415, art. 3 (hereafter Hague Convention on Maritime Neutrality).

13. Seward to Barloza da Silva, Dec. 26, 1864, 3 (ser. 1) OR-Naval 285–287. At the same time, Seward pointedly protested against Brazil's recognition of belligerency as an "unfriendly and wrongful" act on Brazil's part.

14. For an extract from the court-martial proceedings, and Welles's disapproval, see *id.* at 268–269.

15. On this incident, see Bern Anderson, *By Sea and by River: The Naval History of the Civil War* (New York: Knopf, 1962), at 202–204; and Frank Owsley, *The C.S.S. Florida: Her Building and Operations* (Tuscaloosa: University of Alabama Press, 1965), at 137–155.

16. On the British protest, see Russell to Lyons, Nov. 30, 1861, 1 (ser. 1) OR-Naval 159–160. For the text of French note (of Dec. 3, 1861), the Prussian note (of Dec. 25, 1861), and the Austrian note (of Dec. 18, 1861), see 10 *(Supp.) Am J. Int'l L.* 67–72 (1916).

17. On runaway slaves as contraband, see Chapter 5.

18. On prize courts and their functions, see Chapter 8.

19. Seward to Lyons, Dec. 26, 1861, 2 (ser. 2) OR 1145–1154.

20. *See* Law officers (Harding, Atherton, and Palmer) to Russell, Jan. 15, 1862, in

3 McNair, *Opinions,* at 279–287; and Russell to Lyons, Jan. 10, 1862, 1 (ser. 1) OR-Naval 189–190. On the British position in the dispute, see James P. Baxter III, "Some British Opinions as to Neutral Rights, 1861–1865," 23 *Am. J. Int'l L.* 517–537 (1929), at 519–523.

21. On the question of whether the enemy destination must be the *immediate* destination, see the discussion of the continuous-voyage doctrine in Chapter 8. For a thorough account and fair-minded legal analysis of the *Trent* affair, see Bernard, *Neutrality,* at 187–225. On the *Trent* affair, see generally 7 John Bassett Moore, *A Digest of International Law* (Washington, D.C.: GPO, 1906), at 768–779; John Wheeler-Bennett, "The Trent Affair; 1861," 11 *History Today* 805-816 (1961); Case and Spencer, *United States and France,* at 190–249; D. P. Crook, *Diplomacy during the American Civil War* (New York: Wiley, 1975), at 43–60; and Norman B. Ferris, *The Trent Affair: A Diplomatic Crisis* (Knoxville: University of Tennessee Press, 1977).

22. For thorough summations of Confederate grievances against neutrals, see Benjamin to Slidell, Sep. 20, 1864, 3 (ser. 2) OR-Naval 1212–1215; and Benjamin to Slidell, Dec. 27, 1864, *id.* at 1253–1256.

23. *See,* for example, Davis, Message to the Confed. Congress, Jan. 12, 1863, 2 (ser. 4) OR 336–350, at 338–339.

24. For a succinct exposition of the present law on this subject, see 1 Robert Jennings and Arthur Watts (eds.), *Oppenheim's International Law* (9th ed., London: Longman, 1996), at 128–130.

25. *See* British Parliament, H.C., June 7, 1861, 163 Hansard (ser. 3) 762–764.

26. *See* British Parliament, H.C., June 20, 1862, 167 *id.* at 810; H.C., July 10, 1863, 172 *id.* at 554–571; and H.L., July 13, 1863, *id.* at 661–673.

27. For the text of which, see Bernard, *Historical Account,* at 136–137.

28. Modern international law permits neutral states, if they wish, to allow prizes into their territories for sequestration pending a decision by the captor state's prize courts on the lawfulness of the capture. *See* Hague Convention on Maritime Neutrality, art. 23.

29. For Confederate unhappiness of this score, see Benjamin to Slidell, Aug. 4, 1863, 3 (ser. 2) OR-Naval 853–855.

30. *See,* for example, Report Satori to Welles, Dec. 9, 1862, 1 (ser. 1) OR-Naval 579.

31. *See* Seward's characterization of the *Florida*'s actions as "open piracy," in Seward to Adams, Mar. 23, 1863, FRUS 1864(1), at 177. *See also* Seward to Adams, Aug. 15, 1864, FRUS 1865(2), at 270–271; and Union navy secretary Gideon Welles's reference to the *Alabama* as a "piratical steamer," in Welles to McDougal, Jan. 26, 1863, 2 (ser. 1) OR-Naval 58–59. For a lengthy and impassioned defense by Semmes of his actions, see Letter Semmes to the London Times, Jan. 9, 1862, 1 (ser. 1) OR-Naval 640–643. *See also* Chapter 9 for steps which Semmes took to forestall a piracy prosecu-

tion after the war. It may also be noted that, after the war, Confederate navy secretary Stephen Mallory was prosecuted for organizing piratical expeditions. *See* Chapter 9 on this point.

32. Declaration of Paris, Apr. 16, 1856, 115 C.T.S. 1. Over forty states eventually became parties to this agreement, which was the first major multilateral treaty that was freely opened to all states to sign. The Confederacy was not a party, since it was not recognized as a state. The Confederates' observance of the rules of the Declaration was subject to one exception: that they did not support the Declaration's abolition of privateering. On Confederate privateers, see Chapter 1.

33. For the texts of various ransom bonds, see 1 (ser. 1) OR-Naval 653–654, 659, 781–782; and 2 (ser. 1) OR-Naval 331, 685–687, 691–692.

34. Chester G. Hearn, *Gray Raiders of the Sea: How Eight Confederate Warships Destroyed the Union's High Seas Commerce* (Camden, Me.: International Marine, 1992), at 184–186.

35. For the view that the blockade did not make an important contribution to the winning of the war, see Owsley, *King Cotton Diplomacy*, at 229–267. For the opposite conclusion, see David G. Surdam, *Northern Naval Superiority and the Economics of the American Civil War* (Columbia: University of South Carolina Press, 2001).

36. *See* Carl J. Kulsrud, *Maritime Neutrality to 1780: A History of the Main Principles Governing Neutrality and Belligerency to 1780* (Boston: Little, Brown, 1936), at 238–243; and Stephen C. Neff, *The Rights and Duties of Neutrals: A General History* (Manchester: Manchester University Press, 2000), at 22–23, 35.

37. Declaration of Paris, Apr. 16, 1856, 115 C.T.S. 1, art. 4.

38. Davis, Message to Confederate Congress, Jan. 12, 1863, 2 (ser. 4) OR 336–350, at 343. For a thorough statement of the Confederate position, see Benjamin to Slidell, Sep. 2, 1863, 3 (ser. 2) OR-Naval 882–889. For scholarly agreement with this position, see Paul Fauchille, *Du blocus maritime: Étude de droit international et de droit compar* (Paris: Rousseau, 1882), at 112–118; and Owsley, *King Cotton Diplomacy*, at 229–267.

39. Mason to Russell, Feb. 18, 1863, 3 (ser. 2) OR-Naval 695–697.

40. Russell to Mason, Feb. 10, 1863, *id.* at 688–689. *See also* remarks of R. Palmer, British Parliament, H.C., Mar. 7, 1862, 165 Hansard (3d ser.) 1209–1225; and remarks of Lord Russell, H.L., Mar. 10, 1862, *id.* at 1237–1243. On debates in the British Parliament on the issue, see Owsley, *King Cotton Diplomacy*, at 223–228; and D. P. Crook, *The North, the South and the Powers, 1861–1865* (New York: Wiley, 1974), at 177–181.

41. *See* Benjamin to Slidell, Sep. 2, 1863, 3 (ser. 2) OR-Naval 883.

42. Davis, Message to Confederate Congress, Jan. 12, 1863, in 1 James D. Richardson (ed.), *A Compilation of the Messages and Papers of the Confederacy* (Nashville: United States Publishing, 1905), at 287. *See also,* to the same effect, Browne to Mason, Oct. 29, 1861, 3 (ser. 2) OR-Naval 289–290; and Mann to Benjamin, Aug. 15, 1862, *id.* at 515–517 (regarding France).

43. William C. Davis, *Look Away! A History of the Confederate States of America* (New York: Free Press, 2002), at 375–376. *See also* Bernard, *Historical Account,* at 292–295; and Owsley, *King Cotton Diplomacy,* at 203–228.

44. On the cotton embargo, see John Christopher Schwab, *The Confederate States of America 1861–1865: A Financial and Industrial History of the South during the Civil War* (New York: Scribner's, 1901), at 250–252; Owsley, *King Cotton Diplomacy,* at 213–214; and James McPherson, *Battle Cry of Freedom: The Civil War Era* (New York: Oxford University Press, 1988), at 383–386.

45. 4 John Bassett Moore, *A History and Digest of the Arbitrations to Which the United States Has Been a Party* (Washington, D.C.: GPO, 1898), at 4042–4054.

46. *Id.* at 4054–4056.

47. Foreign Enlistment Act 1819 (Great Britain), 59 Geo. 3, c. 69, sec. 7.

48. For a firsthand account of the Confederate navy-building activities, by the major figure in the process, see James D. Bulloch, *The Secret Service of the Confederate States in Europe; Or How the Confederate Cruisers Were Equipped* (2 vols.; New York: Putnam's, 1884). For the principal scholarly accounts, see Owsley, *King Cotton Diplomacy,* at 394–426; Frank J. Merli, *Great Britain and the Confederate Navy, 1861–1865* (Bloomington: Indiana University Press, 1970); and Warren F. Spencer, *The Confederate Navy in Europe* (Tuscaloosa: University of Alabama Press, 1983).

49. Bruce Catton, *Never Call Retreat* (Garden City, N.Y.: Doubleday, 1965), at 136–137.

50. *See,* for example, Bulloch to Mallory, June 30, 1863, 2 (ser. 2) OR-Naval 444–447; Bulloch to Mallory, Sep. 1, 1863, *id.* at 487–489; and Bulloch to Mallory, Oct. 20, 1863, *id.* at 507–511.

51. The leading case concerned the building of the ship *Alexandra. See* Attorney General v. Sillems, 2 Hurstone and Coltman 431 (1863). On the *Alexandra* case, see Frank J. Merli, "Crown versus Cruiser: The Curious Case of the *Alexandra,*" 9 *Civil War History* 167–177 (1963); Merli, *Great Britain and the Confederate Navy,* at 160–177; Spencer, *Confederate Navy,* at 100–104; Wilbur Devereux Jones, *The Confederate Rams at Birkenhead: A Chapter in Anglo-American Relations* (Tuscaloosa: Confederate, 1961), at 42–51; Crook, *North, South and Powers,* at 294–301; Crook, *Diplomacy,* at 131–133; and Hearn, *Gray Raiders,* at 102–109.

52. For documentation on the Union attempt to have the *Alabama* interned in Liverpool, see 2 (ser. 2) OR-Naval 377–393. *See also* Douglas Maynard, "Plotting the Escape of the *Alabama,*" 20 *J. Southern History* 197–209 (1954); Hearn, *Gray Raiders,* at 153–160; and Frank J. Merli, *The Alabama, British Neutrality, and the American Civil War* (ed. David M. Fahey; Bloomington: Indiana University Press, 2004), at 41–88.

53. *See* Hearn, *Gray Raiders,* at 161–236.

54. On the construction and escape of the *Florida* from Britain, see Owsley, *C.S.S. Florida,* at 17–33. On its subsequent raiding career, see *id.* at 61–82, 94–101, 110–128, 142–152.

55. On the career of the *Shenandoah,* see Tom Chaffin, *Sea of Gray: The Around-the-world Odyssey of the Confederate Raider Shenandoah* (New York: Hill and Wang, 2006). For a general account of the Confederate commerce raiders, see generally Hearn, *Gray Raiders.*

56. The Union also supported the rule, confining its captures of enemy property on neutral ships to the two exceptional cases the Declaration of Paris clearly allowed: contraband of war and blockade violation. On blockade violation, see Chapter 8.

57. *See generally* George W. Dalzell, *The Flight from the Flag: The Continuing Effect of the Civil War upon the American Carrying Trade* (Chapel Hill: University of North Carolina Press, 1940).

58. Great Britain-U.S., Treaty of Washington, May 8 , 1871, 143 C.T.S. 145, 17 Stat. 863 (hereafter Treaty of Washington). On the tortuous history of the negotiation and ratification, see Adrian Cook, *The Alabama Claims: American Politics and Anglo-American Relations, 1865–1872* (Ithaca, N.Y.: Cornell University Press, 1975), at 167–206. For the official records of these meetings, see Protocols of Conferences, FRUS 1873 (part 2), at 379–407.

59. The claims concerning the St. Albans and Lake Erie raids, discussed above, were heard by this panel. For further details of the panel's deliberations, see Chapters 8 and 9.

60. Treaty of Washington, art. 6.

61. *Id.*

62. 4 Moore, *Arbitrations,* at 4101–4109.

63. Foreign Enlistment Act 1870 (Great Britain), 33–34 Vict., c. 90, sec. 8.

64. 4 Moore, *Arbitrations,* at 4082.

65. *Id.* at 4075–4081, at 4078.

66. For further strong support for the British position in the dispute, see Bernard, *Historical Account,* at 384–402.

67. On the *Alabama,* see 4 Moore, *Arbitrations,* at 4144–4161. On the *Florida,* see *id.* at 4129–4144.

68. *Id.* at 4082–4097.

69. *Id.* at 4174–4178.

70. *Id.* at 4097.

71. *Id.* at 4115.

72. *Id.* at 4116.

73. *Id.* at 4113–4114. On the indirect claims, see generally Cook, *Alabama Claims,* at 207–240.

74. On the history of such settlements, see Richard B. Lillich and Burns H. Weston, *International Claims: Their Settlement by Lump Sum Agreements* (Charlottesville: University Press of Virginia, 1975). For recent developments, see Burns H. Weston, Richard B. Lillich, and David J. Bederman, *International Claims: Their Settlement by Lump Sum Agreements, 1975–1995* (Ardsley, N.Y.: Transnational, 1999).

75. For confirmation that this is the position in international claims generally, see the later World Court case of the Mavrommatis Palestine Concessions (Jurisdiction), PCIJ Rep., ser. A, No. 2 (1924).

76. Williams v. Heard, 140 U.S. 529 (1891).

77. Act of June 23, 1874, 18 Stat. 245.

78. For the proceedings of this claims panel, see 5 Moore, *Arbitrations,* at 4639–4657.

79. Act of June 5, 1882, 22 Stat. 98.

80. For a summary of this new claims process, see 5 Moore, *Arbitrations,* at 4657–4685. For the legislation terminating the process, see Act of June 2, 1886, 24 Stat. 77.

81. Dalzell, *Flight from the Flag,* at 235.

82. Lawrence, *Neutral Relations,* at 27–30. *See also,* to this effect, Arthur G. Sedgwick, "Unforseen Results of the Alabama Dispute," 41 *Atlantic Monthly* 771–782 (1878), at 781–782.

83. For the diplomatic correspondence on this subject, see 65 B.F.S.P. 393–425.

84. Institute of International Law, "International Duties of Neutral States—Rules of Washington," Aug. 30, 1875, in Scott, *Resolutions,* at 12–14. *See also* 7 Moore, *Digest,* at 671–675.

85. Hague Convention on Maritime Neutrality, art. 8.

8. The Art of Blockade

Epigraphs: The Circassian, 69 U.S. 796 (2 Wall.) 135 (1865), at 151–152; The Bermuda, 70 U.S. (3 Wall.) 514 (1865), at 555.

1. On Confederate blockade running, see generally Francis B. C. Bradlee, *Blockade Running during the Civil War and the Effect of Land and Water Transportation on the Confederacy* (Salem, Mass.: Essex Institute Press, 1925); Bern Anderson, *By Sea and by River: The Naval History of the Civil War* (New York: Knopf, 1962), at 215–232; Stephen Robert Wise, *Lifeline of the Confederacy: Blockade Running during the American Civil War* (Columbia: University of South Carolina Press, 1983); Mark E. Neely, Jr., "The Perils of Running the Blockade: The Influence of International Law in an Era of Total War," 32 *Civil War History* 101–118 (1986); and Hamilton Cochrane, *Blockade Runners of the Confederacy* (Indianapolis: Bobbs-Merrill, 1958). For firsthand accounts, see John Wilkinson, *The Narrative of a Blockade Runner* (New York: Sheldon, 1877); and William B. Watson, *The Adventures of a Blockade Runner; or Trade in Time of War* (New York: Macmillan, 1893).

2. On the Matamoros trade, see James W. Daddysman, *The Matamoros Trade: Confederate Commerce, Diplomacy, and Intrigue* (Newark: University of Delaware Press, 1984).

3. On the Bermuda traffic, see Frank Vandiver, *Confederate Blockade Running through Bermuda, 1861–1865* (Austin: University of Texas Press, 1947).

4. The Circassian, 69 U.S. 796 (2 Wall.) 135 (1865), at 151–152. For a thorough description of this dubious "business," see Young v. U.S., 12 Ct. of Claims 648 (1876).

5. For details of British involvement in blockade running, see Madeline Russell Robinton, *An Introduction to the Papers of the New York Prize Court: 1861–1865* (New York: Columbia University Press, 1945), at 157–164. For formal objections by the Union government to British involvement in the Matamoros trade, see Seward to Lyons, May 12, 1863, FRUS 1864(1), at 597–599.

6. On the effectiveness requirement for blockades, see Chapter 7.

7. *See* Speed v. Smith, 22 Fed. Cas. 908 (No. 13,226) (CC SD Miss. 1869), at 910, for an explicit characterization of a blockade as an "external fence."

8. On the historical development of prize courts, see Carl J. Kulsrud, *Maritime Neutrality to 1780: A History of the Main Principles Governing Neutrality and Belligerency to 1780* (Boston: Little, Brown, 1936), at 13–60.

9. On the admiralty jurisdiction of federal courts, see Erwin C. Surrency, *History of the Federal Courts* (2d ed.; Dobbs Ferry, N.Y.: Oceana, 2002), at 209–228.

10. For a general account of prize law in the period, see Henry W. Halleck, *International Law; Or, Rules Regulating the Intercourse of States* (New York: Van Nostrand, 1861), at 724–774. For a summation of the prize law generally in the late nineteenth century, with surveys of state practice, see M. Bulmerincq (rapporteur), *Commission des prises maritimes* (Ghent: I.-S. Van Doosselaere, 1880), a study done for the Institute of International Law.

11. *See* Henry W. Halleck, *International Law; Or Rules Regulating the Intercourse of States* (New York: Van Nostrand, 1861), at 548.

12. Confederates could be prosecuted and punished for criminal offenses such as treason, as they were regarded throughout the conflict as United States nationals. The ban on punishment protected only *neutral* blockade runners.

13. For a fuller explanation of this distinction, see Chapter 4.

14. *See* Mark E. Neely, *The Fate of Liberty: Abraham Lincoln and Civil Liberties* (New York: Oxford University Press, 1991), at 142–145.

15. Cornelius van Bynkershoek, *Questions of Public Law* (trans. Tenney Frank; Oxford: Clarendon Press, 1925 [1737]), at 74–75 This was also, it may be noted, the incident in which the requirement of effectiveness of blockades was first articulated.

16. *Id.* at 76.

17. *See* The Columbia, 1 C. Rob. 154 (1799); The Vrow Johanna, 2 C. Rob. 109 (1799); and The Neptunus, *id.* at 110 (1799).

18. Yeaton v. Fry, 9 U.S. (5 Cranch) 335 (1809), at 342–343.

19. Ingraham v. The Nayade, 13 Fed. Cas. 55 (No. 7046) (DC D La. 1846).

20. Halleck, *International Law,* at 553–554.

21. Coffey, Running the Blockade from Ports of the United States, July 27, 1863, 10 Op. A-G 513, at 515.

22. The Circassian, 69 U.S. (2 Wall.) 135 (1865), at 151. *See also* The Adela, 73 U.S. (6 Wall.) 821 (1868).

23. *See,* for example, Paul Fauchille, *Du blocus maritime: Étude de droit international et de droit compar* (Paris: Rousseau, 1882), at 326–333. *See also,* to much the same effect, 2 L.-B. Hautefeuille, *Les droits et les devoirs des nations neutres en temps de guerre maritime* (3d ed.; Paris: Guillaumin, 1868), at 230–233. On the effectiveness requirement, see Chapter 7. Also opposed to the intention doctrine was Theodore Dwight Woolsey, *Introduction to the Study of International Law* (2d ed.; New York: Scribner, 1864), at 319.

24. The Adula, 176 U.S. 361 (1900).

25. *See,* for example, Woolsey, *Introduction,* at 350; and Travers Twiss, *The Law of Nations Considered as Independent Political Communities: On the Rights and Duties of Nations in Time of War* (2d ed.; Oxford: Clarendon Press, 1875), at 210–212.

26. Declaration of London, Feb. 26, 1909, 208 C.T.S. 338, art. 17.

27. The Commander's Handbook on the Law of Naval Operations, NWP 9 (Rev. A), FMFM 1–10 (1989), sec. 7.7.4; *reprinted in 73 Int'l L. Studies* 296 (1999).

28. Act of May 20, 1862, 12 Stat. 404.

29. 1 Carlton Savage, *Policy of the United States toward Maritime Commerce in War: 1776–1914* (Washington, D.C.: GPO, 1934), at 446–447.

30. British National Archives, FO5, vol. 1006, n.p.

31. *Quoted in* Stuart L. Bernath, *Squall across the Atlantic: American Civil War Prize Cases and Diplomacy* (Berkeley: University of California Press, 1970), at 14–17. This is an excellent short account of the controversy.

32. Constitution, Art. I, sec. 8.

33. Seward, British National Archives, FO5, vol. 1006, n.p. For an extended defense by Seward of the policy, see Seward to Stuart, Oct. 3, 1862, in 3 Francis Wharton, *A Digest of the International Law of the United States* (2d ed.; Washington, D.C.: GPO, 1887), at 416–427. Opinion was not unanimous on the matter within Britain. For support for the Seward position, see Montague Bernard, *A Historical Account of the Neutrality of Great Britain during the American Civil War* (London: Longmans, Green, Reader, and Dyer, 1870), at 299–307.

34. On the First World War experience, see Edgar Turlington, *The World War Period* (New York: Columbia University Press), 1936, at 67–73.

35. For some consideration of the matter (in the context of the principle of nonintervention in international law), see the World Court case of Military and Paramilitary Activities in and Against Nicaragua (Nicaragua v. U.S.A.), 1986 I.C.J. Rep. 14, paras. 244–245. *See also* Stephen C. Neff, "Boycott and the Law of Nations: Economic Warfare and Modern International Law in Historical Perspetive," 59 *Brit. Y.B. Int'l L.* 113–149 (1988).

36. For a brief account of the Rule of 1756 and the application of continuous voyage to it, see Stephen C. Neff, *The Rights and Duties of Neutrals: A General History* (Manchester: Manchester University Press, 2000), at 65–68. For a more detailed account, see Richard Pares, *Colonial Blockade and Neutral Rights* (Oxford: Clarendon Press, 1938), at 204–224.

37. Welles, General Instructions . . . Regarding the Right of Search, Aug. 18, 1862, in 7 (ser. 1) OR-Naval 656–657. For a condemnation pursuant to these rules, with a detailed analysis of the application of continuous voyage to contraband, see The Stephen Hart, 22 Fed. Cas. 1253 (No 13,364) (DC SD N.Y. 1863).

38. On the capture, see 2 (ser. 1) OR-Naval 97–104. By an interesting coincidence, the captain of the capturing vessel was Charles Wilkes, of *Trent* affair fame.

39. The Peterhoff, 19 Fed. Cas. 316 (No. 11,024) (DC SD N.Y. 1863).

40. The Peterhoff, 72 U.S. (5 Wall.) 564 (1867).

41. On the *Peterhoff* case, see Herbert W. Briggs, *The Doctrine of Continuous Voyage* (Baltimore: Johns Hopkins University Press, 1926), at 55–56; Bernath, *Squall,* at 63–84; and James W. Gantenbein, *The Doctrine of Continuous Voyage Particularly as Applied to Contraband and Blockade* (Portland, Ore.: Keystone Press, 1929), at 68–74.

42. The Bermuda, 70 U.S. (3 Wall.) 514 (1866), at 555.

43. Hobbs v. Henning, 17 C.B. (N.S.) 791 (1864).

44. *See* The William Peel, 72 U.S. (5 Wall.) 517 (1867).

45. Coffey, Running the Blockade from the Ports of the United States, July 27, 1863, 10 Op. A-G 513.

46. The Circassian, 5 Fed. Cas. 712 (No. 2727) (DC SD Fla. 1862). *See also* The Pearl, 19 Fed. Cas. 54 (No. 10,874) (DC SD Fla. 1863).

47. The Circassian, 69 U.S. (2 Wall.) 135 (1865). *See also* The Pearl, 72 U.S. (5 Wall.) 574 (1867); and The Adela, 73 U.S. (6 Wall.) 266 (1868).

48. The Springbok, 72 U.S. (5 Wall.) 480 (1867). *See also* The Bermuda, 70 U.S. (3 Wall.) 514 (1866), at 558, which clearly foreshadowed the *Springbok* decision. The *Bermuda* judgment, however, concerned the application of continuous voyage to contraband rather than to blockade.

49. On the *Springbok* case, see Briggs, *Continuous Voyage,* at 63–79; Gantenbein, *Continuous Voyage,* at 74–77; and Bernath, *Squall,* at 85–98.

50. *See,* for example, Ludwig Gessner, *The Condemnation of the Cargo of the "Springbok" by the Supreme Court of the United States of America* (London: W. S. Johnson, 1869); and Fauchille, *Blocus maritime,* at 333–344. On the British reaction, both official and unofficial, see Bernath, *Squall,* at 150–164. For a summation of views expressed, see 7 John Bassett Moore, *A Digest of International Law* (Washington, D.C.: GPO, 1906), at 727–739. *See also* Briggs, *Continuous Voyage,* at 73–76.

51. Bernath, *Squall,* at 87–89.

52. Travers Twiss, *The Doctrine of Continuous Voyages, As Applied to Contraband of War and Blockade, Contrasted with the Declaration of Paris* (London: Butterworths,

1877), at 32–33. *See also* Travers Twiss, *Belligerent Rights on the High Seas since the Declaration of Paris (1856)* (London: Butterworths, 1884), at 19–32.

53. Nelson to Lawrence, Aug. 4, 1873, in William Edward Hall, *A Treatise on International Law* (4th ed.; Oxford: Clarendon Press, 1895), at 694, n. 3.

54. For defenses of the *Springbok* decision, at least in principle, see Theodore Dwight Woolsey, *Introduction to the Study of International Law: Designed as an Aid in Teaching, and in Historical Studies* (5th ed.; London: Sampson Low, Marsten, Searle and Rivington, 1879), at 366; and Henry Wheaton, *Elements of International Law* (ed. Richard Henry Dana; Oxford: Clarendon Press 1936 [1866]), at 558, n. 231.

55. *See* Law Officers (Harding, Atherton, Palmer) to Russell, Jan. 15, 1862, in 3 Arnold McNair (ed.), *International Law Opinions Selected and Annotated* (Cambridge: Cambridge University Press, 1956), at 286.

56. *See generally* Correspondence Respecting the Seizure of the British Vessels "Springbok" and "Peterhoff" by United States Cruisers in 1863, Cd. 34 (1900).

57. Vernon Harcourt, *Additional Letters of Historicus on Some Questions of International Law* (London: Macmillan, 1863), at 12. *See also*, in the same vein, Bernard, *Historical Account*, at 307–316.

58. 4 John Bassett Moore, *A History and Digest of the International Arbitrations to Which the United States Has Been a Party* (Washington, D.C.: GPO, 1898), at 3838–3843.

59. *Id.* at 3928–3935. The British government was awarded damages for the period during which the ship had been detained by the American authorities prior to its release. There was no award, though, for the condemnation of the cargo, which had been the chief source of controversy.

60. Institute of International Law, "Contraband of War," Sep. 29, 1896, in James Brown Scott (ed.), *Resolutions of the Institute of International Law* (New York: Oxford University Press, 1916), at 129–131, sec. 1.

61. The condemnation was by ten members of the Institute's maritime prize panel. *See* 14 *Rev. de Droit Int'l* 329–331 (1883); *reprinted in* 7 Moore, *Digest*, at 731–732.

62. Declaration of London, art. 30, 35.

63. *Id.*, art. 19.

64. For the leading British case, see The Kim, [1915] Prob. Div. 215. For the leading French cases, see Paul Fauchille, *La guerre de 1914: Jurisprudence française en matière de prises maritimes* (Paris: A. Pedone, 1916), at 412–414, 441–444, 477–479. *See also* Briggs, *Continuous Voyage*, at 107–121.

65. *See* Briggs, *Continuous Voyage*, at 122–144. For a cogent defense of these aspects of the British blockade policy, see H. W. Malkin, "Blockade in Modern Conditions," 3 *Brit. Y.B. Int'l L.* 87–98 (1922–1923).

66. Andrea de Guttry and Natalino Ronzitti (eds.), *The Iran-Iraq War (1980–1988) and the Law of Naval Warfare* (Cambridge: Grotius, 1993), at 24–26.

67. *San Remo Manual on International Law Applicable to Armed Conflicts at Sea* (ed. Louise Doswald-Beck; Cambridge: Cambridge University Press, 1995), art. 148 (emphasis added).

9. Ending a Rebellion

Epigraphs: Thorington v. Smith, 75 U.S. (8 Wall.) 1 (1868), at 7–8; Thomas v. City of Richmond, 79 U.S. (12 Wall.) 349 (1871), at 357–358.

1. This meant that, if the United States continued to enforce blockades against neutral ships after the termination date, then it would thereby become liable, under international law, to pay damages to foreign states whose nationals were affected.

2. *See* In re Milliken, Fed. Dist. Ct., Tenn., 2 Am. L. Rev. 359 (1868).

3. Act of Mar. 3, 1863, 12 Stat. 820, sec. 3.

4. *See* Hanger v. Abbott, 73 U.S. (6 Wall.) 532 (1868). *See also* Levy v. Stewart, 78 U.S. (11 Wall.) 244 (1871).

5. Proc. No. 29, Apr. 11, 1865, 13 Stat. 753. For the legislation authorizing this action, see Act of July 13, 1861, 12 Stat. 255, sec. 4, at 256.

6. Proc. No. 36, May 22, 1865, *id.* at 757. During the interval April 11 to May 22, therefore, the Southern ports were closed by means of *both* belligerent *and* sovereign acts.

7. Proc. No. 44, June 23, 1865, *id.* at 768.

8. Proc. No. 31, Apr. 11, 1865, *id.* at 754.

9. Proc. No. 35, May 10, 1865, *id.* at 757.

10. *Id.*

11. General Orders No. 98, May 27, 1865, 8 (ser. 2) OR 580.

12. General Orders No. 109, June 6, 1865, *id.* at 641.

13. Proc. No. 51, Dec. 1, 1865, *id.* at 774. Martial law in Kentucky was, however, lifted by Proc. No. 49, Oct. 12, 1865, *id.* at 773.

14. Charles F. Dunbar, "The Direct Tax of 1861," 3 *Quarterly J. Economics* 436–461 (1889), at 454–455.

15. Act of July 28,1866, 14 Stat. 328, sec. 14, at 331, which suspended collection until the end of 1867. For a further suspension, see Act of July 23, 1868, 15 Stat. 260. Strictly speaking, this second suspension only ran until the end of 1868. In practice, no effort at collection was made after that time.

16. *See* Chapter 10.

17. Proc. No. 40, June 13, 1865, 13 Stat. 763; and Proc. No. 45, June 24, 1865, *id.* at 769. The contraband restriction was lifted, for both areas, effective September 1, 1865, by Proc. No. 48, Aug. 29, 1865, *id.* at 772.

18. The Reform, 70 U.S. (3 Wall.) 617 (1866).

19. *See* dissenting opinion of Field in Lamar v. Browne, 92 U.S. 187 (1876), at 201. For a useful summary of measures taken to terminate the war, see Grossmeyer v. U.S., 4 Ct. of Claims 1 (1868).

20. Speed, Case of Mrs. Johns, June 14, 1865, 11 Op. A-G 256.

21. John Syrett, *The Civil War Confiscation Acts: Failing to Reconstruct the South* (New York: Fordham University Prress, 2005), at 141–142.

22. J. G. Randall, *Constitutional Problems under Lincoln* (New York: Appleton, 1926), at 328–332. *See also* Jonathan Truman Dorris, *Pardon and Amnesty under Lincoln and Johnson* (Chapel Hill: University of North Carolina Press, 1953), at 227–234; and Syrett, *Civil War Confiscation Acts,* at 137–154.

23. Speed, The Proclamation of June 13, 1865, June 12, 1865, 11 Op. A-G 269. *See* Chapter 1 for the contention that the instituting of the nonintercourse policy marked the formal commencement of the war.

24. Semmes v. City Fire Insurance Co., 21 Fed. Cas. 1051 (No. 12,651) (CC D Conn. 1869); *reversed on other grounds* by 80 U.S. (13 Wall.) 158 (1871).

25. *See* Chapter 1 on this point.

26. Proc. No. 1, Apr. 2, 1866, 14 Stat. 811.

27. Proc. No. 4, Aug. 20, 1866, *id.* at 814.

28. The Protector, 79 U.S. (12 Wall.) 700 (1872). *See also,* following this, Brown v. Hiatts, 82 U.S. (15 Wall.) 177 (1872); Adger v. Alston, 82 U.S. (15 Wall.) 555 (1873); Batesville, Institute v. Kauffman, 85 U.S. (18 Wall.) 151 (1873); and Lamar v. Brown, 92 U.S. 187 (1876).

29. Act of Mar. 2, 1867, 14 Stat. 422. For obvious reasons, the later the date fixed, the more generously were the soldiers being treated.

30. U.S. v. Anderson, 76 U.S. (9 Wall.) 56 (1869). *See also* Adger v. Alston, 82 U.S. (15 Wall.) 555 (1873).

31. Lincoln, Address of Apr. 11, 1865, in 8 Basler, *Works,* at 403.

32. Davis, "Surrender of the Confederacy," Apr. 22, 1865, in Rembert W. Patrick, *The Opinions of the Confederate Attorneys General 1861–1865* (Buffalo: Dennis, 1950), at 580–584.

33. For a thorough and compelling account of the last days of the Confederate government, see generally William C. Davis, *An Honorable Defeat: The Last Days of the Confederate Government* (San Diego: Harvest, 2001).

34. Executive Order, May 9, 1865, 13 Stat. 777.

35. Keppel v. Petersburg R.R. Co., 14 Fed. Cas. 357 (No. 7722) (CC D Va., 1868), at 371.

36. U.S. v. Keehler, 76 U.S. (9 Wall.) 83 (1870), at 86–87.

37. Sprott v. U.S., 87 U.S. (20 Wall.) 459 (1874), at 464–465. *See also,* to the same effect, Hickman v. Jones, 76 U.S. (9 Wall.) 197 (1870). *See also* the Virginia State Supreme Court case Boulware v. Newton, 59 Va. 708 (1868).

38. *See,* to this effect, Prats, Pujol and Co. v. U.S., 3 John Bassett Moore, *A His-*

tory and Digest of the International Arbitrations to Which the United States Has Been a Party (Washington, D.C.: GPO, 1898), at 2886–2900.

39. *See* Dewing v. Perdicaries, 96 U.S. 193 (1878). In American law, as in the English-speaking world generally, the rule is that a person who purchases property from a thief, even if entirely innocently, does not acquire legal title, on the principle that the thief had no good title and so was unable to convey to a buyer any *better* title than he or she possessed.

40. Shortridge v. Macon, 22 Fed. Cas. 20 (No. 12,812) (CC D N.C. 1867).

41. *See also,* to the same effect, the Georgia Supreme Court case Central R.R. and Banking Co. v. Ward, 37 Ga. 515 (1868).

42. *See* Barrett v. U.S., 3 Moore, *Arbitrations,* at 2900–2901.

43. *See* Paolo Mauro and Yishay Yafeh, "The Corporation of Foreign Bondholders," IMF Working Paper No. WP/01/107 (2003), at 23.

44. Mauran v. Insurance Co., 73 U.S. (6 Wall.) 1 (1868). *See also* Williams v. Bruffy, 96 U.S. 176 (1878).

45. Confed. Act of Mar. 17, 1862, 1 (ser. 4) OR 1006.

46. Ford v. Surget, 97 U.S. 594 (1878).

47. Thorington v. Smith, 75 U.S. (8 Wall.) 1 (1868), at 12. It was not a *belligerent* occupier, though, because it was "occupying" its *own* territory rather than that of an enemy power.

48. *Id.* at 12.

49. *See* Hanauer v. Woodruff, 82 U.S. (15 Wall.) 439 (1873), at 449. *See also* the West Virginia Supreme Court case of Caperton v. Martin, 4 West Va. 138 (1870), at 135.

50. Williams v. Bruffy, 96 U.S. 176 (1878). *See also,* to the same effect, Scheible v. Bacho, 41 Ala. 423 (1868); Cassell v. Backrack, 42 Miss. 56 (1868); and Newton's Executor v. Bushong, 63 Va. 628 (1872).

51. *See* William Sumner, "Our Domestic Relations; or, How to Treat the Rebel States," 12 *Atlantic Monthly* 507–529 (1863).

52. William R. Robinson, *Justice in Grey: A History of the Judicial System of the Confederate States of America* (Cambridge: Mass.: Harvard University Press, 1941), at 609.

53. *See* Smith v. Isenhour, 43 Tenn. 214 (1866); State v. McGinty, 41 Miss. 435 (1867); Calhoun v. Calhoun, 2 S.C. 283 (1870); Penn v. Tollison, 26 Ark. 545 (1871); and Scruggs v. Mayor of Huntsville, 45 Ala. 220 (1871).

54. Speed, Provisional Government in Mississippi, Aug. 23, 1865, 11 Op. A-G 322. *See also,* to this effect, Ex p. Bibb, 44 Ala. 140 (1870).

55. Johnson, Message to Congress, Dec. 4, 1865, in 8 James D. Richardson (ed.), *A Compilation of the Messages and Papers of the Presidents* (New York: Bureau of National Literature, 1896–1899), at 3555.

56. Texas v. White, 74 U.S. (7 Wall.) 700 (1869). On this case, see Charles Fairman, *Reconstruction and Reunion 1864–1888,* pt. 1 (New York: Macmillan, 1971), at 628–648.

57. *See also,* to the same effect, the opinion of Justice Bradley in Keith v. Clark, 97 U.S 454 (1878), at 472–473. Bradley was dissenting, but not on this particular point.

58. Texas v. White, 74 U.S. (7 Wall.) 700 (1869), at 733.

59. Horn v. Lockhart, 84 U.S. (17 Wall.) 570 (1873). *See also,* in the same vein, Thomas v. City of Richmond, 79 U.S. (12 Wall.) 349 (1871); and Williams v. Bruffy, 96 U.S. 176 (1878).

60. Sprott v. U.S. 87 U.S. (20 Wall.) 459 (1874), at 464–465. *See also,* to the same effect, Van Epps v. Walsh, 28 Fed. Cas. 986 (No. 16,850) (CC SD Ala. 1870).

61. Oneale v. Commonwealth, 58 Va. 582 (1867).

62. Chicora Co. v. Crews, 6 S.C. 243 (1875).

63. Chancely v. Bailey, 37 Ga. 532 (1868). In technical legal terms, it was said that there was no binding contract because of the absence of (lawful) consideration.

64. Ford v. Surget, 97 U.S. 594 (1878). The effect of the Court's holding was that the later, reconstructed state government was not entitled to repudiate the note issue or to refuse to accept payment in the notes.

65. Scheible v. Bacho, 41 Ala. 423 (1868). *See also,* to the same effect, Phillips v. Hooker, 62 N.C. 193 (1867).

66. *See* Barclay v. Russ, 14 Fla. 372 (1874).

67. Emmerich de Vattel, *The Law of Nations; or The Principles of Natural Law* (trans. Charles G. Fenwick; Washington, D.C.: Carnegie Institution, 1916 [1758]), at 339; and General Orders No. 100, Apr. 24, 1863, 5 (ser. 2) OR 671–682, *reprinted in* Richard Shelly Hartigan, *Lieber's Code and the Law of War* (Chicago: Precedent, 1983), at 45–71, art. 154.

68. *See,* to this effect, Hedges v. Price, 2 W.Va. 192 (1867).

69. Speed, Case of Jefferson Davis, Jan. 6, 1866, 11 Op. A-G 411, at 413.

70. Executive order, May 9, 1865, 13 Stat. 777.

71. Shortridge v. Macon, 22 Fed. Cas. 20 (No. 12,812) (CC D N.C. 1867); Yost v. Stout, 44 Tenn. 205 (1867); and Thompson v. Mankin, 26 Ark. 586 (1871).

72. *See* Speed, Case of Jefferson Davis, Jan. 6, 1866, 11 Op. A-G 411.

73. For an excellent illustration of this point, see the Tennessee Supreme Court case of Hammond v. State, 43 Tenn. 129 (1866).

74. *See* Chapter 3 on this incident.

75. Thomas D. Mays, "The Battle of Saltville," in John David Smith (ed.), *Black Soldiers in Blue: African American Troops in the Civil War Era* (Chapel Hill: University of North Carolina Press, 2002), at 220–222.

76. *See* Chapter 3.

77. For the report of the Wirtz prosecution, see General Orders No. 607, Nov. 6, 1865, 8 (ser. 2) OR 784–792. For the full transcript of the trial, see "Trial of Henry Wirtz," House Exec. Doc. No. 23, 40th Cong., 2d Sess. (1868). *See also* Lewis L. Laska and James M. Smith, "'Hell and the Devil': Andersonville and the Trial of Captain Henry M. Wirtz, C.S.A., 1865," 68 *Military L. Rev.* 77–132 (1975); and Elizabeth D.

Leonard, *Lincoln's Avengers: Justice, Revenge, and Reunion after the Civil War* (New York: Norton, 2004), at 153–163.

78. *See* General Court-martial Orders No. 153, June 8, 1866, 8 (ser. 2) OR 926–928. It appears that the defendant, one James W. Duncan, escaped after one year of detention.

79. General Orders No. 4, Jan. 24, 1866, *id.* at 871.

80. The person was one John H. Gee. *See* General Orders No. 35, Aug. 30, 1866, *id.* at 956–960.

81. *See* Holt to Stanton, Nov. 3, 1865, 7 (ser. 2) OR 782–783, on five cases. It appears, though, that only two of them—those of Duncan and Gee—were actually pursued.

82. On the destruction of ships at sea, see Chapter 7.

83. On the Semmes case, see Dorris, *Pardon and Amnesty,* at 178–186. On the Johnson pardon proclamations, see Chapter 10.

84. For the official report of the Lincoln murder trial, see General Orders No. 356, July 5, 1867, 8 (ser. 2) OR 696–700. For a comprehensive contemporary account, see Benn Pitman (comp.), *The Assassination of President Lincoln and the Trial of the Conspirators* (Cincinnati: Moore, Wilstach and Baldwin, 1865). For more recent accounts, see William Hanchett, *The Lincoln Murder Conspiracies* (Urbana: University of Illinois Press, 1983), at 65–89; Rehnquist, *All the Laws but One: Civil Liberty in Wartime* (New York: Knopf, 1998), at 138–169; and Leonard, *Lincoln's Avengers,* at 67–135. *See also* Joseph George, Jr., "Subornation of Perjury at the Lincoln Conspiracy Trial? Joseph Holt, Robert Purdy, and the Lon Letter," 38 *Civil War History* 232–241 (1992).

85. Ex p. Milligan, 71 U.S. (4 Wall.) 2 (1866). *See* Chapter 6 on this decision.

86. Fairman, *Reconstruction,* at 238–239.

87. On Surratt's trial, see Leonard, *Lincoln's Avengers,* at 235–243, 252–263.

88. *See* Chapter 6.

89. Brian Steel Wills, *A Battle from the Start: The Life of Nathan Bedford Forrest* (New York: HarperCollins, 1992), at 242–249, 325.

90. Randall, *Constitutional Problems,* at 97.

91. Dorris, *Pardon and Amnesty,* at 241–243. The Knoxville indictments included some of the most prominent figures in the Confederacy, including Jefferson Davis and General Edmund Kirby Smith.

92. Act of July 17, 1862, 12 Stat. 589, sec. 2, at 590.

93. Opinion of Adjutant-General's Office, Department of War, June 20, 1867, in 8 Richardson (ed.), *Compilation of the Messages of the Presidents,* at 3750–3754. *See also,* to the same effect, Hoar, The Reconstruction Act, May 24, 1867, 12 Op. A-G 141. These opinions concerned, strictly speaking, not criminal prosecution but rather disqualification from voting pursuant to the main Congressional Reconstruction statute. But the issue at stake was the same—what constituted participation in rebellion. *See* Act of Mar. 2, 1867, 14 Stat. 428, sec. 6, at 429.

94. *See,* to this effect, U.S. v. Rice, 17 U.S. (4 Wheaton) 246 (1819).

95. *See* Speed, Case of Jefferson Davis, Jan. 6, 1866, 11 Op. A-G 411.

96. *See* Stanton to Johnson, Jan. 4, 1866, 8 (ser. 2) OR 843–844.

97. For an exposition of the evidence of Davis's involvement in the Lincoln murder, see Holt to Stanton, Jan. 18, 1866, *id.* at 847–867.

98. Constitution, Art. III, sec. 2.

99. Morton to Johnson, Nov. 14, 1865, 8 (ser. 2) OR 798. Johnson's response was noncommittal. Johnson to Morton, Nov. 14, 1865, *id.*

100. On the issues relating to trial venue, see Speed, Case of Jefferson Davis, Jan. 6, 1866, 11 Op A-G 411.

101. Dorris, *Pardon and Amnesty,* at 294–295.

102. *See,* for example, Senate Res. of Dec. 21, 1865, 8 (ser. 2) OR 843, inquiring why Davis had not been brought to trial.

103. On the Davis treason prosecution, see Randall, *Constitutional Problems,* at 103–117; and Dorris, *Pardon and Amnesty,* at 278–312.

10. Forgiving but Not Forgetting

Epigraph: The Fremont Contract Claims, 2 Ct. of Claims 1 (Dec. 1866 term), at 26.

1. Constitution, Art. III, sec. 2. On the historical roots of the pardon power, see Daniel T. Kobil, "The Quality of Mercy Strained: Wresting the Pardon Power from the King," 69 *Texas L. Rev.* 569–641 (1991).

2. Act of July 17, 1862, 12 Stat. 589, sec. 13, at 592.

3. U.S. v. Klein, 80 U.S. (13 Wall.) 128 (1872), at 139.

4. *See* Stanbery, President's Pardon, Nov. 2, 1866, 12 Op. A-G 81. A specific pardon grant might, however, exclude certain specified penal consequences from its ambit.

5. Ex p. Garland, 71 U.S. (4 Wall.) 333 (1867), at 371. *See generally,* on this subject, Ashley M. Steiner, "Remission of Guilt or Removal of Punishment? The Effects of a Presidential Pardon," 46 *Emory Law J.* 959–1003 (1997).

6. Proc. No. 11, Dec. 8, 1863, 13 Stat. 737.

7. Jonathan Truman Dorris, *Pardon and Amnesty under Lincoln and Johnson* (Chapel Hill: University of North Carolina Press, 1953), at 67–73.

8. Proc. No. 37, May 29, 1865, 13 Stat. 758. On this proclamation, see Dorris, *Pardon and Amnesty,* at 108–115.

9. For the text of a pardon request, see Yulee to Johnson, June 24, 1865, 8 (ser. 2) OR 668–671. The applicant, David L. Yulee, was a former senator from Florida. His request was not granted, although he was eventually (in March 1866) released from detention at Fort Pulaski on parole.

10. On individual pardons, see Dorris, *Pardon and Amnesty,* at 135-152. For a report to Congress on the subject, see House Exec. Doc. No. 16, 40th Cong. 2d Sess.

11. Proc. No. 3, Sep. 7, 1867, 15 Stat. 699. *See* Dorris, *Pardon and Amnesty,* at 339–352.

12. For the pardons over the years of the principal civilian leaders of the Confederacy, see Dorris, *Pardon and Amnesty,* at 244–277.

13. Proc. No. 6, July 4, 1868, 15 Stat. 702. *See* Dorris, *Pardon and Amnesty,* at 352–356. On the position of Davis, see *id.* at 278–312.

14. Proc. No. 15, Dec. 25, 1868, 15 Stat. 711. *See* Dorris, *Pardon and Amnesty,* at 356–361.

15. Bates, Pardoning Power of the President, Feb. 9, 1863, 10 Op. A-G 452; and Speed, The Adelso, Apr. 2, 1866, 11 Op. A-G 445.

16. The Confiscation Cases, 87 U.S. (20 Wall.) 92 (1874); Semmes v. U.S., 91 U.S. 21 (1875); and Stanbery, President's Pardon, Nov. 2, 1866, 12 Op. A-G 81. The possession of a pardon was held, however, to prevent confiscation proceedings from being newly *instituted* after the pardon grant. Speed, Case of Mrs. Johns, Sep. 14, 1865, 11 Op. A-G 356.

17. Semmes v. U.S., 91 U.S. 21 (1875). By *dictum* is meant language that is not essential to the decision reached in the case, i.e., a sort of judicial version of parenthetical remarks.

18. *See* Chapter 4 for further details on this point.

19. *See* Bennett v. Hunter, 76 U.S. (9 Wall.) 326 (1870); and Lee v. Kaufman, 15 Fed. Cas. 204 (No. 8192) (CC Ed Va. 1879).

20. Act of June 8, 1872, 17 Stat. 330.

21. Miller v. U.S., 78 U.S. (11 Wall.) 268 (1871). *See* Chapter 4 for a discussion of this issue. On the Miller case, see John Syrett, *The Civil War Confiscation Acts: Failing to Reconstruct the South* (New York: Fordham University Press, 2005), at 169–174.

22. This was clearly implied by Semmes v. U.S. 91 U.S. 21 (1875), at 26–27.

23. On the First Confiscation Act, see the key cases of Armstrong's Foundry, 73 U.S. (6 Wall.) 766 (1868); and Kirk v. Lynd, 106 U.S. 315 (1882). On this issue, see also Syrett, *Civil War Confiscation Acts,* at 181–184. *See also* the Kentucky Court of Appeal case of Porter v. Botts, 63 Ky. 365 (1866).

24. The property *itself* unquestionably could not be recovered once it had been auctioned off.

25. Brown v. Kennedy, 82 U.S. (15 Wall.) 591 (1873). *See also* Charles Fairman, *Reconstruction and Reunion 1864–1888,* pt. 1 (New York: Macmillan, 1971), at 838–839.

26. Osborn v. U.S., 91 U.S. 474 (1876). *See also* Illinois Central R.R. Co. v. Bosworth, 133 U.S. 92 (1890); and Jenkins v. Collard, 145 U.S. 546 (1892). There was one key proviso: that the proceeds must be held by either the executive or the judiciary at the time of the claim. If they were placed in the Treasury, then an act of Congress would be necessary before there could be a payout. *See* Knote v. U.S., 95 U.S. 149 (1877).

27. For a lucid exposition of this thesis, see the later Supreme Court case of

Austin v. U.S., 509 U.S. 602 (1993). In that case, the issue was the applicability of the Eighth Amendment prohibition against "excessive fines," rather than the reach of a presidential pardon. But the Court's reasoning would seem applicable to both situations.

28. See Chapter 4 on the inauguration of the policy on captured and abandoned property.

29. The Court of Claims, established in 1855, was somewhat misleadingly labeled, since it was not actually part of the judicial branch of the government, but was a sort of advisory body to Congress. Its function was to recommend legislation by Congress, appropriating money for compensation to persons whose claims the Court deemed worthy. For a brief account of the Court, see Erwin C. Currency, *History of the Federal Courts* (2d ed.; Dobbs Ferry, N.Y.: Oceana, 2002), at 470–476. For a more exhaustive history, see Marion Tinsley Bennett, Wilson Cowen, and Philip Nichols, *The United States Court of Claims: A History* (2 vols.; Washington, D.C.: Committee on the Bicentennial and the Constitution of the Judicial Conference of the United States, 1977–1978). The Court, now called the Court of Federal Claims, is now fully a part of the judicial branch of the government.

30. *See* U.S. v. Anderson, 76 U.S. (9 Wall.) 56 (1869) .

31. U.S. v. Klein, 80 U.S. (13 Wall.) 128 (1872). The trusteeship theory, as stated here, was not expounded very clearly in the judgment. There was a strong dissent from Justice Miller, on the thesis that the trusteeship arrangement *only* applied to property taken from persons who were loyal at the time of the capture—with title to property of disloyal persons passing absolutely to the federal government. On this reasoning, disloyal persons had already lost their property irrevocably prior to the receipt of the pardon. *See also* Bernheimer v. U.S., 5 Ct. of Claims 549 (1869), in support of this thesis. For other cases on the effect of pardons on claims for proceeds of captured and abandoned property, see Padelford v. U.S., 76 U.S. (9 Wall.) 531 (1870); Armstrong, 80 U.S. (13 Wall.) 154 (1972); and Pargoud v. U.S., 80 U.S. (13 Wall.) 156 (1872). *See also* Carlisle v. U.S., 83 U.S. (16 Wall.) 147 (1873), for a somewhat different approach to the same result. On the *Padelford* case, see Robert Bruce Murray, *Legal Cases of the Civil War* (Mechanicsburg, Pa.: Stackpole, 2003), at 144–149.

32. U.S. v. Anderson, 76 U.S. (9 Wall.) 56 (1869). *See also* Adger v. Alston, 82 U.S. (15 Wall.) 555 (1873).

33. Haycraft v. U.S., 69 U.S. (2 Wall.) 81 (1875). For a lucid exposition of this admittedly fine distinction between a limitation period and a jurisdictional constraint on a court, see Sierra v. U.S., 9 Ct. of Claims 224 (Dec. 1873 term).

34. Congress occasionally extended the period on occasion in individual cases (as noted below). In 1911, it removed the two-year limit, but only with respect to claims relating to property taken after June 1, 1865. Act of Mar. 3, 1911, 36 Stat. 1087, sec. 162, at 1139.

35. On the possibility of abuse of the pardon power, see Paul J. Haase, "'Oh My Darling Clemency': Existing or Possible Limitations on the Use of the Presidential Pardon Power," 39 *American Criminal L. Rev.* 1287–1307 (2002). On this subject with reference to the pardons by President Clinton in January 2001, see Harold J. Kent, "The President's Conditional Pardon Power," 89 *California L. Rev.* 1665–1720 (2001).

36. Act of Jan. 21, 1867, 14 Stat. 377. *See* Dorris, *Pardon and Amnesty,* at 325–330.

37. Ex p. Garland, 71 U.S. (4 Wall.) 333 (1867), at 370–371. For a later reiteration of this principle, see Schick v. Reed, 419 U.S. 256 (1974).

38. Act of July 12, 1870, 16 Stat. 230, at 235.

39. U.S. v. Klein, 80 U.S. (13 Wall.) 128 (1872).

40. Constitution, Art. I, sec. 9.

41. Joint Res. No. 46, Mar. 2, 1867, 14 Stat. 571.

42. Hart's Administrator v. U.S., 16 Ct. of Claims 459 (1880 term).

43. Hart v. U.S., 118 U.S. 62 (1886).

44. Act of June 23, 1874, 18 Stat. 245, sec. 12, at 247.

45. Rhind v. U.S., in 5 John Bassett Moore, *A History and Digest of the International Arbitrations to Which the United States Has Been a Party* (Washington, D.C.: GPO, 1898), at 4653. On the Geneva arbitration and the distribution of the award money, see Chapter 7.

46. Robert Jennings Harris, *The Judicial Power of the United States* (Baton Rouge: Louisiana State University Press, 1940), at 86–99.

47. Austin v. U.S., 155 U.S. 417 (1894). For another informative exposition of this subtle issue, see Brandon v. U.S., 46 Ct. of Claims 559 (1911).

48. *See,* for example, Act of June 22, 1874, 18 Stat. 606; Act of Feb. 5, 1877, 19 Stat. 509; and Act of June 4, 1888, 25 Stat. 1075.

49. Act of July 28, 1866, 14 Stat. 332, sec. 28, at 336.

50. Fourteenth Amendment, sec. 3.

51. Garland, Pardon—Lawton's Case, Apr. 14, 1885, 18 Op. A-G 149.

52. Act of May 31, 1870, 16 Stat. 140, sec. 14–15, at 143–144. This was the famous "Force Act" of the Reconstruction period. The provisions of the law did not apply to holders of seats in the federal or any state legislature.

53. Act of July 11, 1868, 15 Stat. 85.

54. Act of June 19, 1868, *id.* at 360.

55. Act of June 25, 1868, *id.* at 361.

56. Act of July 20, 1868, *id.* at 386. *See also* Act of July 27, 1868, *id.* at 403, which removed the disabilities of sixteen persons.

57. Act of Dec. 14, 1869, 16 Stat. 607; and Act of Mar. 7, 1870, *id.* at 614. In most cases of Fourteenth Amendment disability removal, the statutory record carefully stated that the law had been enacted by a two-thirds vote of each house, rather than by the mere majority required for ordinary legislation.

58. In March 1871, a mere several dozen persons benefited from congressional generosity. Act of Mar. 3, 1871, *id.* at 694.

59. Act of May 22, 1872, 17 Stat. 142.

60. Dorris, *Pardon and Amnesty,* at 378.

61. Proc. of June 1, 1872, 17 Stat. 956.

62. Dorris, *Pardon and Amnesty,* at 387.

63. Act of June 7, 1872, 17 Stat. 676; Act of June 8, 1872, *id.* at 680; and Act of June 10, 1872, *id.* at 691. The last of these dealt with Vance.

64. Act of Feb. 1, 1897, 29 Stat. 801; and Act of Feb. 25, 1897, *id.* at 821.

65. Act of June 6, 1898, 30 Stat. 432. Curiously, it is not explicitly stated in the statutory record that this act received the concurrence of two-thirds of each house, as did all of the acts removing the disabilities of named persons. Two years earlier, in 1896, the statutory prohibition on military service by ex-Confederates had been repealed. Act of Mar. 31, 1896, 29 Stat. 84.

66. Joint Res. of Aug. 5, 1975, PL 94–67, 89 Stat. 380. The statutory record did not explicitly state that this law had received the required two-thirds vote of each house of Congress, though that was in fact the case.

67. *See* Francis MacDonnell, "Reconstruction in the Wake of Vietnam: The Pardoning of Robert E. Lee and Jefferson Davis," 40 *Civil War History* 119–133 (1994).

68. Dow v. Johnson, 100 U.S. 158 (1880).

69. Hedges v. Price, 2 W.Va. 192 (1867); *followed by* Caperton v. Martin, 4 W.Va. 138 (1870).

70. *See* Arnold v. Kelley, 5 W.Va. 446 (1872). In 1872, the state amended its constitution to prevent the enforcement of existing judgments from actions pursued prior to the statute. *See* Peerce v. Kitzmiller, 19 W.Va. 564 (1882).

71. Mauran v. Insurance Co., 73 U.S. (6 Wall.) 1 (1868).

72. Terrill v. Rankin, 65 Ky. 453 (1867).

73. Capterton v. Martin, 4 W.Va. 138 (1870).

74. Bell v. Louisville and Nashville Railroad, 64 Ky. 404 (1866). *See also,* to the same effect, Lamar v. Browne, 92 U.S. 187 (1876).

75. Hickman v. Jones, 76 U.S. (9 Wall.) 197 (1870). The Court held, however, that trespass, rather than malicious prosecution, was the correct wrong to allege.

76. Act of Mar. 3, 1863, 12 Stat. 755, sec. 4, at 756. See J. G. Randall, *Constitutional Problems under Lincoln* (New York: Appleton, 1926), at 186–214.

77. Act of May 11, 1866, 14 Stat. 46, sec. 1.

78. Ex p. Milligan, 71 U.S. (4 Wall.) 2 (1866). *See* Chapters 2 and 6 on this case.

79. Act of Mar. 2, 1867, 14 Stat. 432.

80. *See* Britton v. Butler, 4 Fed. Cas. 182 (No. 1904) (CC SD N.Y. 1873); *reversing* Britton v. Butler, 4 Fed. Cas. 177 (No. 1903) (CC SD N.Y. 1872).

81. Missouri State Constitution, art. 11(4); *quoted in* State v. Gatzweiler, 49 Mo. 17 (1871), at 22–23.

82. State v. Gatzweiler, 49 Mo. 17 (1871).

83. The North Carolina law is described in Bryan v. Walker, 64 N.C. 141 (1870), at 145-146. *See also* John v. Franklin, 66 N.C. 145 (1872). On the Kentucky law, see Haddix v. Wilson, 66 Ky. 523 (1868).

84. Drehman v. Stifle, 75 U.S. (8 Wall.) 595 (1870). *See also* Clark v. Dick, 5 Fed. Cas. 865 (No. 2818) (CC D Mo., 1870).

85. Mitchell v. Clark, 110 U.S. 633 (1884), concerning a confiscation measure by the armed forces.

86. Beckwith v. Bean, 98 U.S. 266 (1879), at 285–308. *See also* Field's dissent, in similar terms, in Mitchell v. Clark, 110 U.S. 633 (1884), at 647–651.

87. *See* Mullane v. Central Hanover Bank and Trust Co., 339 U.S. 306 (1950).

88. Martinez v. California, 444 U.S. 277 (1980).

89. Mitchell v. Clark, 110 U.S. 633 (1884), at 640.

90. Milligan v. Hovey, 17 Fed. Cas. 380 (No. 9605) (CC D Ind. 1871).

91. Johnson v. Jones, 44 Ill. 142 (1867).

92. Terrill v. Rankin, 65 Ky. 453 (1867).

93. This conclusion was expressly voiced by the North Carolina Supreme Court, in John v. Franklin, 66 N.C. 145 (1872), at 152–153.

94. *See* Chapter 3 for a fuller discussion of this question.

95. Act of Feb. 21, 1867, 14 Stat. 397.

96. Act of July 4, 1864, 13 Stat. 381. *See also* U.S. v. Russell, 80 U.S. (13 Wall.) 623 (1871).

97. For the establishment of the special commissioners, see Act of Mar. 3, 1871, 16 Stat. 521, sec. 2.

98. Pierrepont, Effect of Pardon, Oct. 26, 1875, 15 Op. A-G 60.

99. Act of Mar. 3, 1883, 22 Stat 485, sec. 4. The leading case on this subject of jurisdictional limitations by Congress concerned the constitutionality of this particular provision. *See* Austin v. U.S., 155 U.S. 417 (1894), discussed above. For a reiteration of this policy, see Act of Mar. 3, 1911, 36 Stat. 1087, sec. 184, at 1142.

100. Garber v. U.S., 46 Ct. of Claims 503 (1911). In such cases, victims had two possible avenues of relief, to be discussed below: a civil action for damages against the soldiers themselves; and relief by private act of Congress. For a similar stance in the Confederacy, see Seddon to Milton, July 1864, 3 (ser. 4) OR 560–562.

101. Emmerich de Vattel, *The Law of Nations; Or The Principles of Natural Law* (trans. Charles G. Fenwick; Washington, D.C.: Carnegie Institution, 1916 [1758]), at 320–321. If property was taken from the state's own nationals, then the matter was to be dealt with by the national law of that state, not by international law.

102. Jacobs v. U.S., in 4 Moore, *Arbitrations,* at 3688–3689.

103. Means v. U.S., *id.* at 3706.

104. *See* Chourreau v. U.S., *id.* at 3705; and Bertrand v. U.S., *id.* at 3705–3706.

105. Cox and Cox v. U.S., *id.* at 3678. For the sole case in which compensation was

ordered for the destruction of civilian infrastructure, see the British-American claim of Turner v. U.S. *id.* at 3684–3685.

106. Conard v. U.S., 25 Ct. of Claims 433 (1890). These were the so-called Loudoun County Claims. For an interesting illustration of how this doctrine can work against the material interest of the government, see U.S. v. Pacific Railroad, 120 U.S. 227 (1867).

107. Brown and Sharp v. U.S., in 4 Moore, *Arbitrations,* at 3675–3677.

108. Act of Mar. 4, 1915, 38(2) Stat. 962, sec. 5, at 996.

109. Proc. No. 16, Sep. 22, 1862, 12 Stat. 1267; *reprinted* in 5 Basler, *Works,* at 433–436. It will be recalled that this suggestion of compensation did not appear in the final Proclamation.

110. Act of Mar. 3, 1871, 16 Stat. 521, sec. 2–6, at 524–525. For a masterly general history of this little-known body, see Frank W. Klingberg, *The Southern Claims Commission* (Berkeley: University of California Press, 1955). For a collection of case files of the Commission's work, see Gary B. Mills, *Southern Loyalists in the Civil War: The Southern Claims Commission* (Baltimore: Genealogical, 1994).

111. Dodd v. U.S., 21 Ct. of Claims 117 (1886), at 118.

112. *See* Haym v. U.S., 26 Ct. of Claims 167 (1891).

113. Newton's executor v. Bushong, 63 Va. 628 (1872). The case concerned the payment by the executor of an estate to the Confederate government instead of to the Union-resident legatee, pursuant to Confederate law on confiscation of alien enemy property.

114. U.S. v. Huckabee, 83 U.S. (16 Wall.) 414 (1873). *See also* U.S. v. Keehler, 76 U.S. (9 Wall.) 83 (1870); Keppel v. Petersburg Railroad Co., 14 Fed. Cas. 357 (No. 7722) (CC D Va. 1868); and U.S. v. 1500 Bales of Cotton, 27 Fed. Cas. 325 (No. 15,958) (CC WD Tenn. 1872).

115. French v. Shoemaker, 81 U.S. (14 Wall.) 314 (1872), at 332–333.

116. *See,* for example, Radich v. Hutchins, 95 U.S. 210 (1877); and U.S. v. 1500 Bales of Cotton, 27 Fed. Cas. 325 (No. 15,958) (CC WD Tenn. 1872).

117. Some minor labors remained until 1915, which were dealt with by the Court of Claims. For details, see Klingman, *Southern Claims Commission,* at 185–193.

118. *Id.* at 17–19.

119. Report of Secretary of the Treasury, Feb. 21, 1874, H.R. Exec. Doc. No. 146, 43d Cong., 1st Sess.

120. In the Supreme Court, see O'Pry v. U.S., 249 U.S. 323 (1919); and Mangan v. U.S., 254 U.S. 494 (1921). In the Court of Claims, see Collins v. U.S., 56 Ct. of Claims 41 (1921); and Irby v. U.S., 57 Ct. of Claims 60 (1922).

121. For statutory authorizations to suspend collection, see Act of July 28, 1866, 14 Stat. 328, sec. 14, at 331; and Act of July 23, 1868, 15 Stat. 260.

122. As noted earlier, the policy of gathering the tax by confiscating property was not actually carried out on a significant scale. *See* Chapter 4 on this point.

123. For an able survey of the pros and cons of these alternatives, see Charles F. Dunbar, "The Direct Tax of 1861," 3 *Quarterly J. Economics* 436–461 (1889), at 456–461. He presents a forceful case for the alternative of simply leaving matters as they then stood.

124. Act of Mar. 3, 1891, 26 Stat. 822.

125. There was also an arbitration treaty with Mexico. Mexico-U.S., Claims Convention, July 4, 1868, 137 C.T.S. 331, 15 Stat. 679. This one, however, involved few claims against the United States and is therefore of no importance for present purposes.

126. This reflects the general position in international law, that there is liability only for acts of governments, not of private parties. See, to this effect, various cases in 3 Moore, *Arbitrations,* at 2996–3007.

127. Prats, Pujol, and Co. v. U.S. (Mexico-U.S. tribunal), *id.* at 2886–2900.

128. Great Britain-U.S., Treaty of Washington, May 8, 1871, 143 C.T.S. 145, 17 Stat. 863, arts. 12–17. *See* Chapter 7 for an account of the proceedings of the Geneva panel.

129. *See* 4 Moore, *Arbitrations,* at 3278–3311. The large award was in Syme v. U.S., *id.* at 3290–3292.

130. 1 *id.* at 692–693.

131. McDonald v. U.S., in 4 *id.* at 3683–3684. This was the only claim for cotton destruction which succeeded, because of special facts. The claim had been for over $3 million.

132. *See* Chapter 7 on the unsuccessful claims by the United States for the St. Albans and Lake Erie raids launched from Canadian territory.

133. France-U.S., Claims Convention, Jan. 15, 1880, 156 C.T.S. 181, 21 Stat. 673.

134. 2 Moore, *Arbitrations,* at 1146–1148. The number of successful claims is not given. But the sum awarded was less than 2 percent of the amount claimed by France. George S. Boutwell to Secretary of State, Mar. 31, 1884, *id.* at 1156.

135. Le More v. U.S., 4 *id.* at 3311–3313.

136. Act of Aug. 8, 1790, 1 Stat. 178.

137. Kyle S. Sinisi, *Sacred Debts: State Civil War Claims and American Federalism, 1861–1880* (New York: Fordham University Press, 2003), at 3.

138. *Id.* at 4.

139. Act of July 27, 1861, 12 Stat. 276.

140. Joint Res. of Mar. 8, 1862, 12 Stat. 615.

141. Sinisi, *Sacred Debts,* at 11–12.

142. Act of June 20, 1878, 20 Stat. 206, at 222.

143. Act of Sep. 30, 1890, 26 Stat. 504. The four states were Massachusetts (which received most of the money), Pennsylvania, Iowa, and Missouri.

144. Act of May 27, 1902, 32 Stat. 207, at 236.

145. Act of Mar. 3, 1905, 33 Stat. 1214.

146. New York v. U.S., 160 U.S. 598 (1896).

147. Act of Feb. 14, 1902, 32 Stat. 5.

148. Act of Jan. 17, 1871, 16 Stat. 678.

149. Act of June 1, 1870, *id.* at 640.

150. *See,* for example, Act of June 22, 1874, 18 Stat. 606; Act of Feb. 5, 1877, 19 Stat. 509; and Act of June 4, 1888, 25 Stat. 1075.

151. For the time extension, see Act of Mar. 3, 1883, 22 Stat. 804. For the failure of the claim on loyalty grounds, see Austin v. U.S., 155 U.S. 417 (1894), discussed above.

152. Klingberg, *Southern Claims Commission,* at 145.

153. *See,* on this point, Arthur G. Sedgwick, "The Lobby: Its Cause and Cure," 41 *Atlantic Monthly* 512–522 (1878).

154. Klingberg, *Southern Claims Commission,* at 183.

155. Shorter v. Cobb, 39 Ga. 285 (1869), at 296.

156. Act of June 27, 1890, 26 Stat. 182.

157. For a thorough study of this phenomenon, see Theda Skocpol, *Protecting Soldiers and Mothers: The Political Origins of Social Policy in the United States* (Cambridge, Mass.: Harvard University Press, 1992). *See also* Megan J. McClintock, "Civil War Pensions and the Reconstruction of Union Families," 83 *J. American History* 456–480 (1996).

158. Donald R. Shaffer, *After the Glory: The Struggles of Black Civil War Veterans* (Lawrence: University Press of Kansas, 2004), at 121–137.

159. Act of Feb. 2, 1862, 12 Stat. 337.

160. Regarding the War of 1812 and Indian wars, see Act of Mar. 9, 1878, 20 Stat. 27, sec. 5. Regarding the Mexican War, see Act of Jan. 29, 1887, 24 Stat. 371, sec. 1. The 1887 law, however, expressly excluded from its coverage persons who were still under the disabilities imposed by the Fourteenth Amendment. *Id.,* sec. 6.

161. Act of Mar. 3, 1877, 19 Stat. 403.

162. Act of May 23, 1958, PL 85–425, 72 Stat. 133.

163. Jeffrey E. Vogel, "Redefining Reconciliation: Confederate Veterans and the Southern Responses to Federal Civil War Pensions," 51 *Civil War History* 67–93 (2005), at 67–68.

164. On proposals to this effect, see Eric Foner, *Reconstruction: America's Unfinished Revolution 1863–1877* (New York: Harper and Row, 1988), at 68.

165. For a quantitative survey, necessarily somewhat speculative, on the losses sustained by the Southern states during the war, see Paul F. Paskoff, "Measures of War: A Quantitative Examination of the Civil War's Destructiveness in the Confederacy," 54 *Civil War History* 35–62 (2008).

166. For the leading history of the Reconstruction period, see Foner, *Reconstruction.*

Conclusion

1. Lane County v. Oregon, 74 U.S. (7 Wall.) 71 (1869), at 76.
2. Knox v. Lee, 79 U.S. (12 Wall.) 457 (1871), at 545.

3. *Id.* at 555. *See also* Bradley's separate opinion in Keith v. Clark, 97 U.S. (7 Ott.) 454 (1878), at 475–476. His disagreement with the majority was on a different point.

4. Much of the potential force of United States citizenship as a vehicle of basic civil rights was, however, punctured by the Supreme Court in 1873, in the Slaughterhouse Cases, 83 U.S. (16 Wall.) 36 (1873).

5. Constitution, Art. I, sec. 10.

6. *See* Raoul Berger, *Government by Judiciary: The Transformation of the Fourteenth Amendment* (2d ed.; Indianapolis: Liberty Fund, 1997).

7. Proc. No. 7463, Sep. 13, 2001, 66 Fed. Reg. 48199.

8. Exec. Order No. 13223, Sep. 14, 2001, *id.* at 48201.

9. Act of Sep. 18, 2001, PL 107–40, 115 Stat. 224.

10. *See* Military Order of Nov. 13, 2001, 66 Fed. Reg. 57831; *reprinted in* 41 Int'l Legal Materials 252–255 (2002); and Military Commissions Act of Oct. 17, 2006, PL 109–366, 120 Stat. 2600.

11. Military Commissions Act of Oct. 17, 2006, PL 109–366, 120 Stat. 2600, sec. 7, at 2635.

12. Boumediene v. Bush, 128 S. Ct. 2229 (2008). *See also* Hamdi v. Rumsfeld, 542 U.S. 1 (2004).

13. Padilla v. Hanft, 389 F. Supp. 2d 678 (D.S.C. 2005).

14. Padilla v. Hanft, 423 F. 3d 386 (4th Cir. 2005). The statutory grant was held to be the Authorization of Military Force Resolution, Joint Res. of Sep. 18, 2001, PL 107–40, 115 Stat. 224.

15. For a thorough and dispassionate analysis of the threats to traditional civil liberties posed by the post-2001 war on terrorism, see Louis Fisher, *The Constitution and 9/11: Recurring Threats to America's Freedoms* (Lawrence: University Press of Kansas, 2008).

Index